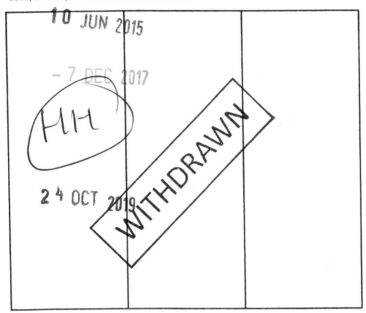

Jack Webster's

ABERDEEN

Jack Webster's

ABERDEEN

BIRLINN

First published in 2007 by
Birlinn Limited
West Newington House
10 Newington Road
Edinburgh
EH9 1QS

www.birlinn.co.uk

ISBN 13: 978 1 84158 478 2
ISBN 10: 1 84158 478 9

British Library Cataloguing-in-Publication Data
A catalogue record for this book is available from the British Library

Design and typeset by Iolaire Typesetting, Newtonmore
Printed and bound by Cromwell Press, Trowbridge

Contents

Acknowledgements

So many people guided me through sources of information that proper gratitude is almost impossible. At the Central Library in Aberdeen, Catherine Taylor proved a tower of strength, quite indispensable in so many directions. Graham Hunter's local knowledge, particularly on university matters, was a revelation, as was Arthur McCombie's, on subjects from the history of education in the city to the rugby in which he was such a memorable participant.

My grateful thanks to those who fleshed out school profiles, including Dr Jennifer Carter (St Margaret's), Irene Burnett and Marjorie Watt (High/Harlaw), Rita Edward, Dr John Halliday (Albyn), (Central/Hazlehead) and Cyria Scott (International).

Gordon Bathgate was my authority not only on his native Torry but on the early days of broadcasting. For the cinema history of Aberdeen I had the co-operation of Michael Thomson, author of the splendid *Silver Screen in the Silver City*, and similar help from Edi Swan, recently the author of a history of His Majesty's Theatre. The sources were impeccable!

Colleagues from my days on *The Press and Journal* could not have been more helpful, from Bob Smith (*The Granite City*) and Bill Mackie (*The Oilmen*) to Jim Kinnaird and Arthur Binnie, who unearthed a truly remarkable story. Fellow-journalist Gerry Davis updated me on Aberdeen Airport and Martin Ray of Aberdeen University was most generous with his own research and writing on Thomas Hardy.

As the Dons' historian, I needed no help at Pittodrie but sought guidance on golf from good friend Ian Edward and on cricket from that inimitable character, Howard O. Smith.

Authoress Diane Morgan, founder of *Leopard*, proved as ever a true custodian of Aberdeen's heritage. Jim Fiddes clarified the origins of Westhill, as librarian Anne Ross did for Dyce. Special thanks to David Catto of Aberdeenshire Libraries who satisfied my curiosity about the notorious Lillie Langtry and the laird of Strichen!

For the early days of Aberdeen I took my cue from historians who had been there before, including two men I was lucky enough to meet. The late Alexander Keith, who gave us *A Thousand Years of Aberdeen*, was a devotee of my own great-grandfather, Gavin Greig, noted playwright, novelist and mastermind of the Greig-Duncan collection of folk song. When I was a young journalist, he was intrigued to find the family connection and could not have been more helpful.

The late Fenton Wyness used to come about *The Press and Journal* office long before he wrote *City by the Grey North Sea*. His nephew, well-known cricketer George Murray, was happy that I should find inspiration in that splendid book. And who could fail to appreciate those two definitive volumes of local history, commissioned by Aberdeen City Council to mark the millennium?

My thanks to managing director Alan Scott and librarian Duncan Smith at Aberdeen Journals, to Stewart Thain of Aberdeen Art Gallery, and my ever-faithful IT guru in Glasgow, Bob Todd, who guided me through the technological minefield. Finally – and with apologies for any omissions – warmest thanks to my 'safety-net' of four trusted early readers: writer and historian Gordon Casely (he also provided the appendix on the coat-of-arms), bookseller extraordinaire Vicky Dawson, and the aforementioned Catherine Taylor and Arthur McCombie.

I'm grateful to so many people and institutions for providing a vast range of photographs for this book. They include: Aberdeen Art Gallery and Museums Collections; Aberdeen City Archives; Aberdeen Journals Ltd (librarian Duncan Smith); Aberdeen Medico-Chirurgical Society; Norman Adams at the Town House; Gordon Bathgate; Gordon Casely; Sir Graeme Catto; Central Library of Aberdeen City Council (particularly Catherine Taylor once again); Siobhan Convery and Mike Craig of the Library and Historic Collections at Aberdeen University; Grampian Television; Graham Jepson (*Aberdeen Magazine*); Jim McColl; McManus Galleries and Museum, Dundee; Diane Morgan; George Murray; National Galleries of Scotland; The National Portrait Gallery, London; Gavin Roberts at Aberdeen Airport; Geoff Runcie of the Chamber of Commerce; Charles Skene; Michael Thomson; The Trustees of the National Library of Scotland; Gordon Wright; and others.

Towards this Book . . .

On the last Sunday of February 1960 I boarded a train at the Joint Station and waved goodbye to family and friends as I headed south from Aberdeen to further a career in journalism. I was joining the newspaper empire of Lord Beaverbrook as a feature-writer on the *Daily Express*, an adventure that would open up a whole new world of excitement, travelling widely to interview the rich, the famous and the notorious.

I went with a lump in my throat and the silent fear of many an Aberdonian – that I might not be up to the task. For all the virtues of our North-east breeding and background, and even a hint that we had a good conceit of ourselves, the major flaw in our character was a lack of true confidence. Across these Grampian lands you were not supposed to get above yourself; and you didn't. So you developed a modesty beyond all good sense, wrapped yourself in a cloak of inferiority and genuinely believed that the smart folk were in places like London, Paris, New York.

On that train journey south, heading for the great unknown, I was mulling over the twenty-eight years of my life so far: born and bred of Buchan farming folk, brought up in the village of Maud where my father, John Webster, was auctioneer at the cattle mart. Childhood memories no doubt glorified the 1930s, that decade of mellow saxophones, elegant women and seemingly golden summers. Then came the upheaval of war, with its blackouts, bombs and bereavements, during which I was transported from the comparative calm of our village life to the greater drama of wartime Aberdeen.

Robert Gordon's College had seemed like a good idea but ended in academic failure. Schooldays were over at fourteen, when I was shown the exit and sent back home to Maud in disgrace. An early heart defect and a bad stammer did nothing to bolster that flagging confidence which would take years to repair. But the fates must have suffered a pang of conscience. A job on the *Turriff Advertiser* in March 1948 was the turning point. Before my seventeenth birthday I was acting editor and two years later the destination was Broad Street, in the heart of Aberdeen, where I would spend the next ten years as a reporter and sub-editor on *The Press and Journal* and *Evening Express*.

All that was now in the past, as the train rumbled south and the next phase of this mysterious adventure awaited. As that life unfolded, it became clearer by the day that the Aberdonian complex of inferiority was ludicrously misplaced. The elementary teachings of Maud School had put into our heads such a sound understanding of the essentials as to carry us to the ends of the earth without fear. Couple that with the basic level of North-east ethics and you were faced with the joyous revelation that if you could do it in Aberdeen you could do it even better elsewhere.

So it was that I kept coming back home, with a fresh appreciation of what I had left. What a city this was! What people! And what changes! On that train journey of 1960, the news to be absorbed had been the announcement that John F. Kennedy was to stand for president of the United States that year, that Princess Margaret was to marry Antony Armstrong-Jones, and that Prime Minister Harold Macmillan was incurring the wrath of the South African government by delivering his 'wind of change' speech to their parliament in Cape Town and urging them towards racial equality. We had not yet become aware of The Beatles.

When I came again to look upon my native heath, another 'wind of change' was blowing, from Bennachie to the Bullers o' Buchan, from Torry to Torphins and all the way across Harry Gordon's familiar territory of Wallfield, Nellfield, Mannofield and Cattofield, down by Constitution Street to his beloved Beach Pavilion and out to that facing North Sea which, for all those centuries, had kept its dark secret. Now all was revealed. Whatever had happened with farming, fishing, granite and textiles in a thousand years of Aberdeen, the best was yet to come. Who could ever have guessed that, in the second half of the twentieth century, nature would excel herself with a munificence that would turn Aberdeen into the oil capital of Western Europe? Canny folk of a bygone age used to have their little joke about God being an Aberdonian. Now the Deity himself had proved it beyond doubt.

These thoughts were in my head one sunny day as I made a return journey by car, driving in from the Stonehaven road and rounding that final bend which stirs the blood of every home-coming exile. For there before you lies the Granite City in all its sparkling splendour, sloping down from the heights of Mastrick to the great North Sea, its familiar skyline standing guard on an impressive heritage.

For those with a writing instinct, there is a temptation to take a closer look at that history. In this particular attempt, the emphasis lies with the people who have passed this way and left their mark on Aberdeen and its environs: from Robert the Bruce, Lord Byron and Bishop Elphinstone to Archibald Simpson, T. Scott Sutherland and Ian Wood, not forgetting Harry Gordon and Buff, Steve and George of *Scotland The What?* No story of Aberdeen would be complete without Alex Ferguson and Willie Miller, raising North-east spirits to the heights and glory of Gothenburg in 1983, when the Dons of Pittodrie took on the greatest club side in the world, Real Madrid, and won. No lack of confidence there! Indeed, the late Chris Anderson, vice-chairman of Aberdeen Football Club, made the valid point that the success in football terms arose in tandem with the oil industry. He firmly believed that that modern bonanza had instilled a new confidence in Aberdonians, spreading itself to all other aspects of local life. At last, perhaps, the native caution had been cast aside.

It is a curious fact that history, the overall story of mankind which should surely be the most fascinating of all subjects, has generally had a bad press. Voltaire thought it 'nothing more than a tableau of crimes and misfortunes', while the blunt Henry Ford of motor-car fame dismissed it as 'more or less bunk'. Carlyle called it 'a distillation of rumour' but may have been nearer the mark when he said history was 'the essence of innumerable biographies'. In his wisdom, Winston Churchill reminded us that a nation forgetting its past has no future. He added: 'If we open a quarrel between the past and present we shall find that we have lost the future.'

Whatever the opinions, history is for sure a day-by-day progression, without break, a never-ending chronicle that stretches from the mists of obscurity to the topical tales of yesterday. All is grist to the mill. On the basis that journalism is the first draft of history, I have had nearly sixty years of recording those fresh events, some of which will eventually take their meaningful place in the context of time.

This book is by no means a definitive history of Aberdeen. That has been tackled by many distinguished historians, not least the thirty-eight academics whose combined efforts produced two massive and well-researched volumes a few years ago. Instead, this is merely the attempt of one lone journalist casting an eye over his native corner and trying to make some sense of its intriguing background. If I had a speciality in journalism it was in seeking out people who made their mark in this world – and trying to discover what made them tick. So let's see what we can make of it all, this Granite City of Aberdeen . . . And Twal' Mile Roun'.

CHAPTER I

A Taste Of Aberdeen

It was one of the simple joys of growing up in rural Aberdeenshire to step outside on clear frosty nights and view a ghostly shimmer in the sky that stirred an excitement in the breast of a country child. Most times it was the aurora borealis, those merry dancers in the sky; at other times, no more than the glow of city lights in the distance. Either way, to the young imagination they became the Northern Lights of Aberdeen, to be enshrined one day in a song that would become the anthem of Aberdonianism.

That city of Aberdeen, encased in its Grampian cocoon, was a symbol of many things, from granite, fishing and, eventually, oil to a self-engendered reputation for meanness – as well as the most distinctive dialect of the Lowland Scots tongue. Not least, Aberdeen was the focal point of a county to which it was inextricably bound. In the great shift of population that began with the Industrial Revolution, that rural hinterland of Aberdeenshire had made a monumental contribution to the genetic base of the city with a calibre of human being well-seasoned to the back-breaking task of turning a sour and grudging land into some of the finest cattle country in the kingdom. So whatever the definition of a Glaswegian or a Dundonian, you didn't have to be born in the city of Aberdeen to call yourself an Aberdonian. That was claimed as an indisputable birthright by the country cousins who carried that label to the far corners of the earth with pride and passion.

From a childhood of the 1930s, I can still relive a day out in Aberdeen. First, the twenty-eight mile drive from Maud in the little green Austin 8 (RG 6502), negotiating that ultimate stretch of dual carriageway (then called 'the double road') that brought the excitement of the Gordon Barracks at the Bridge of Don. There, marching across the parade ground, you would spot many a country lad, not long from the plough, now drilled into military precision and ready for a posting to Gibraltar or Singapore. Crossing the Bridge of Don to King Street, before reaching the main thoroughfare of Union Street, you were soon consumed by the magic of the big city: the clank of the tramcars, the clop of the dray horse, the smell of hot butteries in the Empress Café or the linoleum in Raggie Morrison's. From the easy sway of the countryside, this was life at the top end. Aberdeen was surely the gateway to that wider world lying always to the south.

Those memories were vividly with me as I came again, seventy years later, to reacquaint myself with Aberdeen for the purpose at hand. On such a perilous venture, you must prepare for the fact that, whatever changes may or may not have taken place in what you are seeing, the one

Union Street in days of trams, horses and carts, c. 1900

certainty is that changes will have taken place within you, the observer. So the perspective will inevitably be different.

To gain a broad, initial sweep of Aberdeen, I drove down town from Hazlehead towards the Castlegate on a fine summer evening when the traffic had largely gone and there was time to appreciate the surroundings, letting loose the imagination on how this fine city grew out of the bare braes of nothing to become the handsome, thriving place it is today. You are not far down Queen's Road when you glance the now-silent quarry of Rubislaw to the left, a treasure of grey granite that lay undiscovered from the beginning of time until the 1800s, when it became the fashionable stone that gave the Granite City its name. That biggest of man-made holes, so dramatic in its depth as to become a tourist attraction in its day, is now filled with water, a non-descript loch rimmed by expensive houses and spacious company headquarters symbolising another of nature's hidden mysteries which would revolutionise the fortunes of Aberdeen in the second half of the twentieth century.

So you drive down Queen's Road, regal in the sparkling rock of its mansions, not least in number 50, built as his own home in 1887 by a master mason in the city, John Morgan, who also built Queen's Cross Kirk, which comes next on your itinerary. These magnificent designs were the brainchild of John Bridgeford Pirie, a much-neglected Aberdeen architect who was still only forty-one when he died in 1892. So you branch down Albyn Place, enhanced in its elegance by the gardened terraces of Queen's and Rubislaw to the left until you reach Holburn Junction, at

John Morgan's house, 50 Queen's Road

the top end of Union Street. As you view the mile-long stretch of the city's main thoroughfare, it is hard to imagine that it didn't exist until the 1800s, and that its construction became a major feat of engineering involving archways from below Market Street as far up as Diamond Street, taking in Union Bridge which carried the new street across the chasm of the Denburn. All of that without a mechanical digger in sight.

Like Princes Street in Edinburgh, of course, Union Street has lost much of its grace, replacing elegant shops and finance houses with some of the gaudy vulgarity of modern commercialism. The cheapening of the facade does not, however, detract from the magnificence of the concept as it strikes its way to the very heart and focal point of Aberdeen, which has for long been the Castlegate.

If our short journey from Hazlehead has taken us across acres once trod by Robert the Bruce, Mary, Queen of Scots, Lord Byron and so many others, it has been no more than a taste of what Aberdeen has become. The whole spread of the modern city, from its architecture to its industrial and cultural life, its ancient schools and universities, raises wonder at the calibre of our forefathers as they tackled the deprivation of primitive times and struggled, step by step, to give us the quality of life we enjoy today.

Union Street, looking west

CHAPTER 2

Where It All Began

If this is not quite a tale of two cities, it is most definitely a tale of two burghs which, within the memory of our grandparents, had their own separate identities, complete with councils and provosts, prides and prejudices, and inevitable rivalries. It was as recently as 1891 that they came together as the one city of Aberdeen.

That evening drive from the heights of Hazlehead and ending with the majestic sweep of Union Street was wholly within the former burgh of New Aberdeen. Turn left at the Castlegate, however, and King Street will guide you just as surely to the historic setting of Old Aberdeen, the impressive crown of King's College heralding an atmosphere not unlike that of Oxford or Cambridge. Before there was a King Street, in the early 1800s, that linking route between the two burghs rose from Broad Street to the Gallowgate, Causewayend and Mounthooly, dropping down to the High Street which carried you into the heart of the university town. King's College, founded in 1494, lies there to this day with all its academic grace. Past the Old Town House and across the main thoroughfare, you reach the ancient Cathedral of St Machar, named after one of the disciples of Columba and set in what is surely the most picturesque corner in the joint city of Aberdeen.

It stands in that leafy avenue called the Chanonry, once the centre of religious life in the North-east and home to the clergy, though the manses of that time did not survive the Reformation. However, two of the ruins were rescued by the Marquis of Huntly and converted to his town residence. That same site in time became Chanonry Lodge, still to this day the home of the principal of Aberdeen University and closest neighbour to the cathedral. Indeed, the university acquired the later mansions of the eighteenth and nineteenth centuries as they became home to many of its professors.

With all that in mind, I took a stroll down the Chanonry and could feel again that melancholy which lingers in the silence of a cathedral. History hovers over St Machar's like a guardian angel, its voice a whisper in the casting trees of an autumn day. On that solitary walk I was thinking of my old friend Flora Garry, a truly authentic voice of North-east poetry, who was born in 1900 and lived to within weeks of her centenary in 2000. At the back end of the First World War Flora came as a student to King's College, fresh from her Buchan background of hard times on the land. She, too, had come this way to sample the evening sophistication of Old Aberdeen,

St Machar's Cathedral

gazing in through the windows at dinner parties, all candlelight and flowers, where the professor's wife would preside 'in low-neckit goon'. Her thoughts would stray to her humble folks back on the croft at Glenardle, pleitering through dubs and drudgery and making sacrifices for the daughter's learning.

'Fine,' says I to masel
'Fine to be up in the wardle,'
An thocht wi a groo, on the brookie pots
In the kitchen at Glenardle.

The poem forming in Flora Garry's head captured the contrasting lifestyles and came to the fore many years later as 'The Professor's Wife'. The irony of the denouement was that, with 'the aul' folks lyin quaet in the kirkyard at Glenardle', the student herself ends up as a professor's wife. And that is exactly what happened to Flora Garry in real life. Behind those Chanonry casements of today Flora would still find the minister of St Machar's Cathedral, as well as the principal of the university, but little else to suggest academia. Within the high walls of those magnificent properties, built by great architects of two hundred years ago, you are today more likely to find an oil executive side by side with at least one distinguished member of the Aberdeenshire aristocracy who keeps up the tradition of Lord Huntly four hundred years ago. Happily, in the twenty-first century they remain a sociable bunch, gathering as a community in each other's mansions for occasional drinks parties and festive fun.

Their fine homes cluster round the Twin Towers of St Machar's Cathedral, a spiritual treasure that symbolises the history of the Kirk-toun of Aberdon, which became known as Old Aberdeen. Famous for its magnificent heraldic ceiling, it gained the status of cathedral in 1131 but owed its overall beauty to a succession of 'Building Bishops', as they were called. Those towers became a landmark for ships at sea and for those reaching Aberdeen by the slope of the Grampians. The present building dates back to Bishop Kininmund of 1355, while the kirkyard outside includes the burial ground of local people like Gavin Dunbar, Bishop of St Machar's and Chancellor of Scotland in the sixteenth century; the Glover family whose son Thomas gained fame in Japan; and the last provost of Old Aberdeen.

For all the antiquity of Old Aberdeen, however, the irony remains that it became a burgh of barony only in 1498, by which time the younger neighbour of New Aberdeen had been a royal burgh for more than 300 years. Whatever their respective ages, the signs are that there were inhabitants in these parts some 5,000 years before Christ, continuing in their various civilisations through the Ages of Ice, Stone, Bronze and Iron, but with scant evidence of what was happening in those days. For certain, there was a settled community by 1800 BC.

Old Aberdeen would grow in a crook of the Don on the south bank of the river with access to the north via the ancient Brig o' Balgownie, regarded as a feat of engineering when completed in 1320 at the insistence of Robert the Bruce. If Old Aberdeen was destined to be a small town it would at least bask in the prestige of the cathedral and eventually a university, along with a highly impressive bishop's palace, with large courtyard of four towers, a great hall, a hospital and chambers for the chaplains. The intelligentsia lived here, believing they were a superior breed to their neighbours, with whom they sought very little contact. By 1636, however, Old Aberdeen was still little more than a one-street town of 800 citizens, increased only modestly by the population of King's College, which was itself of minor proportion at that time. But one man above all had left his mark on this old town.

CHAPTER 3

The Man Who Founded King's

Bishop William Elphinstone, priest, lawyer, diplomat and lecturer at the University of Paris, must go down as one of the greatest figures in the history of Aberdeen. Best remembered as the founder of King's College, this illegitimate son of Glasgow first arrived to be Bishop of Aberdeen in 1483. Within a few years, however, he had taken on the greater mantle of Chancellor of Scotland under James III, attending Parliament, playing a major part in the affairs of the nation, and becoming widely accepted as Scotland's leading man of his day.

During thirty years he absorbed himself completely in the life of the town with all the feelings of a native, a powerful force behind the building of a better St Machar's Cathedral, a church for the Grey Friars, the old Bridge of Dee, and, of course, the University and College of St Mary, which became known as King's. St Andrews had had a university since 1411 and Glasgow since 1451 and now it was Aberdeen's turn. Whether it was entirely his own idea remains unclear but Elphinstone, a man of vision and good contacts, was certainly the driving force, first in making the tiring journey to Rome to gain approval for the idea and then in raising the funds to make it all possible. The actual papal bull which sanctioned the arrival of Aberdeen University in 1494 came from one of the notorious Borgia family no less, Pope Alexander VI, but Aberdonians were magnanimous enough to forgive his sins.

In presenting his case to the Pope, Elphinstone had claimed that Aberdeen was an oasis in the midst of a population that was 'rude and ignorant of letters, and almost barbarous' and therefore in need of his civilising idea. That was overstating the case but it served his purpose, which almost certainly carried an element of vanity. A university would surely raise his own status to the level of the leading clergy in Glasgow and St Andrews. Once he had secured his funds the building proceeded and the university was in operation by 1497, with construction work continuing until 1505. The first principal, who arrived in 1500, was the Dundonian Hector Boece, a product of St Andrews and the University of Paris, where he was a professor when Bishop Elphinstone lured him to Aberdeen.

Elphinstone himself was the chancellor and among his early staff was James Cumine, the first professor of medicine to be appointed in Britain. Oxford and Cambridge did not follow suit until the 1540s. Aberdeen University is therefore credited with having produced the very first qualified doctors in the English-speaking world. Not every faculty was as far advanced as the medical faculty and indeed Bishop Elphinstone was still deeply involved in working out his plans for the university when he died in 1514, a worn-out man aged eighty-three. In the decades that followed, King's College lapsed into some decline and that helped to promote the rival institution that was Marischal College, not that it was greeted with much acclaim when another such institution existed so near at hand.

The last Catholic principal of King's was Alexander Anderson, a substantial figure who, in the Reformation upheaval of 1560, armed his students and drove out the Reforming mob which was set to storm the college precincts. Along with some of his professors, Anderson had previously gone to Edinburgh to take issue with John Knox and his Reformers. He even secured from Queen Mary an injunction that the college should be 'unhurt, unharmit, unmolestit, inquietit' by any of her subjects. But his days were numbered and in 1569 the regent Earl of Moray, the most powerful man in Scotland, came to Aberdeen with his commissioners and summoned Anderson and his colleagues to an inquiry at the Kirk of St Nicholas. Predictably, they refused to sign the Confession of Faith and were promptly removed from office. Anderson, who lived out the rest of his life in Aberdeen, was succeeded at King's by Alexander Arbuthnot of Pitcarles in the Mearns, a highly popular figure who was also a close friend of Andrew

The crowning glory of King's College

Melville, the leading churchman and educationalist of his day, who hailed from Baldowie in Angus and became principal of Glasgow University in 1574.

Royal Rebuke

But for all his fine human qualities, Arbuthnot was not a success. Whereas Andrew Melville had hoped that the modern methods of discipline through which he himself had revitalised Glasgow University would be introduced at King's College, there was no sign of such progress. Parliament appointed a commission to see what was happening at King's, and Arbuthnot was roundly censured by King James himself, a royal rebuke that may have contributed to his death when he was just forty-five. Parliament eventually came up with a New Foundation for King's, in which the subjects to be taught included physiology, geography, astrology, history and Hebrew and one regent was to 'propound the principles of reasoning from the best Greek and Latin authors'.

Scottish education was on the move. Edinburgh University was founded in 1583 and ten years later Aberdeen was presented with that second college by George Keith, the fifth Earl Marischal. At twenty-seven, Keith had succeeded to one of the most powerful titles and inheritances in the land, with castles the length and breadth of Scotland. Of all the nobles in the North-east, he was the only one who could stand up to the power of the Gordons. Now, as the corresponding figure to Elphinstone of Old Aberdeen, he was giving rise to Marischal College, with a preamble which said that learning in the north of Scotland was still generally deficient. Therefore, the earl wanted to establish 'a public gymnasium where young men may be thoroughly trained and instructed in the humane arts and in philosophy and a purer piety . . .'

George Keith, the Earl Marischal
who founded the college

If vanity was part of Elphinstone's drive it could not be ruled out in the case of the Earl Marischal either. With the idea of a second university less than two miles away seeming ridiculous, his stronger motive was to establish a Protestant institution, balancing up the lingering Catholicism of King's, even if that had been largely purged by then. After the Reformation of 1560 Keith was at least spared the long journey to Rome to seek approval, gaining it instead from the General Assembly of the Church of Scotland and proceeding at a much faster rate than was possible for Elphinstone.

Rivalry with King's

The scheme of education was almost identical to that of the New Foundation for King's. In presenting a new university to the North-east, however, he was almost beaten to it by Sir Alexander Fraser, the virtual founder of the burgh we know today as Fraserburgh. It is an extraordinary story. Having converted the little village of Faithlie into a burgh of barony, Sir Alexander persuaded James VI to grant him, in 1592, authority for a university with the same privileges as those of any other university in the land. He took upon himself the financial burden of erecting such an institution, a rather foolhardy enterprise, one might think, considering the location in a remote corner of Scotland and with an established rival in Aberdeen, less than fifty miles away. The Scots parliament did come to his aid with the cost, at least to the extent of granting him funds belonging to the churches in the neighbouring parishes of Philorth, Tyrie, Crimond and Rathen.

Completing the buildings by the end of the sixteenth century, Sir Alexander appointed the new minister at Fraserburgh, the Rev. Charles Ferme, as principal of his university. Ever a man with an eye to the future, he had had this appointment in mind when he chose his new minister. Mr Ferme had previously been professor of philosophy at Edinburgh University, in days when the interchange between church and education was a common feature of professional life.

Fraserburgh University opened its doors in 1600, on the corner site of High Street and Denmark Street where the Alexandra Hotel became known to future generations. (There is still a street called College Bounds in the town today.) Sadly, little evidence survives to tell us of the scholastic life except that the university closed after five years. A man of strong conviction, Principal Ferme became embroiled in the religious turmoil that followed the Reformation. He incurred royal displeasure, was denounced by the Privy Council and was sent to prison in Stirling and at Doune Castle before serving three years of detention on the island of Bute. In his absence, and with no successor appointed, teaching at the university collapsed. Thus the vision of Sir Alexander Fraser was brought to a sad end, leaving us to speculate on what might have happened if Principal Ferme, a man of undoubted brilliance and high ideals, had not been removed from his task to be remembered only as the first and last principal of Fraserburgh University.

Three Universities

Fraserburgh University was called back into service in 1647 when the plague broke out in Aberdeen and students and professors from King's College arrived to take up their abode, reviving memories of that brief academic venture. (Similarly, refugees from Marischal College found a temporary home in Peterhead which, thereafter, liked to claim some form of university connection, however tenuous, if only to be upside-down with its neighbour!) It tells us something about the educational climate of the North-east that, in those early days of the 1600s, Aberdeenshire alone could boast three universities while the whole of England had only Oxford and Cambridge. It has to be said, however, that both the Aberdeen universities had a strong element of the secondary school about them, with children enrolling as early as twelve and graduating by sixteen. In all truth, King's College was struggling to raise itself from the period of depression and return to the dynamism it had known in the days of Elphinstone and Gavin Dunbar, another distinguished Bishop of Aberdeen.

Most of the benevolence of the time was going either to Marischal College or Aberdeen Grammar School. In 1619, when the Protestant Bishop of Aberdeen, Patrick Forbes, was instructed by James VI to look into the affairs of the two universities he reported that King's was in a miserable state, its funds in a condition of 'abominable dilapidation' and its resources handled with as little skill as if 'nather a God hade been in heaven to count with, nor men on earth to examine their ways'. By another visitation in 1638, however, matters had improved substantially.

In 1623 the minister at King Edward, Dr William Guild, presented the town with a house in the Broadgate to provide a spacious gateway for Marischal College, the appearance of which was blighted by the high tenement houses that had been built across the street. (Dr Guild would no doubt have had similarly generous thoughts if he had lived in the twentieth century and found his eye just as offended by the monstrosity of St Nicholas House. Some lessons are never learned.)

Outwith the universities, much of the educational focus landed on Aberdeen Grammar School which benefited from the fact that it came under the aegis of the town council, a privilege shared with Marischal College. That status of municipal institution was the first essential difference between the Grammar School and its later rival, Robert Gordon's College, both of which became fee-paying schools for boys. Gordon's was a privately funded institution from the time it was built in 1732 and, in educational terms, that turned out to be the most significant event in Aberdeen during the first half of the eighteenth century.

CHAPTER 4

A Town on Fire

Historians will debate whether the Romans ever reached as far as Aberdeen, though Agricola, who was governing Britain for the visitors in that first century after Christ, did come north around AD 83 to engage the locals in the Battle of Mons Graupius, believed to have been fought somewhere near Bennachie. His victory over the Caledonian men led to Roman settlements in the North-east but the fierce fighting of the local tribes put an end to his grand plan to conquer the whole of Britain. Within a few years he was heading back south, speaking of a place called 'Devana' which is taken to be Aberdeen. The Romans did, of course, return at a later stage, setting up camp at Peterculter, but whether they ventured into town is a matter of speculation.

More to the point, the origins of the burgh once known as New Aberdeen are to be found at Gilcomston, with a couple of the standing stones that were part of a Bronze Age circle in what became Hill Street. Gilcomston, then, had a community living high between the two streams of the Denburn and the Gilcomston Burn, with a vast stretch of water spreading to the east, called the Loch, and taking in the area we know as Woolmanhill, Loch Street, Spring Garden and Maberly Street. With the River Don to the north, the Dee to the south, the beach to the east and the extensive Stocket Forest to the west, the bounds of Aberdeen were more or less set. Until around 1200, however, there were very few certainties about its history, an observation that could be extended to the history of Scotland itself.

The various religious orders played a big part in the life of the community, having acquired large parcels of land and property in Aberdeenshire. In 1240 Alexander II, King of Scotland, handed over his palace and gardens in Schoolhill to the Dominicans, or Black Friars, who established their monastery. Twenty years later, the Carmelite Friars built a house at the Green, while the Grey Friars arrived in Broadgate much later.

Dee and Don

Meanwhile, there was a movement of population from Gilcomston down the Denburn to the Green, which would become the site of the burgh of Aberdeen. It had grown together from clusters of hamlets between Dee and Don, sheltered by half a dozen hillocks with names like

Castle Hill, St Katherine's Hill, Gallow Hill, Woolman Hill and School Hill. Even then, the communities of the North-east were trying to form some kind of economic co-operation, stretching from Aberdeen to Inverness, as shown in a royal charter granted in 1179 by William the Lion. He also granted Aberdeen a charter, giving goods belonging to the burgesses immunity from all tolls and customs at markets and fairs throughout Scotland. Most of all, it established a Merchant Guild which, for centuries thereafter, would provide the rulers of the burgh.

Aberdeen of the 1200s was doing well in the matter of royal charters, bringing privileges of land protection as well as those trade immunities. But the ambience of the place was not for the faint-hearted as far as cleanliness and hygiene were concerned. In fact the filth and squalor of domestic homes and narrow streets deep in mud were beyond belief; middens and pigsties everywhere gave rise to an unbearable stench as roaming dogs, cats, pigs and poultry matched the population level of the humans. Even ladies of the highest order, it was recorded, seldom had a bath or changed their underclothes.

There were no stone-and-lime houses in the burgh till the sixteenth century; instead, wooden houses thatched with straw, broom or heather were ready victims in the event of fire. One such outbreak, in 1244, more or less destroyed Aberdeen and might have seemed like a blessing in disguise since it wiped out so much of the filth and squalor, giving an opportunity for new beginnings. However, the rebuilding programme brought still more wooden houses – bigger and more spacious and readily available from the resources of the Stocket Forest – and completed in good time for another such blaze twenty years later.

The town destroyed by that fire of 1244 was really no more than a big village of about 1,500 people, running from Castle Hill, round the Shiprow and the Green but not reaching as far as the area we know as George Street. Curling round from north and west were those forest lands of Stocket, including Foresterhill, reaching down towards Gilcomston. Between Dee and Don and stretching inland to the Justice Mills you found not only crofts but royal residences, in the days when the monarch moved around the country. King William the Lion, for example, had built himself a palace overlooking the estuary of the Denburn at the other end of that slope which began at the Kirk of St Nicholas.

CHAPTER 5

Robert the Bruce in Aberdeen

A man with the fancy name of Ricardus Cementarius became the first provost of Aberdeen in 1272 and it is no surprise to find that, with a moniker like that, he was a mason, engaged on work at the original castle on Castle Hill which was in need of repair. In his day the burgh was administered in four quarters, each under the charge of a baillie (Aberdeen always used the double 'l'). Those quarters were named as the Futty, the Green, the Even, and the Crooked. The Even lay north of the Green and west of the Guestrow and the Gallowgate, while the Crooked lay north of the Castlegate and east of the Guestrow and the Gallowgate.

Of course, democracy had not yet raised its head and municipal government was in the hands of a powerful elite drawn from the burgesses of guild. There is evidence of cloth-making as an occupation but even then it was fish-curing that was the main industry. The English were buying pickled Aberdeen salmon for their soldiers and the cured fish gained such a reputation on the Continent that it was given a name of its own, 'Habberdine', believed to have come from the Dutch way of saying 'Aberdeen'. Meanwhile the country folk of the North-east were bringing in wool and hides from their animals and trading them, along with the fuel of wood and peat, for the fish of the Futty folk and the cloth of the local weavers. That rural trade remained the town's biggest business.

Aberdeen had fared well under a succession of kings from David I, who became King of the Scots in 1124, bringing unity to Scotland and a stability to the rule of his own family who survived for the next four reigns. All that came unstuck, however, in 1286 when his descendant, Alexander III, was thrown from his horse and killed at Kinghorn in Fife. This glory period in Scottish history ended with dilemma. Alexander's heir was his little granddaughter Margaret, known as 'The Maid of Norway', who was the child of his own daughter Margaret and King Erik of Norway. One tragedy followed another when young Margaret died in Orkney at the age of eight. The situation became more bizarre when a German lady claimed that she was the rightful Queen of Scots, one of a dozen or more people with the same idea. The King of England, Edward I, entrusted with the task of deciding who should take the throne, plumped for John Balliol, who had sworn his loyalty.

Hammer of Scots

By 1296, however, the new King of Scots had turned against Edward, and that was how the War of Independence was brought to the gates of Aberdeen. Edward, who became known as the Hammer of the Scots, came north with his vast army, accepted Balliol's abdication and proceeded in triumph, crossing over the hills to Deeside and arriving in Aberdeen on Saturday, 14th July 1296. He was there to receive homage from his people, many of them county families with land in England as well as Scotland, before returning south. Scotland's champion of freedom, William Wallace, proceeded to rout the English at the Battle of Stirling Bridge in 1297 but was defeated by Edward at Falkirk the following year. Edward, who was back in Aberdeen in August 1303, had set his sights firmly on Scotland and two years later the greatest stumbling-block to that ambition was removed. Wallace was betrayed and taken to Smithfield, London, where he was hanged, drawn and quartered.

In all history, William Wallace was without doubt the country's finest patriot, selfless in a way that could not be said of Robert the Bruce, who generally had an agenda of his own when he was fighting for Scotland. That appalling death of Wallace, however, stirred a new determination in the Scottish people, and Bruce, perhaps with the thought that he might have been more of a support to the country's hero, took up the cudgels and became a real hero himself. The man who had once sworn loyalty to Edward was now ready to be crowned King of Scots, an event that happened at Scone on 27th March 1306. The Hammer sent his English army northwards, determined to re-establish himself in Scotland and ready to follow in person despite his age and failing health. But he didn't make it, dying on the journey near Carlisle in August 1307.

The English forces continued, however, defeating Bruce at Methven in Perthshire and sending the king and his queen and party scampering over the hills to seek refuge in Aberdeen. It was the beginning of a deep association with the burgh in which he never forgot the friendship and loyalty they received in their time of need. Sending his queen and family to Kildrummy Castle to escape the English army, Bruce put them under the protection of his young brother, Sir Nigel Bruce, and the Earl of Atholl. But the English caught up and, as the queen and family made their escape, Nigel Bruce put up a heroic fight to keep them at bay. He was finally captured and taken to Berwick,

Robert the Bruce, who spent more time in Aberdeen after Bannockburn than anywhere else

where he was hanged. As an even more gruesome end to that particular tale, the Earl of Atholl was not only executed in London but his severed head was given its place on London Bridge, alongside the bleaching skull of William Wallace!

Though they escaped from Kildrummy, Robert the Bruce's two sisters, Mary and Christian, were betrayed at Tain and handed over to the frightening prospect of Edward's men who kept them in iron cages for years thereafter. Christian survived to spend her last years in Aberdeen, living at the family palace in the Green.

Earl of Buchan

But if Bruce had many friends and supporters in Aberdeen, he did have one sworn enemy not far away: John Comyn, the Earl of Buchan and a member of a powerful North-east family. The two men finally came face to face in a church in Dumfries in 1306, when Bruce was trying to make some kind of overture. Instead, passions ran high and in the ensuing row he plunged his dagger into Comyn and killed him. Bruce was excommunicated for his troubles. Having disposed of the Comyn threat, his finest moment still lay ahead: at the Battle of Bannockburn in 1314, where he became a national hero. After Bannockburn, Bruce spent more time in Aberdeen than anywhere else in Scotland, sharing, with his family, a warm affection for the place, a fact not widely appreciated. He never forgot the loyalty of the inhabitants and the refuge they provided, not least in his time of serious illness. His second daughter, Matilda, married Thomas Isaacs, a burgess and town clerk of Aberdeen, who lived at Exchequer Row, where they brought up their daughters Catherine and Joanna. Matilda died in 1353.

Bruce and his family came to regard Aberdeen as 'their own romantic town', and his favours in its direction were far in excess of those accorded to places like Edinburgh and Perth which might have seemed further up the pecking order. So it is all the more surprising that a town so partial to its king, and so royally rewarded, took so long to remember him with a statue. That honour had been reserved most dramatically in the triangle by His Majesty's Theatre for William Wallace, an incomparable hero of course, though there is no real evidence that he ever set foot in the town. Not until 2006 did Aberdeen City Council set out to rectify the omission. It agreed to launch a competition, inviting designs for a statue that would occupy a prominent position in the city centre.

Death of Bruce

With the death of Robert the Bruce in 1329, Aberdonians mourned not only a heroic king but their own great benefactor. Sadness was compounded by the fact that David, his son and heir, was only six years old, laying Scotland wide open to the designs of the English whose reigning king was now Edward III, grandson of the Hammer of the Scots. And just as his grandfather had used John Balliol as his puppet to gain power in Scotland, so did the king use Balliol's son

Edward for a repeat performance. In August 1332, Edward Balliol landed with an English army in Fife, defeated the Scots at Dupplin in Perthshire and promptly had himself crowned King of Scots. So, in the chaos of the time, Scotland had two kings, with the young David Bruce (David II) sent to France for his own safety.

He returned when he was eighteen and Aberdeen's fortunes began to rise once more, just as they had done in his father's time. He held his first parliament in the town in 1342, reopened a mint in Exchequer Row for the encouragement of trade and picked up on that family feeling that Aberdeen was home. But luck was not on his side. He invaded England and was taken prisoner at the Battle of Neville Cross in 1346, when the English put a ransom on his head. Aberdeen was among the burghs that sought to meet the ransom, some of which was paid in wool from the North-east. He was held prisoner for eleven years and died in Edinburgh in 1371.

David was succeeded as king by his nephew, Robert II, who had acted as guardian during his uncle's imprisonment. He would now be the man to found the Stewart dynasty. He was also to father the boy Alexander, who became known as the Wolf of Badenoch, a wild bandit who gained control of the whole North and North-east of Scotland. The Wolf's son, another Alexander Stewart, was in much the same mould. He occupied Aberdeen and became the Earl of Mar by threatening the widowed countess that he would burn down Kildrummy Castle if she didn't marry him.

CHAPTER 6

Was Shakespeare Here?

In the fifteenth century, the civic leadership of Aberdeen was characterised by struggles among the most prominent families, with names such as Marr, Fyfe, Chalmers, Collinson, Menzies, Rutherford and Cullen featuring prominently. The Chalmers family was dominant when the Menzies name appeared on the scene. Gilbert Menzies arrived from Perth, became a baillie in 1412, dealt in land and by 1423 was provost. It was the beginning of a dynasty that would hold sway over Aberdeen's affairs for the next 200 years, during which members of the family would occupy the provost's chair for 114 years, one of them for twenty-nine years in succession. This was autocracy run wild, from a family which mixed in the highest circles of nobility, even royalty, and certainly proved themselves administrators of good calibre. For more than three centuries the estate of Pitfodels was the family's main base.

The original Gilbert Menzies was provost four times and the town's commissioner to Parliament three times. However, the Menzies family found a serious rival with the emergence of Sir John Rutherford of Migvie and Tarland, who was elected provost eleven times and represented Aberdeen in Parliament. The sixteenth century began with Menzies domination but ended with a Rutherford in charge. Trouble boiled up in the council when John Cheyne of Fortrie, an advocate who became provost in 1593, led a protest to the Privy Council with an indictment of the Menzies family which claimed that for eighty years the liberties and privileges and free election in Aberdeen had been 'pervertit and abrogat by the unlauchful usurption of the provostrie by the race of Menzies'. The action failed and Cheyne was out of the council at the next election, though he did find his way back in time to be provost.

At the distance of five hundred years it is hard to envisage the tenor of daily living and, not least, to connect with the old Scots tongue, expressed in words and spellings quite different from the later vernacular of our native North-east. Elements of Latin and Chaucer are to be found within the speech. Indeed, the overall view of our ancestors in that period is of a rustic peasantry living out drab and dreary lives in conditions of hardship and squalor. In an age without newspapers, radio or television you wonder how they knew what was going on in the world. All communication came by the speed of horse and coach.

Yet any idea of anarchy and lawlessness must be judged against the reigning structure of society, from governments and town councils to trade organisations and commercial enterprises, where much diligence was applied. Our ancestors were keen to learn and by no means did drabness dictate every aspect of their lives. There is a vivid record, for example, of how Aberdonians reacted in 1511 when word spread that Margaret Tudor, James IV's young queen, was to pay them a visit. Their efforts at giving her a right royal welcome benefited from the fact that the queen was accompanied by that most brilliant of court poets, William Dunbar. He was there to immortalise the event and Aberdeen most certainly put on the style, the town council having resolved to 'receive our sovereign lady the queen as honourably as any burgh of Scotland except Edinburgh and to make large expenses thereupon'.

Orders were given to remove all middens from the streets, to empty, redd and clean them, and to clear away all pigsties. The queen was met outside the town by the burgesses in their Sunday best, four of the handsomest dressed in velvet, and carried into town under a pall of crimson velvet with guns going off all round. It was said that a procession of girls greeted her at the gate and the streets were hung with tapestries and there were pageants at every corner. There was a combined choir and orchestra of young ladies, 'all clad in green of marvellous beauty' and 'with hair detressit' hanging like golden threads under white embroidered hats. They played on timbrels and 'sang richt sweetly'. At the Cross there was an abundance of wine and the crowd convoyed the queen to her lodgings. While the Reformed Kirk didn't encourage excess in public festivals, it was not a spoilsport altogether.

Again, with James VI of Scotland expected in Aberdeen in 1580, the council decided to decorate the town and lay on theatrical displays. An opportunity to make merry was seldom missed, brightening up the more sober aspects of life in those days. When James then became James I of England in 1603 his accession was another occasion to be celebrated in a grand manner. The people of Aberdeen were summoned to the church by the sound of trumpet and drum to 'prais God for his gratious and mervellous providence' and thereafter to light bonfires through all the streets, ring the bells, make merry and express 'the joy and glaidness of the hartis of the people'.

The Cullens were among the richest and most influential of the merchant families in Aberdeen around 1500 and beyond. A later member of the family, Alexander Cullen, who was elected provost several times around 1600, was the man who gave the freedom of the burgh to Laurence Fletcher and his group of London theatricals called 'His Majesty's Servants'. It was Aberdeen's first visit by a touring repertory company, and the significance of this story from 1601 is that the company was said to have included among its strolling players no less a figure than William Shakespeare himself. The bard was certainly a member of Laurence Fletcher's company in London, and one of his editors, Charles Knight, believed it was the Aberdeen visit that gave him the idea for *Macbeth* and claimed he had gone to Forres to gain local colour. It is an intriguing thought, if lacking in proof.

William Shakespeare, believed to have visited Aberdeen in 1601

CHAPTER 7

The Reformation

Though the overthrow of popery at the Reformation led to a massive amount of trouble in central Scotland, Aberdeen escaped the worst of the damage when it came to church property. This was the biggest revolution in European history but, when it had all settled down, the North-east still had many Catholics in positions of power, people like the Earl of Huntly, Principal Anderson of King's College and the provost of Aberdeen, Menzies of Pitfodels. Aberdonians were not in favour of destroying local property so many of the Roman Catholic monuments survived into the days of the Reformed Church. However, Reformers from Angus and the Mearns did invade the town in January 1560 and proceeded to demolish the monasteries of the Black Friars in Schoolhill, the White Friars at the Green and the neighbouring Trinity Friars.

They pillaged the Grey Friars' church in the Broadgate but were interrupted by protesting townsfolk. They then headed for King's College and St Machar's Cathedral and inflicted serious damage on the latter, though the Catholic Earl of Huntly had removed most of the valuables. The local council sold the ornaments of St Nicholas Church for the common good, the sole buyer being Provost Menzies of Pitfodels himself, paying a total of £45. The provost held on to his office, and the money paid for the effects of St Nicholas was used to repair the harbour and maintain the Bridge of Don and the town's defences. Principal Anderson of King's College was suspected of having sold books and other effects belonging to the college.

Whatever was happening elsewhere in Scotland with the Reformation, the whole upheaval was confined to a matter of days in Aberdeen. Though the three monasteries were destroyed, the only human casualty seems to have been a monk who was cremated by accident. The Roman bishop kept his job and Provost Menzies slipped across from his Catholic faith to become an elder of the Kirk no less. Aberdonians can handle situations like that! The impression of bitter conflict that attaches to the Reformation would more properly apply, as far as Aberdeen was concerned, to a century later when Presbyterians and Episcopalians were at each other's throats.

John Knox, Scotland's Protestant reformer, paid his one and only visit to Aberdeen in 1564, though not much of it is recorded except that he stayed for six weeks and preached several times in St Nicholas. Knox, incidentally, was not forthcoming about his ancestry but there was a belief that he was rooted in the Buchan family of Knox from the parish of Strichen. His grandson, Nathaniel Welsh, attended Aberdeen Grammar School in 1622.

Witchcraft

If the Reformation did away with many practices of the past, that of burning witches at the stake was not one of them. In fact it became more prevalent. Aberdeen had an epidemic of witch-hunting at the end of the sixteenth century, and in 1596–97 alone, twenty-four women and two men died in the most unspeakable manner. Two women were starved, branded and prodded with sharp stakes until they died while the others were simply burned, much to public satisfaction. James VI of Scotland was among those with a horror of witches, reflecting a widespread public fear of their activities at the time, though, in all truth, most of them were no more than harmless old hags. They would hold their gatherings at the Mealmarket, the Market Cross or the Castlegate but their favourite meeting point was St Katherine's Hill, roughly where the Adelphi is today.

Their main night of the year was 14th September, the Feast of the Holy Rood, on the eve of which they would gather for their allegedly devilish rituals. Their leader was Thomas Leis, son of a notorious woman called Janet Wischert, whose fellow members of the cult had names like Bessie Thom, Isobel Cockie, Christen Mitchell, Isobel Brown and Isobel Manteith. An undesirable character called Andro Man, himself arrested for witchcraft, escaped the law by turning witch-finder and putting many an old soul to her unthinkable death. The evidence against them was frequently nothing more than hearsay and superstition as they were despatched to the Tolbooth en route to the stake. In days of little public entertainment, the roasting of human beings became a spectator sport, with crush-barriers to contain the enthusiasm.

CHAPTER 8

Mary, Queen of Scots

With the Reformation splitting Scotland into the rival camps of Catholicism and Protestant-ism, Mary, Queen of Scots decided to return from France. Both sides were trying to woo her; the Protestant parliament led by her own illegitimate half-brother, Lord James Stewart, and the Catholics by the most powerful figure on their side of the fence, the Earl of Huntly. Huntly's plan was that Aberdeen would become the focal point for the Catholics, with Mary established at the head of a vast army, in an attempt to bring Scotland back to the old religion. The idea was that they would march south to Edinburgh and begin the overthrow of Protestantism. But matters didn't go Huntly's way. Mary gave to Lord James Stewart the earldoms of both Mar and Moray, which made him a neighbour of Huntly, his sworn enemy. On her return to this country she landed at Leith, as advised by her Protestant parliament, and turned

down Huntly's invitation, the latter returning to his North-east stronghold of Strathbogie. In the summer of 1562, however, Mary did arrive in Aberdeen and was put up at the bishop's palace in the Chanonry.

Meanwhile, in a family feud between the Gor-dons and the Ogilvies, Huntly's third son, Sir John Gordon, inflicted serious wounds on James Ogilvie of Cardell and was arrested in Edinburgh. He escaped and returned to Aberdeenshire. As Queen Mary held court in Aberdeen, one of the first to seek an audience was the Countess of Huntly, who had come with the twin purpose of pleading for her son, Sir John, and inviting the queen to visit them at Strathbogie. On both counts she failed, Mary insisting that Sir John give himself up. Anticipating the outcome of all this, the Earl of Huntly had gathered an army of a thousand men and marched down on Aberdeen, encamping at Cullerlie, twelve

Mary, Queen of Scots stayed at the bishop's palace in Aberdeen in 1562 miles away. And there he would be met by Lord James Stewart, now the Earl of Moray, who had mustered a superior force.

It was all over next day, as Huntly withdrew to the Hill o' Fare. Well outnumbered, his men were driven into the glen of Corrichie Burn; Huntly himself fell in the battle and five of the Gordons were convicted and hanged a couple of days later in the full public view of the Castlegate. His son, Sir John, captured once more, was brought into town to meet his fate. For the act of decapitating him, it is said that the Earl of Moray forced Queen Mary to witness the gruesome deed from the window of the marischal's house, a particularly distressing experience since it was strongly hinted that Sir John had been her lover.

But nothing is forever in history. For all the Catholicism of the Huntly family, the earl who succeeded his father after Corrichie Burn took part in an unthinkable episode in June 1597. It followed a battle in which the Earl of Argyll and seven thousand Highlanders invaded the Gordon territory, determined to put Huntly in his place. The neighbouring Forbeses were no friends of the Gordons and lay ready to assist the invaders. But Huntly and his fellow leading-lord of the faith, the Earl of Errol, mustered 2,000 retainers, met the Celts between the Cabrach and Glenlivet, and sent them into retreat.

The Protestantism of Knox was on the ascendancy, however, and within the Kirk of St Nicholas that Sunday in 1597, the 6th Earl of Huntly and the 9th Earl of Errol publicly renounced the Pope's authority and were received into the Protestant religion. They both made full confession of their defection and accepted the Protestant religion in the presence of a crowded congregation of 'noblemen, barons, gentlemen and common folk'. The bishop absolved them and Huntly struck a peace pact with his enemy, Lord Forbes, burying all quarrels as the two men shook hands in the kirk. All this in the presence of the king's commissioner, who delivered a wand of peace to the earls and received them back to royal favour. They partook of communion and there was music and toasts and everyone entered into the spirit of jolly celebration. Despite all this, however, it took only a few years before Huntly was excommunicated by the General Assembly because he was still adhering to the Catholic faith.

CHAPTER 9

The Troubles

By the time James VI of Scotland left in 1603 to become James I of England, the Episcopal rule of bishops had largely been imposed upon the Church of Scotland, much to the chagrin of the Presbyterians. The first General Assembly after the union was held in Aberdeen in 1605, when John Forbes of Alford was chosen as moderator. James's son, who would become Charles I, was born a weakling with so many problems that he was not expected to survive. So he was sent to spend his early years at Fyvie Castle, under the care of Sir Alexander Seton and his wife, Lilias Drummond (she who was starved to death and became known as the Green Lady ghost of Fyvie). Sir Alexander was an able law-yer and statesman who had been poli-tical adviser to the boy's father, James VI, and later chancellor of Scotland.

Charles I spent his early years at Fyvie Castle

But the boy revived, except for his stammer, and eventually returned to London, where he became an accom-plished scholar, succeeding his father in 1625. Aberdeen rejoiced in his corona-tion but trouble would soon build up for the new king. He ran into the National Covenant, which arose to fight the Divine Right of Kings and the imposition of the Episcopal system on the Church of Scotland. His intro-duction of the new Prayer Book, with-out much thought for Scottish feelings, aroused resentment north of the border and was met with opposition right across society, including the nobility, who asked him to reconsider what he was doing.

But the king was not for turning. In fact he made it plain that opposition from now onwards would be regarded as treason. It was a step too far. Within days the opponents had drawn up the National Covenant, cleverly worded in that it expressed loyalty to the king but nevertheless made it clear that those who signed it would have to defend the Kirk, the laws and the liberties of Scotland that Charles seemed to be undermining. Though cautious at first, the burghs mainly came down on the side of the Covenant and, in March 1638, commissioners from the Convention of Royal Burghs brought a copy of the National Covenant to Aberdeen to gain the endorsement of the town council. But canny Aberdonians had a habit of avoiding religious issues like the Reformation and the Covenant and the council refused to back it. Within a few weeks they were found to be the only royal burgh to have taken that action, citing their loyalty to the king as the reason.

There were influences at work, however, as the second Marquis of Huntly, a leading nobleman in the North-east and a staunch supporter of the king, was spurred into action, especially when he found that his aristocratic enemies, such as the Frasers and Forbeses, were supporting the Covenant. Huntly knew he could muster a sizeable army at short notice and it became clear that both sides were lining up for trouble. Just how serious that trouble might become was hardly foreseen.

Earl of Montrose

In July of that year eight leading Covenanters, including the Earl of Montrose, arrived to give further publicity to their cause, only to find that the council, having been given a second chance to support it, had simply confirmed its rejection. The visitors were offered the customary Cup of Bon Accord, which they declined, being more interested in pursuing their purpose. The snub did not go down well. They had hoped to preach their message from the Kirk of St Nicholas but found the doors locked and barred. Instead, they held their meeting at the Castlegate but the crowd was disappointing and the signatures were few. Delighted to hear of Aberdeen's response, Charles I sent his thanks, along with a hint that rewards would follow. A few weeks later he granted the town its Great Charter, a raft of privileges obtained to this day.

Actually, public opinion in the town was divided between the two factions. But with the news that Montrose was forming a Covenanting army, Aberdeen was preparing to defend itself against attack in the spring of 1639. They dug trenches, lined up their twelve cannon and organised the men of the town into troops, gathering at the Links for drill. A royal proclamation read out at the Market Cross appointed the 2nd Marquis of Huntly as the king's lord lieutenant in the north and ordered all men between sixteen and sixty to join him.

The Covenanting army of 9,000 men under the Earl of Montrose arrived in Aberdeen on 30th March 1639 and encamped where the Beach Ballroom stands today. The events of that time are graphically recorded, thanks to an Aberdeen lawyer called John Spalding (he gave his name to the subsequent Spalding Clubs), an early historian of the town's affairs. Spalding was

The Earl of Montrose, who arrived in Aberdeen at the head of an army of 9,000 Covenanters on 30th March 1569

able to report on how the Covenanting army came in by the Overkirkgate, through the Broadgate and the Castlegate and down to the Links, heavily armed and with horses, trumpeters and drummers creating a colourful spectacle. They sat down and unfolded their breakfast 'piece' which they rested on their knees.

It was the start of a troubled time of bloodshed and treachery. Montrose and his men would soon be heading out of town towards Kintore to see if he could track down Huntly and his Royalist troops. Before leaving, however, he established the Earl of Kinghorn as military governor of Aberdeen, taking over control of the town and billeting 1,800 men in local houses. Kinghorn demanded that the town should sign the Covenant. When Montrose returned, he appeared at Greyfriars Kirk and told the people of Aberdeen that, as well as signing the Covenant, they must surrender their arms – and pay up 100,000 merks as well as the full cost of the keeping the army in Aberdeen. It was an impossible demand and finally he had to settle for 10,000 merks.

Huntly Under Arrest

Now that Aberdeen had been dealt with, Montrose returned to the unfinished business of finding Huntly and his army who were somewhere in the North-east. The wily Montrose decided to summon him to a meeting in Aberdeen, with a guarantee of safe conduct, and Huntly duly arrived with two of his sons. The meeting took place in the earl marischal's house in the Castlegate, where Montrose was staying, and they were entertained to dinner in apparently convivial circumstances. When asked to drop the Royalist cause, however, Huntly refused to resign his commission as the king's lieutenant and retired to bed. He awakened next morning to find himself under guard, about to be taken to Edinburgh Castle as the prisoner of Montrose.

His eldest son, Lord Gordon, volunteered to go with his father but the other son, Viscount Aboyne, stayed behind with revenge in mind. He stirred support from North-east aristocrats who set a trap for a gathering of Covenanters near Turriff. Led by Sir George Ogilvy of Banff, the Royalists scored a victory in a fairly minor battle that came to be known as the 'Trot o' Turra'. Thus encouraged, the Royalists entered Aberdeen and claimed the town for King Charles. Aberdonians were suffering from their position on the dividing line between the Covenanting south and the Royalist north and, with a population split between the causes, they became a pawn in the hands of the two sides.

Now it was the turn of Montrose to come storming back to Aberdeen, at which point the Royalists scattered and disbanded, leaving the townsfolk to face the anger of the Covenanters, who accused them of supporting the opposition. Local Covenanters were out to welcome them – and Aberdeen was back in their hands, with Patrick Leslie elected as provost and more and more Covenanters joining him on the council. Following the return of Montrose and his men, Aberdonians were haunted by a horrifying incident, remembered as The Massacre of the Dogs. Since Covenanters were in the habit of wearing blue rosettes as a sign of true-blue Presbyterianism, some teenagers rounded up all the dogs they could find and tied such rosettes round their necks. Meant as a joke, it was taken as an insult to the faith of the Covenanters, who proceeded to slaughter every dog in sight.

Then an extraordinary thing happened. Back south, the same Montrose who had led the Covenanters, changed sides and became the king's man, an enthusiastic Royalist with the title of marquis, and the rank of lieutenant-general in His Majesty's service. In September 1644 he headed once more for Aberdeen, this time in charge of a large Royalist army, consisting mainly of Irish Highlanders. Crossing the Dee to Crathes he approached the town, encamping by Garthdee and sending a commissioner and a drummer-boy to demand immediate surrender in the name of the king. If that was refused, he would give them time to evacuate old men, women and children, warning that those who remained could 'expect no quarter'.

The Covenanters refused to surrender, vowing that they would spend the last drop of blood defending the town. The commissioner and the drummer-boy were returning to camp, under the flag of truce, and were crossing the Green when the boy was shot dead by a trooper of the Fife regiment. When he heard the news, Montrose broke into a fury, guaranteeing that all hell was about to be let loose. The Battle of the Justice Mills is sometimes called The Fecht of Aberdeen. It was on an unlucky Friday, 13th September 1644, that Aberdeen suffered such a ferocity as had never been inflicted upon a Scottish burgh. The Aberdonians gathered on that high ground that would later be known for its Justice Mills Baths and Odeon cinema. They fought bravely but were no match for the Irish, who were hardened veterans.

Shocking Times

In his days as a Covenanter, Montrose had at least held his men under rein when he took the town in 1639. But this was different. As the Irish troops pursued the retreating Aberdonians down the Hardgate, Windmill Brae and into the Green, brutally hacking them to death, their leader heard the screams and witnessed the carnage but did nothing to stop it. Rape, pillage and murder were the order of the day, with men forced to strip before being killed – to spare their clothes from the bloodstains. These vivid word-pictures came from the same John Spalding who was recording the history of Aberdeen in those shocking times. He described how corpses lay naked where they fell, with burial forbidden. Translating from his old Scots of the time, 'the wife dare not cry nor weep at her husband's slaughter before her eyes, nor the mother for the son, nor daughter for the father, which, if they were heard, then they were presently slain . . . And nothing heard but pitiful howling, crying, weeping, mourning through all the streets.'

When the atrocity drew to its bloody end after three days of unthinkable violence, there were 160 men and countless women and children lying dead in the streets of Aberdeen. Again thanks to John Spalding, there is in existence a roll of honour, at least for the men who were accounted for, showing that those who stood and fell in the defence of their town ranged from lawyers, merchants, tradesmen, musicians and even schoolboys. Whatever is regarded as lawful in the name of war, supporters of both Covenanters and Royalists in Aberdeen were united in their condemnation of what had happened. The fact that Irish Catholics were mainly involved made it all the worse in the eyes of Scottish Protestants.

The Troubles, as they were known, were not yet over, Aberdeen having to endure the alternate occupation of rival forces, never on the winning side and longing for nothing more than a peaceful existence. Montrose went on his warring way, with a succession of victories over the Covenanters across the land, and he and his Irishmen were back in the North-east on several occasions. But he kept his forces out of town. On their first return, a month after the massacre, surviving men refused to take up arms and women fled through an early snowstorm, carrying their children on their backs.

Charles Beheaded

Meanwhile, in the wider world, Charles I ran into a succession of troubles, was put on trial at Westminster and beheaded on 30th January 1649. Montrose, who was abroad when he received the news, was reported to have fainted. He then vowed to avenge his monarch's death and undertook an invasion of Scotland on behalf of the new king, Charles II. But that ended in disastrous failure and he was taken prisoner by Macleod of Assynt, who delivered him into the hands of the Covenanters. He was put on trial as a traitor to the Covenant and sentenced to death. The hanging took place on 21st May 1650. By the custom of the time, his body was cut up and distributed among the main burghs of Scotland. Aberdeen received one of his arms and displayed it publicly on an iron spike at the Justice Port, one of the entrance gates to the town. Aberdonians were deeply upset by the execution of Charles I, remembering the king who had spent his early years at Fyvie Castle. No such sympathy was expressed for the dreaded Montrose, with whom justice had finally caught up.

But Aberdonians were greatly enthused by the accession of Charles II, all the more so when it was announced that he was coming to visit Aberdeen. To a rousing reception, he duly arrived on 7th July 1650, when he was presented with the keys of the burgh by Provost Robert Farquhar of Mounie. The royal entourage was conveyed to the old 'stane hoose' of the Menzies family in the Castlegate and entertained that evening at a lavish reception, the like of which Aberdeen had never known. Crowds gathered in the Castlegate for a glimpse of the royal party, which included one of the king's favoured women, listed in the burgh records as 'the Maiden', believed to have been Catherine Green, by whom he later had a son. She was, of course, just one in a long line of his royal mistresses, the most notorious of whom was Nell Gwyn, the Covent Garden orange-seller-turned-Drury-Lane-actress by whom he had another of his illegitimate offspring. On a night of raucous revelry in the Castlegate matters seemed to get out of hand somewhat, not only in the opinion of local ministers but of the general citizenry as well. As guardians of morality, the clergy sent William Douglas, professor of divinity, to have a word with the king and to suggest, as his parting thought, that if he had to 'do it', would he at least close the windows!

Charles II was crowned at Scone on 1st January 1651 and came back to spend a week in Aberdeen in the following month. By August he was marching into England with a Scottish army of 13,000 men but was defeated by Oliver Cromwell's forces of twice that number at Worcester. Within weeks he became a fugitive on the Continent and did not show face again until the Restoration of the Monarchy in 1660.

He was the last reigning monarch to visit Aberdeen until Queen Victoria in 1848, when she landed on her way to Balmoral. The Restoration of the Monarchy was another cause for jollification among Aberdonians, who joined in a thanksgiving service at St Nicholas Kirk, drank toasts at the Market Cross and lit bonfires in the streets and candles in their windows.

But if the main point of the Restoration was the return of Episcopacy, Aberdeen folk maintained their usual control over such enthusiasms. That hard-headed approach to doctrine gave such matters a limited place in their priorities. After all the traumas of recent times, from plagues to a decade of civil war, they now looked forward to a restoration of their own – to peaceful times in which they could get on with the more normal daily life of Aberdeen.

Charles II visted Aberdeen in 1650

CHAPTER 10

From Black Death to Typhoid

It hardly compared to the plague of 1647, when a quarter of the population was wiped out, but the events of 1964 were bad enough when an outbreak of typhoid catapulted Aberdeen into the headlines of the world. In an age of sensationalism, the Granite City became the Forbidden City as Aberdonians were rushed to hospital in the spreading panic of an epidemic. Cut off from the outside world, with bells around its neck, Aberdeen became the city no outsiders would dare approach, nor would they welcome a visitor from within its bounds.

Schools, cinemas and dance halls closed, business dipped and holiday bookings collapsed as a modern world, attuned to its daily dose of tabloid sensationalism, soaked up scare stories that reached the absurdity of a Continental journal saying the dead were being borne from the streets and cast into the sea! In fact, the number of people affected was 469 and the only death was not directly connected to the outbreak. At the root of the whole drama was a batch of corned beef on sale in a shop at the top of Union Street. The city's medical officer of health, Dr Ian A.G. MacQueen, became a media figure with a hint of hyperbole but the poor man had important news to disseminate, warnings to give, and his task was not an easy one. When the City Hospital reached its limit, patients were taken to Tor-na-Dee and it was from there that the first victim was released. Evelyn Gauld took her place in the typhoid story, presented with a sash which showed that Aberdeen had not lost its sense of humour. The inscription said 'Typhoid Queen, 1964'!

Dr Ian A.G. MacQueen, medical officer in typhoid outbreak of 1964

When the all-clear approached after four weeks, the first person to lend support to a favourite city stepped from The Royal Yacht *Britannia* and gave the world a signal that all was now well in Aberdeen. Large crowds turned out in gratitude to Queen Elizabeth as she came among the medical people who had fought the outbreak. The effect was almost immediate. As the city came back to life, holiday bookings were restored, business picked up, and Aberdonians thought twice about eating corned beef again!

At least they were luckier than their forefathers who had none of the modern medicines. The Black Death that spread across Europe reached Aberdeen in 1350 and struck again in 1401. For 300 years, in fact, there was hardly a generation that escaped the dreaded bubonic plague. A typhus epidemic in the 1860s killed 600. That other scourge, leprosy, gave rise to a lepers' croft, in an area near St Peter's Hospital, now bounded by King Street, Nelson Street, Mounthooly and Advocates Road. The plight of the lepers is hard to contemplate. With no attempt at a cure, the only aim was to protect the healthy and that was achieved with a firm set of rules which, for example, forbade a leper from drinking or washing in burns used by healthy people. To break the rules meant death by hanging, with a gallows situated nearby for convenience!

Even when leprosy died out, the plague remained a nightmarish prospect. In 1647, as Aberdeen drew a sigh a of relief that the fearful days of Montrose and his massacre were over, Provost Patrick Leslie announced that the dreaded bubonic plague had reached Inverbervie, just twenty miles away. Though no one was to know it, this would be the very last time the disease would hit Scotland. It seemed determined, however, to go out with one final flourish as the worst-ever outbreak, killing nearly a quarter of the burgh population of 8,000. Provost Leslie managed to pinpoint the source – a woman who had been allowed to move from the infected area of Brechin to Pettymuck, near Aberdeen, where two of her children had died of the plague, one of them having attended school in Aberdeen and mixed with many people.

Armed guards, provided by the 600 burgesses of guild and craft, were supposed to control all movement at the burgh gates but Provost Leslie raged that they had not done their duty. Ministers took the opportunity to call for moral hygiene as well as physical, urging the magistrates to clamp down on 'the many whoredomes and abominations in this city', with special reference to women who sold ale round the doors. One such married woman, Isobel Kempt, was chosen as an example by the magistrates, who not only banished her from the burgh but threatened to drown her if she ever showed face again.

With all these hazards of health, there was still only one medical practitioner in the town. An embarrassing episode took place in 1496 when Aberdeen agreed to entertain eight followers of Perkin Warbeck, a Flemish imposter who laid claim to being the Duke of York and to whom James IV gave in marriage his relative, Lady Catherine Gordon, daughter of the Earl of Huntly. Aberdeen's hospitality was poorly rewarded when it was discovered these visiting cads had left behind a legacy of syphilis. The magistrates quickly realised the implications of this outrage and made their own piece of medical history in becoming the very first authority in Britain to issue a public regulation against venereal disease.

CHAPTER II

The Finest Square in Scotland

As you survey the grand sweep of Union Street today (forgetting for a moment some of the modern blights upon its grandeur) it is hard to envisage an Aberdeen in which no such street existed. The burgh was indeed a very different shape in the seventeenth century, by which time several people were leaving to posterity a clear picture of its character and appearance. Baillie Alexander Skene of Newtyle and Sir Samuel Forbes of Foveran were putting down their impressions of the burgh. But the best guide to its appearance came from Robert Gordon of Straloch (an estate near Newmachar), grandfather of the benefactor who gave us the Robert Gordon's College of today. Gordon was the first MA of Marischal College, who became the great geographer of his day. His Scottish atlas of 1648 was hailed as 'one of the most notable accomplishment of our nation in a noteworthy age'.

Both he and his son James, the minister at Rothiemay who made a famous plan of the city, were clear in their detail – a picture that was complemented by a German visitor, Richard Franck, who set down his outsider's view in 1658. So what was Aberdeen's appearance all those years ago? For a start, it is interesting to pinpoint the quality of house construction at the start of two centuries. In 1500 there wasn't a single private house that was built of stone and lime; but by 1700 the majority of homes in Aberdeen had the benefit of such stability.

Richard Franck speaks of stone-and-timber construction and streets that were large and spacious. The Gordon account speaks of buildings of three or four storeys, with galleries projecting to the street and hung with tapestries and decorations on festive occasions. The houses were said to be clean and beautiful, both inside and out. There was, of course, a downside to the story. After a serious fire in the Gallowgate in 1716 the council had to forbid the thatching of houses with heather or straw. Five years later, an outbreak in the Broadgate led to the introduction of a fire brigade, and another in the same street forced the town council to insist that outer walls had to be made of stone or brick, with roofs of slate or tile. This marked the beginning of granite as a facing for dwelling-houses. Trees were becoming a feature of Aberdeen and Gordon of Rothiemay described the town, when seen from a distance, as if it stood in a garden or little wood. Therein lies a hint of the size of Aberdeen four hundred years ago.

With more than 200,000 people today, it is hard to fathom a time when the population ranged between six and eight thousand. There were two main focal points in the Aberdeen of that time – the Castlegate and St Nicholas Church, both of which were regarded with a fierce local pride. Alexander Skene described the former as a marketplace 'larger than in any town in the kingdom'. To Aberdonians, the Castlegate was simply the finest square in Scotland. Around it were thirteen main thoroughfares, stretching from the Gallowgate to Regent Quay and from Castlehill to Woolmanhill. The Green and Schoolhill were regarded as residential suburbs, with the merchant princes occupying their small estates a few miles inland. But there was not much cultivation beyond a mile-deep belt of land, made up of crofts and market-gardens that arched round from Dee to Don. In those days before our rural forefathers broke their backs and sometimes their spirits in turning thrawn land into the fertility of a later age, Gordon of Rothiemay gave it this description: 'The country is barren-like, the hills craggy, the plains full of marshes, the fields covered with heather or pebble-stones, the cornfields mixed with these but few.'

Back in Aberdeen, the town had developed on a series of modest hills. The Gallowgate had houses on either side, running down towards the Broadgate, which had indeed been broad and impressive until the town's living quarters became congested. Near Marischal College and the beautiful Greyfriars Church the planners decided to use the space for a double row of houses, which became the Guestrow. In the developing pattern, the Upperkirkgate ran from the Broadgate to the parish kirk of St Nicholas West, while the Netherkirkgate took a near-parallel route towards the East Kirk. Local pride in St Nicholas Kirk knew no bounds, stirred by the clock in the steeple and the bells that rang out to crystallise a local feeling that here was the spiritual heart of Aberdeen. On the purely aesthetic level, James Gordon wrote: 'There is no church so neat and beautiful to be seen in Scotland.' The St Nicholas of today dates back to 1751, designed by James Gibbs, a famous local architect, and ranks as Aberdeen's finest building of the eighteenth century. The fact that he moved to

St Nicholas Church. The present building dates from 1751

London may explain why Gibbs' reputation is not more widely recognised in his native city. Among his many commissions, he designed St Martin-in-the-Fields and St Bartholomew's Hospital in London and influenced church architecture in colonial America.

But there was still no Union Street. Nor was there a Market Street or a St Nicholas Street. The lower end of where Union Street is today was completely built over, with two narrow openings on to the Castlegate. The most interesting building in that fine square was the Town House, or Tolbooth, which in those days combined a municipal purpose with that of town jail.

Criminals at Large

The hooligan element in times gone by was sometimes no less than we know today and security could become a standing joke. Well ahead of the modern 'open prisons', Aberdeen had some weird and wonderful tales to tell. One particular murderer managed to release himself and his fellow prisoners and, proving that a sense of humour is no modern phenomenon, he chalked on the door: 'Room to let'! Alexander Keith of Balmoor, an upper-crust character serving a sentence for debt, escaped the Tolbooth in a trunk, which his sisters and some women friends directed to the pier. From there, a boat took him to his castle at Boddam, near Peterhead, while the town had a search party of sixty men pursuing him, in vain, for a fortnight. The creditors to whom Keith owed money raised an action against the magistrates for the sum they were owed.

Other gentry in debt, like Viscount Frendraught and James Crichton of Kinaldie, were also on the run from the Tolbooth. But nothing quite matched the exploits of another landed toff, John Leith of Harthill, who elevated farce beyond the point of a joke with a brand of thuggery that is hard to imagine, even in our own disturbing days of callous criminality. Having terrorised Aberdeen and the Garioch for years, he was finally brought to justice after the Christmas service in St Nicholas Kirk in 1639, when he created a scene, abused Provost Leslie and resisted the town's officers who tried to remove him. When facing the magistrates immediately after the service, he became even more offensive, calling the presiding provost 'a doited cock and an ass', tearing up the charge-sheet, hurling a pen-holder and ink-stand at the clerk's face and cutting him 'to the great effusion of his blood'. Sent to the Tolbooth, Leith tried to burn the place down and then demolished part of the thick stone wall. When friends smuggled in arms, he attacked his jailers with dirks, knives and cudgels and found great amusement in taking pot-shots at passers-by from his cell window. After further outrages, he was finally removed to Edinburgh, where they were better versed on security. That much-revered historian of the time, John Spalding, was suffering a severe dose of naivety when he lamented the misfortunes of John Leith and wrote: 'Pitiful to see ane gentleman chief of ane clan, of good rent, so extremelie handlit.'

CHAPTER 12

From Combs to Crombie Coats

At the start of the 1600s Aberdeen had no factories as we came to know them. Staple products of the local economy came instead from the farmers of the hinterland who killed their own cattle and brought the skins to town, selling them to local shoemakers or to merchants who exported them to England and beyond. The same happened with sheepskin. Indeed, Aberdeen's export of hides, pork and woollen goods and, not least, the salmon caught in the Dee and Don, was growing into substantial business. Ships from Aberdeen began to penetrate the markets of the world, the Aberdonian John Burnett leading the way among Scottish skippers who reached America, taking goods from the North-east to Virginia and bringing back tobacco.

Through to the 1700s Aberdeen would gain a worldwide reputation for its woollen goods, with merchants like George Pyper, a local burgess, buying up wool and spreading it among hundreds of women around the North-east, knitters and spinners who worked from home and returned it as stockings and gloves. In the seventeenth century tweed and plaid led the way in manufactured exports, with large quantities going to Danzig in Poland and Campvere in Holland, two of the main destinations for Aberdeen goods. Salmon from Dee and Don went to Holland, France and Spain while London came more into the picture after the Union, with fast little coastal craft running salmon to the English market. For all that, Aberdeen's own fleet was comparatively modest, sometimes no more than ten small ships and fifty seamen. It was Dutch boats that plied most of the trade, which explains why Aberdeen Town Council was so unwilling to seize their vessels when war broke out with Holland in 1665.

It was the firm of Leys, Masson and Co. that established the linen industry at Grandholm in 1749, with town premises in Market Street, where the Douglas Hotel later stood. Their Grandholm Mill was on a massive scale, with a main building of seven storeys, an eighty-acre bleach-field and a canteen for its thousand employees, all within a complex that included a mile-long canal and a bridge over the Don.

The Crombie company, previously based at Dyce, brought its heavy tweed-making to that same Grandholm Mill when it was vacated by Leys, Masson and Co. in 1859, and, by the start of the nineteenth century, Aberdeen was giving work to 2,000 people in the woollen industry. The Crombie name, made famous around the world by its overcoats in particular, was led to success by James Crombie until his death in 1878. His family kept up the good work for the next fifteen years, when Alexander Ross, who had started as a junior in the company, took over as managing director and further enhanced the Crombie name. After his death in 1923, his son, John A. Ross, along with J.E. Crombie (grandson of James) sold the shares to Salts of Saltaire but continued to run the business. Both men served on Aberdeen University Court and gained a name as philanthropists. The link with the Crombie family ran through to the twenty-first century in one of the North-east's most distinguished citizens, David Paton of Grandhome [*sic*], a well-known chartered surveyor with an impressive range of public service, whose mother was a Crombie. David and Juliette Paton still live on that leafy estate by the Don which has been the family home for three hundred years.

David Paton, a distinguished member of the Crombie family

Nearer the town itself, the Broadford Mill became a major producer of linen, bought in 1810 by an Englishman called John Maberly, who gave his name to the street. A keen educationist, Maberly also started a bank in 1818 and entered Parliament; but not everything was a success. The bank went down the drain, he gave up politics and in 1835 sold the Broadford Mill to Richards and Company, which built up the workforce to an impressive 2,200 and survived until modern times, though much of the textile industry had gone out of existence. Flax had a minor place on the industrial scene while cotton manufacturing had was brought to Aberdeen in 1779 by Gordon, Barron and Co., with a mill at Woodside and a hand-loom weaving shop in Schoolhill, at the corner of Belmont Street, later the site of the three churches. (Their employees included William Thom the poet.)

At the same time, Forbes, Low and Co. built their factory on the Denburn at Poynernook Road, and by 1815 those two firms between them were employing 2,500 adults and 1,500 children, the men earning up to twenty-five shillings a week (£1.25 today), the women up to ten shillings and the children up to five shillings. Still in the cotton industry, Thomas Bannerman and Co. had built the Banner Mill but sold it to Robinson, Crum and Co., a firm headed by Robert Crum, whose family lived in Rouken Glen House, Glasgow. By 1857 that was the only cotton mill left in Aberdeen, with a staff of 645. It went out of business in 1904, along with Hadden's Mills.

Paper Mills

In 1696 Patrick Sandilands began paper-making at Gordon's Mills on the River Don, an experiment ahead of its time but one which made him a pioneer of an industry that would take

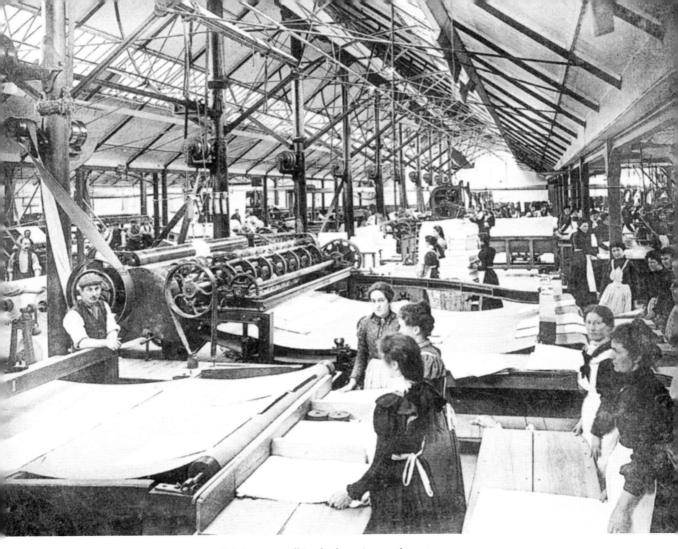

Pirie's paper mill in the late nineteenth century

its significant place in the economy of Aberdeen. After fishing, the paper industry was the largest employer, coming into its own at Culter in 1751, in the aftermath of the '45 Rebellion, when a mill was founded by Bartholomew Smith. Gaining a name for high-quality utility paper, it was followed in 1771 by the Stoneywood paper mill, the biggest in the district, which was owned by Alexander Pirie and Son until it became part of the Wiggins Teape organisation. Next door was the Mugiemoss paper mill, founded by Provost John Dingwall and taken over in 1821 by Charles Davidson and Sons, who dealt mainly in paper-board and wrapping paper.

Down river at Gordon's Mills, the Donside Paper Mill turned out its products in the former meal and flour mill of John Forbes White. It became part of the Inveresk Paper Company in 1927 and was once the biggest producer of newsprint in the United Kingdom.

By 1871 there were five paper mills around the town, employing 2,500 people, the remaining one being a subsidiary of Stoneywood known as Pirie Appleton and Co. which turned out a large percentage of Britain's envelopes at its Union Works near the Joint Station and later at Dyce. The level of employer responsibility in the area can be gauged from the fact that Pirie's built a school and paid for the education of their workers' children. This was typical of good labour relations in the paper industry.

Industry in Aberdeen was stretching over a remarkable range of products, showing the versatility of the local population. In the 1800s it ranged from nails, ropes, straw hats, pins, paints, sails and soap to pharmaceutical goods (William Paterson and Sons), quills and matches. The best-known brewery was that of William Black, whose Devanha products were in demand as far as London.

The engineering that blossomed with the Industrial Revolution included names like Barry, Henry and Cook, William McKinnon, and James Abernethy and Co. at Ferryhill. Head of the McKinnon company was that public-spirited gentleman John Gray, whose foresight gave Aberdeen its Gray's School of Art in Schoolhill, which opened in 1884 and became such an integral part of what is now the Robert Gordon University. John Gray's company specialised in plantation machinery for the milling and grinding of sugar, coffee, rice and cocoa in the Far East and in Africa, a worldwide trade that put it firmly in the vanguard of the United Kingdom's exporting business.

Guns and Shells

But the largest of the engineering firms was J.M. Henderson in King Street, again with a big overseas business that ranged from building dams and barrages in Egypt and Portugal to major construction work as far afield as China, Australia, South Africa and Jamaica. The company was founded in 1866 by John MacDonald Henderson, with its premises in Jopp's Lane, and specialising in the machinery required in the granite, stone and allied trades. By 1873 it had built the first aerial cableway in Britain, which led to contracts all over the world for quarrying, open-pit mining and dam, lock and bridge construction.

The company's success brought a move to King Street in 1878, with a purpose-built factory that covered four and a half acres. That remained the manufacturing base until 1985, when Henderson's moved to Arbroath. During the Second World War the factory switched exclusively to howitzer guns, ammunition hoists, Bailey bridges, mine-sweeping equipment, tank components and shells. In the post-war years new opportunities arose with coke ovens for the National Coal Board and British Steel plants, which became the company's main production line. So the story of Henderson's continued into the second half of the century, headed by its managing director, Richard E. Spain, who became a leading figure in the life of the city. After the move to Arbroath, the offices were sold in 1991, breaking the final link with Aberdeen after 125 years.

The Combworks was an interesting feature of the local industrial scene, founded by John Stewart in 1830 and reaching a workforce of 700 at its headquarters in Hutcheon Street. In the early part of the twentieth century it was the world leader in its field, producing 25 million combs per year, by which time it was headed by Sir David Stewart of Banchory-Devenick, who had been provost from 1889 until 1894. (He also funded the Burns statue in Union Terrace).

Moving from the traditional horn material into plastics after the Second World War, the Combworks spread itself into a wider range of products, including tableware.

The construction industry in Aberdeen would take on a whole new dimension with the arrival of oil but, long before that, it had established itself on a national basis. Symbolic of that industry was the firm of William Tawse Ltd., founded in 1896 by the manager of Fyfe's quarry at Kemnay. The main thrust of the family enterprise, however, came from the second William Tawse, a man of genius who played a major part in so many aspects of North-east life. A native of Yorkshire, he arrived in Aberdeenshire at an early age and was schooled at Kemnay and Robert Gordon's College, gaining a name for the breadth of his reading, his immense vocabulary and the skill of his literary style. With all that talent and culture behind him, William Tawse then entered the family business with a dynamism and good judgement that propelled it to new heights.

Hydro Schemes

William Tawse Ltd built bridges, harbours, aerodromes, dams and reservoirs for the hydro-electric schemes and hundreds of miles of the nation's highways – and fulfilled major Government contracts in both world wars. It became an important part of a consortium that also included Alexander Hall and Son the builders, G.W. Bruce Ltd, concrete specialists, and general contractors like W.J. Anderson, who built the King George VI bridge over the River Dee. An enthusiastic Gordonian, William Tawse became a power in the affairs of his old school, and was associated in many of its major developments with his friend Dr Walter A. Reid, chairman of governors at Gordon's College. Sadly, Mr Tawse died in 1940, while in the prime of his life.

In the modern age of debate about renewable sources of power, it is interesting to recall their vital importance in days gone by. Windmills are mentioned in the charter of 1271 and the generic name gave rise to Windmill Brae, where one was built in 1678. In a town full of mills, it is not surprising that Aberdeen was experimenting with tidal power, even if it was a venture that did not succeed.

Outwith the manufacturing industries, Aberdeen was not averse to a flutter on foreign investment. The local council joined the bandwagon of the Darien Scheme in the 1690s, when Scotland staked half her wealth on an ill-fated attempt to colonise the Isthmus of Darien (later known as Panama). Despite the unmitigated disaster, Aberdeen managed to recover most of its investment after the Union of Parliaments in 1707, the English having played a part in scuppering the Scottish plan in the first place.

CHAPTER 13

Granite Stirs to Life

Whereas most of Aberdeen had been built of freestone, with King's College the classic example, it was not until after the Jacobite Risings that the potential of local granite became a serious interest. If oil was to create an unexpected revolution more than two centuries later, the existence of granite was a much more obvious asset on the North-east doorstep. Around Aberdeen lay the largest expanse of high-quality granite rock in the whole of Britain, fanning out from nearby Rubislaw, with its grey stone, reaching northward to Peterhead, with its red hue, and westward to the village of Kemnay with its distinctive near-white. It was London's decision of 1764 to pave its streets with Aberdeenshire granite that caused the first big stir in local quarries. But it was the creation of Union Street that led to Aberdeen's name as the Granite City. Union Bridge became a good advertisement for the sparkle and durability of the native stone and Dancing Cairns, one of the earliest quarries to be opened up, later supplied the portico of the Music Hall.

The granite industry, however, found its focal point in what became the world-famous Rubislaw Quarry, a spectacular chasm eventually plunging to a depth of seven hundred feet, complete with a rather precarious-looking viewing platform to facilitate its role as a public attraction. This had the appeal of a Grand Canyon at domestic level. It had provided the foundation materials for both the Forth and Tay rail bridges – and a large part of the city that was created in the nineteenth century. But the site of Rubislaw, right in the heart of what would become the residential and highly fashionable west end, would limit its life as an active quarry, given the blasting activity required. Other factors would also intervene to end its days.

Before all that, however, the old hand-polishing of granite, which had existed since 1770, was replaced after 1832 by the invention of an Aberdeen businessman, Alexander Macdonald, whose machinery opened up a new prosperity for sixty polishing yards. Mr Macdonald, who had been making chimneys, paving-stones and headstones in a small way, went to an exhibition at the British Museum during a visit to London. Evidently, the art of polishing granite had been lost from the days of the Pharaohs until 1820, when the Italian explorer Girolamo Benzoni came back from Egypt with specimens that had been polished 5,000 years earlier. These were on show at the British Museum, prompting Macdonald to carry out his own experiments and to come up

Rubislaw Quarry, the biggest man-made hole in Europe. Queen's Road is on the right

with a quick method of polishing granite. His first example of a polished monument was sent back to London and installed at Kensal Green Cemetery.

Granite that was dressed and polished was now being exported in large quantities, with the Americans as main customers. Machinery was now coming into its own, giving new opportunities to skilled engineers in Aberdeen who were diversifying from their more accustomed role of turning out agricultural implements. On the bigger construction side of the industry, the scale can be gauged from the peak year of 1898, when enough granite was quarried in Aberdeenshire to provide stone for 747 new buildings. Despite all that, however, the granite industry gained a rather false reputation as far as its importance to the local economy was concerned. The spectacular nature of quarrying operations and the fine appearance of granite buildings belied the fact that it was not a huge employer of labour. Aberdeen industries that ranged from textiles, food, drink and tobacco to metal and wood-working, paper-making, printing and fishing all came further up the pecking order than granite.

But the industry did create its own human stories. On the death of his father in 1846, John Fyfe from Newhills took over the family quarrying business at Tyrebagger when he was just sixteen. Within ten years he was on the move to Kemnay, where there were better granite deposits, as well as a transport service with the coming of the Alford Valley Railway. John Fyfe, who was also a contributor to the Forth and Tay Bridges, now had the biggest quarrying company in the north, involving himself in projects much further afield like the Thames Embankment in London. Nearer home, he built the Victoria Bridge in Aberdeen, well below the commercial rate as a contribution to the city, and gave £1,000 towards the new frontage of Marischal College. That magnificent advertisement for North-east granite came straight from his Kemnay quarry and was given its royal opening by Edward VII in 1906, the year of John Fyfe's death.

With the inventive genius so often found in men of that calibre, he was the one who designed and erected the aerial cable and hoisting apparatus that became known as the Blondin, a spectacular operation at quarries like Rubislaw and Kemnay. It took its name from Charles

A stunning view of Marischal College

Greyfriars Church

Blondin, the French acrobat who not only crossed Niagara on a tightrope but repeated the performance blindfolded, then with a wheelbarrow, a man on his back – and on stilts! James Taggart from Port Elphinstone was another sixteen-year-old who served his time as a stone-cutter in Aberdeen before making his mark on the merchant side of the industry. He emigrated to America but returned to form his own business – and to become lord provost of the city during the Great War.

Into the twentieth century the granite industry was prospering, both in house-building and the export of monuments. The Aberdeen stone was on its way to countries like Japan for the building of temples and China for the equally ornate creation of pagodas. With the outbreak of the Great War, industrial Aberdeen was kept busy on diverted projects. But granite suffered in the ensuing conflict, after which there was unspoken anticipation of a revival, based on the need for war memorials. The expected post-war building boom did not materialise, however, and by the 1920s there was competition from granite imported from the Continent. Ironically, after that war, the Germans were selling us gravestones and war memorials!

The fortunes of the industry fluctuated between the wars, the number of manufacturing firms shrinking from eighty-five in 1919 to forty-nine in 1939. Architectural fashions had changed and by 1958 that number had fallen to thirty-four, with a few firms, like the Pittodrie Granite Turning Company, surviving in the 1960s through specialised markets. By the time the oil industry was establishing itself, the Aberdeen Granite Association had come to an end and there were only two firms in the city who were still processing. Jointly employing about 120 people, they were two of the greatest names in the history of granite – A. and J. Robertson Ltd and John Fyfe Ltd.

With the decline of granite, the arrival of oil was an uncanny coincidence, needing time to imprint itself on the psyche of a cautious North-east populace. Gradually, however, they realised that whatever bounties had been bestowed on Aberdeen over the centuries, this fledgling industry of oil would far outdo the combined benefits of everything else. It would be a matter of significance not only in creating 50,000 jobs in and around Aberdeen and her offshore waters but in bringing a major revolution in the economic fortunes of the whole nation.

CHAPTER 14

Ship that Ruled the Waves

At the beginning of the nineteenth century shipbuilding was an active business in Aberdeen, with three yards in particular giving a lead. Alexander Hall and Co. (formed 1790), J. Duthie, Sons and Co. and John Vernon and Sons, along with others, were producing more than twenty ships a year. The port itself was employing 200 seamen transporting upwards of £80,000-worth of local goods to the Continent. Aberdeen's first steamboat was launched from the John Duffus yard in 1829 and its first iron ship came from the John Vernon yard in 1837. Two years later, Alexander Hall followed with the town's first clipper, the *Scottish Maid*, which took its place on the London coastal trade.

In 1845 another Aberdeen ship, the *Torrington*, went to challenge the American vessels in the Chinese opium trade. By the middle of the century Aberdeen was heading for the heyday of the clippers, having already produced three of the fastest wooden tea vessels in the *Stornoway*, the *Chrysolite* and the *Cairngorm*. The shipyard of Walter Hood and Co. gained prominence when it built a whole fleet of clippers for George Thompson's Aberdeen White Star Line. The *Jerusalem* and *Thyatira* were described as masterpieces.

But it was another of the Hood ships that gained the greatest glory and stirred excitement in Aberdeen. That was the *Thermopylae*, launched in 1868 and hailed as the queen of the clippers. Her greatest rival was the *Cutty Sark*, completed a year later at Denny's of Dumbarton and taking its name from that most famous of long poems, 'Tam o' Shanter' by Robert Burns. The *Cutty Sark* proved to be the last sailing clipper, now a national monument with her own special dock at Greenwich. In 1872 she was engaged in a race with the Aberdeen ship on a straight run back to Britain from Shanghai. The *Cutty Sark* was well ahead but lost her rudder in heavy seas so a fairer contest was arranged for the following year when the *Thermopylae* once again came out on top. She then set a record for all sailing ships by completing 380 miles in a day.

Another of Aberdeen's clipper builders, the Duthie family, gained their own distinction by running the first mercantile service between London and Australia and sending the first ships to South America for guano. Among their best-known vessels was the *Australian*, chalking up a voyage in 1869 that was claimed by a Melbourne newspaper to have compared favourably with anything achieved by the tea clippers. Some members of the Duthie family actually commanded ships which they had built and one of them, Alexander Duthie, designed the most celebrated of

The record-breaking clipper *Thermopylae* in Sydney Harbour, 1870

all their boats, the *Port Jackson*, an iron four-masted clipper which, in this case, was built by Hall and Co. She was the last to fly the Duthie flag before the firm was taken over by Hall, Russell and Co.

Agricultural produce from the rural hinterland had once provided good business for Aberdeen Harbour, with the 1849 figures showing that 7,800 cattle and 687 tons of meat were loaded on to boats that year. By the following year, however, the railways claimed their first consignment of cattle for the journey south and that was soon to be the favoured mode of transport.

CHAPTER 15

The Birth of Banking

With a reputation for shrewd judgement and an instinct for canniness, it was not surprising that Aberdonians should be lured into banking. Outside Edinburgh, Aberdeen was the first town in Scotland to have its own bank. In 1749 four local merchants, Livingston, Mowat, Bremner and Dingwall by name, formed the Aberdeen Banking Company but within a few years they had been forced into liquidation by the combined efforts of otherwise deadly rivals, the Bank of Scotland and the Royal Bank of Scotland.

That did not go down well in a city strong on pride, and the town council was soon advising its inhabitants to shun the notes of southern banks. It encouraged a second attempt, which resulted in another Aberdeen Banking Company, floated in 1766 with capital of £72,000. This time it was a huge success, maintaining a dividend of eight per cent and paying bonuses that raised the issued capital of £30,000 to £200,000, with a reserve fund of £50,000. In the manner of these things, and after a faltering spell, it was taken over by the Union Bank in 1849, but its headquarters on the site of the Earl Marischal's house in the Castlegate remained the Union's head office in the city until it, in turn, was taken over in more recent times . . . yes, by the Bank of Scotland. The big boys win in the end.

Before that, however, the success of the local bank had produced a rival, the Commercial Banking Company of Aberdeen; but that too was taken over, this time by the National Bank of Scotland, which became the National Commercial and then the Royal Bank of Scotland! But the Aberdonian spirit is nothing if not optimistic. Encouraged by low interest rates, a third local venture emerged as the Town and County, with a capital that was soon standing at £750,000. In 1908 it amalgamated with the latest of the Aberdeen banks, the North of Scotland Banking Company, a successful union which was later taken over by the Clydesdale Bank.

CHAPTER 16

Davie do a'thing

In these early days of the twenty-first century Aberdeen can claim a list of business and professional figures to match that of any comparable city on earth. The scale of influence these men had is massive, whether we speak of Ian Wood taking his place on the worldwide scene of oil, Fred Duncan leading the field as the United Kingdom's main supplier of fresh provisions with his Grampian Country Foods, Moir Lockhead of FirstGroup running trains and buses throughout Britain and across the United States, or Stewart Milne spreading his name down the United Kingdom as a house-builder with a golden touch, although this touch proved more elusive in his other role as chairman of Aberdeen Football Club.

There were financial figures like Martin Gilbert handling billions in his Aberdeen Asset Management, or his close friend, and fellow-Gordonian, John Sievwright, who was running the entire global market and investment banking business of Merrill Lynch from his base in New York while keeping a business foothold in his native Aberdeen.

There was a time, however, when the burgh could match that level of eminence, from a population only a fraction of what it is today. Just before the current crop of high-fliers emerged, historian Alexander Keith was lauding their predecessors, more in terms of intellectual genius, and saying their like had never been seen before or since. Some of that brilliance had been found in distinguished families like the Gordons, Keiths and Forbeses.

But the best example came from an inter-twining of families with a central character known as Davie do a'thing, a mathematician whose life story takes us back to the Union of the Crowns in 1603. Davie's real name was

Davie ('do a'thing') Anderson

David Anderson, part of a Deeside family that once owned Candacraig, later to be the home of comedian Billy Connolly. Davie's own base was Finzeauch at Keig, by Alford, and his family had already made useful contributions to the life of Aberdeen, of which he himself was a burgess.

Aberdeen was Scotland's principal port at a time when international trade was blossoming and ships were increasing in size. But in a harbour that was virtually the estuary of the Dee, it had one major problem. A colossal boulder that gloried in the name of Craig Metellan (or the Maitland Rock) sat plumb in the middle of the harbour entrance and imposed severe limitations on the size of vessel that could enter the port. Somehow, this abominable obstacle had to be removed so the town council offered a fee of sixteen guineas to anyone who could do it. Davie do a'thing took up the challenge and struck on an ingeniously simple way of doing it. Having measured the highs and lows of tidal movement, he fixed a series of empty barrels to the rock at low tide and allowed their buoyancy to lift the mighty rock as the water rose and carried it up the channel. Some accounts of this public spectacle say Davie seated himself on the rock, cheered on by an admiring crowd.

Two hundred years later, when a corresponding piece of clearance was undertaken in the Thomas Telford scheme, named after the renowned builder of bridges, harbours and roads, the cost was £80,000, to be measured in many millions today. Davie did the job for those sixteen guineas, and completed it in a hour. As a baillie and dean of guild, Davie also had much to do with building the

breakwater to protect the mouth of the Dee, as well as the Bow Brig over the Denburn. He is credited, too, with having designed a steeple for St Nicholas Kirk. Davie's half-brother Alexander was professor of mathematics in Paris and his sister Marjory married Andrew Jamesone, the contractor who built the bridge over the Don at Balgownie. More to the point, she became the mother of the famous George Jamesone, the 'Scottish Van Dyck' with a worldwide reputation, who studied in the Antwerp studio of Rubens when Van Dyck himself was a pupil.

Jamesone, who painted a portrait of his uncle, returned to Aberdeen around 1620 and was soon in demand with the Scottish aristocracy. When Charles I visited Edinburgh in 1633 he was invited to paint his portrait and later went to London to paint the queen. (He also did a remarkable portrait of the Duke of Montrose at his height). In that shocking case of neglect, Jamesone's splendid house in Schoolhill,

George Jamesone, Aberdeen's famous portrait painter

George Jamesone's house in Schoolhill

with its turreted windows and magnificent garden, was demolished in 1890 to accommodate a depot for the horses of Wordie the contractor.

But we are far from finished with this remarkable family. Davie married Jean Guild, daughter of Matthew Guild, an armourer who became deacon of the local Hammermen for six terms in succession. From the Earl Marischal, Davie had bought the property of the Black Friars in Schoolhill and the widowed Jean would later gift that property to the town council to fund the education and maintenance of orphan children. Appropriately, that would eventually become the site of Robert Gordon's Hospital (the college of today) which had similarly philanthropic aims and for which the town council was among the trustees.

Tree of Life

Jean's brother, the Rev. Dr William Guild, was to add still more distinction to the family connection. A graduate of Marischal College, he was only twenty-two when he published in London his first treatise, *The New Sacrifice of Christian Incense* (or *The True Entry to the Tree of Life*). Appointed as chaplain to Charles I, Dr Guild acquired the deserted monastery and chapel of the Trinity Friars and presented them as a meeting-place to the Trades of Aberdeen. Acclaimed as one of the most distinguished names in the history of the city, he became principal of King's College and is remembered as the first patron and most famous benefactor of the Incorporated Trades, which still look after his monument in St Nicholas kirkyard.

But Davie do a'thing and his wife Jean had yet more contributions to make to this tale of distinction. Their daughter Janet married John Gregory, minister at Drumoak, and gave them grandsons who would add their own lustre. For example, James Gregory, who became professor of mathematics at St Andrews and then Edinburgh University, revealed his genius when he wrote his first book on optics at the age of twenty-four, announcing on the title page that he was 'An Aberdonian Scot'. He also risked inbreeding by marrying his close relative, Mary Jamesone, daughter of the famous artist. Gregory gained fame in his own lifetime as the inventor of the reflecting telescope, which was perfected by Isaac Newton; indeed, in scientific distinction, he was regarded as the latter's equal. Demonstrating to his students one day, he was suddenly struck with blindness and died within days. He was in his thirty-seventh year. His brother David was another extraordinary character – laird of Kinnairdy, librarian at Marischal College and said to have fathered thirty-two children in his two marriages. He also invented a revolutionary gun which he sent for comment to Isaac Newton who persuaded him not to unleash such a devastating weapon upon humanity.

Prof. James Gregory invented the reflecting telescope

The Gregory branch of Davie do a'thing's family proceeded to chalk up an impressive record of fourteen professors, seven of them coming from the aforesaid David. The matter becomes too complicated for full explanation, but suffice to say that within this galaxy of genius one of them was the inventor of that incomparable laxative known the world over by the name of Dr Gregory's Powder. A dynamic dynasty indeed.

CHAPTER 17

Jacobite Risings

For Aberdeen, the two biggest events in the first half of the eighteenth century were the Jacobite uprisings of 1715 and 1745. In the first of those attempted rebellions, the Earl of Mar raised the standard of revolt on the Braes of Mar, precisely where the Invercauld Hotel at Braemar stands today. Opposing the Hanoverian monarchy and set to restore the Stuart kings to the British throne, he proclaimed James Edward Stuart – the Old Pretender, who landed at Peterhead from France and proceeded to Aberdeen and then Fetteresso – as king. There he met up with the Jacobite magistrates of Aberdeen, along with professors from the two colleges, before moving on to hold court in Scone Palace. But the Jacobites began to look like a lost cause and the Old Pretender retreated to Montrose and fled to Rome. The Earl of Mar and others took to the hills. The town's Jacobite council gave up office and the 1715 Rising was over. Little more would surface for the next thirty years.

Before then, however, there were rumblings that another Jacobite Rising was stirring. The Marquis of Tweeddale, a principal secretary of state, warned the Aberdeen council that an invasion in favour of a Popish Pretender was likely to happen with the backing of the French. The central figure would be Charles Edward Stuart, otherwise known as the Young Pretender or Bonnie Prince Charlie, seeking to succeed where his father had failed in 1715. From the Continent he landed at Eriskay in the Hebrides in 1745 and a few weeks later raised his father's standard at Glenfinnan. Bonnie Prince Charlie gathered the support of his clansmen and began the march south. After victory at Prestonpans, defeating Sir John Cope (commander of the forces in Scotland and the man ridiculed in the song 'Hey! Johnny Cope'). he invaded England and advanced as far as Derby. There, however, he was persuaded by his commanders to turn back, on the basis of poor support in England, and thereafter was chased and routed by the Duke of Cumberland, second son of George II and England's military commander.

This was where Aberdeen came into the picture in the '45 Rebellion. In February 1746 Prince Charlie and his men reached the town in full retreat, dallying only briefly before heading north to Inverness. The excitement of the time was heightened just a few days later, on 25th February, when the Hanoverian troops arrived in town looking for billets as they prepared for the final assault. Their leader himself arrived two days later. Already known as the Butcher of Cumberland on account of his brutal methods, the duke, still only twenty-four years of age, was greeted by a deputation of magistrates and conveyed to his lodgings in the Guestrow. Crowds lined the streets for this royal arrival, while Jacobite supporters stayed very much under cover, but were rounded up wherever they could be found. One Jacobite spy was caught and brought in from Strathbogie, and crowds headed out to the Bridge of Don to watch the spectacle of his public hanging.

As the civic leaders continued to fawn over the dreaded Butcher, he in turn accepted their good wishes and invited 'all the respectable people in the town' to a ball at Marischal College on 3rd March 1746. He was said to have put on a fine display of cordiality, showing 'sincere marks of respect for both the ladies and the gentlemen'. Searching for suitable barracks to house his troops, Cumberland noticed that the newly built Auld Hoose of Robert Gordon's was not yet occupied and proceeded to commandeer it. So, before it had a chance to serve its intended purpose of educating and caring for poor boys in Aberdeen, the brand-new building, which still stands in Schoolhill today, became known as Fort Cumberland, invaded by the king's men, who treated it with no respect and caused much damage to the fabric.

Suspecting that his enemies in the North-east were lying low and might rise up in his absence, Cumberland decided to leave a garrison of 200 men at Schoolhill. So there was nervous excitement in Aberdeen for the next few weeks as he prepared his plans and finally headed out of town on 6 April, leading the rear division of his army. They were on their way to Culloden, a mixture of English and Lowland Scots who would defeat Prince Charlie and his Highlanders ten days later on what remains the last major battle to have been fought on British soil. Cumberland and his troops returned in triumph in time for their leader to receive the Freedom of Aberdeen. Nor were they in any hurry to leave their barracks at Schoolhill. Anxious to regain their Auld Hoose for its intended purpose, the governors of Gordon's were frustrated for another year or more. It was not until the late summer of 1747 that they finally won control and saw the last of the Hanoverian troops. Damages were claimed and a royal cheque for £290 arrived in due course.

Scots Giants

We are now mid-way through that eighteenth century which produced an extraordinary collection of world-class citizens, giving us what became known as the Scottish Enlightenment. Putting their ages in context, David Hume, the great philosopher of his day, was thirty-five at the time of Culloden. Adam Smith, the leading economist who gave us *The Wealth of Nations*, was twenty-three. James Watt of steam-engine fame was a lad of ten, while Sir Henry Raeburn, the famous portrait painter of the time, and John McAdam, who gave us roads, both came along ten years later, followed in 1759 by the national bard, Robert Burns.

They were men of international calibre from one small country where the population was not the five million of today but no more than a million. The North-east could lay claim to some of their roots. Adam Smith's father was born at Mains of Seaton, James Watt belonged to a Kintore family and Robert Burns's father grew up near Stonehaven, part of a family that farmed at Bralingmuir and Clochnahill. In fact, William Burness (as he then was), the main influence on his famous son's life, was the only one of that family to leave the North-east, going south to look for work as a gardener and enabling the county of Ayr to claim Burns and bask in his reflected glory. Aberdonians mumbled that there was undoubted poetic genius, if no poetic justice!

How Union Street Began

Even in the years after Culloden the street pattern of Aberdeen was little more than the random layout that would have greeted Robert the Bruce nearly five hundred years earlier. But times were indeed a-changing. After a land-clearing operation, dwelling-houses began to appear close to what is now the Grammar School, in streets that came to be known as Northfield Place, Loanhead Terrace and Jack's Brae, with a meal-mill at the corner of Leadside Road. In 1755 this was counted a suburb of Aberdeen, with a population of about a thousand, soon to spread southward across the Denburn and up Windmill Brae until the Hardgate became another suburb.

Such were the limitations of the time – a time when the popular hostelry of the town was the New Inn, looking on to the Castlegate at Lodge Walk (named after the adjacent headquarters of the Aberdeen Lodge of Freemasons). As well as a wide range of local patrons, the New Inn could claim many passing celebrities of the day, including Dr Johnson and his biographer, James Boswell, and later Robert Burns, when he came back to visit the land of his father. Johnson and Boswell arrived on 21st August 1773, when the doctor ate several platefuls of Scotch broth with barley and peas in it, and seemed very fond of the dish. They met up with prominent professors but also went to tea with Boswell's cousin, Miss Dallas, 'a sensible cheerful woman to whom Dr Johnson, in his mischievous way, threw out some jokes against Scotland'.

Further development of Aberdeen became possible with the draining of the loch, that marshland with a running burn that occupied the area we know as Maberly Street, Spring Garden and, of course, Loch Street. In 1790, that paved the way for George Street taking shape, with ten more streets arising within that pattern, taking names like Virginia, North, Marischal, Belmont, Queen, Carmelite and St Andrew. The old gateways to the burgh, known as ports, were being demolished at points like the Gallowgate and Netherkirkgate, with private houses being built at Woolmanhill. Charlotte Street emerged in honour of George III's queen.

But the most significant development of all was yet to come, prompted by the fact that Aberdeen was still burdened by approach roads unworthy of its importance. To reach the burgh the traveller had to cross primitive little paths that wound their way over the Denburn at the Bow Brig or came over the Spital Brae from the Brig o' Balgownie, en route to the Castlegate. At the end of the eighteenth century, a road surveyor called Charles Abercrombie came up with a solution that would revolutionise the appearance of Aberdeen. Backed by Provost Thomas Leys of Glasgoforest and the town council, Abercrombie produced a plan that caught the imagination of the public with its vision, opening the way for the modern city of later times. Indeed, the rate-payers themselves had been pushing for some such plan of entrance to the town.

Major Feat

From the central point of the Castlegate, said Abercrombie, let us drive two main thoroughfares to the north and west. Thus he gave birth to the two arteries that would open the way to the north, via King Street, and create the main thoroughfare of Union Street from which the rest of Aberdeen would fan out. King Street had few complications but Union Street was a bold suggestion, considering the crossing of the Denburn would entail a major feat of engineering. That would call for all the ingenuity of David Hamilton, the Glasgow architect whose design was chosen from the seven submissions.

The smooth contours of Union Street today give little hint of that landscape when it was first suggested. For a start, St Katherine's Hill sloped down between the Castlegate and what is now St Nicholas Street and would have to be levelled down. On top of that, the whole area was a clutter of housing, commonly described as 'the jungle', and that would have to be cleared away. But this was just the beginning. The main task would be to bridge the valley of the Denburn. For that purpose, the ground beyond St Nicholas Street had to be levelled upwards to form a base for the new bridge. Estimates for the building of Union Street up to that point, including the main bridge and the smaller ones spanning Carnegie's Brae and Correction Wynd, amounted to £6,493. Buying the property between the Castlegate and the Denburn was to cost £20,000, a figure which soon rose to £30,000.

Union Street's link-up with the Castlegate was officially opened in 1801, the street having gained its name from the union between Great Britain and Ireland. The rest of the project came in stages. For the Union Bridge, John Rennie, the engineer who was also building the Aberdeenshire Canal to Inverurie, was engaged as adviser. David Hamilton had originally planned a bridge of three arches, with a total span of 124 feet. But the contractors bungled the estimates and had to abandon the work, having completed only the foundations and the piers to carry the arches. John Rennie's assistant, Thomas Fletcher, suggested a single-arch bridge of 130-foot span, which was submitted to Thomas Telford. With modifications, Telford approved the plan at a total cost of £13,342. When it was finally completed in August 1805, the overall cost of the street was a great deal more than the first estimates, contributing to the fact that the building of its main thoroughfare was to put Aberdeen into a state of bankruptcy.

With fewer problems, the building of King Street was well ahead of Union Street, linking up with the Broadgate and the Gallowgate via Queen Street and West North Street. As King Street took shape, the first building of any size to arise was St Andrew's Chapel in 1817, built at a cost of £6,000 to the design of Archibald Simpson, Aberdeen's noted architect.

Union Bridge, c. 1815

King Street gave rise to offshoots like Frederick Street, where a school for six hundred pupils was built in 1835, each pupil paying a weekly fee of three-halfpence. Wales Street gave us the butcher market in 1806, Nelson Street arose in honour of Trafalgar while, at one corner of the Castlegate, they built the Royal Athenaeum, appropriately, considering its Greek origins, a library and reading room but later to change its purpose from literary to culinary nourishment as the most upmarket restaurant in town. The Society of Advocates built premises at the corner of Back Wynd but, on moving to Concert Court, it left its former home to a chequered career, in which it housed the Conservative Club and later became a restaurant under the name of the Queen's Rooms. Its purpose changed once more with the arrival of the cinema, and on Hogmanay night of 1912 it opened as the Queen's Cinema, which survived on Union Street for nearly seventy years, finally closing in 1981 and finding a new identity as the Eagles nightclub.

Golden Square

With Union Bridge now pointing the way to the west end, Union Street became the catalyst for the contours and character we begin to recognise. Union Terrace and Golden Square took shape and by 1818 there was Diamond Street, Chapel Street and Dee Street, followed by Crown

Street, Huntly and Affleck Street, named after the deacon-convener who, in 1824, presented the George Street United Presbyterian Church with the first gas lamp in Aberdeen.

Any mention of Aberdeen's design leads inevitably to its great architectural figure, Archibald Simpson, son of a merchant from the narrow confines of the Guestrow, near Broad Street, where he was born in 1790. His schooling was cut short at the age of fourteen, when his father died, so he took an apprenticeship with a mason in the Castlegate. By twenty, however, he had found his way to an architect's office in London before heading for Rome, where he studied the ancient buildings that would shape his ideas. It was the good fortune of Aberdeen that he was back home by the age of twenty-three, devoting the rest of his life to enhancing the beauty of his native city. The Roman style was right for the granite stone that would be his

Archibald Simpson, great architect of his day

material, as he set out to create the Music Hall in Union Street, the old Infirmary at Woolmanhill, the Medico-Chirurgical building in King Street and onward to the older part of Marischal College, the Royal Athenaeum and, one of his best, the head office of the North of Scotland Bank at the corner of King Street and the Castlegate.

His talent for domestic planning becomes clear in Rubislaw Place, Waverley Place, Victoria Street and Albyn Place (number 28 was his own special favourite) and never better than in the beautiful lines of Bon Accord Terrace and Crescent as well as Bon Accord Square, where he made his own home at number 31. Archibald Simpson compressed all that and much more into the limited lifetime of fifty-seven years. By the time he died he had moved home from Bon Accord Square to 1 East Craibstone Street.

A few substantial private houses already stood on what became the west end of Union Street but development at the other end of the street was more sluggish. On its north side, in fact, the stretch between St Nicholas Street and Union Bridge lay vacant for twenty years, except for the occasional arrival of a circus. In 1830 St Nicholas kirkyard was extended to take in part of that space and an impressive frontage was designed by city architect John Smith. At precisely the same time, Smith showed his mettle when he submitted a design for the wings that would flank the famous Auld Hoose of Robert Gordon's, and won the commission against competitors who included Archibald Simpson. By the 1840s, loyalty to the monarch was expressed in the names of Victoria Street and Albert Street as they stretched towards Albyn Place and Carden Place, those handsome streets that marched in unison towards the further majesty of Queen's Cross.

Back towards the central regions, Woolmanhill retained a village atmosphere with its local gathering-point of Corbie Well, before it became Union Terrace Gardens. On the lower side of Union Bridge they were laying the foundation stone of the new Trades Hall, built to the design

Queen's Cross in more sedate times, c. 1900

of John Smith's son William and opened in 1847. By 1830 a new Bridge of Don had opened up the way to the North-east, at a cost of £26,000, while a widened Bridge of Dee improved access to the south. As the city we know began to blossom, so did the population increase in proportion. Whereas it had stood at around 6,000 at the time of the Union of Parliaments in 1707, the areas of Old Aberdeen and Gilcomston came within the count half a century later – and by the census of 1841 the figure had gone up to 63,000.

CHAPTER 19

The Scandal of Slavery

Among the native characteristics, Aberdonians have gained a reputation as an honest, decent, hard-working breed who could teach the world a thing or two about humanity. If anyone should have missed out on this piece of essential intelligence, we are more than willing to put them in the picture, for good measure adding modesty to the string of virtues. What we are less likely to reveal, however, is that Aberdeen had a reputation in days gone by for something less savoury – the kidnapping of children and selling them off to the slave trade of the American plantations. In the eighteenth century, with ships from Aberdeen involved in the North American routes, there were local merchants including the town clerk depute and some baillies who were prepared to add to their legitimate business by indulging in such disgraceful behaviour, no doubt seeking justification in the fact that other Scottish ports were engaged in the same activity.

Their infamous plan of kidnapping would include young lads from the country districts, often lured into the greater excitement of the town – and into the grip of the merchants who would then lock them up in a barn in Rennie's Wynd, near the Green, or in the cellars of a nearby house by the steps which lead up from the Green to Union Street. The overflow was imprisoned in the Tolbooth to await the ship's departure. Parents of those missing youngsters would sometimes hear the alarming news and come desperately to view their offspring through the windows. But such was the power of those merchant monsters that, when one distressed father tried to raise an action, he couldn't find a single sheriff's officer in Aberdeen who was prepared to cite the defendant. Everyone knew about this evil trade but seemingly could do nothing about it.

In the few years leading up to the '45 Rebellion, around 600 youngsters were despatched to slavery, in most cases never to appear again. But there was one notable exception. Among those sent into slavery in 1741 was Peter Williamson from Hirnley in Aboyne, described as 'a rough, ragged, humle-headed, long, stourie, clever boy'. He stormed back on the Aberdeen scene in 1758, by which time the scandalous operation had come to an end. After serving as a soldier, he had managed to have his kidnapping translated into print and there he was, back home and trying to hawk his story on the streets of Aberdeen. Regarding this as an outrage, the local magistrates had him arrested and sent to prison, fining and banishing him from the town.

Williamson went to Edinburgh, where he managed to raise an action against the baillies, in which he was awarded £100 of damages and £80 in costs. He then brought a civil action against the particular people who had kidnapped him and in 1786 was awarded £200 in damages and a 100 guineas in costs. The defenders tried their hand at corrupting the law but came unstuck at the Court of Session. Those who were named and shamed by Williamson included merchants John Elphinston, George and Andrew Garioch, John Burnet, James Abernethy, Alexander Gray, saddler James Smith and ship's captain Robert Ragg. Peter Williamson settled to a life of prosperity in Edinburgh, became a banker, a wine merchant and a publisher, the man who produced Edinburgh's first directory. It was the satisfactory end to an otherwise appalling episode in the darker side of Aberdeen's history.

Peter Williamson (right), the slave who
pursued his kidnapper

CHAPTER 20

Towards Foresterhill

With all-too-vivid memories of the plague and leprosy, now mercifully under control, Aberdeen was conscious of its need for a proper hospital. Moves were made ahead of the '45 Rebellion and by 1740 they had laid the foundations of Aberdeen Infirmary, known to generations as Woolmanhill. (It was built on artist George Jamesone's large garden which stretched all the way back from Schoolhill.) The cost of the original building was £500. Extensions were added, but by 1840 they had to put up a completely new building at a cost of £16,700. Originally the infirmary had a section set aside for lunatics, the violent ones held in secure cells, but there was a clear need to separate the patients. Land was found for a new building on what was later the site of the Royal Mental Hospital.

The opening of an operating theatre at Woolmanhill was a mixed blessing for medical students, who had to pay two guineas a year just to attend with the physicians and surgeons. In 1831 the students opened their own research establishment in St Andrew Street, where they dissected dead bodies obtained by mysterious means. Remembering the exploits of Burke and Hare, the two murderers who supplied corpses for anatomists in Edinburgh, locals called their premises 'Burkin' Hoose'. Nothing much was said about this dubious operation until a dog was found one day chewing away at human remains. A mob burst in, to be confronted with more corpses, and Burkin' Hoose was burned to the ground. Such were the excitements of nineteenth-century Aberdeen.

As a house of correction for delinquents, an institution called the Bridewell was built in Rose Street, with an impressive entrance from Union Street. Another reformatory for delinquents was built at Oldmill, while a house of refuge was opened for the elderly at Oakbank. Later, those two buildings switched their functions. Both were brought to life by a distinguished provost of Aberdeen, Alexander Anderson, who was handling the estate and fulfilling the wishes of his uncle, Dr George Watt of Old Deer, a general practitioner who left £40,000.

Matthew Hay

The development of health care in this country took a major step forward under Benjamin Disraeli's administration of 1868, with a bill enabling Scottish local authorities to deal with infectious diseases. One result of that, in 1877, was the building of the City Hospital near the Links, creating the fever hospital of Aberdeen, followed by the setting up of a city health department to deal with sanitary and health services as well as housing congestion. When the need for hospitals intensified after the First World War, the town council took over responsibility for Oldmill, which had served as a military hospital during the war and later became known as Woodend.

These major changes in the health services of the city involved in turn three substantial figures – J.R. Simpson (later knighted), who became medical officer of health for Calcutta; Dr Matthew Hay, who led the department while occupying the chair of forensic medicine at Aberdeen University; and Dr J. Parlane Kinloch, who reorganised the city's hospital services and became chief medical officer for the Scottish department of health in 1928.

Professor Matthew Hay, the 'father' of Foresterhill

But something much bigger was in the wind. On the basis that most visionary schemes begin in the brain of one individual, it is Matthew Hay who must be given credit for the idea that a new hospital covering all branches of care should be combined with a medical school. He put forward the idea as early as 1920 and even pointed to the most appropriate site – the slopes of Foresterhill, looking down towards the city. His plan was taken up by Dr Ashley W. Mackintosh, president of the Medico-Chirurgical Society, to which Hay had first stated his case. Mackintosh called a conference of all appropriate bodies, from Corporation to university and the medical professions and gained general approval for the idea. The first practical move concerned a new Sick Children's Hospital, for which there had already been a fundraising scheme since 1914. The original plan had been to build it behind Holburn West Church, but that was revamped under the new initiative and Lady Cowdray opened the hospital, with its 134 beds, in 1928, by which time the subscription list had reached £140,000.

The main project, the creation of a new Aberdeen Royal Infirmary to replace the old one at Woolmanhill, would obviously be on a much larger scale. Bringing it to fruition, however, ran into controversy when Matthew Hay's successor as medical officer of health, J. Parlane Kinloch, had other ideas for the local health service. It took the diplomatic hand of Lord Provost Andrew Lewis to bring harmony to a delicate situation. The lord provost, a leading shipbuilder in the city, made it his personal crusade in which he also launched an appeal for £400,000 in 1927. A considerable part of that sum was already on its way, with donations from Lord and Lady Cowdray, Sir Thomas Jaffrey and Sir Robert Williams of Park, and the balance was more than met as the people of Aberdeen and the North-east took an intense personal interest in raising the funds for a major centre of healing they were proud to call their own.

The new Aberdeen Royal Infirmary, opened in 1936 by the Duke and Duchess of York

The gleaming white building that arose on the green slopes of Foresterhill, with its sense of space and fresh air, was the envy of many a visitor from the industrial south, more accustomed to their own blackened buildings of smoke and grime where good health did not spring readily to mind. In 1936, the Duke and Duchess of York, soon to be King George VI and Queen Elizabeth after the monarchy's crisis of that year, came to Aberdeen to perform the opening ceremony. By then, public generosity had more than met the cost of £525,000. Five hundred beds were already in place and Professor Hay's dream took a further leap forward when the subsequent buildings included a maternity hospital and the university medical school, making Foresterhill one huge modern complex at the forefront of healing and teaching.

There would be just three years leading up to the Second World War and three years after it before the North-east's pride and joy, built and run by public generosity, was swallowed up in the National Health Service of 1948. If that diminished the sense of local achievement and responsibility, it did at least bring the broader benefits of a health service for all, with whatever imperfections were to follow. But the dream was not yet complete. Teaching in the medical faculty of Aberdeen University was still centred largely on Marischal College and it was not until the latter part of the twentieth century that the final initiative began. Regarded as the last piece of the jigsaw, what became known as the Matthew Hay Project would bring all teaching to the medical campus at Foresterhill, in a £16-million facility standing side by side with the splendid Institute of Medical Sciences, the new Children's Hospital, the Maternity Hospital and the Royal Infirmary itself.

The new building would include everything from the department of anatomy, a lecture theatre and a museum on the history of medicine to the provision of teaching for undergraduates and postgraduates and ongoing training for all health-care staff, including doctors and nurses. The project, undertaken by the university and NHS Grampian, was due for completion by 2008 and was seen as a flagship in the university's Sixth Century Campaign which was seeking to raise £60 million. As leader of fundraising for the Matthew Hay Project there could have been no more fortunate choice than that distinguished Aberdonian, Sir Graeme Catto, former vice-principal of Aberdeen University who, by the year 2000, was professor of medicine at the University of London, vice-principal of King's College, London, and dean of Guy's, King's and St Thomas's medical and dental schools.

Sir Graeme, who was also president of the General Medical Council, brought with him a wealth of experience from those London teaching hospitals and was well placed to put Aberdeen in a position enjoyed by no other Scottish university. In his fundraising campaign Sir Graeme, whose father was the long-time doctor to Aberdeen Football Club, enlisted as a public patron no less a favourite than Sir Alex Ferguson, who had already brought his own share of glory to the city.

Elsewhere in the story of Aberdeen's health care, Woodend Hospital would also expand while the old infirmary at Woolmanhill became a convenient casualty and outpatient centre in the heart of the city, all under the North-eastern Regional Hospital Board. In association with the others, Morningfield Hospital continued its long-standing role of handling incurable illness, having been founded in 1857 at Belleville in Baker Street before moving to Morningside in 1884. Other hospitals included the Royal Cornhill, with the adjoining Ross Clinic, Woodlands Hospital at Cults and Tor-na-Dee at Milltimber.

From a different era, the private nursing homes, well remembered by an older generation of Aberdonians, had names like the Armstrong on Albyn Place, the Kepplestone near Rubislaw Quarry and the Northern, again on Albyn Place but later renamed the Watson-Fraser and removed to the Foresterhill site. The successor to those nursing homes in modern Aberdeen is the Albyn Hospital in Albyn Place.

There is a revealing footnote to the story of Matthew Hay, throwing some light on his character. In 1905 he demonstrated that a typhus epidemic was transmitted by body vermin, but refrained from publicising his discovery. Four years later, a French scientist was awarded the Nobel Prize for exactly the same work!

CHAPTER 21

King's and Marischal Unite

After centuries of separate identity, the two colleges of King's and Marischal did the sensible thing and headed towards partnership as the University of Aberdeen, which became a reality in 1860. Both had undergone physical changes earlier in the century, Archibald Simpson having designed a west front for King's in 1825, while Marischal had followed up with a complete rebuild at a cost of £30,000. Though King's College had once opposed the idea of amalgama-tion, it took the initiative for the events of 1860, with an agreement on how the faculties would be divided up. When the two united, the Duke of Richmond and the Earl of Aberdeen became joint chancellors while the Rev. Peter Colin Campbell, formerly of King's, became the first principal of the united body.

Compromises and sacrifices are inevitable when organisations merge, and the joining of King's and Marischal colleges lost Aberdeen one of the greatest scientific brains the world has ever known. Of the competing professors of natural philosophy, James Clerk Maxwell, who held the chair at Marischal, was the junior of the two, having not yet reached thirty. So he went quietly on his way to London and Cambridge and, in the short time left to him, became the father of modern physics, establishing the theory of electromagnetism as well as the nature of Saturn's rings, paving the way for radio and infra-red telescopes, demonstrating colour photography with a picture of tartan ribbon,

James Clerk Maxwell, father of modern physics

and publishing his famous *Treatise on Electricity and Magnetism* in 1873. A native of Edinburgh, James Clerk Maxwell joined Newton and Einstein as one of the three most important figures from the physical sciences. Albert Einstein, who publicly acknowledged Maxwell's greatness, was born in 1879, ironically the year of Maxwell's premature death at the age of forty-eight. His wife Katherine came from Aberdeen.

The amalgamation of King's and Marischall coincided with the introduction of university courts and general councils in Scotland, with changes that included the right to return one Member of Parliament, in conjunction with Glasgow. There would be six new chairs, as well as the admission of women to study for degrees, an official recognition of the Students' Representative Council, the introduction of a faculty of science and major alterations to traditional courses. The medical course, for example, went from four years to five while the arts degree, previously based on a four-year course of fixed subjects, was opened out to so many options that there was said to be more than 600 different routes to the same degree! All this imposed a financial strain that was poorly served by the Treasury grant and was eased only by the generosity of Andrew Carnegie. The restructuring of Marischal College was another heavy cost in the offing, a plan that would bring the famous granite frontage on Broad Street to fruition, along with the realignment of the adjacent and historic Greyfriars Church.

Charles Mitchell funded the Mitchell Hall and Tower

Mitchell Hall

As so often in life, there would be men of the moment: saviours arising with perfect timing to maintain a local tradition of generosity. Such a man was Charles Mitchell, an Aberdeen graduate who had become principal of the Newcastle ordnance firm of Armstrong, Mitchell and Co. He came forward with an initial £20,000 to build a graduation hall, a student union and an anatomy department, and to heighten the university tower to 235 feet, giving us the Mitchell Hall and Mitchell Tower. By a cruel twist of fate, Charles Mitchell died the night before the hall and the union were due to be opened. But the spirit of generosity towards his old university was extended by his son, Charles W. Mitchell, who made a further donation of £6,000 and offered to take over any debt on the buildings providing 'it does not much exceed £20,000'.

He was not alone. That other gentleman of good public spirit, Lord Strathcona, in delivering his rectorial address, announced that he was giving £25,000 as an incentive to further fundraising. The money was forthcoming and the grand scheme came into being with a lingering regret that Greyfriars, Aberdeen's last pre-Reformation church, had had to be largely rebuilt in the process. One other regret, for those fascinated by the homes of the famous, was the necessary demolition of 64 Broad Street where Byron and his mother had lodged when he was a boy. Lord Strathcona was one of those shrewd North-east figures little understood by the general public. As plain Donald Smith, he joined the massive Hudson Bay Company as a clerk but became its chief shareholder and then governor. Still in North America, he was largely responsible for rescuing the Canadian Pacific Railway in 1880 and later became high commissioner to Canada. Without too much fuss, he devoted his wealth to hospitals and education.

Charles W. Mitchell died just eight years after his father and, sadly, did not live to see the final outcome of Marischal College and all that his family had done to enhance it. The reopening of the college was part of a four-day celebration in the autumn of 1906, also serving as a belated quater-centenary of Aberdeen University, which was due in 1894. There were banquets, receptions, graduations and other grand ceremonials. Elaborate French menus and wines revived memories of a bygone age of opulence, much of it at the expense of the said Lord Strathcona, who had now become chancellor of the university. It all culminated in a right royal day, Thursday 27th September, when King Edward VII and Queen Alexandra, in full regalia, came in stately procession to Marischal College to perform the inauguration. The crowd scenes in Broad Street as the king and queen approached can still be seen in archive film which manages to convey the flavour of a very different era.

The renovation of Marischal gave only temporary respite to the problem of accommodation, leading to an expansion at King's College – it became known as New King's – when the north side of Regent Walk was developed to house the English, history, French and German departments, some of which had been transferred from Marischal. The church reunion of 1927 meant that the divinity classes of the Church of Scotland could be moved to the former United Free College, which became better known as Christ's College at Holburn Junction. With that shift of emphasis from Marischal to King's, and the later building of the new Royal Infirmary taking some medical classes to Foresterhill, there was strong speculation that Marischal College might be sold to the Corporation, an interesting consideration which was revived with more success in the twenty-first century.

Floodlights

When Marischal College was floodlit for the first time, it somehow symbolised a feeling of hope for the future as the survivors of 1918 resumed studies in a mood of abandon. Men like novelist

Eric Linklater were at the forefront of a social scene perhaps never equalled for its vibrancy. Into the thirties, the Mitchell Tower proved too much of a temptation for daredevils like Charles Ludwig from 5 Rubislaw Den South, a medical student of German origin whose family came to Aberdeen to trade in herring. He speeled to the top and left proof of his feat, variously reported as being a mock skeleton and a chanty! The same Charles Ludwig did something even more dangerous when, again as a student stunt, he went hand-over-hand across the Blondin cable that spanned the heights of Rubislaw Quarry. Graduating as a doctor, he passed up the chance of a medical commission in the Second World War, preferring to join the RAF, where he met his death as a pilot in 1942.

Charles Ludwig's family connections are interesting. His sister Barbara married John Foster, a legendary teacher at Gordon's College, and his nephews included Jonathan Foster, distinguished classics scholar and lecturer and later an Anglican priest in Harrow, and Charles Foster, still prominent in Aberdeen as a musician and instrument-maker, and mastermind of the medieval and Renaissance music group known as the Kincorth Waits.

Meanwhile, back at the campus, the university authorities had displayed a shrewd business sense in quietly buying up property in Old Aberdeen, paving the way for the post-war development so essential to cope with an explosion of the undergraduate population. In light of today's numbers, running to 13,500, it is hard to imagine that at the beginning of the twentieth century they stood nearer the 600–800 mark and, even by the 1950s, had not reached much beyond 2,000. Apart from new college buildings which arose in the old town and at Foresterhill, the student union was moved from Marischal to the corner of Upperkirkgate and later extended to the former home of Aberdeen University Press. There was also a fresh need for student accommodation, the situation having gone beyond the scope of the traditional Aberdeen landlady. Halls of residence became the fashion, with the former estate of Seaton House by the River Don now a central point of living.

Keith's Quibbles

Because the affairs of town and gown had always been so closely linked, with the character of the university deeply influencing the progress of Aberdeen as a civilised community, Alexander Keith, distinguished man of letters and himself a graduate, became concerned about changes taking place at his alma mater. The claims of superiority for Scottish education had owed a lot to that broad base of learning which contrasted with the early specialisation of the English system. It was the encroachment of the latter upon his native land that worried Keith and encouraged him to express himself in print in 1972. Recalling from a bygone day the four-year all-round arts degree that demanded exact knowledge, a sternly disciplined mind and an infinite capacity for hard work, he extolled the thorough grounding of that system which, he said, 'armed the Aberdeen graduate for successful combat in any intellectual armageddon anywhere'.

It was essentially a cultural training, with practically everyone passing through it before they proceeded to other faculties. The result was that society was supplied with doctors, scientists, lawyers, clergymen and others who were not limited to the boundaries of their own professions. They were broadly-based human beings. Now, he feared, the emphasis was on training instead of education, with the temptation of soft options gaining ground not only among students but also with educational legislators. Across the seven seas, travellers from Aberdeen had always found that their great advantage in life was simply in being Aberdonians, such was the reputation of the breed, based on proven high standards of performance. Keith was making the point that such standards were largely set by professors and lecturers who were themselves Aberdonians or Aberdeen-bred academics. He was thinking, for example, of intellectual giants like Alexander Bain, world-renowned philosopher and psychologist; William Minto from Alford, one of Bain's most brilliant students who succeeded him in the chair of logic in 1880; and Herbert John Clifford Grierson, scholar and critic – all graduates of Aberdeen.

His second quibble was that in the rapid expansion of students and staff, the home-grown teacher had been swamped by those from over the border, where clearly they hadn't come up the Aberdeen way! In the modern world, Keith would have started a war with the so-called politically correct, while no doubt collecting a fair measure of support for his outspoken view. Whatever his doubts, he would surely have conceded that the injection of professors from beyond the Grampian cocoon had always contained a fair measure of talent, indeed genius, ranging from the university founder himself, Bishop Elphinstone from Glasgow, to England's Professor R.V. Jones, one of Churchill's back-room boffins during the war who came to Aberdeen as professor of natural philosophy in 1946 and spent the rest of his life there.

In addition, Keith could hardly have denied the merit of giants like Dugald Baird, the Greenock man who was regius professor of midwifery at Aberdeen from 1937 till 1965 and who changed mortality rates with his concept of social obstetrics, battling to save women from 'the tyranny of excessive fertility'. (His wife was the distinguished Dr May Baird and their son Euan gained his own high profile as boss of the massive Schlumberger organisation and chairman of Rolls Royce.)

Into the twenty-first century Keith would have faced a massive injection of world-class academics, stirring an intellectual excitement and a high hope that Aberdeen would move into that informal list of the top 100 universities in the world. This modern initiative has come from a man well within Keith's own limits of approval – Principal C. Duncan Rice, a born-and-bred Aberdonian and local graduate to boot.

Origins apart, the university's reputation has involved a remarkable array of skill, not least in

Professor Dugald Baird attacked the mortality rates

medicine, spectacularly represented by the coincidence of three colleagues, John A. MacWilliam (physiology 1886–1927), Sir John Marnoch (surgery 1909–32) and Sir Ashley W. Mackintosh (medicine 1912–28). MacWilliam was said to have the widest reputation for his research into cardiac functions. Marnoch was noted for the sheer beauty of his operations, while Ashley Mackintosh goes down as the most distinguished academic ever registered at the university.

Among other names to catch the eye was J.J.R. Macleod, who followed MacWilliam in the chair of physiology in 1928, having been a young man in the department earlier in the century when they narrowly missed fame as the discoverers of insulin, the successful treatment for diabetes. MacWilliam had been leading the research in which they concentrated on giving extracts from the pancreas by mouth instead of bypassing the digestive system and injecting into the bloodstream. When Macleod later became a professor in Toronto, he used the Aberdeen experience to lead his team of Frederick Banting and Charles Best towards perfecting the use of insulin in 1921. He shared the Nobel Prize in 1923 and came back home as a professor, when he confirmed that insulin had certainly been discovered at Aberdeen University. They had indeed tried to inject it, unfortunately without success, and the problem had not been solved until his Toronto days.

Distinguished names extended to the university library, where an Inverness man, Peter John Anderson, became something of a legend in his tenure from 1894 till 1926, to be followed by another of the North-east's most distinguished figures, Dr W. Douglas Simpson, who held the post for the next forty years till his sudden death in 1968. As an area where education had long been a god on its own pedestal, the North-east had certainly produced a remarkable array of distinguished academics, often whole families from humble origins. Names like the Nivens, the Gregories and the Fordyces stood out, as did the Ogilvies, who produced the headmaster of Gordon's College, the headmaster of George Watson's in Edinburgh, the director of the Church of Scotland Training College and HM Inspectors of Schools in Scotland.

John Marshall Lang, who was inducted as minister at Fyvie in 1858 and later became principal of Aberdeen University, managed what Keith called 'the procreational schizophrenia' of producing one son who was moderator of the General Assembly of the Church of Scotland and another who became Cosmo Lang, the distinguished Archbishop of Canterbury from 1928 till 1942. As another consequence of increasing numbers at Aberdeen University, Alexander Keith lamented the inevitable loss of rapport between professor and student, in which the former had good knowledge of the talent within his ranks and would have batches of them along for an evening at his house. That would even apply to the principals, like Sir George Adam Smith, whose reign from 1909 till 1935 was marked by Sunday afternoon gatherings at Chanonry Lodge, where he kept himself in touch with undergraduate life. In summary, Alexander Keith was harking back to a time before the Education Act of 1918 when all Scottish learning came from the belief that the foundation of knowledge was general intelligence, and that by the training of the mind in subjects that induced accurate thinking students could in time apply their mental powers to any subject of their choice.

CHAPTER 22

A Panoply of Principals

The men who would lead the joint university from its inception in 1860 until the twenty-first century turned out to be a varied and colourful collection. Establishing the new order was the main preoccupation of the first two principals, Peter Colin Campbell and William Robinson Pirie, but by the arrival of the third incumbent there was time to look around to see where the future might lie. That late-Victorian task belonged to Sir William Duguid ('Homer') Geddes, distinguished poet and scholar, who was followed by John Marshall Lang, the former minister of Fyvie Parish Church.

Sir George Adam Smith was the Victorian scholar, born in Calcutta, who was a minister in Aberdeen before he became professor of Hebrew at the Free Church College, Glasgow, in 1892. A prolific writer (his books included *Modern Criticism and the Preaching of the Old Testament*), he returned to Aberdeen as principal of the university in 1909. His grandson is well remembered in modern times as Alick Buchanan Smith, Conservative MP for North Angus and Mearns, who died in the prime of life.

Sir George was succeeded in 1935 by William Hamilton Fyfe, whose widowed mother had struggled to bring up her family. But young William won a scholarship to Fettes College, Edinburgh, and went on to distinguish himself at Oxford. He was one of the young followers of the future Archbishop of Canterbury, William Temple, in his drive to open up the universities to members of the working class. He was headmaster of Christ College in Sussex before his appointment as principal of Queen's University, Kingston, Ontario. He re-crossed the Atlantic to take up his appointment in Aberdeen, a city he knew through his wife, whose father, Dr J.F. White, was a brother-in-law of the same Sir William Geddes who had already been principal of Aberdeen University.

Tom Taylor

Knighted in the fashion of the time, Sir William Fyfe was followed into the principal's chair by a typical North-east lad-o'-pairts, Thomas Murray Taylor from Keith who, with his wife, the former Dr Helen Jardine, became the first-ever partnership of Aberdeen graduates to occupy

Chanonry Lodge. A man of striking appearance, with an intellect to match, Tom Taylor was dux of Keith Grammar School in 1915 and, rejected for military service, went on to a first-class honours degree in classics in 1919, collecting both the Fullerton and Ferguson scholarships. Thereafter he took the legal route with a call to the Scottish Bar, rising to the appointment of senior advocate-depute in 1934. Returning as professor of law at Aberdeen, he had the privilege of delivering the eulogy on Winston Churchill when he received an honorary degree, a memorable speech which delighted even the old warrior himself. In 1945 he became a King's Counsel and was off to the sheriffdom of Argyll and Renfrew, only to return three years later as principal of his old university – the first-ever lawyer to occupy the position. He was knighted in 1954. Sir Thomas, who came from a substantial Banffshire family, was courteous in an old-fashioned way but his manner was sometimes taken for aloofness, especially by journalists, who found him difficult.

Sir Thomas Taylor with the Queen at opening of Crombie Hall, 1960

Edward Maitland Wright

When Sir Thomas died suddenly in 1962 the memorial tribute was paid by his successor, another remarkable scholar, Edward Maitland Wright, whose father owned Wright's Washall Soap factory near Leeds. But the business collapsed, his parents separated and young Edward supported himself from the age of fourteen by teaching French. By that age, no one had taught him any mathematics, so he tackled the subject himself, became a master at Chard Grammar School at the age of seventeen, and pursued his studies to an external BA at London and went on to Jesus College, Oxford. He rowed for the college, learned to fly and met his future wife, Phyllis, who was cox of the women's eights.

This extraordinary character became a lecturer at Christ Church, Oxford, and was already professor of mathematics at Aberdeen University by the age of twenty-nine. Having been a research student of the great G.H. Hardy, Britain's outstanding mathematician of the century, Wright teamed up with his mentor to become 'Hardy and Wright', co-authors of the popular textbook, *An Introduction to the Theory of Numbers*. After all that, the principal's office at Aberdeen

University might have seemed like an anti-climax, but that was his appointment in 1962, leading the university through a hectic period of expansion till his retirement in 1976, just escaping the first wave of cuts that would have tested his ingenuity. The fact that Edward Wright could be harsh and dictatorial raised a theory that he had expected to return in triumph to Oxford and, on realising his career would end in Aberdeen, he was doubly determined that he would at least be master of his own house. So said *The Times* in its obituary. Knighted in 1977, Sir Edward was equally determined to live on, and in characteristic fashion, he did. In fact he died in February 2005, just a few days before he would have entered his hundredth year. Happily, he survived long enough to see his son John, professor of pure mathematics at Reading, move back to the chair of mathematics at Aberdeen University in 2004, a man hailed by those qualified to judge as a mathematician at least on a level with his father.

Thomas Alexander Fraser Noble

After the eccentricities of Wright's career, it was time for a return to the more recognisable profile of Thomas Alexander Fraser Noble, a headmaster's son from Morayshire who, with his wife Barbara, followed the Taylor example and became the second couple of Aberdeen graduates to occupy Chanonry Lodge. Fraser Noble was born in 1918 but his father died when he was eight, leaving his mother with two boys to bring up. From Nairn Academy he went to Aberdeen University when he was sixteen and graduated with first-class honours in classics in 1938 and economics in 1940. Off to war with the Black Watch, he was then transferred to the Indian Civil Service, where he performed with distinction in the North West Frontier Province, right through to the end of British rule. Shouldering heavy responsibility there, he was awarded the MBE.

He returned to his old university to be a lecturer in political economy in 1948, at the same time as his older brother Donald returned to Aberdeenshire to be editor of the *Turriff Advertiser*. Ten years later, Fraser Noble was appointed secretary and treasurer of the Carnegie Trust for the Universities of Scotland, taking him all over Britain and the United States and giving him an insight into the problems of running a university. This equipped him admirably for the appointment of vice-chancellor of Leicester University in 1962, heading into that decade of student unrest which led to direct confrontation with the authorities and the occupation of his administrative buildings. It took all the diplomacy of Fraser Noble to bring peace to a troublesome situation and set the pattern for solutions elsewhere.

With that behind him, he was entitled to anticipate better times when his alma mater invited him to be principal of Aberdeen University in 1976. But luck was not on his side. From student upset to trouble of another sort, this time from Government policy demanding unprecedented cuts in university spending. In disturbing times, he faced the frustration of a retrenchment that brought him criticism, though he retained the respect and affection he had engendered at Leicester. Both universities honoured him with substantial buildings that bear his name, and his other recognitions included a knighthood. When Sir Fraser took up his appointment in 1976 he was one of three Aberdeen graduates who were principals of Scottish universities. The others were George Burnett, who had been principal of Heriot Watt University since 1974, and William Cramond, who had just taken over at Stirling University. Sir Fraser retired in 1981, back to the Nairn he knew so well, and died in August 2003.

George McNicol

If the clouds were gathering in Fraser Noble's time, the storm broke fiercely over his successor, George Paul McNicol, who was said to have presided over the most perilous decade in the history of Aberdeen University. Times were dire, with staff cuts and tumbling grants and little shelter from the odium aroused in the public mind. George McNicol sought to steer the university through troubled times, even producing a stream of innovative ideas, although not all achievable. All that seemed a far cry from his early days at Glasgow University, where he graduated in medicine in 1952 and before going on to Washington University, Missouri, on a Harkness Fellowship, and then back to Glasgow as a reader. He was editor of the *Scottish Medical Journal* from 1969 to 1971, after which he went to Leeds University as professor of medicine. Despite the difficulties of his Aberdeen days, he nurtured a successful Centre for Continuing Education and brought in a summer school to open up a university path for those with a disadvantaged educational background.

John Maxwell Irvine

Full acknowledgement of those difficult years was made by his successor, John Maxwell Irvine, who looked forward to better times when he became principal in 1991. Maxwell Irvine was an Edinburgh man, a product of George Heriot's who graduated in mathematical physics from Edinburgh University before gaining his MSc at the University of Michigan. For the next twenty-nine years he was to be found at Manchester University (apart from a spell at Cornell), pursuing a distinguished career in theoretical physics and gaining the chair of that subject in 1983 and the deanship of science in 1989. Among his many appointments, he was a consultant to the UK Atomic Energy Research Establishment at Harwell. In his five years in Aberdeen he presided over a large recovery in staff and student numbers as well as the widespread celebration of the university's quincentenary. In 1996 he left for the post of vice-chancellor of the University of Birmingham.

C. Duncan Rice

The man who straddled two centuries as principal and vice-chancellor of Aberdeen University was another of that North-east breed in whom the natives take a fierce pride. The name of

Professor C. Duncan Rice, who became
Principal in 1996

Charles Duncan Rice resonated with an older generation who remembered that distinguished figure as rector of Peterhead Academy in the earlier part of the twentieth century. But this was his grandson of the same name, born and raised in Aberdeen and gravitating from the Grammar School to the university, where he gained a first-class honours degree in history in 1964. He taught briefly in the city and completed an Edinburgh doctorate before heading for the United States, spending much of his professional career at Yale and New York Universities.

At New York, Duncan Rice became dean of the faculty in 1985 and vice-chancellor in 1991. On top of his academic distinction, however, he gained a name as a fundraiser, playing a key role in one of the most successful campaigns ever known in American education. Incredibly, that campaign raised more than a billion dollars in ten years. In 1996 he succeeded Maxwell Irvine as principal of Aberdeen and re-established himself in the North-east land he knew so well. Essential fundraising for the university was not forgotten, with an eye on the potential of that exiled North-east community in America. Back home, Duncan Rice also spread his talents across the national scene, serving on the boards of Scottish Opera, the Heritage Lottery Fund and Scottish Enterprise Grampian. Along the way he collected an honorary degree from New York University and fellowships at Harvard and Yale. On returning with her husband, his American wife Susan made her own mark on Scottish business life, first with the Bank of Scotland and then as chief executive of Lloyds TSB Scotland.

CHAPTER 23

A Chain of Lord Provosts

If the modern fad for league tables and listings were to focus on the lord provosts of Aberdeen, seeking out the most dynamic, the name of Alexander Anderson would be hard to beat. Of course he had the advantage of living in a nineteenth century in which the pragmatic spirit could operate with more independence than is granted by modern bureaucracy, where so much of local government is dictated by national policy. The son of a Buchan minister, young Anderson went from Strichen School to the familiar route of Aberdeen Grammar and Marischal College before becoming a high-profile lawyer in the city firm of Adam and Anderson.

Long before his town council days he had displayed an astonishing breadth of enterprise. In 1836, for example, he was the power behind the formation of two major North-east institutions, the Northern Assurance Company and the North of Scotland Bank, both hugely successful ventures swallowed up in the modern manner by Commercial Union (later Norwich Union) and the Clydesdale Bank. Even in those far-off days Aberdeen's entrepreneurs were by no means confining their business interests to the local scene. Nor did everything go well for them. Anderson had a cousin, George Smith, a native of the Buchan village of Old Deer who gave up medical studies at Marischal, tried farming at Turriff and finally made a fortune in real estate in America. He became better known as Chicago Smith, a much-lauded benefactor in the parish of Old Deer, even if his activities, along with those of his Strichen cousin, raised a few question marks.

Sensing opportunities in what was then the small town of Chicago, lying between New York and the prairies of the west, he suggested that his cousin's legal firm of Adam and Anderson should float and promote the Illinois Investment Company. So in 1837 Alexander Anderson did indeed persuade many Aberdonians to invest, but the end result of what was no doubt a well-intentioned venture was a total loss of around £100,000 for those North-east speculators. Only the principal partner, Chicago Smith himself, seemed to emerge without damage to his bank account. As for Anderson, he simply continued on his enterprising, if unconventional, way, managing to avoid too much blame for his part in the American fiasco and retaining a fair measure of public respect. His next ploy was the Aberdeen Market Company, which led to the building of the first New Market in 1842 and virtually created Market Street itself. In 1844 he challenged the high charges and the monopoly of the local gas company by starting a rival – and forcing the older company to accept amalgamation.

Perhaps most of all, he was a principal figure in creating the railway system of the North and North-east, having floated the Aberdeen Railway Company in 1844, with a capital of £900,000, to build a line from Aberdeen to Forfar. He then promoted bills which brought us the Deeside and Buchan railway lines and the building of the Great North of Scotland Railway to Keith and Alford. Was there no limit to Anderson's energies and determination to succeed? He would brook no opposition to his various schemes and managed, skilfully, to further the ends of himself and his friends by demonstrating clear benefits for the public interest. Furrowed brows questioned, for example, how he had financed his railways through the North Bank. But the general public was just glad to have them.

His public spiritedness was put to the test in 1859, when he was invited to stand for the town council. At the very first meeting after his election, he was invited to become lord provost! It could have happened to no one but Anderson. With customary vigour, he set about providing a modern water supply and revolutionising the sewage system, two essentials for the needs of an expanding city. For the new waterworks at Cairnton, he persuaded Queen Victoria to perform the opening, despite her resistance to such duties, especially after the death of Prince Albert. Indeed, it was his second royal success since Albert's death in 1861. Anderson was behind the plan to honour her prince consort with a statue and secured her presence in what was the first public engagement of her widowhood. The statue originally stood at the corner of Union Street

Alexander Anderson, hailed as the greatest Lord Provost

and Union Terrace and, in a day of heavy rain, the queen performed the 'unveiling' from the shelter of the Northern Assurance building across the street.

During his provostship Anderson's town residence was at 198 Union Street, before he moved to 14 Union Terrace. Even in retirement, however, as factor to Lord Saltoun, he was modernising Fraserburgh Harbour to become Scotland's premier herring port and founding the City of Aberdeen Land Association whose members acquired vast areas around Rubislaw and Torry. In addition to all that, when you consider that Alexander Anderson had planned new roads and civic layouts, pressed for the new Grammar School in Skene Street and the new Town House at the corner of Broad Street, there can be little argument that he was the man above all others who set the pattern of the Aberdeen we know today. Queen Victoria knighted him during the visit of 1863, and it was at that stage that the term lord provost was brought into use. The ring-road of Anderson Drive, the longest street in Aberdeen, is another reminder of the man.

A footnote to the fabulously rich cousin, Chicago Smith from Old Deer: he came home from America to live at Westhall, Oyne, and then North College, Elgin, before settling at the Reform Club in London. There he moved among the frock-coats and tile-hats of Victorian society, re-reading the novels of Sir Walter Scott and walking in the parks. He died on 11th November 1899 and is buried at the New Cemetery in Elgin.

In an age of colourful lord provosts, Sir Alexander Anderson had been preceded by people like George Thompson of Pitmedden, founder of the Aberdeen Line, whose ships were known worldwide for their comfort and efficiency, and George Henry, senior partner in the Coffee Company and said to be a relative of Patrick Henry, famous orator of the American Revolution. Anderson was followed in the civic chair by Alexander Nicol, a shipping man who owned Aberdeen's first clipper, the *Scottish Maid*, and then by William Leslie, the man who designed Dunrobin Castle in Sutherland. During Leslie's time, the city boundaries were extended to embrace Ferryhill, Mannofield and Kittybrewster; the Victoria Park became the city's first public area; and the freedom was given to prime ministers W.E. Gladstone and Benjamin Disraeli.

Other names to hold office in Victorian times included the formidable Peter Esslemont (1880–82), founder of the well-known city store of Esslemont and Macintosh, who had the pleasure of accepting from Miss Charlotte Duthie of Ruthrieston part of the lands of Polmuir and Ferryhill, from which they created the Duthie Park. This charming attraction, still popular now, was opened on a showery day in September 1883 by HRH Princess Beatrice. Miss Duthie's brother Alexander had been a lawyer with Adam and Anderson (that name again). For this purpose, the town bought the adjoining estate of Arthurseat, which belonged to Arthur Dingwall Fordyce, grandfather of the laird of Brucklay. Peter Esslemont went on to become Liberal MP for East Aberdeenshire in 1885.

Another distinguished architect took his place in the lord provost's chair in 1883. James Matthews, a pupil of the famous Archibald Simpson, presided over interesting times. He himself had been the architect of such notable buildings as the Grammar School, the Free Church College, the large auditorium of the Music Hall, Her Majesty's Theatre (the Tivoli) in Guild Street and the Palace Hotel, as well as country residences like Ardoe House and Brucklay Castle. In Matthews' time they built Rosemount Viaduct and Union Terrace Gardens. He was followed into office by a banker, William Henderson of Devanha House, a native of New Aberdour. It was Henderson who arranged a £30,000-extension to the old Royal Infirmary to mark Queen Victoria's jubilee, for which he attended the special service in Westminster Abbey. The statues of Sir William Wallace and General Gordon were presented in his time.

Sir David Stewart of Banchory, head of the Combworks and lord provost from 1889 to 1894, was another busy man. In his time the burgh boundaries went out to include Woodside, Ruthrieston and Torry, while the public library was opened in 1892, followed by the burgh courthouse and the police building in Lodge Walk.

In the early nineties the city received its electricity supply, the statues of Robert Burns and Queen Victoria found their resting places, and Aberdeen welcomed two notable figures to receive the freedom of the city. They were the great Scots-American philanthropist Andrew Carnegie and the famous journalist and explorer, H.M. Stanley, who was sent by his newspaper, the *New York Herald*, to find David Livingstone in the depths of Africa ('Dr Livingstone, I presume?'). His instruction had come from James Gordon Bennett, whose father of the same name was born in Banffshire and was the founder of the *New York Herald*.

Each lord provost was managing to leave the mark of his tenure with something of significance to the city. One of the greatest was Daniel Mearns (1895–98), who tackled slum clearance, prepared harbour and fish-market reforms, instigated the fire station in King Street at a cost of £16,500 and the model lodging house in East North Street at £11,000, and was responsible for the esplanade stretching from Dee to Don. On top of all that, he was a decent and humorous man and a great favourite with the public. That may explain why Sir John Fleming declined the invitation to stand against him in 1895. He bided his time and became lord provost as the successor to Danny Mearns in 1898. This gave John Fleming a place of special poignancy, in that he would be the last to hold office in the nineteenth century and the first in the twentieth century, straddling that landmark and seeing out the Victorian age with the death of the Queen in January 1901.

CHAPTER 24

The First Train Arrives

In trying to imagine what life was like in previous centuries, it has been one of my enduring puzzles to understand how people managed to move and communicate when there was no faster vehicle on land than a horse-drawn carriage, and had to negotiate long journeys on roads which were no better than dirt-tracks. The condition of the roads at least began to improve with the arrival of that distinguished Scotsman, John McAdam, born in the town of Ayr in 1756, just three years before Robert Burns made his appearance a few miles away at Alloway. McAdam was an engineer and inventor who returned from a profitable spell in New York with the thought of applying his skills to the improvement of our roadway surfaces. His method of crushing stones and binding them with gravel revolutionised the whole process and led to his name being immortalised in the phrase 'tarmacadam roads'. But another hundred years would pass before there was such a thing as a motor car to use them.

In the meantime, human movement on land was confined to the coaching services, which did at least benefit from those road improvements. Earlier historians have recorded that, by 1819, the mail-coach leaving London on a Monday didn't arrive in Aberdeen until the Thursday afternoon, as if indicating a measure of tardiness. (Some critics of the modern second-class post might be impressed by such speed!) So the North-east's network of public transport 200 years ago depended on coaches fanning out in all directions, from Perth to Peterhead. From the days of the old turnpike roads (a phrase still used in America but not here) it is a touching link with the past to find that many of the old toll houses still survive. The one in Queen's Road became a grocery and is now a restaurant.

But so much would change with the arrival of the railways. The English saw their first passenger train in 1825, running between Stockton and Darlington, to be followed a year later by the Monklands Railway in Scotland. How the various local enterprises proceeded to become an integrated system would confuse all but the dedicated railway enthusiast. Enough to say that surveys about a possible link between Aberdeen and Perth began in 1837 and you could bet that a leading figure in those exciting new ventures would have been none other than Alexander Anderson, the same controversial figure and future provost already mentioned, the man who floated the Aberdeen Railway Company in 1844. It was not until 1850 that Aberdeen welcomed its first train, steaming into the terminus of the day which was Ferryhill before it was moved to Guild Street. By then, the Aberdeen Railway Company had teamed up with the Scottish Midland Railway to become the Scottish North-Eastern.

Anderson was involved in another of the companies, the Great North of Scotland Railway, which would drive routes through to Inverness and out by Kintore to Alford and again northwards into Buchan. That particular line would take in Dyce and Ellon and divide itself at the central Buchan point of Maud Junction, one branch going to Peterhead and the other to Fraserburgh, passing through Anderson's native village of Strichen, which he was determined to include.

Cruden Bay Hotel

Whatever the hardships of the time, there was of course a glamorous side to life for those who could afford it. The railway company built the spacious Cruden Bay Hotel, complete with golf course, as an attraction which would need a railway line to accommodate its guests. So they interrupted the Buchan line at Ellon to take a branch route to Boddam. That would conveniently pass through Cruden Bay, where the hotel guests alighted and were transported in an electric tramway to the very portico of the entrance. From its opening in 1899 you would find the rich and famous taking in the splendours of that fine coastline by Slains Castle, which inspired Bram Stoker in his creation of *Dracula* to the extent that he took a cottage there. In the 1920s and beyond you would also find among the guests at the hotel North-east exiles like B.C. Forbes, the poor boy from New Deer who became the millionaire founder of *Forbes* magazine of business in New York, coming home to entertain his family in friends. The Cruden Bay was a smaller version of that other splendid railway hotel at Gleneagles which would arise on the Perthshire landscape in 1924. But whereas Gleneagles went on to become one of the most famous hotels in the world, Cruden Bay was never a commercial success and became a hospital during the Second World War, before being demolished in 1947.

Before everyone had a motor car, hotels and railways had a natural affinity. The finest hotel in Aberdeen in those days was the Palace, situated on Union Street at the corner of Bridge Street, where the C&A store would later stand, and linked into the Joint Station with lifts and a covered walkway, by which the porter carried your luggage straight to the platform. As for the railway from Aberdeen to Banchory, it was opened in September 1853 and extended to Aboyne six years later, with the intention of carrying on the Braemar. But Queen Victoria did not wish her privacy at Balmoral disturbed and bought up the land by which the intrusion might arrive. There would no doubt be a right royal rumpus if the monarch tried that today, but in more respectful times they quietly terminated the Deeside line at Ballater in October 1866 and that was the end of that.

In his grand plan for spreading the railway network around the North-east and beyond, Alexander Anderson had a rival in John Duncan, an Aberdeen advocate who was chairman of

The old Palace, Aberdeen's no.1 hotel, opposite King Edward's statue

that Deeside Railway and later presided over the Great North of Scotland Railway itself. Their competing schemes went to Parliament for decisions but John Duncan, ever mindful that Anderson's movements were worthy of scrutiny, had the suspicion that the directors of the North Bank were behind Anderson's railway plans even though the man himself had already resigned from the board. Duncan went as far as to suggest that the financing of the Buchan line had involved some juggling of bank funds; more precisely, taking £36,000 from the till. That landed him in court, where he lost his case, and he settled out of court in the bank's action for £10,000, paying out £250 to each of four directors as well as legal fees. None of that prevented the North Bank from facing a financial crisis in 1848, incurring losses of £250,000.

The Joint Station, which had become the focal point of railway activity in Aberdeen, was in need of reorganising in the early part of the twentieth century, a task entrusted to a highly skilled railway engineer, James A. Parker, who built nine new platforms. The railways were the flavour of the time, not only with passengers but with commercial ventures, including the cattle trade that had once depended on the sea to take its products to the more populated areas of the south. But nothing stands still. Road haulage began to develop after the First World War, to the extent that the 1,400 vehicles licensed in Aberdeen in 1938 had expanded to 2,515 by 1948. The advantage was that a lorry could deliver from door to door and save double loading. After the Second World War, in the Labour government's enthusiasm for nationalising anything that moved, both the trains and the road haulage industry were taken into state control.

Bustle of the Joint Station on Fair Friday in the 1950s

Dr Beeching

While more cars and lorries filled the roads of Britain, the railways went into a decline that was tackled in the early 1960s when the Government appointed a man called Dr Richard Beeching as chairman of the British Railways Board. His main preoccupation was to produce a plan of streamlining the nation's network. The doctor used his scalpel to devastating effect, removing many of the branch lines altogether. Whatever the economic necessity might have been, the Beeching Plan cut the heart right out of many a rural community, the local station having become so often a focal point of village life.

The irony, as far as it affected the North-east of Scotland, was that no sooner had he destroyed the Buchan railway to Peterhead and Fraserburgh than nature produced its surprise of an oil industry, calling out for a rail service that would have been kept busy transporting pipelines and much more for years ahead. With the oil coming ashore at Cruden Bay, on one side of Peterhead, and a massive gas terminal required at St Fergus, on the other, the inadequate roads of

Buchan could have been spared the ridiculous volume of lorry traffic that was to follow. This was merely symptomatic of what was happening elsewhere on the roads of Britain, as traffic built up to a widespread congestion and the logic of diverting people and products to the railways began to reassert itself.

But if the trains had revolutionised transport in the nineteenth century, it was the aeroplane that would take travel to new dimensions in the twentieth. The Wright brothers, Orville and Wilbur, gain the credit for that first modest flight at Kitty Hawk, North Carolina, in 1903. But spare a thought for a brilliant young naval architect at Glasgow University, Percy Pilcher, the same age as Wilbur Wright but several years ahead in perfecting powered flight. About to demonstrate his invention on 30 September 1899, and unwisely defying bad weather so as not to disappoint the large crowd, he crashed to the ground and died two days later, aged thirty-two. Such is the margin between fame and oblivion.

CHAPTER 25

Charm of the Tramcars

The tramcar, which wormed its romantic way into public affection, first appeared on the streets of Aberdeen on 31st August 1874 after a private company had gained parliamentary permission to introduce this novel form of transport to the city. With tramlines embedded in the street, the system began with two routes, one from Queen's Cross to the North Church in King Street and the other from St Nicholas Street along George Street to Kittybrewster, a single track running for three miles, with passing places.

Union Street, when pedestrians ruled, c. 1900

The original rolling stock consisted of seven tramcars, drawn in relays by eight horses each, working shifts of three and a half hours. In 1880 the system was extended to Woodside, Mannofield and down King Street, and in 1888 the Union Street line was doubled. Further extension took the trams to the Bridge of Don in 1892, the Bridge of Dee in 1894 and Rubislaw in 1896 but, in keeping with the times, they did not run on a Sunday. After their first year, drivers were paid twenty-four shillings a week (£1.20) for a fourteen-and-a half-hour day, with two hours of a break for meals. The upkeep of a horse was eleven shillings (55p) a week and its average life on the rails was five years.

But the days of the horse-drawn tram were coming to an end with the century itself and the new-fangled idea of electrification became a possibility. The private company that brought the tramcar to Aberdeen in the first place did not, however, relish the task of finding additional capital and the corporation bought over the whole system for £103,785. The transfer took place in August 1898 and the first electric tramcar travelled from St Nicholas Street to Woodside on 23rd December 1899. By July 1902 the trams were running on a Sunday and the whole system had been electrified at a cost of £156,000. The route to the beach, with its open-topped upper decks, began in 1901, followed two years later by the Ferryhill and Torry lines.

While the Corporation transport carried 17,676,000 passengers in 1907, that figure had risen to more than 77 million by 1939. But, as ever in this bewildering world, nothing endures for long. For all the public affection for the tramcars, the progress of mankind had brought another dimension to the transport scene. The cars and lorries now pouring on to the streets and highways of the land presented a problem if not a danger for the public passenger, who had to board and leave the tramcar at its fixed distance from the kerb. You were at the mercy of the motorist, who could normally pass the tram on its left-hand side.

Yes, the good old trams did have disadvantages and their days were clearly numbered. But the clank and sway and charm of their movement gave rise to a warm nostalgia which stirs again even in the twenty-first century for anyone who happens to visit a city like Melbourne, Australia, where they have found new ways to retain them. Ironically, they are even finding their way back to the streets of Britain.

So the corporation began to introduce buses to the streets of Aberdeen in 1921, and within ten years those tramlines to Ferryhill and Torry were no more. That left the longer-standing routes which were a familiar recitation to anyone worthy of the Aberdonian name. The No. 1 was that longest of all routes, running from the Bridge of Dee, up Holburn Street and down Union Street and King Street to the Bridge of Don. For most others, the focal point was the Castlegate, the No. 2 running from there to Mannofield, the No. 3 to Queen's Cross and the No. 4 to Hazlehead. The Nos. 5 and 6 circled gracefully in opposite directions, like country dancers parting and meeting up again, one going from the Castlegate via Union Terrace to Rosemount and Beechgrove, along Fountainhall Road to Queen's Cross (acknowledging its colleague coming in the other direction) and swaying down Albyn Place to Holburn Junction and Union Street on its way back to the Castlegate.

Apart from the seasonal route from the Castlegate to the beach, that left the No. 7, which started at the door of Raggie Morrison's general store in St Nicholas Street and powered its way

The Castlegate, still busy with trams in 1949

out George Street, past Isaac Benzie's and northward to Kittybrewster, veering right at the Northern Hotel before negotiating Great Northern Road towards the dominion of Woodside.

The Last Night

But all that would come to an end in the aftermath of the war, buses taking over on the Mannofield route in 1951, Rosemount in 1954, Woodside in 1955, Hazlehead in 1956 and the bridges route in 1958. That final night of the tramcars must find its tear-filled place in any history of Aberdeen. Having arranged a funeral pyre at the beach, the Corporation released those wonderful machines, one by one on a free-wheel basis, to gather momentum as they sped to a fiery cremation. Grown men cried. I was duty reporter on *The Press and Journal* that Saturday night and can claim to be the last person ever to travel on an Aberdeen tramcar. As the last victim began its journey to hell, I jumped on the platform, with an uncharacteristic display of bravado, and jumped off again in time to prevent another tragic tale!

Depots for those tramcars were to be found all over the city, from Constitution Street, Market Street and Mannofield to the former militia barracks in King Street and the Queen's Cross garage which became the site of Grampian Television when it opened in 1961. By the time the tramcars disappeared altogether, there were 140 buses plying the streets of the city.

The electricity that powered the tramcars was also the great new source of energy available to the domestic customer and others. The wife of Lord Provost Stewart switched on the first ten street lamps in Union Street and Castle Street on 27th February 1894 and the first thirty-five customers were connected a week later. Though the Corporation's generating station was originally in Cotton Street, the new century saw the main centre of output transferred to Millburn Street, on the site of the old Dee Village. Cotton Street became the gas headquarters in 1905. As with most new developments, there were doubts and suspicions in the public mind about this new-fangled business of electricity. An Aberdonian who became a distinguished psychiatrist tells the story of his grandfather answering the door of his little cottage in Woodside where a salesman was trying to convert him to this brand new form of lighting. The old man listened grimly to the sales talk and then, with that not unfamiliar hint that Aberdonians have the gift of far-sightedness, replied: 'Electricity? Na, na. It'll juist be a passin' fad!'

CHAPTER 26

Mart Day at Kittybrewster

The coming of the railways, which linked Aberdeen to the south in 1850, opened up a whole new artery of prosperity for the city. But the farming industry of the North-east hinterland would also play a major role – and one too easily forgotten – in boosting Aberdeen's fortunes of that period. The livestock auction companies were opening up, with headquarters in Aberdeen and branch marts spread around the North-east. What is now the combined Aberdeen and

When the trams gave way to pigs, near Kittybrewster Mart

Northern Marts complex at Thainstone, near Inverurie, a smart-casual kind of place with a multiplicity of functions, was once a major feature of the city, based around the Central Park at Kittybrewster, near the Northern Hotel and the Astoria Cinema and next to the football home of the Parkvale junior club.

Particularly on a Friday, the country came to town, farmers stuffing tobacco into their short-stemmed pipes and heading for the drama and camaraderie of their favourite destination, whether it was the Central Mart on Great Northern Road, or the family firms of Middleton or Reith and Anderson, round the corner on Belmont and Berryden, all competitors within a few hundred yards of each other.

Meanwhile, their douce wives were jumping gingerly on a No. 7 tramcar as it shoogled its way from Woodside, via Great Northern Road, George Street and St Nicholas Street to that junction with Union Street then known as the Queen. (Victoria's statue became a popular rendezvous point for Aberdonians.) There they would alight at the door of Raggie Morrison's, the best-known general store in the city (it stood where Marks and Spencer is today) and rummage their way to an appetite which would take them the short distance to Isaac Benzie's in George Street. That was the more upmarket shop where they could sample sophistication before enjoying lunch (or their 'denner', in North-east terms).

There would be time for an hour or two with Clark Gable or Spencer Tracy at the new Astoria Cinema back at Kittybrewster before the reverie of romance was interrupted by the reminder that Sharnydubs awaited, in all the grind of its reality. It was time to rejoin their matter-of-fact menfolk as they revved up the old jalopy for the bumpy ride to deepest Buchan or wherever – those men of solid worth from whose lips, unlike the Hollywood Romeos, the word 'love' may never have been allowed to escape.

Home it was to the dubs and hard graft of another week, pleitering among pigs and poultry, mucking the nowt and trying to make ends meet in a constant struggle against the odds. Country folk had a lot to teach the world about hard work and endurance, patience and good humour and simply making the best of what you have in this life. At least that's how it was as far as the middle of the twentieth century, before the countryside was uprooted from a sound and settled and decent way of life for a man and his wife and their family and turned into a conglomeration of disparate elements, some farming or nearly so, but many others so alien to the tradition of centuries as to baffle the indigenous population. That is, if you could find an indigenous soul left to baffle.

Thainstone

But that was what they called progress which, in the modern manner, led to the amalgamation of those three companies into Aberdeen and Northern Marts. Again, following the industrial trend towards out-of-town sites, that company proceeded to uproot itself from the bustling north side of Aberdeen and move the eighteen miles to Inverurie. Ever so subtly, the true flavour of the countryside began to fade. Smart suits replaced the hairy jackets to which the scent of Bogie Roll had clung so distinctively. And with it, to a large extent, went the authentic dialect of the North-east, once so crisp and natural and expressive but rising now with alien effort to the lips of a new and apparently sophisticated generation.

Whatever agriculture gained by the removal to Thainstone, the city of Aberdeen lost a vital link in its contact with that rural hinterland which had played such an important part in its own origins. The livestock companies had not been alone in boosting the prosperity of Aberdeen. Others, trading in everything from farm seeds and feeding-stuff to fertilisers and agricultural machinery, sprouted in all directions, adding to the city economy with names that gained household status, like Gavin and Gill, Barclay, Ross and Hutchison, George Sellar, R.G. Garvie, Reid and Leys, all the way to distinguished nurseries in the trees, seeds and shrub business like William Smith and Son, Benjamin Reid and Son, Springhill Nurseries and names that spread the fame of North-east roses, like Anderson's and Cocker's.

The manufacture of fertilisers had long been a major part of this burgeoning industry, and here we come across a name which deserves to be up there among the best but is sadly neglected to the point of oblivion. James Robertson, a farmer's son from Ardlaw of Pitsligo in the Buchan district of Aberdeenshire, had entered King's College, Aberdeen, at the age of twelve, and graduated for the ministry but engaged in a common practice of the time which was switching between preaching and teaching. By the tender age of twenty-six he was headmaster of Robert Gordon's, sorting out the indiscipline and educational deficiencies of his predecessor to great effect, a feat all the more commendable since he was of dwarf-like proportions, short and sinewy and hideously out of shape. Switching back to the ministry, he became professor of church history at Edinburgh University and moderator of the General Assembly of the Church of Scotland.

More to the point of our immediate interest, James Robertson set about testing the theories of a German scientist on the question of applying dissolved bones for the growth of crops. As the father of fertilisers in the North-east of Scotland, he was the man who sparked off a whole new industry for their manufacture, with the Miller family's factory at Sandilands, John Milne's factory at Dyce, and the fertiliser works of Nalco at Waterloo Quay and the North-Eastern Agricultural Co-operative at Bannermill.

As with the marts, amalgamation became the fashion of the century. In 1924, the Grandholm Wool Mills were bought by Salts, followed by the Donside Paper Mills amalgamating with the Inveresk group. In 1922 the Great North of Scotland Railway and the North British Railway became part of the new London and North-Eastern Railway while, in the same year, the paper works of Pirie and Sons joined up with Wiggins Teape, and the *Aberdeen Daily Journal* and the *Aberdeen Free Press* combined as the *Aberdeen Press and Journal*, later to become part of the Kemsley Empire of London.

CHAPTER 27

A City Takes Shape

The Aberdeen we know today was taking shape more recognisably within that last third of the nineteenth century. Much of it had to do with the building of the Joint Station in 1866, a major upheaval when you consider what it meant in demolishing existing buildings to make way for the railway lines that would plough their way through the centre of the town. Until then, the trains which had first puffed their way into Aberdeen in 1850 came with little disturbance, approaching from the south by means of a viaduct that followed the edge of the Dee estuary and, from the north, along the route that had been cut for the old Aberdeen–Inverurie Canal. Now they would be linked by a route cutting through the Denburn valley and meeting up at a brand new station called the Joint, to the south of Union Street. The demolition work required for these dramatic changes certainly added to the general congestion in districts like the Gallowgate, Causewayend, College Street and the Shorelands, overcrowded areas already suffering a typhus epidemic that had raged in the town during the mid 1860s. Six hundred people died.

But Aberdeen was booming commercially and its expanding trade demanded a bigger harbour, an extension that took place in 1868. In addition, the municipal boundaries were spreading out by 1871, northwards as far as the Bedford Road we know today, westward to the Forest Road and Ashley Road areas, to Westburn Park and down towards Great Southern Road. Old Aberdeen and Woodside still retained their independence and would remain as separate police burghs until as recently as 1891, when these communities were finally brought together. Whereas Aberdeen had consisted of only thirty streets at the start of the nineteenth century, that number had soared to five hundred by the end of it.

Into the expanding geography of Aberdeen came housing developments and street names like Jasmine Terrace, Roslin Terrace, Baltic Street, Cotton Street and King's Crescent. The contractors cutting their railway line through the Denburn built Craigie Street, while Rosemount was developing into Watson Street, Ann Street, Mount Street and Upper Stocket Road. Rubislaw was being opened up by Sir Alexander Anderson and James Matthew, the architect, with Queen's Terrace forming an extension to Rubislaw Terrace and Prince Arthur Street taking shape as an improved link between Albyn Place and Carden Place. There was also much building activity around Holburn Street, the Hardgate, Ferryhill and Cuparstone Road, though the name of Union Grove was still a private house within its own grounds.

The grandeur of Aberdeen: Rubislaw Terrace

Bridge Street, Broad Street and Schoolhill

In 1866, an article about Union Street in the *Aberdeen Journal* said, 'The feus in the west end have of late been filling up well with houses admirably suitable for so important and splendid a thoroughfare.' It added that Bridge Street was being built to give access to the brand new station, remarking on the high, imposing buildings being erected to take advantage of the new opportunities for commercial enterprise. By 1871, therefore, the general pattern of the Aberdeen we know today was taking on a settled appearance, rounded off in splendid fashion with the opening of the handsome new Town House at the corner of the Castlegate and Broad Street.

Heading west from Schoolhill, the Viaduct would open up Rosemount, while the tramway system now sped us to Holburn Street, King Street and Ferryhill, Mannofield and round by Rubislaw. The trawling fraternity was building its houses in Torry, just as at a later date many a reluctant farmer, persuaded by his wife to retire to a suburban 'semi' in the city, chose the north side by Kittybrewster, where he would at least be kept in touch with his rural roots, especially at the mart on a Friday.

Broad Street, when Byron lived there. On the left, two students in the arched pend which led into Marischal College. Past the clock and turret, Byron and his mother lived on the first floor in the accommodation with six windows looking on to the street

Broad Street, once the town's main thoroughfare, took on a brand new look in 1906 when Marischal College was given its spectacular frontage of granite. On that same street a century earlier, they may not have paid much attention to the lady with the crippled son who occupied a first-floor flat at number 64. Who was to know that the lad called George Gordon, a pupil at Aberdeen Grammar School, would one day emerge as the great Lord Byron, world-famous poet and wild man of literature whose mother was a Gordon of Gight, from the edge of Buchan? In late-Victorian times the ground-floor of Mrs Byron's house became the bookseller's shop of the remarkable John Mackintosh, who served customers as an interruption to his real calling in life, which was to write scholarly books like his *History of Civilisation in Scotland*. There are still many alive who remember his son and namesake, better known as Johnny Mac, the eccentric head of history at Robert Gordon's College, where he taught from 1920 until 1958.

Schoolhill was developing into the charming corner of the city it remains to this day, despite having lost one of its treasures in 1886, when they pulled down the magnificent home of Aberdeen's greatest artist, George Jamesone, to provide a depot for Wordie the carter's horses. Jamesone's wonderful garden had stretched back from Schoolhill to Woolmanhill and Loch Street. The old Grammar School was giving way to Gray's School of Art and moving to its present Skene Street site in 1863. The art school was designed to match up with the new art gallery, and John Gray, who gifted the school, achieved a further ambition when they linked the two buildings with an archway, better known as the vaulted gateway which leads you into Robert Gordon's College.

That corner was completed in 1925, when Lord and Lady Cowdray gave the city its impressive Cowdray Hall, with a handsome frontage forming the War Memorial, which was unveiled by King George V. The adjacent Rosemount Viaduct now had the public library, next to the South Church and then His Majesty's Theatre, one of the finest in Britain. Aberdonian humour soon branded that trio as 'Education, Salvation and Damnation!' They all came under the sword of William Wallace, cast in glorious pose across the street in that triangle, enhancing the contours that extended along Union Terrace and dipped dramatically into the gardens below.

Babbie Law's, Falconer's, E and M's

Holburn Junction was still known locally as Babbie Law's, named after a great local character who, until 1885, ran her licensed shop as a welcome howff for carters with a thirst as they transported granite down town from Rubislaw. Babbie once prophesied that, whereas the centre of Aberdeen had formerly been the Green and then the Castlegate, her own Holburn Junction would claim the distinction one day. In modern times, she could be right.

The massive soap works of Ogston and Tennant was eventually swallowed up by the giants of Unilever while many well-known local names were disappearing completely: names like Saint the draper, Steele the hatter, Hampton the art-dealers, Stephen the picture framer; bakers like Johnston and Laird, Garden and Raeburn, Lockhart and Salmond; and booksellers such as Murray, Brown and Co. and A. and R. Milne. National names began to appear on the streets of Aberdeen, starting with Woolworth, which opened in October 1919. By the Second World War, the Scottish Co-operative Wholesale Society was buying an assortment of businesses, from taxi firms and laundries to funeral undertakers.

Union Street was developing fashionable shops like Falconer's, Esslemont and Macintosh,

Watt and Grant's and Morrison's, while the hotels springing up included the Northern at Kittybrewster, the Douglas in Market Street and the Gloucester in Union Street, formerly the Forsyth. The ring-road, from the old Bridge of Dee to Great Northern Road, was started in 1929 at an estimated cost of £140,000 and the king and queen came to open the new Bridge of Dee in 1942, naming it the King George VI. When Glenburnie Distillery in Rubislaw Den North ceased to exist in 1857 it was then occupied by George Washington Wilson, Aberdeen's great pioneer of photography. Despite so much expansion of the city, however, house-building had not reached the Rubislaw Quarry by the end of the First World War. King's Gate had not begun its advance towards the green fields.

Yet Aberdeen of the 1800s was more industrialised than we sometimes imagine, with a broad spectrum of occupations. Statistics of employment in 1861, for example, show there were 700 seamen in the merchant service, though only 175 were classed as fishermen. There were 400 gardeners and nurserymen, 487 blacksmiths, 111 stone quarriers and 280 stone-cutters and polishers. Predictably for the time, domestic service dominated the job opportunities for women, the Aberdeen figure reaching the surprising number of 3,836. The town's main manufacturing interests were listed as flax, wool, cotton, wincey (wool and cotton material for shirts), combs, paper and envelopes. By 1871 the number of people employed in manufacturing was given as 9,000.

CHAPTER 28

A Public Library at Last

For a city that has always counted itself in the forefront of education, it is a surprising fact that early attempts to establish a public library in Aberdeen were met with formidable opposition. For once, no blame could be attached to the town council, which was perfectly willing to discuss the matter. It was the democratic vote of a public meeting in July 1871 that strongly rejected adoption of the Public Libraries Act. A report of the time said the citizens were 'not rising to the position of appreciating the privilege sufficiently high'. It took a further thirteen years before the distinguished Professor Alexander Bain, seconded by Baillie George Walker, managed to persuade Aberdonians at a meeting in the Music Hall on 25th March 1884. Opinion was swayed, no doubt, by an offer from the directors of the Mechanics' Institution in Market Street to hand over their building and library to the town council for the purposes of a library.

Professor Alexander Bain, philosopher with world-wide reputation

It soon became clear, however, that the premises were inadequate and Lord Provost Henderson instigated a new building fund from which would emerge the Central Library in Rosemount Viaduct. Awakening to the virtues of such a facility, everyone from business and professional people to employees in shops, offices and factories, weighed in to reach the £10,000 cost and to take pride in their achievement. The library took shape as a three-storey building in Renaissance style, designed by Alexander Brown of Messrs Brown and Watt and clearly visible from Union Bridge. When the opening day arrived – Tuesday, 5th July 1892 – crowds lined the street in great excitement. Flags, bunting and flowers were everywhere, while the band of the Aberdeen Artillery Volunteers entertained from across the street at the Wallace Statue.

As the dignitaries arrived in a carriage procession from the Town House to the far end of

Union Terrace, the biggest cheer was reserved for the man who would declare open the new building and whose name was synonymous with libraries – the great Andrew Carnegie, Scots-American industrialist and philanthropist. The presence of his wife and sister-in-law proved an attraction to the ladies, who were even then delighted to catch sight of the latest in American fashions.

Carnegie, the richest man in the world and one of the contributors to the cost of building the library, was the most recent burgess of Aberdeen and appeared at the ceremony with his ticket tied to his silk hat with a broad red ribbon. In his prayer of dedication, the minister of Queen's Cross United Free Church, the Rev. Professor G.A. Smith, called for 'the dispersion of ignorance and prejudice, for the growth of mutual understanding and sympathy among all classes of the community, for the education of children, the equipment of men for public counsel and debate and for the awakening of genius and invention'. In congratulating Aberdeen on its forward thinking, Mr Carnegie said education and free libraries were the only guarantors of a peaceful, progressive and law-abiding society. That evening, Alexander Robertson, the city librarian, provided two brakes so that all twelve of his library staff could go for a drive up Deeside, stopping at Banchory House to give three hearty cheers for Mr and Mrs Carnegie, who were staying as the guests of Lord Provost (later Sir David) Stewart, on their way to their summer residence at Loch Rannoch.

Aberdeen Central Library, opened in 1892

With the extension of boundaries in the previous year taking in the burghs of Old Aberdeen and Woodside and the fishing village of Torry, the new citizens were looking for a library service of their own. Branch libraries were financially out of the question but a reading room was opened at the Town House in Old Aberdeen in 1893. Electric lighting was installed in the new Central Library in 1895, replacing the old gaseliers, which were the chandeliers of the gas age.

Mr Robertson resigned his librarian's post in 1899 and the rush of applicants from all over Britain included a dentist, a tailor, a retired minister, a journalist and a number of teachers and booksellers. When the short-leet of six included the name of a journalist there was an outburst of protest at the *Aberdeen Journal*, for the applicant, George Milne Fraser, was a reporter on the rival *Aberdeen Free Press*. A native of Methlick, Mr Fraser had been an apprentice stone-cutter but an accident in an Aberdeen granite yard lost him an eye and he switched to journalism. To the consternation of the *Aberdeen Journal*, however, he was the man who landed the job. His substantial knowledge of the North-east and an enthusiasm for local history played a major part in the development of the public library over the next thirty-eight years.

The inimitable Marcus Milne took over before the war but he was soon off to the services, posted to India. In the upheaval back home, the bombing of London and other cities destroyed thousands of volumes at the premises of book suppliers. With social activities severely restricted in the wartime blackout, the reading habit was very much on the increase. Meanwhile the library staff was coping with extra duties which ranged from night-time fire-watching to a more bizarre role as the city's Casualty Recording Service. Linking up with the emergency services, including the hospitals and the mortuary at Berryden, one male and two female members of staff were on stand-by duty each night, waiting for the next German air-raid. With a total of thirty-four raids and extensive casualties (detailed elsewhere), messengers were despatched on their bicycles to collect details of the dead and wounded.

When it was all over in 1945, the protective sand-bags were removed from the windows and the blackout curtains put up for sale. Marcus Milne and other members of staff were welcomed back from the war. One of the first developments thereafter was the introduction of school visits, in which hundreds of children went to the library each year as part of their curriculum. With the city population heading for 183,000 and housing in short supply, the Corporation began the building of a Northfield estate in 1950. In the same year the first mobile library took to the road, serving outlying areas and causing a stir of curiosity and appreciation to the extent of 76,000 book borrowings in its first year. By 1955 Northfield had grown to the extent of 2,500 houses, meriting its own branch library, which was built in Byron Square, at the heart of the new community. That movement of population meant the closure of the East Branch and the one at Powis, but by 1968 the library had a presence in almost every area of the city, contradicting the forecast that the arrival of television in the mid 1950s would bring a serious decline in leisure reading. In 1967 local librarians played their part in establishing a school of librarianship at Robert Gordon's Institute of Technology (now the Robert Gordon University), only the second such school in Scotland.

Marcus Milne retired in 1968, having established himself as one of the city's best-known personalities, a popular speaker at clubs throughout the North-east, a good friend of the blind and an enthusiast for the organisations of Rotary and Freemasonry. He died in November 1989 in his eighty-seventh year. He was succeeded by his deputy, William Critchley, a highly popular appointment for a man who joined the staff in 1940 at the age of seventeen. After war service he studied for the fellowship of the Library Association and worked in Berwick and Motherwell before returning to Aberdeen. Bill Critchley broadened the scope of the library and put it in the forefront of provision for the Open University, of which he was a strong supporter. Tragically, however, he died at the age of forty-nine, sadly missed as a wise and kindly man.

Appropriately, the man who filled the post was his own deputy, Peter Grant, who had shared his plans and hopes for the library service. But uncertainty lay round the corner in the shape of local government reorganisation in 1975. As it turned out, the new city district of Aberdeen would stretch to embrace an area from Dyce in the north to Peterculter and Cove in the south, with the library authority serving a population of 210,000. A planned extension to the Central Library fell victim to cuts in public expenditure and staff frustration found its way into the newspapers, with talk of 'drabness, smelliness and brown linoleum – and the charm of a model lodging house!' But matters improved in 1978 when work began on the first phase of a scheme that would take four years and £1.5 million to complete. A second phase was completed in 1982 when the library was graced with a visit from Queen Elizabeth the Queen Mother.

Before the Central Library came into existence, the independent Woodside had taken pride in its own Anderson Library, the centenary of which was celebrated in 1983. At a civic lunch, Lord Provost Collie welcomed five descendants of the eponymous Sir John Anderson, along with family members of the architect, the legal adviser and the first librarian. The centenary also marked the library's first venture into narrative publishing, the story of Sir John and his Woodside Library being recorded in the publication of *The Admirable Mechanic*, written by Moira Henderson, at that time the reference services librarian. In 1990 the library gained its first writer-in-Residence, Hugh Scott, an established author whose work benefited aspiring writers and resulted in a publication, *The Book of Poems*. In further reorganisation, the libraries department became part of a new city arts department in 1989, which happened to coincide with Mr Grant's decision to retire after sixteen years in which he had greatly improved the image of the service and gained a personal reputation as a well-informed book-man. The library now became the responsibility of the city arts officer, Ian McKenzie Smith, under a new umbrella organisation in which the former deputy, Alan Fulton, became head of library services. The centenary of the Central Library was celebrated in 1992.

The Co-opy

Of all the institutions in Aberdeen, as in other communities throughout the land, none was closer to the heart of the people than the one they knew familiarly as 'the Co-opy', or the Northern Co-operative Society to give it its more formal name. Considering its scope and power, it would have seemed unthinkable to previous generations that the retail organisation so much at the centre of their daily lives would not survive the full run of the twentieth century.

The main appeal of the Northern Co-op was not so much bargain prices as the fact that every pound spent over the counter brought back a dividend, usually upwards of three shillings (15p today) and paid out twice a year, in May and November, when the working-class needed extra money for rent, rates and other household expenses. As a disciplined means of saving, it was a godsend to many a hard-pressed family. Little wonder that, by the end of the First World War, the membership had reached 87,000 – a figure that was roughly the same as the number of households in the city.

Built up as a working-class movement in the face of a predominantly capitalist system, it perished in the second half of the twentieth century, ironically through a period when socialism in this country had risen to power before losing its appeal in the rush of modern commercialism. By the time of Prime Minister Blair's administration in 1997, the old-style socialism of the Attlee government in 1945–51 was but a distant memory. Even with Labour in power, capitalism now had the support of an affluent society.

It was a different world from the founding days of the co-operative movement. In Aberdeen, it had its origins at the Broadford works in 1833, when 150 employees formed a society for supplying them with meal, groceries and spirits. But this and other attempts did not succeed and it fell to a certain William Lindsay, publisher and local leader of the working-class Chartist movement, to bring them all together. A follower of Robert Owen, the social reformer and idealist who created the model community of New Lanark in the early 1800s, Lindsay called a meeting in the vestry of Dr Brown's Church in Belmont Street. That led to the formation of the Northern Co-operative Company, with capital of £1,000 in one-pound shares.

The first shop opened in the Gallowgate on 4th July 1861 and branches of the Co-op were soon to be found in every working-class district of the city as well as in surrounding towns like Stonehaven, Banchory, Kemnay, Inverurie and Oldmeldrum. Retail trading was conducted

The Commerce Street Co-op, at the beginning of the twentieth century

mainly in the shops but there was also a substantial array of street vans, with a delivery service of groceries and bread. The headquarters was based in Loch Street, where there was also a large departmental store complete with restaurant. This was, in practice, a superstore before we came to know the term at national level. A furniture department included an upholstery workshop and there were also drapery saloons and a boot-and-shoe section. The Co-opy was going from strength to strength. By the late 1960s it was building a brand-new flagship store in George Street, giving it the modern-sounding name of Norco House, with an exterior design that was officially deemed futuristic but more generally regarded as an architectural monstrosity, rather resembling a wedding-cake.

In the mid 1970s Norco undertook its most ambitious project of all, building a gigantic superstore on its existing site at Berryden Road which also included its own bakery, dairy, meal-mill and sausage factory, grocery and drug warehouses, and a transport department. Strangely, with such a large and loyal customer base – and a guarantee of ultimate business – the only venture to fail was the funeral department! It began in 1908 and closed down in little more than a year. With insufficient turnover, it must have been a good year for the living.

With more than two thousand workers, the Co-op was regarded as a responsible employer, leading the way with paid holidays, a superannuation fund and sickness pay, and taking an active part in educating its members. Junior employees were given an incentive to attend evening classes. Into that structure came the recreational elements of bowling club and rifle range – and an active band of Women's Co-operative Guilds, contributing to charities and local social services as well as giving an outside interest to the many housewives who did not readily have that opportunity in days gone by.

By its very nature, the society was closely linked to the Labour movement, with prominent trade unionists to be found among the twelve elected directors who ran it with a small executive. Predictably, it was not universally popular, especially among private traders, but it prospered in its day as a business and a base for working-class togetherness. Everybody could rattle off their Co-opy membership number, even when the institution itself had faltered and passed away.

That day loomed when it became clear that all was not well with the Co-opy. As debts began to mount, the much-vaunted Norco House in George Street closed its doors in 1987, giving way to the John Lewis Partnership. New-style shopping arcades and multi-national superstores were the popular fashion in a new generation. Norco was now disposing of its comparatively recent expansions in places like Westhill, Ellon, Banchory and Elgin and selling off its dairy business to the Kennerty company. With reports that it had overstretched itself, the great Northern Co-operative Society finally crashed in 1993 with massive debts. For a proud institution that had served the citizens well, it suffered the ignominy of seeing the liquidators preparing to sell off the last outpost, the Berryden complex, that had once been regarded as the jewel in the Norco crown. In fact it had proved to be the biggest nail in the company's coffin.

Royal Visitors and Others

The monarchs of this country have made a habit of visiting Aberdeen at least once during their reign and that was a matter more easily achieved when Balmoral became a royal residence. Queen Victoria was there in 1863 to unveil the statue of the prince consort at the corner of Union Street and Union Terrace. Three years later her own statue was unveiled by the Prince of Wales at the corner of Union Street and St Nicholas Street, but was removed to Queen's Cross.

Her son, King Edward VII, paid that visit of 1906 to perform the opening of the new-style Marischal College, an event recorded on film and reappearing from time to time. His son, King George V, followed the royal pattern in 1925, when he came to open the new Cowdray Hall and Museum, adjoining the Art Gallery. On that same day the War Memorial, forming the front of the Cowdray Hall, was dedicated by the moderator of the General Assembly of the Church of Scotland and the United Free Church, and over the weekend 20,000 people filed into the hall to see the Shrine of Remembrance.

The Prince of Wales, who had laid the foundation stone at the new Royal Infirmary, was invited to perform the opening ceremony in September 1936, by which time he was being overtaken by events. When his father died in January of that year he became Edward VIII, the king who would never be crowned. Surviving an assassination attempt in August, he would end that year by giving up the throne in favour of the woman he loved, the American divorcee Mrs Wallis Simpson. In his absence, the infirmary was declared open by his brother, the Duke of York, who in the monarchial crisis was crowned King George VI, father of the future Queen Elizabeth. (Ironically, the Prince of Wales was in Aberdeen that same day, on the more personal business of meeting Mrs Simpson at the Joint Station!)

George VI was not unfamiliar with Aberdeen hospitals. As a young naval officer at the beginning of the First World War, he was brought ashore for an appendix operation at the Northern Nursing Home (later the Watson Fraser) in Albyn Place. As king, he would also return in 1942 to open the new Bridge of Dee which bears his name. His Scottish wife, now better remembered as Queen Elizabeth the Queen Mother, was a frequent visitor to Aberdeen, attending the Mod in 1946, opening the Beach Boulevard and receiving the freedom of the city in 1959, and giving her blessing to the new home of Aberdeen Journals at Mastrick in the 1970s.

Other distinguished visitors to the city included Winston Churchill, who first appeared in

The Prince of Wales laying the foundation stone of Aberdeen Royal Infirmary, 1928

1904 and made his last visit on 27th April 1946, when he came to receive the freedom of the city, driving in an open car from the Town House to the Music Hall. He waved cheerfully to the crowd, though carrying the huge disappointment that, having become the country's saviour and hero as prime minister in the Second World War, he lost Number 10 in the general election of 1945, even before that war was finally over.

In 1919 Field Marshal Douglas Haig, fresh from the tragedy of the First World War in which he was our commander-in-chief, had been another recipient of the city's freedom. A few years later he was followed north by David Lloyd George, prime minister during the First War, who was said to have added to Haig's complications by trying to control the warfare strategy. The freedom of the city was due to be bestowed on the first Lord Cowdray, who had been so generous to Aberdeen, but sadly he died two days before the ceremony.

CHAPTER 31

Thomas Hardy Comes to Town

More needs to be said about William Minto from Alford, already mentioned as the brilliant student who succeeded Professor Alexander Bain in the chair of logic and English literature in 1880 – not least for his connection with that great English novelist, poet and dramatist, Thomas Hardy. Having gained a triple honours degree at Aberdeen and begun an academic life as assistant to Professor Thomson in natural philosophy, Minto gave it all up for journalism, heading south to London, where he became editor of *The Examiner* and leader-writer on the *Daily News* and *Pall Mall Gazette*. Fleet Street gave him that entrée to notable writers of the day, including Thomas Hardy, a contact made initially after Minto wrote a review of *Far From the Madding Crowd* in 1874. The two men became friends.

When Minto returned to Aberdeen to resume his academic career, taking over Bain's chair, there was some criticism that he had stayed too long in London. That was outweighed by the advantages, however. He brought back 'the heady aroma of Fleet Street', said W. Keith Leask, having met so many significant people and known their minds. He impressed his students with his sensibilities, like that of the old medieval wandering scholar. To them, Minto's style of teaching English was a new experience. Sadly, he was struck down by illness when only forty-seven and died on a bitter day in 1893. He was a much-loved character, and witnesses told of the desolation that descended on his class when the news was brought to them in the middle of a lecture.

Professor Sir William Ramsay wrote that he and Minto had been drawn together by the romantic side of modern literature. They believed that 'the aim and crown of all literary education is to understand and appreciate the spirit of our age'. If William Minto had lived for the full span of his career he would have looked forward to a memorable occasion at Aberdeen University in 1905. On that April day he would have renewed his friendship with Thomas Hardy, who was coming to receive an honorary Doctor of Laws, the first of five degrees that would come his way. (Oxford, Cambridge, St Andrews and Bristol were much later in thinking about it.)

The invitation seems to have surprised him, since he had no connection with Aberdeen and he confessed that he 'didn't know a soul up that way'. The catalyst for the Hardy honour was thought to be J.M. Bulloch, a distinguished native and graduate of Aberdeen, co-founder of the student magazine *Alma Mater* and author of a history of the university. He was also the Aberdeen representative when the four Scottish universities produced that excellent musical anthology *The Scottish Students' Song-Book*.

Like Minto, John Malcolm Bulloch met Thomas Hardy in his years as a journalist in London, having gone there from the *Aberdeen Free Press*. On the day after the graduation Hardy was also to be a guest at the opening of the Sculpture Gallery, an extension to Aberdeen Art Gallery. So, for the two events, Sir James Murray, chairman of the Art Gallery, hired a special train at his own expense and filled the seven carriages with a remarkable array of personalities. As it left Euston Station at 10.45 p.m. on the eve of the graduation, the passengers accompanying Thomas Hardy included Lord Reay and Professor J.B. Bury, editor of Edward Gibbon's *Decline and Fall*, both of whom were to receive honorary degrees at the same ceremony; the novelist Maarten Maartens; the poets Arthur Symons and William Watson; a number of Royal Academicians; an envoy of the Pope; and journalists from all the national newspapers.

One journalist described the journey in these terms:

In the splendid sleeping carriages we had a smooth run but the early morning was cold and we lost a little time in Cumberland and Westmorland on account of a snowstorm. Two breakfast cars were added at Stirling and nearly all the passengers enjoyed a good meal soon after passing Perth. Mr Thomas Hardy, with pensive face and simple manner, sat in a smoking room and chatted of many things.

As the train arrived in Aberdeen, less than two hours before the graduation ceremony, the city was 'sparkling with frosted snow like a Christmas card'.

In his subsequent autobiography, Thomas Hardy wrote that he was hospitably entertained at the Chanonry Lodge, Old Aberdeen, by Principal and Mrs Marshall Lang, which was the beginning of a lasting friendship. Principal Lang presided at the graduation ceremony, which took place at noon in the Mitchell Hall. Presenting Hardy for his degree, Professor Neil J. Kennedy said:

Perhaps it is not the least of his successes to have done for Wessex what Scott did for the Borders and the Highlands. He has described the scenery, the placid rustic folk, their instinctive wisdom racy of the soil, their ways, thoughts and morals, the effects of collision with the modern struggle for life, and the traditions of the noble dames of Wessex, as only one could do who knew and loved what he described . . .

Thomas Hardy (*Far From the Madding Crowd*) was honoured by Aberdeen University in 1905

In catching the moment of graduation, one journalist wrote:

The novelist with the grey moustache, the thick grey eyebrows and the clear, meditating eyes ascended the platform, and there was great gusto in the cheering by the students and in their thunderclap when the cap was placed on his head. Mr Hardy himself was outwardly unmoved. His face was placid rather than triumphant as he sat at the table signing the roll, and yet he must have been gratified by the welcome of so many eager young men.

There was an evening reception in the Mitchell Hall at Marischal College, made lively by Scotch reels and bagpipers, and next day the opening of the Sculpture Gallery was followed by a Corporation dinner at the town hall. On the Sunday morning Thomas Hardy visited spots in and around Aberdeen associated with Byron and lunched at the Grand Hotel (later the Caledonian) as the host of Sir James Murray. There he crossed hands in 'Auld Lang Syne', drawing towards a close the whole Aberdeen episode which, he said, was of a most pleasant and unexpected kind, remaining with him like a romantic dream. Hardy said he was deeply struck by the energy and earnestness of the Aberdeen people, 'so unlike the apathetic people of the south'. As a trained architect himself, he spoke of the granite houses, said he liked the red granite but thought the grey version would be improved by a mixture of the warmer colour.

Appropriately, before leaving the city, he went to Allenvale Cemetery to visit the grave of his old friend Professor William Minto, whom he had known since 1875. Then he joined the evening sleeper train, engaging in conversation with the lord provost and remarking, 'It is the most hospitable city I have ever been in.'

CHAPTER 32

From Fleming to Mitchell

The end of a century is a peculiar phenomenon, experienced recently when we said goodbye to the twentieth and couldn't quite articulate the feeling – not to mention the fact that we couldn't agree on whether the milestone should be December 1999 or December 2000! To many, it seemed like saying farewell to an old friend, the century which had bred us and reared us and by which we gauged all the events of our lives.

The civic leader at the start of the twentieth century, Sir John Fleming, was a native of Dundee who had come to Aberdeen as a timber merchant, entering the town council in 1891. It was during his time that the burgh was given the enhanced status of 'a county of a city', giving him the added honour and responsibility of lord lieutenancy. Fleming was a man of interesting pedigree. From fairly modest origins his Dundee family had spread out towards various branches of fame in banking and land ownership, his brother Robert having founded the Scottish–American Investment Trust and pointed the way to other institutions of that concept around the world.

Sir John's nephew, Valentine, was killed in the First World War but not before he had fathered two sons destined for fame: Peter Fleming, the renowned explorer and travel writer, and Ian Fleming, the creator of 007 himself, Commander James Bond. Having started his own small timber business in Dundee, John Fleming and his wife walked out one evening in December 1879 to observe the drama of a gale that was lashing the city. As they gazed towards the railway bridge over the river they saw an avalanche of red cinders cascading in the sky, little realising that they had just witnessed the Tay Bridge rail disaster in which the girders collapsed and took a train and its passengers to their deaths.

By now John Fleming was extending his business to Aberdeen, in time for a house-building boom that taxed his ability to supply enough timber. Soon he had moved from a room in the Douglas Hotel to 58 Queen's Road, prospering enough for further moves to Richmondhill House and finally the splendid residence of Dalmuinzie at Murtle. His timber business was based at the Albert Sawmills on Albert Quay, from which he took time to immerse himself in local politics in the 1890s and beyond. A major topic of civic interest at the time was the expansion to a new style of Marischal College, carrying with it the complication of the neighbouring and much-valued Greyfriars Kirk. Attempts to placate the more sensitive of feelings were not entirely successful, but the result was a blending of the two buildings and Lord Provost Fleming played a major part in keeping it all in perspective. The university felt indebted to him for his handling of a delicate situation and his reward was an honorary LLD.

In the poignancy of his time, John Fleming had lived through the Crimean War (from which he had clear memories of Florence Nightingale), the Indian Mutiny, the American Civil War and the assassination of Abraham Lincoln, through to the Boer War in which, as lord provost of Aberdeen, he saw the men off to South Africa and welcomed them back. He was there at the time of Queen Victoria's death in 1901 and was heading down Regent Street towards Westminster for the coronation of her son, King Edward VII, when the news vendors proclaimed it postponed because of the king's appendicitis.

Sir John stood for Parliament in 1917 and was returned as the Liberal member for South Aberdeen. He died on a trip to South Africa in 1925. In a memoir written for his family's consumption in 1922, Sir John reflected on the calibre of the man who was standing for civic office. Even in Victoria's time, it seems, many of the best citizens tended to shun the ordeal of an election, for reasons that resonate in more recent times. He wrote:

John Fleming, Lord provost with a
James Bond connection

The best of business men can decide rightly in most matters on their own initiative but quite often cannot put their reasoning into words. They are *doers* but not *talkers*, and refuse to sit through hours of tedious talk on committees where their shrewd business sense is out-voted by glib-tongued but ill-informed fellow-members. The consequence is that a large proportion of town councillors are men, although as a rule honest and well-intentioned, of little mark in the community; many indeed fond of the limelight, finding in many instances that it pays to be in the public eye.

Rose Fleming

There are two interesting postscripts to the Sir John Fleming story. First, the timber firm he started in the 1870s still exists in the Aberdeen of the twenty-first century, remaining in the family until 2006 when it was sold by his great-grandson, Mark Fleming, who lives at Keig, near Alford. Secondly, Sir John's daughter, Rose, lived to be a hundred and wrote her memories of life in the home of an Aberdeen provost in Victorian times.

She paints a vivid picture of Richmondhill House, of croquet lawns and summer houses, of walking to Albyn Place School, always known as 'Mackie's' as it belonged to Mr Mackie, who had been their neighbour. There was the Boer War, after which several generals came to receive the freedom of the city. Rose sat on the knee of General Sir Hector MacDonald, once a hero but later ordered to be court-martialled for some trouble in Ceylon. The poor man shot himself. Her father had started public lectures in the Music Hall, from which Rose remembered Sarah Grand, famous authoress of the time, and Edward Whymper, the first man to climb the Matterhorn. When her father was assessor to the rectors of the university, he was host to people like Andrew Carnegie.

Rose married the Rev. John Coutts, minister of Ferryhill Church, whose family came from Tarland. And they produced among their five distinguished sons a governor general of Uganda, a courageous fighter pilot, and two who became notable soldiers in the Second World War. Ben Coutts was seriously wounded at Tobruk (and then torpedoed on the way home) and later became highly popular in Scottish farming and broadcasting circles after the war. Frank became Brigadier Coutts of the King's Own Scottish Borderers, who came to train for the Second Front at Hayton Camp, Aberdeen, and in the Buchan village of Maud in 1942–43. After the war he played rugby for Scotland and eventually headed up both the Royal British Legion and the Earl Haig Fund.

Rural Connection

As you cast an eye over the list of distinguished men who became provosts of Aberdeen, you find very few who originated in the city itself. This merely reflects, once again, how the rural North-east has always played a major part in populating the city. Even today, there are few families of long-rooted connection who cannot tell you of their beginnings in the farms and villages beyond the boundaries.

As for that watershed of a new century, with its changing moods and attitudes, there were the early rumblings of left-wing politics which would spread in the new age until a North-east man, Ramsay MacDonald from Lossiemouth, would become the first Labour prime minister in 1924. Labour had already gained a toehold in local politics, with two members elected to the town council. Such history was made by James Forbes, a shoemaker, for St Machar, and George Maconnachie, printing compositor, for St Andrews. Not much more was immediately discernible on the local scene, however, and the lord provosts continued to be men of business orientation or professional distinction and it would take another half-century before socialism established its grip on the running of Aberdeen.

Sir John Fleming's successor, James Walker of Richmondhill, was in the familiar mould of prominent fish-trade capitalists and he was followed in 1905 by Alexander Lyon, of Garioch farming background but born in Footdee, his father having started a hide and tallow business in George Street. Lyon's activities ranged from leading the layout of the Westburn, Stewart and Walker Parks and Union Terrace Gardens, developing the tramway system and reorganising the fire brigade, to campaigning against diseased meat, clearing the slums of the Gallowgate and Exchequer Row, and bringing a campanologist from Belgium to look after the bells of St Nicholas. He was also involved in the widening of Union Bridge and College Street and in improving the amenities at the beach.

His time as lord provost also covered the royal opening of the new-style Marischal College in 1906, giving him the privilege of greeting King Edward VII and Queen Alexandra when they arrived from Ballater at Ruthrieston Station and escorting them for the rest of the visit. The effort was well rewarded at the end of the day, however, when he received his knighthood.

The extension of Aberdeen's water supply had been hottering for some time, with two schools of thought. Some favoured tapping into the River Avon in Banffshire while others wanted to stay with their own River Dee. The new lord provost, Alexander Wilson, a lawyer born in Drumblade (another country boy), moved the adoption of the Avon scheme at the town council debate of 1909 but was defeated. A bill to the same effect was thrown out by the House of Lords. Wilson founded the Aberdeen Society of Solicitors, and was to the fore in the building of both the Masonic Hall in Crown Street and the Sculpture Gallery at the Aberdeen Art Gallery.

Taggart's Own

It was back to the country for the next lord provost, with the familiar name of Adam Maitland, whose family had farmed Balhalgardy of Inverurie since before the Battle of Harlaw and was still there in modern times. Starting as a bookkeeper with the *Aberdeen Journal*, he moved to J. and W. Henderson, the builders' merchants, where he became a partner. His tenure at the Town House ended with the First World War, when he was succeeded by James Taggart, another Donside man, this time from Coldwells of Inverurie, who followed his apprenticeship as a stonecutter in Aberdeen by emigrating to the United States. Returning in 1879, he started in business as a granite merchant, a name which soon established itself in Great Western Road. Having entered the town council in 1899, he became lord provost in 1914, with a

James Taggart, popular lord provost during the First World War

very different prospect before him. Immediately, he set about forming an artillery brigade which became known as Taggart's Own and spent the rest of that tragic war trying to keep up the morale of his community. So much of civic routine is affected by war, but when it was over in 1918 he diverted his energies towards a new hospital for sick children. In his fundraising efforts he put Lord Cowdray at the top of the list and, having explained the purpose of his visit, Taggart heard his lordship say: 'Well, how much do you want?' The lord provost made his equally forthright reply: 'How much have ye got?'

James Taggart, who was knighted in 1918, was president of Aberdeen Burns Club and the Scottish Cyclists' Union and first president of Aberdeen Rotary Club. In the aftermath of the First World War, he was still in office to present the freedom of the city to Douglas Haig, whose name is synonymous with that conflict. Taggart died in 1929 and his portrait hangs in Aberdeen Art Gallery.

His successor, from 1919 till 1925, was a fish salesman with the unusual name of William Meff, who had joined the Harbour Board in 1892 and the town council in 1894. It was during his time as lord provost that the Labour wing of the council began to assert itself, bringing scenes of confrontation with Meff and others of a more traditional nature who were not comfortable with the new obligations being placed on local authorities. Housing, for example, was becoming a local matter. Though knighthoods were by no means a guarantee for the city's lord provosts, their frequency had increased in recent decades and Meff became Sir William after receiving King George V and Queen Mary in 1925, when they came to add royal approval to that opening of the Cowdray Hall and War Memorial.

Andrew Lewis

A well-deserved knighthood also came the way of the next incumbent, Andrew Lewis, whose family was well established in engineering and trawling and who established a shipyard on the banks of the Dee. A man of drive and vision, he managed to extend his spirit of enterprise for the good of the community as well. Sir Andrew had barely warmed the civic chair when he was faced with the potential turmoil of the General Strike in 1926. Aberdeen escaped the worst of the troubles and a local emergency committee managed to keep order. The 1920s brought that serious movement to replace the Royal Infirmary at Woolmanhill, which would have a basic requirement of £400,000. Andrew Lewis launched his appeal and for most of his provostship pursued that dream of a brand new infirmary. When he emptied his last collection box, his appeal had gathered £407,000. Retiring from the provostship in 1928, he stepped up to receive his knighthood and lived on till 1952, dying at the age of seventy-seven.

A man from Lower Donside was next on the parade of provosts, James R. Rust occupying the chair from 1928 till 1932 and adding to that list of Aberdeen streets which bear the names of civic heads. A city businessman, Provost Rust had joined the town council in 1914 and served as the city treasurer who carried through important deals in real estate that would make way for future expansion. Hazlehead Estate, for example, was bought in 1920 for £40,000, paving the way for

Hazlehead golf course, to be followed by the lands of Kincorth for £45,000 and Hilton and Rosehill for the purpose of housing schemes. In his time he welcomed Miss I. Burgess as the first woman to take her place on the town council, but had the less comfortable task of coping with the national recession of the early 1930s.

The professional tone of the Aberdeen provosts altered somewhat with the next two appointments, which would take us through most of that decade leading up the Second World War. Henry Alexander, who took office in 1932, had been editor of the *Aberdeen Free Press*, the daily paper owned by his family, until it amalgamated with the *Aberdeen Daily Journal* in 1922 to become *The Press and Journal*. As a graduate of Aberdeen University, Alexander was the first Master of Arts to lead the city in a long time and, as a mountaineering enthusiast, he wrote a very fine book, *The Cairngorms*. On the civic side, he was deeply involved in a grand scheme of town planning for roads and housing schemes, which brought us, for example, the ring-road of Anderson Drive and the suburb of Kincorth. Having sampled a journalist at the head of its affairs, the city continued the habit with Edward G. Watt, a colleague of Henry Alexander, who edited the sister paper of the *Free Press*, the *Evening Gazette*. Another graduate of Aberdeen University, Watt was much involved with the Territorial Army, having commanded a reserve battalion of the Gordon Highlanders in the First World War. His time as lord provost coincided with the opening of the new Royal Infirmary at Foresterhill in September 1936, for which he made a further appeal for £100,000 to cover the cost of medical equipment.

By the time of his departure in 1938 the war clouds were gathering, with the prime minister, Neville Chamberlain, returning from his ill-fated meeting with Hitler in Munich. The search for a new lord provost in Aberdeen came down to a contest between George Duncan, a well-known lawyer and convener of the education committee, and Thomas Mitchell, a local baker, the latter winning out by a narrow margin.

Tommy Mitchell

Just as Sir James Taggart had been the right kind of lord provost to bolster morale during the First World War, so was Tommy Mitchell the best possible choice for that same role in 1939. He was the pawky, cheery, archetypal Aberdonian who would invariably produce some gem of local wit and humour to relieve tension when matters became too serious. Sticking to the local dialect, and without a hint of condescension, Tommy Mitchell was as much at home with the cleaning wifies at the Town House as he was with the king and queen. They all loved him. He caused hilarity when King George VI came to open the new Bridge of Dee during the war. Delivering the loyal address, Tommy suddenly threw away his piece of paper, saying, 'Ach, I've lost my place.'

His journey to the lord provost's chair had started in vastly different circumstances. Born in an upstairs room of what became known as Morris's Hotel in Oldmeldrum (his mother was the proprietor's daughter), he was an unwanted child, given away within hours to foster parents who had a croft at Daviot. Starting work as a farm servant at £8 a year, Tommy Mitchell also learned to be a baker, moving into the big city first as an employee, before deciding to buy a bankrupt bakery business in George Street. It cost him £115. Building up a prosperous enterprise in both George Street and Queen Street (it had no connection with that other well-known bakery of Mitchell and Muil), he then turned his attention to public service, culminating in his election to Aberdeen Town Council in 1928.

Winston Churchill with Sir Thomas Mitchell during an Aberdeen visit

Tommy Mitchell was nearly seventy, however, before be became lord provost, just in time for that crucial role he would play during the Second World War. He worked tirelessly during that upheaval, when Aberdeen became one of the most bombed cities in Britain. Tommy Mitchell raised enough money from his public appeal to build four Spitfires, which carried names with Aberdeen and North-east connections. With nine arduous years in the civic chair, he was still in office at the end of the war when the city conferred its freedom on Winston Churchill, with whom Tommy had already formed a friendship. Though defeated in the general election of 1945, Winnie was still the national hero warmly welcomed to Aberdeen on that memorable Saturday of 27th April 1946 with crowds lining Union Street. The two old warriors drove together in an open car from the Town House to the Music Hall for the freedom ceremony.

With a fine sense of occasion, Tommy Mitchell made a phone-call one day in wartime to that hotel in Oldmeldrum which hosted his birth, just hours before he was given to foster parents. 'I've never spent a night in your hotel,' he said, 'but I want to sleep there tonight. This is a very special day for me and I'll sleep in the kitchen if necessary.' A puzzled proprietrix gave him a room, and all became clear next morning when she opened her newspaper. In the Honours List of that day, the unwanted baby, born in the hotel seventy-two years earlier, had just become Sir Thomas Mitchell! One of the truly great lord provosts, the wonderfully warm and witty Tommy stepped out to public acclaim that morning, glad that he had made his sentimental journey to the place of his birth. Sir Thomas became such a favourite with the Royal Family that the Queen Mother came to visit him at the Watson Fraser Nursing Home in Aberdeen just before he died in 1959. He was ninety. His parting words to her were: 'We've done a lot of things together, your Majesty!'

CHAPTER 33

Gateway to the World

Industries come and go according to the times, but the importance of the harbour has remained high in terms of the trade and prosperity it has brought to Aberdeen. The harbour existed long before there was shipbuilding of any significance, and various Acts brought expansion during the 1800s, with an expenditure of £1.7 million and a rise in the port's vessel tonnage from 17,000 in 1810 to 120,000 by the end of the century. The harbour covered an area of 370 acres, consisting of the Victoria and Upper Docks on the northern side the Albert Basin in the middle and the fish market, which belonged to the town council, extending to the west.

As a seafaring city, Aberdeen had maintained a strong connection with most parts of the world, but the glory days as an independent port faded with those wonderful clippers. The last sailing ship built in Aberdeen was the *Alexander Nicol* in 1876. Interestingly, as the last clipper took to the water, Alexander Hall was launching the first warship that Japan had ordered to be built for herself. The *Jho-Sho Maru* was an armour-plated corvette, a vessel said to have been ordered on the suggestion of Thomas Glover, an Aberdonian by adoption (he was born in Fraserburgh), who was working as a civil engineer in Nagasaki, a name that would find its place in the history of the Second World War when the Americans dropped their second atomic bomb to end that war in Japan.

Glover played a major part in introducing railways to that part of the world and he returns to our story later. But as a further point of interest, at his coal mine in Japan the engineering department was run by young Alexander Hall, a member of the Aberdeen shipbuilding family. Tragically, Alexander died in Nagasaki at the age of twenty-eight, a few years after that Japanese corvette had been launched at the yard back home.

For much of its early maritime history, however, Aberdeen had not exploited the fishing potential as well as it might, leaving much of the enterprise to the Dutch. It was herring that changed the picture around 1870, when fishermen cottoned on to the possibilities and boats began arriving from England. It was a trade that would move on more significantly to Peterhead and Fraserburgh, but it led to the creation of a trawler fleet, a fashion that was established by a certain William Pyper, owner of *The Toiler*, a converted tug which made her first trip with trawl gear in March 1882.

Just as woollen goods, linen and granite had brought bouts of prosperity to the city over the years, it was now the turn of the trawlers to add wealth to Aberdeen. *The Toiler* was followed by

Herring boats sail into Aberdeen Harbour

the first locally built iron steam-trawlers, the *North Star* and the *Gypsy*, and a whole new industry was born. The value of its landings rose from £10,000 in 1882 to a staggering £264,000 a little over ten years later. The town council had already rebuilt the hamlet of Fittie for the fishermen, with its North and South Squares still a picturesque attraction to this day. By the end of the 1800s there were 200 trawlers in the Aberdeen fleet, employing 1,800 men, with a further 4,300 people working in the curing yards and 500 in ancillary businesses.

As a measure of what the new prosperity was doing for Aberdeen, in the twenty years up to 1902 the shipyards of Alexander Hall, John Duthie and Hall Russell had built no fewer than 267 trawlers, at an average cost of £4,500. And the best was yet to come. The herring industry was bringing in two-thirds of the value of Scottish fishing, one half of it landed within fifty miles of Aberdeen and the bulk of it going to cured herring markets abroad. But there is always a pitfall. Big catches brought not only inflated hopes but also an over-supply of the cured herring market, and a subsequent crisis. The North Bank, which had been the main financing agent of all this prosperity, took a serious blow but did at least have the good sense to stay with the industry until it was restored to good health.

Meanwhile the white fish industry was progressing well, the landing values rising from £882,000 in 1907 to £1.5 million in 1913. The reward was that Aberdeen became the premier trawling port in Britain. However, foreign boats were beginning to land a quality of fish regarded by the local fleet as being substandard, as a result of which the Aberdeen fish salesmen took action of their own to discriminate against foreign landings. During the 1920s Aberdeen slipped from first to third place among British ports, behind Hull and Grimsby, but even by the outbreak of the Second World War there were said to be no fewer than 40,000 people dependent, one way or another, upon the fishing industry in Aberdeen.

A trawler under construction at the Hall Russell Yard, 1959

As well as the catching of fish, the city has been prominently involved in the experimental work of the industry. In 1929 the Torry Research Station was established to study the subject of fish preservation, its discoveries in quick-freezing and cold storage leading to the building of those large factory trawlers that undertake so much of their work at sea. Still on the scientific side, the Torry Research Station was preceded by another research station, the Marine Laboratory of the Department of Agriculture and Fisheries, which studied the life and habits of fish and sent a fleet of vessels with frogmen and underwater cameras to pursue the study at sea.

Back at the shipyards, many a smaller company went out of existence at the turn of the century, leaving only Alexander Hall and Co. and Hall Russell from the building yards of a generation earlier. John Lewis and Sons opened up as shipbuilders in 1916, at the height of the First World War, and by 1935 had launched forty-six cargo boats, many of them going to Australia and the Far East. During the war, the three yards were building anything from frigates and corvettes to minesweepers and tank landing-craft and were heavily involved in repair work. Hall Russell had come into existence in 1867, when Alexander Hall and Co. opened a branch next door to their original yard for the purpose of building iron ships. Ironically, it was the branch that bought the share capital of Alexander Hall in 1953 and then took it over completely. Around 1950, shipbuilding in Aberdeen was employing 3,000 people, with marine engineering taking up another 1,000.

The fortunes of Aberdeen Harbour would, of course, change dramatically in 1969–70 with the discovery of North Sea oil, the fuller story of which comes later. With the announcement of one oilfield after another, the harbour became a scene of curiosity for large crowds who had never seen vessels quite like those required for the exploration of this new industry. It soon became clear that Aberdeen was the ideal base for this bonanza now turning up on its North Sea doorstep and that the harbour management would have to ascertain quickly what the needs of the oil companies really were.

As things stood, access to the Victoria and Upper Docks was available only through lock gates at periods before and after high tide. Such restrictions were no use to the oil companies, who needed round-the-clock operations. To open those lock gates, however, meant a reconstruction of all quays within the enclosed dock to cope with the water pressure. It was just the beginning of vast changes to accommodate the biggest industrial happening in the history of the North-east. Who could have imagined that, by 1985, there would be upwards of 800 firms in Aberdeen and the North-east devoting themselves entirely to the offshore industries of oil and gas, bringing work to 65,000 people?

All this development at Aberdeen Harbour had to be planned and financed while keeping in mind, with characteristic canniness, the uncertainty of how long the oil industry would last. As a finite commodity, its eventual demise was the greatest certainty of all. Future possibilities would include a return to traditional cargoes like fish, grain and fertiliser, encouraging cruise-ships, ferry-boats to the Continent, and perhaps a leisure industry by the waterside. Beyond that, who knows what the future holds for Aberdeen Harbour when the last Stetson disappears over the horizon and the story of oil takes its place in history?

CHAPTER 34

How the Houses were Built

Though the city's population was increasing rapidly in the latter part of the 1800s, it was not until the very end of the century that the council began to pull down slums and build its first council houses – fourteen tenements in Urquhart Road and Park Road. It was left to private builders to keep pace with the growing numbers. The First World War was over before various housing acts spurred on the municipal programme, the first post-war building being developed as the Garden City scheme at Torry, followed by Hilton. The Mansefield Road district of Torry, along with the Pittodrie and School Road areas, were laid out in the later twenties, while the Corporation was also going ahead with clearing the slums in Guestrow, Longacre, Shuttle Lane, the Denburn, Young Street and Berry Street, and the occupants being moved to low-rent accommodation in Seaforth Road, Sunnybank Road, Errol Street, School Road and Torry. Soon there was a criticism that the slums had merely been moved.

Meanwhile, in the private sector, Aberdeen was extending its boundaries in all directions, with villas and bungalows spreading out to the Rubislaw and King's Gate areas, to Westburn Road, Stockethill, Duthie Terrace and the Bridge of Don. Yet as recently as 1918 you would have found at the west end of the town just a few old cottages in that stretch between Kepplestone and Woodend. With housing came schools at Torry, Hilton, Powis and Linksfield and new churches at Hilton, King Street and Seaton. Between the two world wars Aberdeen built 11,400 houses, of which 6,400 came from the Corporation. But in 1938 there were still 27,000 city dwellings without their own toilets. After the war, the housing shortage was met by the novelty of the 'prefabs', temporary-looking, separate little homes which were then replaced by multi-storey flats. The few prefabs that were spared demolition turned out to be durable enough to last a human lifetime and every bit as acceptable, aesthetically, as the skyscrapers. As planning convener back in 1928, Sir Henry Alexander came up with a scheme which caught on elsewhere and was concerned not so much with building as with the prevention of it. It was the green-belt idea, setting out an area around the city in which nothing could be developed except under the strictest scrutiny.

CHAPTER 35

Education for All

Scotland played a major part in fostering education in the old colonial days, largely through the churches. But with more than half a century of home rule established, it is surprising to find that many parts of the former British Empire, including India, are still without compulsory schooling. For a country which prides itself in a long tradition of education for all, it comes as a further surprise to find that into the second half of the nineteenth century there were still close on 3,000 children in Aberdeen who had no chance of attending a school, at a time when the total population was just around 75,000. That meant only 4,000 had a school to go to. All that would change with the Education Act of 1872, which made it compulsory for children to be instructed between the ages of five and thirteen. At that point, there were only thirteen town schools in the city, apart from the Grammar School, Robert Gordon's, the High School for Girls and St Margaret's.

Within the next ten years, however, they had built Commerce Street, the Middle, Causewayend, Ferryhill, Mile-end and Skene Street Schools and enlarged the existing ones to a capacity of nearly 8,000 pupils, double that of 1872. By the early 1890s there were twenty-two elementary schools, including King Street, Rosemount, Ruthrieston and Ashley Road, with a roll of 19,000, in addition to the 1,750 attending the Grammar, Gordon's and the High and another 1,250 at other institutions. Walker Road and Kittybrewster were built before the end of the century.

All this was set against a background of rapid expansion in the city. After a mid-century period of stagnation, Aberdeen was enjoying a new growth and prosperity by the 1870s, the census of that time showing a ten-year rise in population of more than 14,000. The needs of education were already becoming more of an issue nationally, not least because Britain was facing economic competition from countries like Germany and would have to look to her laurels if she were to maintain her pre-eminence. In any case, for all our reputation in matters of education, were we really as good as we imagined?

Doubts in that direction were being expressed by people like William Lyon Playfair, Member of Parliament for the Universities of Edinburgh and St Andrews (yes, universities had their own MPs well into the twentieth century). In a powerful speech in the House of Commons he warned against nourishing our Scottish pride with the traditions of the past. He said: 'It is quite true that Scotland was once a nation with nearly universal education. But it is not true now.' The national system didn't meet the needs of even one-sixth of schoolchildren, he said, and the efforts of the various religious bodies had by no means made good the deficiencies. His views were supported by a commission set up to examine the matter, reporting that a drastic overhaul of the system was required.

So the revolution began. Within twelve months school boards had to be elected in every parish and burgh, which meant no fewer than 986 of them in Scotland. The initial task, to be completed within nine months, was to take a census of how many children were of school age in the area, and how many actually attended. The funding of schools would come from a government grant, from the local rates and from fees paid by the pupils since education was not yet free. In 1874 the ratepayers' contribution in Aberdeen was twopence in the pound. Against that, the total wage bill for all teaching staff was £2,973! A hundred years later, that corresponding figure was £5 million.

But if the criticism of schooling at that time has a familiar ring today, the position of the churches wasn't much better. In 1872 they were reported to be in great distress, suffering from falling attendance, with masses of 'heathens' who never went near a church, and a general attitude of hostility to any form of religious influence and privilege. It is hardly surprising, then, that they were desperately holding on to whatever authority might still remain in their grasp. Among the more articulate members of the school boards, one of the key issues concerned what kind of religious education, if any, was to be supported in Aberdeen. Was it to be a 'sectarian' or a 'secular' education? There were suspicions that the 'secular' lobby was gaining the upper hand, though there were differences of opinion as to what the word actually meant. In the event, the chosen board turned out to be a well-balanced blend of intellectuals and men of business, a union of town and gown, well capable of handling balance-sheets, salary negotiations and property deals.

Only one 'secularist' made it through the election. But who was going to argue with the calibre of the man when he turned out to be none other than Alexander Bain, philosopher of international renown and at that time professor of logic at Aberdeen? His leanings were balanced by the Rev. W.R. Pirie, a former moderator of the General Assembly of the Church of Scotland who went on to be principal of Aberdeen University. Whatever else, the churches had always played their part in education, at home as well as abroad, and they were prominent again with providing teachers, the Church of Scotland opening a training college in 1873, followed by the Free Church two years later. In 1906 they combined with the Aberdeen Training Centre (commonly known as the 'TC') in St Andrews Street, adding a Demonstration School to assist in the practical training of students. It later became known as the College of Education. In 1928 a Training College Hostel was built at Hilton at a cost of £81,000.

Administration passed from the local school boards to education authorities in 1919 but the costs began to rise. In 1909–10 it had taken £5 13s 3d (£5.66) per annum to educate a child. Twenty years later it had gone up to £16 and by 1969 the cost was £237 per annum, at a time when Scottish education was certainly losing its proud boast of superiority. Those education authorities in turn gave way to education committees within the local authority and, with the rise of a Labour majority on Aberdeen Town Council in the middle of last century, there were shocks in store for the Grammar School and the Girls' High, frowned upon in some quarters for their fee-paying status.

They were indeed fee-paying but, whereas Gordon's College had always been in the independent sector, the Grammar and Girls' High came under the control of the council. They were nevertheless schools of the highest calibre, to the point of social comparison where, in the eyes of many Aberdonians, the Grammar was just ahead of Gordon's. It certainly had a longer history and could claim a fine line of distinguished former pupils, including George Gordon, later Lord Byron. In the more radical realms of mid-twentieth-century politics, however, such a reputation could raise paranoia among those with a mission, and the power, to iron out the inequalities of life.

So it was no surprise when Aberdeen Corporation removed the fee-paying status of the Grammar and Girls' High, abolished their primary departments, turned them into co-educational schools and took away their names. The Grammar became Rubislaw Academy and the Girls' High changed to Harlaw Academy – area schools like any other under the council's jurisdiction. With the later change in control from a Labour town council to a more moderate Grampian Regional Council, the Grammar regained its proper name but all else remained.

CHAPTER 36

Independent Schools

Outwith the system of district education in the city, Aberdeen has long been able to claim a rich seam of single-sex schools that held their own with the best of establishments in the other Scottish cities, both academically and in the field of competitive sport. Politically, there was always an element of opposition from those who cried 'elitism' and to whom such fee-paying schools were abhorrent. Nevertheless, a place within their walls was still the ambition of many a bright youngster whose parents could not have afforded the fees. But money or social background would never be an obstacle as long as the system of bursaries could be maintained. In other words, in some of the country's finest academic establishments there would always be a place for the most promising of Aberdeen children.

For boys, the choice was Aberdeen Grammar or Robert Gordon's College, while girls could aim at the High School for Girls, St Margaret's School for Girls, or Miss Oliver's, later known as Albyn School and retaining its single-sex status until 2005, when it accepted boys as well.

Aberdeen Grammar School

By far the longest history belongs to the Grammar School, dating back 700 years or more and well established even before William Wallace and Robert the Bruce were fighting the cause of Scottish independence. (It needs to be identified as the school of New Aberdeen, to avoid confusion with the Grammar School of Old Aberdeen, known as the Barn, which survived until the late nineteenth century.) Until the present, handsome construction in Skene Street, the site of the Grammar School was always to be found at Schoolhill, uncomfortably close to what became its chief but much younger rival, Robert Gordon's Hospital. Successive buildings were repaired or replaced, but the last one to stand in Schoolhill took shape in 1757, precisely on the site that was known in modern times as Gray's School of Art, now part of the Robert Gordon University.

In all truth, the Grammar was a modest little place, a single-storey horseshoe with four rooms and a hall, staffed by a rector and three teachers. With a roll of around 200, the classes were therefore large by modern standards, pupils remaining with the same teacher until they

James Melvin, outstanding headmaster of the
Grammar School

finally passed into the rector's class. The most distinguished rector of the nineteenth century was Dr James Melvin, widely acclaimed as the finest Latinist the North-east ever produced, who sometimes found himself teaching classes of more than a hundred.

And these were not the mealy-mouthed, well-disciplined youngsters we sometimes imagine our forebears to have been. In those days Grammar School boys were not alone in their reputation for unruly and riotous behaviour, known to seize control of the school building and defy the town council authorities on matters like school holidays. Such behaviour, which followed the Grammar even to its present site, was not to be condoned but was perhaps explained by a frustration with the narrow curriculum, largely confined to Latin, Greek, ancient history and geography. Surprisingly, for more basic subjects like English and mathematics they had to move round the corner for brief sessions at Drum's Lane or Little Belmont Street, where the town schools taught the subjects.

By the mid 1800s there was a general demand throughout Britain for a broader curriculum and Aberdeen was no exception. What's more, for over a hundred years that modest little building in Schoolhill had lived in the physical shadow of the highly impressive Auld Hoose of Robert Gordon's, less than 200 yards away, and suffering the ignominy of being mistaken for its gatehouse! It was time for a move and various plans were considered. A site on Union Street, where Gilcomston South Church was later built, was the first choice, but when that was abandoned other options were considered – Skene Square, Justice Mill Lane, Ferryhill, Albert Terrace, Crown Terrace and Carden Place. The final choice of Westfield Model Gardens, where the Grammar stands today, was heavily criticised as being too far from the city centre. But the project went ahead and a brand new school in gleaming white granite, enhancing the architecture of the city, opened its doors in October 1863.

Despite the criticism of remoteness, there was enough enthusiasm among the citizens of Aberdeen to raise almost the entire cost from public subscription. Now they had a Grammar School in which they could take real pride, teaching not only the classics but English, mathematics and so much else, all under one roof. The Grammar had always been fee-paying, though coming under the aegis of the local authority. Strangely, until 1881 the pupils could choose the subjects they wished to study and paid only for the classes attended. This left too much spare time for mischief and accounted for much of the rowdiness. Despite the vast difference in scale, that little building in Schoolhill had created a heritage second to none, claiming a remarkable output of distinguished sons. Its scholars had included Alexander Bain, world-famous philosopher, and that great poet of the age, George Gordon (Lord Byron), the crippled lad whose daily walk took him round from his mother's modest home in Broad Street past the Kirk of St Nicholas to Schoolhill.

In its later incarnation, the Grammar maintained that reputation, extending it to art, music and drama and turning out such memorable performers as Andrew Cruickshank (Dr Cameron in *Dr Finlay's Casebook*) and Steve Robertson of *Scotland the What?* Its journalists included Kenneth Peters, former editor of *The Press and Journal*, and Harry Reid, former editor of *The Herald*.

An earlier Grammar School at Schoolhill

The Grammar produced a Nobel Prize-winner in J.J.R. Macleod (for the discovery of insulin) and two winners of the Victoria Cross: Robert Grierson Combe, who trained as a chemist in Aberdeen and emigrated to Canada, came back to fight in the First World War and was killed in action in 1917; and John Alexander Cruickshank, who collected his Victoria Cross as a pilot in Coastal Command during the Second World War, sinking a German U-boat while his own plane was under attack while he was suffering from seventy-two different wounds! Happily, he survives to this day and walks to Rubislaw Church every Sunday from his home in Anderson Drive.

Not least, Grammarians excelled on the sports field, with outstanding figures like Dr J.R.S. Innes, Scotland's rugby captain; Dr D.W.C. Smith, who not only managed the British Lions at rugby but played soccer for the Dons of Pittodrie; Eric Watt, who was Scotland's most capped hockey player; and Marjorie Coutts, more recently captain of the Scottish women's hockey team. Academically, its pupils in modern times have included the principal of Aberdeen University, Professor C. Duncan Rice.

Even after the move to the present school, the numbers remained quite small until the opening of a primary department, known as the Lower School, in 1881. The catchment area was mainly the city, but the railways provided for country boys coming to town, then the needs of overseas families sending their sons home for that prized education led to the opening of a boarding house in Queen's Road. It ran from the 1930s until after the Second World War, when it was taken over by the Scottish Youth Hostels Association.

Strong competition from Gordon's College and the Central School put the Grammar under pressure and the man credited with turning it into the modern school of the twentieth century was H.F.S. Morland Simpson, an Englishman who came from Fettes College in Edinburgh to be rector in 1893. In his time, two wings were built in 1913, a technical department and gymnasium were added and sport was elevated in the curriculum with Rubislaw Field opening in 1916 and its pavilion becoming a memorial for the men of the First World War. It was Simpson's idea to have a statue of Byron in front of the school, which was erected in 1923, but his other ambition, for a swimming pool, was not realised until 1963. Expansion led to the former Westfield School being incorporated into the Grammar in the 1920s and Rosemount School following the same route in the 1970s.

However, the nature of Aberdeen Grammar School began to change after the Second World War. Its local authority bosses decided to abandon fee-paying in 1947–48, presenting the democratic stance of entry-by-ability, and following that up with the phasing out of the kindergarten and lower-school departments. The process was taken a stage further in 1973, when the local authority decided that the catchment of the Grammar, broad in its scope down the centuries, should be narrowed to the role of a local school, part of the plan to turn all city secondaries into district academies. In addition, it would no longer be exclusively a boys' school.

However much the hackles of Grammar traditionalists began to bristle, open fury was unleashed when the same authority took the ultimate step of changing the name. What was seen as the final insult to a great heritage came with the announcement that it would now be known as Rubislaw Academy, with a subtitle of 'Aberdeen Grammar School' in parenthesis. For several years it toiled under what was regarded as a monstrous moniker, until the fates intervened with a new form of local government called regionalisation. The Labour town council which had brought about the changes was no longer in control of such matters. So in 1977 Grampian Regional Council, responding to a vociferous campaign by former pupils, gave the Grammar back its proper name and salvaged, to some extent at least, the honour of the school.

If that had been a burning issue, a more literal interpretation of the phrase reared its disastrous head on 2nd July 1986, when fire broke out and largely destroyed the main core of the school. Buildings can at least be replaced but the biggest heartbreak was the loss of the library, generally regarded as better than those of Eton or Harrow. That library had been created out of the old school hall in 1963 and had just undergone a refurbishment. With great spirit, the school continued to function by means of a temporary 'village' on the lawn and it was not until the first anniversary of the disaster that Grampian Regional Council took a final decision to rebuild, albeit on a smaller scale, reducing the roll to a thousand and bringing it all to one site. It was a further two years before the work began but, if there can be any consolation in a devastation like that, it meant that the Grammar now had a modern, purpose-built school, ready for the needs of a new century.

Robert Gordon's College

In terms of its history, second place goes to Gordon's College, the other boys' school in Aberdeen but one with a vastly different story to tell. Whereas the Grammar had always been within the control of one local authority or another, Gordon's was an independent school from the very beginning and remains so today. That independence, however, comes at a price. Parents at such a school pay not only the fees to educate their children but also the taxation which incorporates a certain sum, the purpose of which is . . . to educate their children! Yet not a single penny of that money is returned from a state that totally escapes the multi-million-pound burden of financial responsibility and calmly appropriates the cash for other purposes. Mercifully, down the years, there have been people of greater principle than the politicians.

The Auld Hoose of Schoolhill, now well through its third century, was the brainchild of one such man: the eponymous Robert Gordon, an aristocrat from the Gordon family at Pitlurg, near Ellon, which was a branch of the Gordons of Huntly. Young Robert, son of a lawyer, grew up in the fashionable Huxter Row that ran between Broad Street and the Castlegate, where their local hostelry was the original Lemon Tree Hotel, later demolished in 1867 to make way for the Town House at the corner of Broad Street.

Not long after graduating from Marischal College in 1689 he was taking his shrewd business brain off to Danzig in Poland, at that time a huge country which included the Ukraine and did brisk business with Scotland. There, for the next thirty years, he operated as a merchant and

The original Lemon Tree Hotel, demolished to make way for new Town House in the 1870s

amassed such a fortune that his philanthropic instinct was busily engaged on what to do with it. Robert Gordon, the bachelor, did not take long to make up his mind. Retiring to Aberdeen in 1720, aged fifty-two, he set about preparing his dream – to provide live-in care and education for boys in his native city whose parents could not afford to keep them at school. He himself chose the Schoolhill site that formerly housed the palace of Scotland's King Alexander II, who handed it over as a Dominican priory in 1240, and there he would sit alone and visualise the dream he would never see in reality. That would come after his death in 1731, when he so gorged himself at dinner in a friend's house one evening that he fell ill and died of suspected food poisoning.

Robert Gordon, founder of Robert Gordon's

But he had laid it all out in his will, or Deed of Mortification as it was called. And within a short time, with upwards of £10,000 in hand, that classical central building we still know today as the Auld Hoose took shape. However, with Robert Gordon laying down some sound financial rules about first restoring the level of his investments, there was a delay in bringing into operation what would be known as the Robert Gordon Hospital ('hospital' was a usage of the day, employed on similar projects by men like George Heriot in Edinburgh and the

The Auld Hoose, which dates from 1732

Hutcheson brothers in Glasgow). That delay would bring about a dramatic turn of events, involving the Jacobite Rising of 1745, already related on p. 56.

For the next 131 years it served the needs and intentions of the time until the whole concept of those 'hospitals', praiseworthy in their day, simply ran out of favour. In 1881 the governors came up with a revolutionary plan that would send the boys home to live with their own families and bring a broader spectrum of society into what would now be called Robert Gordon's College, incorporating an evening school with the day school.

Out of that structure in 1909 came Robert Gordon's Technical College, later to become the Institute of Technology and ultimately the Robert Gordon University, which would spread itself around Aberdeen till it found a natural focal point at Garthdee House, overlooking the Dee. That was courtesy of its generous benefactor, T. Scott Sutherland, architect, entrepreneur and eloquent town councillor, who not only gave over his estate within his own lifetime but added a gift of £50,000 before moving into 27 Albyn Place as a more suitably sized home for him and his wife. Himself a Gordonian, Tommy Scott Sutherland set the scene for a university that would blossom in many directions, not least as a centre of academic excellence for the oil industry. He wrote a book called *Life on One Leg*, for that was all he had, having lost the limb in a childhood accident. His determination to succeed was shown in his prowess as a sportsman, extending to the tennis court, where his agility on one leg and a crutch was a feat to behold.

The university still occupied the east side of the Schoolhill quadrangle, and in the 1980s, with space at a premium, there was a suggestion that Gordon College itself might move out to a green-field site at Slopefield, later known as Counteswells. Apoplexy among former pupils, spluttering about the unthinkable idea of leaving the spiritual home of the college, might not in itself have averted the outrage. But other considerations, like planning permission and local objection, did. So moves were set afoot to effect the eventual departure of the university instead. Counteswells became the school playing-field.

Gordon's College had come through a twentieth century of memorable milestones, with buildings including a swimming pool that would pave the way for Olympic performers like Athole Still, David Carry and, the most notable of them all, Ian Black, hailed by many as the greatest swimmer Britain has ever produced. (He returned to the college as head of the Junior School.) If the twentieth century belonged to Ian Black, his nearest rival emerged in the twenty-first when David Carry gave Scotland a sensational start to the 2006 Commonwealth Games in Melbourne by winning two gold medals in the 400-metre freestyle and the 400-metre medley. As part of his triumphant return to Aberdeen on a fine spring day, David was led down the main drive of the college by the pipe band, complete with his medals, before taking the stage of the MacRobert Hall to address the entire school.

Academically, Gordon's produced some of the top medical men of the earlier days, and in modern times claimed such outstanding figures as Sir Ian Wood, the Aberdonian above all who took his place in the international oil industry; investment high-flyers in Martin Gilbert, founder of Aberdeen Asset Management, the biggest financial organisation in North-east history, and his friend and classmate John Sievwright, boss of global markets and investment banking at Merrill

Lynch in New York; Lord Sutherland of Houndwood (Stewart Sutherland from Hilton Drive) former principal of Edinburgh University; and Don Cruickshank, chairman of the London Stock Exchange.

It could also claim writers like John R. Allan and Robert Kemp; entertainers in Buff Hardie and Robbie Shepherd; and a new-age politician in Michael Gove from Rosehill Drive, top debater and former president of the Oxford Union, who entered Parliament in 2005 with a forecast from leading Conservatives that he could become their prime minister one day. Rising through the ranks of the Liberal Democrats at local and national level, Nicol Stephen reached new prominence in 2005 when he succeeded Jim Wallace as deputy first minister of the Scottish Parliament. A special niche in Gordon's College legend, combining academic brilliance and athletic prowess beyond compare, must go to St Clair Taylor from Raemoir, near Banchory, who, born in 1928 and a pupil during the Second World War, was held in rapture by his contemporaries as a god-like creature despite his own chronically modest nature. Taylor proceeded to a career as a research scientist in animal breeding at Edinburgh's Roslin Institute, where they created Dolly the Sheep.

Meanwhile, Gordon's College went co-educational in 1989, the governors making it plain that it was a matter of principle and not economic necessity. On that score, Gordon's has maintained a system of bursaries which enables 250 of the 1,000 pupils in the senior school to attend with financial assistance, the highest percentage of any school in Scotland. That money came not only from the Aberdeen Endowment Trust, which handled the original Robert Gordon investments, but from Aberdonian well-wishers like Peter Scatterty, a farm servant from the Garioch who went to work in the gold mines of South Africa and, on his death in the 1930s, left the college around £50,000. He was not a Gordonian.

Ronald Burnett, the modern dux of 1935, became depute city chamberlain and left a legacy of £1.4 million when he died in 1996. Legacies apart, one Gordonian stood out with the distinction of having given the college a fortune – in his own lifetime. The generosity of Robert Crawford from Hollybank Place was all the more laudable in that his own bursary was withdrawn in 1939, when he reached his third year and was adjudged to have fallen short of the academic standard. After war service he joined a solicitor's office in London and, without a single school or university qualification to his name, worked his way through internal examinations to become an indispensable authority on maritime law, with a raft of clients that included C.Y. Tung of Hong Kong, the man who bought the *Queen Elizabeth*, and Aristotle Onassis, the Greek ship-owner. In fact, the one-time telegraphist in Aberdeen Post Office would find himself on board the fabulous yacht *Christina* with Mr Onassis and his glamorous mistress, opera singer Maria Callas, for company. He was a close witness to that ill-fated romance as well as Onassis' subsequent marriage to his trophy wife, Jacqueline Kennedy. Robert Crawford held Miss Callas in the highest regard. His opinion of the White House widow was rather different! So he took his place among the Gordonians of great heart, without whom many an able but less fortunate youngster in Aberdeen would not pass through that vaulted gateway en route to the Auld Hoose.

By a coincidence of events, Gordon's College had a vintage decade in the 1930s, in which it gained not only the physical features of the MacRobert Hall (mainly a gift from Lady MacRobert of Douneside), a Sillerton House for boarders, a swimming pool and library, but also scholarships from people like Peter Scatterty (mentioned above) and the Otaki prize which takes the school captain to New Zealand every year. That latter award is in memory of a former pupil, Bisset Smith, who captained a New Zealand merchant ship, ss *Otaki*, during the First World War and bravely tackled a German battleship, for which he was given a posthumous Victoria Cross. The 1930s also brought the first Founder's Day, one of the ideas of the reigning headmaster, I. Graham Andrew, who carved out a special niche in the ten years from 1933. His successors from wartime onwards were David E. Collier, John Marshall, George Allan and Brian Lockhart, who guided Gordon's through its 250th anniversary in the year of the millennium and was succeeded by Hugh Ouston, former deputy head of George Watson's in Edinburgh.

St Margaret's School

By the early years of the twenty-first century the trend towards co-education had left Aberdeen with only one single-sex school: St Margaret's. With the Grammar and Harlaw Academy (formerly the Girls' High) already well established in the new fashion, Gordon's College followed suit in 1989 and Albyn welcomed its first boys in 2005. Whether the moves were a matter of principle or economic necessity hardly matters. Smaller independent schools, proud of their ability to produce well-rounded individuals, were certainly the most vulnerable in terms of financial survival. Following a review of independent education in Aberdeen in the 1980s there was indeed an attempt to merge Gordon's College (then with 1,150 boys), Albyn (490 girls) and St Margaret's (430 girls), involving two years of serious negotiation to find an acceptable structure. The idea was that Gordon's and one of the girls' schools would combine as a large, co-educational establishment, with the other continuing as a single-sex school for girls.

Though loss of identity for one of the girls' school was always a difficulty, they did reach the day when a protocol of agreement was due to be signed. But the St Margaret's delegation came with the news that they had a problem with parents and were therefore unable to sign. They withdrew, and the plan fell apart. In 2000 Gordon's College headmaster Brian Lockhart produced a further plan to bring his school into union with Albyn but that also came unstuck. By 2005, therefore, St Margaret's School for Girls was on its own, not only flying the flag of independent, single-sex education but proud of its position as the oldest all-through girls' school in Scotland.

It began in 1846 when Miss Ann Stephen opened a day school in the drawing-room of her parents' house at 1 Union Wynd. It was one of many small schools of its type which existed in the nineteenth century. The fact that it survived beyond most was due to a distinguished line of headmistresses who, in the first seventy-seven years, were also the owners of the school. Those ladies and their staffs built an impressive level of academic achievement, creating an ethos that was much admired. Ten years after it began, Miss Stephen and her family moved to 13 Union Row and the school took on the name of Union Row Academy. In 1874 she retired to 9 Albert Street, where she lived until her death in 1922 at the age of ninety-seven.

When the school expanded under the subsequent ownership of the Misses Isabella and Jean Duncan, it moved to a larger house at 31 Union Grove and finally, in 1890, to its present home at 17 Albyn Place. There, it would soon have new neighbours next door, in the shape and rivalry of the Girls' High. It was only with that move to Albyn Place that Miss Stephen's creation took on the name of St Margaret's, appropriately, as the queen of Scotland who married Malcolm Canmore remains our only female royal saint, having been canonised in 1250 for her piety and charitable works, especially in the cause of education. In 1934 they were granted an achievement of arms by the Lord Lyon, consisting of a shield bearing the arms of St Margaret, surmounted by the triple-storied castles that symbolise the city of Aberdeen.

When Isabella and Jean Duncan retired in 1923, St Margaret's was purchased by a group of friends led by Mr Edward Watt, prominent newspaperman and future lord provost, who set it up as an independent school run by a council and recognised as a charity, just like most other independent schools. In the upheaval of the Second World War, St Margaret's was requisitioned as a Government food office and day pupils were transferred to the boarding house at numbers

The grandeur of Aberdeen – Queen's Gardens, near the Cross. During the Second World War,
day pupils as St Margaret's were transferred to the school's boarding house at nos. 6 and 7.

6 and 7 Queen's Gardens, with the boarders evacuated to Glenbuchat Estate on Donside, the owner of which, Colonel Barclay Milne, the Liberal MP, had a daughter Jean as a pupil. They later moved to Blackhall Castle, Banchory, and finally to Woodlands, Cults. The original Miss Stephen was enterprising enough to take boarders in 1856, a tradition that lasted for 133 years. St Margaret's was the first girls' school in Aberdeen to teach gymnastics and had introduced swimming at the Beach Baths by the 1930s. A strong musical tradition was established by the gifted David Murray (formerly of Turriff Academy), who taught music at the school and was organist at St Machar's Cathedral, where they continue to hold the annual St Margaret's Day service.

Nor has it been without its distinguished former pupils. A modern audience will recognise the name of Tessa Jowell, a prominent member of Tony Blair's Cabinet as secretary of state for culture, media and sport. As Tessa Palmer, she arrived from England in 1953 at the age of five, when her father, Kenneth Palmer, came to Aberdeen as a chest specialist and her mother, Rosemary, as a radiologist. The Palmers began their twenty-seven years in Aberdeen with a house in St Swithin Street, ending up in the Chanonry. Tessa spent her entire school career at St Margaret's, inspired by memorable teachers like Mrs Downie and Miss Merchant. From there it was on to an arts degree at Aberdeen University where she was president of the women's union, in tandem with Bill Taylor for the men. In those carefree days of long walks on the Beach Promenade she had no thoughts of a political career.

St Margaret's can also claim one of the most distinguished Aberdonians of all time in Mary Garden, a world-class operatic singer who was once bracketed with President Theodore Roosevelt in a public vote as one of the two best-known personalities in the United States. Miss Garden (originally Mary Davidson) was a St Margaret's girl before the family emigrated to America, paving the way for an operatic career centred largely in Chicago and Paris. From her home on the Champs Élysée she was the darling of the Paris crowds, closely involved both musically and personally with Claude Debussy, who asked her to create his famous role of Mélisande.

Mary Garden, world-class opera singer and Debussy's Mélisande

A mixture of fame and notoriety greeted her 'Dance of the Seven Veils' in Richard Strauss's *Salome*. When the police chief of Chicago declared it indecent, Mary told him with native bluntness to go pursue Al Capone instead! From prima donna she made the unusual switch to manager of the Chicago Grand Opera company. Back in Europe, she was courted by royalty, a welcome guest at Windsor where she once met that other great diva, Dame Nellie Melba, who allegedly behaved very badly. Mary, who had reservations about Melba, said she was a wonderful singer – as long as you kept your eyes shut!

No man kept his eyes shut when Mary was around. Sixty-five at the outbreak of war in 1939, she caught the last plane out of Paris before the Germans arrived and came home to Aberdeen, where she spent the last twenty-eight years of her life. Local memories of Mary Garden are mainly of a ladylike figure in those post-war years, veiled and glamorous and gliding down Union Street with all the aura of a faded Hollywood star. She frequented the coffee houses and tipped outrageously, though in fact she had outlived her means. Respectful to a fault, the average Aberdonian stood back in awe and came to know very little about her. Mary Garden died in 1967, having ended her days in the psycho-geriatric surroundings of Daviot. According to Frederic Mohr's dramatisation of her life, there were only fourteen people at her funeral, with no one to claim her ashes.

A distinguished list of former pupils also includes women like Susan Raeburn QC and Sheriff Deirdre MacNeill, while Hilary Henderson (Mrs Douglas) became the first woman academic registrar in Scotland when she was appointed to the Robert Gordon University in 1992. Other names remembered include Sandra Inkster, wife of MSP Lewis Macdonald and herself a local councillor; Dr Jennifer Carter, distinguished lecturer at Aberdeen University who counted Gordon's College headmaster Brian Lockhart and Lord Provost Jim Wyness among her students; and Kate Lewis of the shipyard family, who became Lady Fraser of Allander and helped her husband with the Allander Trust.

Since its establishment as an independent school in 1923, St Margaret's has been headed by Miss Mary Bell (1923–29), Miss Mabel Holland (1929–52), Miss Edith Currie (1952–70), Miss Marjorie Bosomworth (1970–88), Miss Lorna Ogilvie (1989–98), Miss Anne Ritchie (1998–2000), Mrs Lyn McKay (2001–06) and Mrs Anne Everest (from 2007), a former staff member who returned from her years as a deputy head at Gordon's College.

The name of St Margaret's has now been taken by many others around the world, to the extent that they form an international sisterhood stretching from Canada to Australia and Japan. Needless to say, St Margaret's School for Girls in Aberdeen is a prominent member of the group.

Albyn School

From an age when many an independent school was owned by the head teacher, 'Miss O.'s' is still remembered as the popular name of that rather exclusive establishment for girls in Queen's Road. It stood for Miss Oliver's, one of four distinguished figures in the history of what is now Albyn School. In a final act of devotion, instead of selling it to a successor, the lady forfeited any profit for herself by handing over the school to a charitable trust. But the story goes back to 1867, to another remarkable lady who laid the foundations. Miss Harriet Warrack, born in Aberdeen in 1826, was the daughter of James Warrack of 33 Dee Street, whose business interests included a brewery at Gilcomston and a grocery and tea dealer's shop at 50 Union Street. A lady of enterprise and energy, she opened Miss Harriet Warrack's School at 8 Waverley Place and was soon planning a boarding house for out-of-town girls, with its initial base at 30 Fountainhall Road.

Miss Warrack, who played a pioneering part in broadening out the educational opportunities for women, was joined in the early 1880s by Alexander Mackie, who helped to run what was now called the Union Place Ladies School. Mackie, who would take his place among the distinguished four, was born on the Delgaty Castle estate near Turriff, where his father was gardener, and graduated with honours from Aberdeen University. Having considered divinity, he became assistant to the famous Professor Alexander Bain and decided his true vocation was as a teacher of English language and literature.

Miss Warrack thought so highly of her young graduate teacher that, when she retired from active work in 1886, she passed over to him the full control of the school which was about to move to numbers 4 to 6 Albyn Place, diagonally opposite St Margaret's, and to become known as Albyn Place School for Girls. To most people, however, it was better known as 'Mackie's', such was the reputation of the principal, a debonair gentleman who was the very opposite of the Victorian martinet: breezy and good-humoured, using wit and irony, even sarcasm, together with a balanced charm to run a school where teachers were left simply to teach and the girls were encouraged to learn.

Mackie was a poet, author and able public speaker whose reputation spread across the world, leading to an extensive lecture tour that took him from New York to Montreal, Toronto and across Canada to that other Banff and the Rockies beyond. It may have been a step too far. A man of robust good health, he nevertheless fell ill soon after his return and people were shocked by his sudden decline. Hours after the school closed for the summer holidays of 1915 he died peacefully at home, before his sixtieth birthday. His wife Philippa was the daughter of Dr Robert Gordon Rattray, medical superintendent of the Royal Infirmary.

By 1920 Albyn had come into the hands of the memorable Miss E.C.S. Oliver, heralding another great era in the history of the school. Under her leadership it made a dramatic leap forward, first with a move from the cramped environment of Albyn Place to the more spacious surroundings of Queen's Road. The school had already acquired No. 21 as a boarding house and quickly bought up the properties on either side. Now they had tennis courts on site, and electric lighting instead of gas. Miss Oliver developed the curriculum and ethos of the school, with a vigorous involvement in the arts, sport and political and moral debate complementing rigorous academic expectations and strict standards of courtesy and deportment. This was laced with the originality and strength of Miss Oliver herself, giving all-day parties for the whole school, smoking, and being followed into the French lessons by her dachshunds! She remained a revered and respected figure.

The interruption of the Second World War brought the usual upheaval, with the Air Raid

Precaution authorities taking over 23 Queen's Road and some pupils being sent to Blelack, near Dinnet, and others to Tillypronie House. When ill health forced Miss O. to retire in 1948, she arranged for a board of governors to run her school as a charitable trust. For its headmistress, the new board appointed Miss Walker, noted for her kindliness and tact, 'a gentle, wise hand' as she was described. She was followed in 1958 by another inspired choice, Miss Dorothy Kidd, who was destined to complete that quartet of significant figures, dominating Albyn in every respect for the eighteen years till 1976. In her time the school opened the new hall, gym and science laboratories which rightly bear her name. It celebrated its centenary in 1967. When she died in 2004 a memorial service was held at Rubislaw Church, with an address by Sheriff Muir Russell. It was time to reflect on a rather special lady who was remembered and revered by former pupils and staff alike.

Her successor, Miss Christine Campbell, who had previously been head of St Bride's in Helensburgh, was a highly popular figure whose time was cut short by illness. Her early death shocked the community. That thrust Miss Catherine Morrison, head of English and a long-time servant of Albyn, into the role of acting headmistress, pending the appointment of Miss Norma Smith, a scientist, who guided the school sensitively through the next fifteen years and was able to oversee the building of the new science block. The legacy was then placed in the hands of Mrs Sheena Taylor, assistant head of Torry Academy, whose time at Albyn was brief and fraught with controversy, leading to her departure after two years. Miss Jennifer Leslie, who had been deputy head, then took over and played a crucial role in maintaining the ethos and standards of the school.

In the years surrounding the millennium, there was an attempt to amalgamate some of Aberdeen's independent schools, including Albyn, but the merger failed to materialise and Albyn gained a new lease of life, appointing Dr John Halliday as headmaster when Miss Leslie retired in 2002. Dr Halliday, a graduate of Exeter and Cambridge and former lecturer at the German University of Passau, had previously taught at Dollar Academy, was head of German at Merchiston Castle, Edinburgh, head of modern languages and housemaster at Sedbergh School, Cumbria, and headmaster of Rannoch School, Perthshire. He also had the distinction of being Albyn's first male head since the days of the famous Alexander Mackie a century earlier.

But change was still in the wind. From its long tradition as a girls' school, Albyn embarked on a move towards full co-education in 2005, accepting the first thirty boys into the primary section. With an upbeat mood, it was announced that the annual turnover of £1.9 million in 2002 had risen to more than £3 million by 2006. In the same year, celebrations were under way for the centenary of the Former Pupils' Club, with concerts, dinners, gatherings and a civic reception. Miss Harriet Warrack would have been delighted. Albyn's former pupils have included Audrey Margaret Geddes, in 1973 the first woman to be admitted as a member of the Stock Exchange; Professor Tessa Holyoake, director of the Leukaemia Research Institute at Glasgow University; Hilda Brown, professor of German at Oxford and vice-principal of St Hilda's College, Oxford; and Perpetua Pope, the well-known Edinburgh landscape artist.

Aberdeen High School for Girls (Harlaw Academy)

The story of Aberdeen High School for Girls has strong similarities to that of the Grammar School, inasmuch as they both became high-profile, single-sex, fee-paying schools under the management of the local authority, albeit with vastly different spans of history. The High School began life in Little Belmont Street in 1874 in a charming little Grecian building that had previously been known as the Town School and would later become part of the Central School. But it soon outgrew the accommodation and moved to 19 Albyn Place in 1893. The existing building on that two-acre site had originally been the Asylum for Orphan Girls, erected through the generosity of Mrs Emslie, widow of a wealthy Aberdeen merchant, who spent £15,000 on the construction and gave a further endowment of £40,000. Her architect was none other than the city's most distinguished figure of his profession, Archibald Simpson.

The orphanage, which trained girls to be domestic servants, had been closed in 1890 but was bought by Aberdeen School Board, which paid £4,500 and enlarged it for the new role as the High School for Girls. As such, it became the biggest girls' school in town. As they were town council schools, the fee-paying status of both the Grammar and the High was removed in the aftermath of the Second World War and the parallel fate was extended in the 1970s, when they also became co-educational schools for their respective areas, as part of the comprehensive system. Again like the Grammar, the High was not only to lose its primary department but was also to suffer the loss of its name, to be replaced by one that would approximate to the district it served. Thus it became Harlaw Academy, a decision that was met with the same kind of hostility as arose when the Grammar lost its name.

As so often, the ultimate custodians of a school, its essential spirit and traditions, tend to be the former pupils who have built an emotional attachment to the place and will fight with nostalgic fervour in its defence. Both Grammar and the High were in the battle to win back their traditional names but, whereas the former won the battle, the latter was unsuccessful. In sweeping away the ethos of those more privileged establishments, town councillors were accused of political spite. Naturally, they appointed head teachers who were sympathetic to the new order, so in their campaigns to regain the old names the former pupils' clubs could hardly count on support from that quarter. In the subsequent history of the Girls' High, one head teacher described the former status of his school as 'anathema to me'. Former pupils were upset when the portraits of headmistresses were removed to less prominent positions and the dux board disappeared, along with the tradition of prize-giving – deemed no longer appropriate in the new order of comprehensive education. Be that as it may, the High School did have a heritage that could not be ignored. Prizes were restored.

The move to Albyn Place had come a year after the University of Aberdeen first admitted women, a development raising questions that were pertinent to High School girls, ranging from 'What are they being educated for?' to 'Will it put men off them?'! Within the few remaining years of the Victorian era, however, those girls were giving their own answers, using the new-found opportunity as a springboard towards professions like medicine and law that had previously been the preserve of men. Dipping a toe in political life, even if they still didn't have the vote, a girl like Mary Bisset was soon gaining the highest award for public services in India while Mary Reid was becoming Lady Mayoress of Cape Town. High School girls were teaching in colleges and universities around the world, with the Former Pupils Club, founded in 1899, counting its members in places like Shanghai, Singapore and New Zealand.

Dorothy Kidd went as far as to lend her talents as headmistress to the neighbouring Albyn School for Girls while Dr Mary Esslemont became one of the outstanding medical figures of her generation, the first woman president of the Students' Representative Council at Aberdeen University and the first woman chairman of the British Medical Association. Dr Esslemont was the granddaughter of Lord Provost Peter Esslemont and daughter of George Esslemont, both Liberal MPs and partners in the family business of Esslemont and Macintosh. She received the freedom of the city in 1981.

One girl, recollecting her late-Victorian schooldays, spoke of the hideous clothing of the day, shapeless dresses with humped shoulders, with at least two petticoats, black ribbed stockings and black lacing boots. The hairstyle was better favoured, everyone wearing it long and flowing so that 'when not frizzled with hot tongs, but just carefully brushed, it looked very pretty'. The teachers were tightly packed into woollen dresses, with beautiful hour-glass waists and elegantly frizzed heads 'fringed à la Princess of Wales'. By her gentleness and sympathy, Miss Iverach instilled an admiration for good manners and toleration. 'We certainly needed both,' said the lady observer, 'for we were extremely class-conscious and contemptuous of each other's home background and personal appearance.'

Into the upper school came a brilliant young teacher, straight from university, by the name of Miss Annand. Her appearance was staggering, the Titianesque red hair rippling over her head without help from a hairdresser, her invariably blue frock hanging in loose pre-Raphaelite simplicity and her slender neck rising from the petals of a daisy frill. Add to that 'the piquancy of Miss Annand's stimulating personality' and the lady thus extolling her beloved teacher's virtues, without realising it, was also being influenced by her literary talents, unaware that she would yet emerge as Rachel Annand Taylor, the distinguished poetess. The High School did well for writers, none more outstanding than Nan Shepherd, novelist and critic and close friend of Neil Gunn and Charles Murray, arguably the greatest vernacular poet the North-east has produced. Nan Shepherd's novels, from *The Quarry Wood* to *A Pass in the Grampians*, dealt with the development of a young woman growing up in her native area.

But the contribution to the arts did not stop there. With the emergence of the movies, the High School girl known as Lois Obree moved from the role of prominent stage actress to that of internationally famous film star, under her professional name of Sonia Dresdel. From the 1940s to the 1970s you would find her in such films as *The Clouded Yellow*, with Trevor Howard, Jean Simmons and Kenneth More; Graham Greene's *The Fallen Idol*, with Ralph Richardson, *The Trials of Oscar Wilde* and *Where I Live*, perhaps best remembered for its theme tune, the Charles Williams compostion 'Dream of Olwyen'. Sonia Dresdel had blossomed in school drama, which had been her springboard to a place at RADA. And when the drama group marked its golden jubilee in 1955 the High's famous film star came back to play the lead in *Iphigenia in Tauris*. The last appearance in her native city came in 1974, when she returned to His Majesty's to play the lead in William Douglas-Home's comedy, *Lloyd George Knew My Father*. That nostalgic occasion was heightened by the appearance of two others in the cast, North-east favourites Dennis Ramsden and his wife, Christine Russell, fondly remembered from their regular visits with the Whatmore Players.

Though the world of film-making, with its early mornings and tedious routines, had claimed her talents, Miss Dresdel made plain her preference for the live theatre. She said: 'How I long for those footlights and my beloved audience; for the unexplained thrill of "curtain up"; for the satisfying glow of mind and body when the show is over; for the weariness that sets in later in the dressing-room; for the people who thank you with tears for "a wonderful performance".'

Blazing the trail for women in broadcasting was another High School girl, Elizabeth Adair, whose father was the first manager of His Majesty's Theatre and who introduced to the airwaves such exquisite talents as writer Jessie Kesson, a product of Proctor's Orphanage at Skene. Julie Davidson was another writer and broadcaster to gain prominence. Among world-class performers to emerge from the High in the second half of the century were the glamorous rock singer Annie Lennox, who left in 1972, having straddled the two systems, and that exquisite opera star of modern times, Lisa Milne. Lisa, who grew up in Sycamore Place, showed early promise with the youth theatre company Giz Giz but sprang to prominence when Hughie Green and his highly popular

Annie Lennox, international singing star

Opportunity Knocks came to His Majesty's Theatre in the late 1980s. She brought the house down that night, giving notice of a very special talent. Proceeding to the Royal Scottish Academy of Music and Drama in Glasgow, Lisa studied with the celebrated Aberdeen-born singer Patricia MacMahon and was soon appearing with Scottish Opera and taking her place on platforms across the world, a singer of unlimited prospects.

Annie Lennox, who was born on Christmas night of 1954, recalled that she came from a two-roomed tenement in Hutcheon Street, passed the entrance test before she was five and found the High 'a very posh school, where you had to wear a uniform with a hat and proper gloves and shoes. You had to shake the teacher's hand and curtsey when you left class at the end of the day'. But she was soon singing and playing the flute and eventually gained a place at the Royal Academy of Music in London. Determined to be a singer/songwriter, she worked in shops, bars and restaurants, and that was where she met a customer who happened to be a music publisher.

Annie teamed up with Dave Stewart, a talented musician, to become The Tourists. Interestingly, the High School had a Continental teacher called Marguerite Feltges who popularised the word 'Eurythmics' in the Aberdeen vocabulary. It was a form of dancing that promoted harmony between mind and body, created by Rudolph Steiner. Annie and Dave later changed their band name and became even more famous around the world as the Eurythmics. Annie's rise to fame as a pop diva of spirited reputation was not surprising when you consider that she came from a family of deep conviction. Her grandfather was Archie Lennox of Cornhill, a Hall Russell shipyard and railway worker whose campaigning in the class struggle of the 1930s turned him into a veteran activist of the Communist Party. Archie lived to within six months of his centenary in 2002, dying five months after his younger brother, Lord Provost Robert Lennox. (It's interesting to note that even before it became the co-educational Harlaw Academy, the old Girls' High was claimed by historian Fenton Wyness, who attended when little boys were welcomed into the nursery class!)

In an illustrious history from 1874, the Girls' High ran for most of a century with only four head teachers. John McBain came first but there is still living witness to his three female successors, Lucy Ward, Beatrice Rose and Margaretta McNab, formidable ladies who commanded the respect of their day. Miss Rose did the honours on the death of her predecessor, Miss Ward, first among the nine children of a prosperous lord mayor of Leicester. On her appointment as English mistress in 1894 – and as an amusing sign of the times – her father accompanied her to ensure that she would be quite safe in the far-north citadel of Aberdeen. But Miss Ward was well able to look after herself, soon to become the outstanding figure in the school. By 1912 she was headmistress and was just fashioning the school as she wished when the First World War broke out. The High School became the First Scottish General Hospital and the pupils had to be scattered to houses throughout Aberdeen, until their return in 1919, by which time the roll had increased from 500 to more than 800. Even after retirement in 1929 Miss Ward remained secure in her adopted city, becoming a member of Aberdeen Town Council, serving the Children's Court and finding time to embark on a journey round the world. Her successors, Beatrice Rose (1929–55) and Margaretta McNab (1955–71) maintained that level of integrity and respect throughout the remainder of the time when it was the High School for Girls.

In 1971 it entered the modern phase of comprehensive education, with Alexander Chalmers as headmaster, followed in 1985 by Norman Horne and in 1993 by John Murray. A whole new chapter of school history lay ahead, embracing the changes in systems, teaching methods, parental attitudes and social behaviour that have spread themselves across modern society. It is no easy task. Harlaw Academy, with its 940 pupils, is not alone in coping with the extremes of high achievement and learning difficulties, affluent homes and poverty. In his 2005 report, John Murray reaffirmed his commitment to the system by saying: 'Leading a comprehensive such as ours is challenging. But I am encouraged by my firm belief that, if all schools in Britain were truly comprehensive in the manner of Harlaw Academy, we would live in a happier and more successful country.'

As a footnote, the initial determination of the former pupils to retain a separate High School FP Club identity gradually softened to an acceptance of their successors in Harlaw Academy. In varying degrees of comfort, they are now bedfellows, bracketed under a joint name.

Central/Hazlehead Academy

Outwith the stratum of fee-paying schools in Aberdeen, there was one above all else that held a reputation for a high consistency in educational matters. Indeed, the Central School, which lay between Schoolhill and Little Belmont Street, was championed by many who felt it was the equal of anything in the city. Without frills, it simply got on with the job of high-calibre teaching, under the tutelage of men like the legendary Jock Robertson, educational giants who settled for nothing but the best.

With 181 pupils and three teachers, it opened its doors in Little Belmont Street in 1894, taking over the building so recently vacated by the High School for Girls. In 1900 it became known as the Central Higher Grade School, and was reconstructed five years later with a new building of three floors and a circular tower at the street corner, providing a main entrance and opening out to a wide hallway and staircase. In 1924 the school acquired an assembly hall, notable as the former City Church in Belmont Street, once the place of worship for Mary Slessor, the Aberdeen girl who gave her life to missionary work in Africa. Despite another minor change of name, the school would be known to generations simply as 'the Central' which, from the outset, took its unique place in Aberdeen as the only non-fee-paying senior secondary school in the city and, for a long time, the only co-educational one as well.

It set its own entrance examination for pupils leaving primary schools at eleven and twelve years of age and, by the 1930s, the roll stood at around 800. They came from all over town and from all kinds of backgrounds. In the words of Harry Gordon's song, there were folk 'fae Wallfield, Nellfield, Mannofield and Cattofield, folk fae Constitution Street and folk fae Rubislaw Den'. They met and mixed quickly in a camaraderie that lasted a lifetime, many couples choosing to send their children to their old school even when they could have afforded the most expensive private ones.

Like many others in that earlier period, the Central undertook pupil-teaching, in which pupils still at school were given training and undertook teaching duties, an imaginative scheme that led many to choose it as a career and produced a raft of headmasters, lecturers and professors. Since many parents could ill afford to keep their children at school beyond the minimum leaving age of fourteen, there was a special obligation on pupils to work hard and make the most of their time. Motivation was therefore no problem for the staff, a lesson from harder times that must raise a wish in many a teacher's mind in these more affluent and undisciplined days. Because of this, the Central gained a reputation for conscientious students, standing them in good stead when seeking jobs that were hard to find.

The first headmaster, A.G. 'Toby' Wallace, supervised the whole development of the new school from 1894, taking it to the full curriculum as known from 1920 onwards. He was succeeded in 1926 by John W. Robertson, one of the most gifted mathematicians and brilliant teachers of his day. Better known as Jock, he elevated the Central to the very front rank of Scotland's secondary schools, renowned for its results in the leaving-certificate examinations and university bursary competitions.

Jock Robertson knew all his pupils, assessed their capabilities, opted for shrewd comment rather than praise (noting poor performance by teacher as well as pupil!) but was nevertheless a master of motivation. Honoured by his alma mater, he retired in 1954, to be followed by Alexander Goldie, in time for the Central to change its name to Aberdeen Academy. During the 1960s Mr Goldie saw the school roll rise to 1,400 and in 1970 he masterminded the revolutionary move from the heart of town to the sylvan west end, where it now became known as Hazlehead Academy. Thus he guided the gradual change from a selective senior secondary to a comprehensive, retiring in 1975 as only the third headmaster in more than eighty years.

Within those years the two world wars brought the customary disruption of the time. The 1914–18 conflict meant a move up Skene Street to share accommodation with the Grammar School, while the Central buildings were used to house the residents of Woodend Old People's Hospital. They, in turn, were making way for the large number of casualties coming home from the battlefields of France. A similar pattern resumed in the Second World War, again making way for the old folks from Woodend. Sharing with the Grammar School developed into a two-shift system, alternating between 8 a.m. and 12 a.m., and 1 p.m. and 5 p.m. In the notorious black-out, with no street lighting and lack of transport, that meant many a pupil walking to school in the pitch black of a winter morning or similarly walking home after dark. As the modern Hazlehead Academy, the school became popular with those outwith the immediate zone who were exercising a parents' right to choose their school. The city's education committee, however, managed to set a limit on that particular intake. In 1994 the school that had grown out of the old Central celebrated its centenary, complete with civic reception and a major exhibition of its background at James Dun's House Museum, which had once been the janitor's house.

Former pupils came from far and near, an occasion to remember what a galaxy of varied talent the old Central had produced. From an embarrassment of riches, it is hard to reduce the list to: Lord Provost George Stephen (1899–1900); Harry Gordon (1904–07), Aberdeen's own comedy legend; Edwin Maxwell (1918–24), Cambridge professor and author of text-books on calculus; James Shewan (1922–28), head of microbiology at Torry Research Station; distinguished Scots poet Alexander Scott of Glasgow University (1933–39); George Chalmers (1933–36), one of the RAF's famous 'Dambusters' of 1943; Bertha Wernham (1936–41), first woman judge of the Supreme Court of Canada; George Richardson (1938–42), principal of Keble College, Oxford; the singing sisters Laura Brand (1945–51) and Anne Brand (1947–52), who gained fame on programmes like *The White Heather Club*; Graham Leggat (1946–52), memorable footballer for Aberdeen and Scotland; Edi Swan (1947–53), first technical director and historian of H.M. Theatre; Brian Wood (1961–67), reigning rector of Hazlehead Academy; and Derek Rae (1978–84), the broadcasting voice and face of Association Football in the United States and one of the organisers of the World Cup in that country.

The Central also had a remarkable record of long-serving teachers, not least Miss Rita Edward, a pupil from 1937 to 1943 and a teacher from 1948 till 1987, a fifty-year connection that ended at Hazlehead. Former pupils regard her as the custodian of their heritage.

International School of Aberdeen

The arrival of a North Sea oil industry, involving so many people from abroad, inevitably gave rise to an international school, the only one of its kind in Scotland. Even before the oil began to flow, the school was already well established, catering mainly for the children of those who had come to partake in the biggest industrial revolution ever to hit Aberdeen and the North-east. Originally known as the American School, it opened its doors in 1972 at a former convalescent home at Cults, before spreading to the present campus at Milltimber, where it expanded from the manor house of Fairgirth on the North Deeside Road to become a purpose-built school. The annual fees were £600. Owned at first by Mr A.J. McCormick, it started with thirty-six pupils and eight teachers but soon built up a roll of more than 300, headed by the energetic Dr Duane Mead from Michigan.

With divergent opinions about how the school should develop, a consortium of oil companies stepped in and bought the property in 1979, setting up a company to act as landlords, thus ensuring that, when the school buildings were eventually sold, the sponsors would get some return on their investment. Although the programme of studies employs the best examples from Britain, America and other countries, the students graduate from the International School of Aberdeen with a diploma based on an American-style curriculum. They may also choose to earn the International Baccalaureate Diploma.

All graduates from the school are prepared for entry to colleges and universities and more than 90 per cent elect to do so each year. By the very nature of the oil industry, there is a regular turnover of pupils, many returning to the United States and elsewhere. Not surprisingly, a fair proportion of former pupils have found careers in the oil industry that brought them here in the first place. Though the dominant influence is American, there are more than thirty nationalities in the total enrolment, with native languages which range from Spanish and Portuguese to Norwegian and Japanese. Families from around the world choose to send their children to Aberdeen.

Even parents from the United Kingdom, involved in the peripatetic life, choose the Aberdeen option, on the basis that it is easier to move within the international school community. The smaller student-teacher ratio is among other attractions. As might be expected, the facilities within the ten-acre campus are of the highest order, taking in everything from spacious classrooms with internet connections to computer laboratories, a full-sized gymnasium and a large playing-field which includes an artificial surface. Basketball takes its place in the sports schedule and football comes in the connotation of soccer rather than the heavy-padded American variety.

The International School, with director Daniel A. Hovde as its head in the twenty-first century, links into the local scene at every turn, participating in festivals, visiting museums, theatres and historical sites, and entering schemes like the Duke of Edinburgh Awards. A Grampian Police liaison officer works with the students on health and safety, as well as on matters of alcohol and drugs education. But the International School was not the only one identified with the oil industry. The arrival of so many families from France gave rise to the Total French School, housed in the grounds of Aberdeen Grammar but not part of it. It was the only school in the United Kingdom, outside London, where all instruction was given in French.

The Barn

The Grammar School of Old Aberdeen, distinct from the Aberdeen Grammar School of today, had its own considerable history and was commonly known as the Barn. It originally stood by the gate of King's College and later in School Road, catering for country boys as well as those from Old Aberdeen. It closed its doors in the latter part of the nineteenth century, at the same time as Robert Gordon's Hospital was changing over to the college we know today. It was Gordon's, rather than Aberdeen Grammar, that inherited its role of preparing country boys for university.

The Gymnasium

Still in the vicinity of School Road and the Chanonry, Aberdeen could claim another remarkable little institution known as the Gymnasium, or the Gym, or even Chanonry House School, founded by the Rev. Alexander Anderson, a Presbyterian minister who 'came out' at the Disruption and who produced a fine calibre of scholar. The Gym offered a much wider curriculum than elsewhere and, when a Commission examined the rather dubious state of Scottish education in 1866, it came to the conclusion that there were only six establishments in the country that could be classed as genuine secondary schools. Aberdeen claimed one half of that distinction, with its Grammar Schools of the Old and New towns, and the Gymnasium.

CHAPTER 37

Rowett and Macaulay

In a North-east of Scotland that can pride itself in a monumental reclaiming of a sour and grudging land, turning it into some of the best cattle country in the kingdom, and forging a distinctive human character in the process, it is wholly appropriate that food and land research have found an international base in Aberdeen and twal' mile roun'. The first Lord Strathcona endowed a chair of agriculture in 1910 and Aberdeen Town and County Councils, then weighed in with financial support to buy the estate of Craibstone, on the northern outskirts of the city, to create an experimental farm.

Within that same momentum, the development commission founded an institute for research in animal nutrition, but it had no home until 1920, when the problem was solved from a rather unexpected source. Through his friendship with the chief biochemist, a colourful London wine merchant called John Quiller Rowett decided on a generous donation towards what became the Rowett Institute for Animal Research, opened at Bucksburn in 1922 and gaining a worldwide reputation that survives to this day. Rowett, who was patron of Shackleton's expeditions to the Antarctic, had a near-monopoly of the rum trade and was said to have been running illicit drink into the United States as a bootlegger during Prohibition. Aberdonians acknowledged his generosity and were grateful.

When the Institute and the College of Agriculture came together, they were headed by one of the great Scots of the century, Sir John Boyd Orr, the beetle-browed biologist, who later went to Washington as the first director of the United Nations Food and Agriculture Organisation. His efforts in improving the world food situation brought him the Nobel Peace Prize in 1949. It comes almost as an incidental piece of information that such a giant of a man, called away from his early researches in a basement room at Marischal College, crowned his heroism in the First World War by gaining the Military Cross at the Battle of the Somme and the DSO at Passchendaele.

The North-east's contribution to the science of agriculture took another step forward in 1930, when Thomas B. Macaulay, a former president of the Sun Life Assurance Company of Canada, whose father came from Fraserburgh, gave the money to create the Macaulay Institute for Soil Research. For that purpose, they bought Craigiebuckler House and fifty acres of land in the west end of Aberdeen and proceeded to advance the work of reclaiming land to provide soil surveys for farmers and to create a soil map of Scotland. The Institute's first director, Sir William Ogg, became director of the Rothamsted Agricultural Institute in 1943 but returned to the chairmanship of the North of Scotland College of Agriculture.

CHAPTER 38

A Gordon for Me!

Though first swallowed up in an amalgamation called the Highlanders, and more recently the Royal Regiment of Scotland, it is the name of the Gordon Highlanders that stands out among all things military in the hearts and minds of Aberdonians. There is hardly a family of North-east origin that has not had a father, son, uncle or brother connected at one time or another with the local regiment. Its origins go back to the late 1700s, with a demand for men to serve in the colonial expansion of the British Empire, and the East India Company leading the way in raising regiments for service. That coincided with the outbreak of the French Revolution in 1789 and the later appearance of Napoleon Bonaparte, bringing a major threat to the monarchies of Europe and exposing Britain to possible invasion. With the British Army at a low ebb, there was a massive recruitment drive, led by the king's representatives across the country.

In earlier times, the 4th Duke of Gordon had been successful in raising regiments, such as the Northern Fencibles, but they were available for home defensive purposes only. This time he was authorised by George III to raise a Regiment of Foot, which he accomplished in 1794, under the name of the 100th Regiment. The 900 men who joined up came almost entirely from the duke's own estates across the North and North-east of Scotland, one half of them from Aberdeenshire and the rest with clan names like the MacPhersons, MacDonalds and the Camerons. From wherever they appeared, they had as an enlisting incentive the rather novel offer of taking the King's shilling along with a kiss from the duke's attractive wife, Jane Maxwell, who became better known as Duchess Jean.

An enthusiastic aid to her husband's recruiting activities, Duchess Jean was a most personable member of London society, both socially and politically, enjoying a close association with the bachelor prime minister of the day, William Pitt the Younger. As a frequent guest at 10 Downing Street, she would not have missed an opportunity to discuss the threat from republican forces in France. Her personal interest included the fact that she had three daughters married to dukes and a son who would become the 5th Duke of Gordon.

The number of the new regiment was changed to the 92nd but they became better known as the Gordon Highlanders, who proceeded to prominence in the wars against France in Europe and in the Peninsular War, where they played a memorable part under the command of the famous Sir John Moore and then the future Duke of Wellington. With Sir John Moore they fought a notable rearguard action, culminating in the defeat of the French at Corunna, but sadly at the expense of Sir John's life. The wearing of black buttons on the spats is said to be a tribute to his memory. The Gordons were to the fore again at the Battle of Waterloo in 1815, in the final overthrow of Napoleon, and indeed wherever the action was to be found. After the Crimean War of 1854 they were off to the east for the first time, with the outbreak of the Indian Mutiny, and took in the Afghan War before dropping in to South Africa on the way home, for the first Boer War of 1881.

When the north-west frontier of India was in revolt, and the tribesmen had occupied the village of Dargai, a hard-fought action was ended only when the Gordons were sent in from reserve and, within forty minutes, captured a position which had been defying a whole brigade. They did so to the skirl of the pipes, an episode of North-east folklore which made Piper George Findlater from Turriff a household name. Under heavy fire and shot through both ankles, Findlater dragged himself to a nearby boulder and, propped against the rock, continued to play the regimental march, 'Cock of the North', and didn't stop playing until Dargai had been taken. Passing into North-east folklore, it was an incident that gained him the Victoria Cross from the hand of Queen Victoria herself. Back home, he married his cousin, Nellie Findlater, and settled into the small-farm tenancy of Bridgend, Forglen, near his own birthplace at Mill of Turriff. From there he moved to Cairnhill of Forglen. With the outbreak of the Great War, however, he volunteered and was off with the Gordons once more, in time to be wounded at Loos. Piper Findlater V.C., local hero, became a well-known figure, leading the Turriff Pipe Band and playing at agricultural shows and functions. He died at Cairnhill in 1942 and is buried in Forglen Cemetery.

For the Great War of 1914–18 the Gordons were stretched to eleven battalions, accommodating a total of 50,000 men, of whom 29,000 became casualties, including 9,000 killed. So you found them all the way from Mons to Loos, from the Somme to that Third Battle of Ypres which became known as Passchendaele after the local village of that name. In that last encounter, which involved some of the most furious fighting of that ghastly war, the Gordons little knew that a German corporal facing them over the trenches had the name of Adolf Hitler. His day would lie ahead, as leader of the next catastrophe to plague civilisation.

In the Second World War the Gordons were again prepared, as part of the 51st Highland Division, storming into action at Abbeville but left to stem the enemy while the great evacuation of Dunkirk took place in 1940. A division of North-east men, taking on a whole German army, was finally cut off and left with no option but to surrender at St Valery-en-Caux. I had a first-hand account from my own father-in-law, Nelson Keith from Fraserburgh. Before they were marched off to spend the next five years in German prison camps, they were met by Erwin Rommel, the German commander, who came among them and handed out cigars, deeply admiring their courage, as he later revealed. Those who defended Le Havre were successfully evacuated and formed the basis of a revived 51st, ready for action again in the North African desert in 1942.

This time they were under the command of General Montgomery, who led them to victory at El Alamein against none other than the same Erwin Rommel, en route to Sicily and Italy.

Gordon Highlanders march through Banchory in 1938

Then it was back home to regroup for the final push of D-Day in 1944. Those men from Aberdeen and the North-east were returning to the beaches of Normandy, with one memory and one objective: St Valery. As they powered along the French coast, fighting for every field and cow-shed, they blasted the Germans out of position till the precious moment beckoned. What could have been more fitting than to hand over the task of recapturing St Valery to the 51st Highland Division. What a welcome from the local population! Those brave soldiers had come back to settle an account. Victory was on its way. When it was all over, the infantry regiments were each reduced to one battalion in 1948, the Gordons becoming part of the Highland Brigade. In August 1949 Aberdeen bestowed its highest honour on the regiment: the freedom of the city.

In the post-war years the Gordon Highlanders were despatched to trouble spots wherever they arose, from the Berlin blockade to Malaya, Cyprus, Kenya or Borneo. There were postings to Germany, Singapore and Northern Ireland for a generation of North-east soldiers whose fathers and grandfathers had fought in two world wars. Defence cuts brought a reduction in military personnel, always a matter of public outcry where you find that loyalty to local regiments such as the Gordons of the North-east, the Black Watch of Perthshire, the Highland Light Infantry of Glasgow. In 1994 the axe fell on the Gordon Highlanders as a separate regiment, forcing them into a union with the Queen's Own Highlanders. Further amalgamation made them part of the Royal Regiment of Scotland in 2006, a year in which the spirit of the Gordons was fortified in their refurbished museum at Viewfield Road, for which the Prince of Wales performed the opening.

It is the way of the world, a bewildering world in which the enemy is no longer that clearly defined adversary on the battlefield. New generations face a battle against the hidden forces of terrorism that had not even been dreamt about in the hell of Passchendaele or the tragedy of Dunkirk. Sadly, it seems, the human race will forever find its way to conflict.

CHAPTER 39

The Romance of Gandar Dower

It would have taken a huge leap of imagination back in 1934 (when it came into being) to picture the growth Aberdeen Airport would achieve during the second half of the twentieth century. The catalyst for its development was, of course, the oil industry, which expanded the passenger business and, due to its need for a shuttle service to and from the North sea oil platforms, turned Aberdeen into the biggest helicopter base in the world.

By 2005 what had become, rather grandly, Aberdeen International Airport was dealing with 3 million passengers a year, offering 400 departing flights each week, with twenty-one international destinations and twenty-three domestic ones. These included good connections to all parts of the world through the hub airports of London, Paris, Amsterdam and Copenhagen. The airport was contributing more than £127 million a year to the local economy, a figure set to rise with the number of airlines then operating from Aberdeen. Fifteen new routes were introduced in 2005 alone, making it the British Airport Authority's fastest-growing Scottish airport. In the same year, Aberdeen City Council paved the way for the future by lifting a long-standing restriction on operating hours so that fixed-wing aircraft were given round-the-clock freedom. That tied in with a 25-year master-plan, launched for public consultation, which envisaged a further £50 million investment, a £10 million runway extension to bring the United States and the Middle East within direct range, and an expansion of the terminal buildings to cope with a doubling of passenger numbers.

By contrast to these developments, the humble origins of such a major British airport present a touchingly romantic tale. It all began with an extraordinary character called Eric Gandar Dower who, as a schoolboy in Brighton in 1909, motorcycled to Dover to witness the arrival of Louis Blériot as he completed the crossing of the English Channel for the very first time. That so fired the boy's imagination that he became a pilot in the Royal Naval Air Service during the First World War, after which he went to Cambridge, where one of his friends was Robert Cowell Smith from Banchory. The two young men were driving London buses during the General Strike when their conversation turned to aviation, Smith suggesting that Gandar Dower might think of starting a flying school in Aberdeen.

A few years later, that was what brought this Biggles-like character on a reconnaissance flight over the North-east, landing on a likely field by the Far Burn of Dyce in his little Blackburn

In the cockpit – Gandar Dower, founder of Dyce Airport

Bluebird and attracting a crowd now filled with curiosity. Gandar Dower later recalled two impressions. Having never been to Scotland before, he expected to find all the men wearing kilts! And having landed his aeroplane on alien soil, he now had to decide what to do with it overnight. The solution was to have it towed from Dyce into the city and parked at the garage of Aberdeen Motors in Union Row!

From that visit, however, Gandar Dower made a monumental decision: 'I'll build an aerodrome here for Aberdeen – and start an airline.' From scenes like these . . . The Depression of the early 1930s delayed his plans, but by 1934 he proved as good as his word and the aerodrome was opened in July of that year, sporting four grass runways. Dyce had no electricity in those days so he had to pay for a cable to be extended from Stoneywood.

A single-engine plane came in to land one day, piloted by a friend of Gandar Dower, Captain Neville Stack. He was due to fly Prime Minister Ramsay Macdonald to Ireland next day but when the two men dined at the Palace Hotel that evening Gandar Dower questioned the wisdom of crossing the Irish Sea with the one-engined Leopard Moth. His offer of a Dragon with two engines was accepted and the prime minister was flown safely to the Emerald Isle. A week later that Dragon crashed while taking off from Dyce!

He founded Aberdeen Airways, later renamed Allied Airways (Gandar Dower) Ltd, the controlling company responsible for the development of airlines and the fleet of planes. Other companies registered included an Aberdeen Flying Club to provide social amenities and a Flying School to teach enthusiasts. With what was claimed as 'the finest aerodrome in Scotland', those were exciting times for the North-east, Gandar Dower now establishing routes that could take you to Glasgow, Thurso, Orkney and Shetland and, eventually, to Norway.

The brave venture of this flamboyant character was, of course, interrupted by the Second World War, when the airport and buildings were requisitioned and Dyce was used for military purposes. But the company was still allowed to operate until that post-war period when airlines were nationalised. Gandar Dower had gone off to serve in the RAF and, sensing that the incoming Labour government of Clement Attlee would kill off his enterprise, he decided to stand as a Conservative candidate in the 1945 General Election. Opposing the popular figure of Sir Archibald Sinclair, Liberal member for Caithness and Sutherland and air minister in Churchill's wartime government, he was given little hope. But as sometimes happens with adventurous spirits, he won!

However, men like Gandar Dower were cast aside in that bleak post-war period when the state took control with companies like British European Airways and the British Overseas Airways Corporation. In his disappointment, he retreated to Guernsey with memories that extended far beyond his passion for flying. With his theatrical flair, it was not surprising to find that he wrote songs for music-hall stars like George Robey and gained a place at the Royal Academy of

Aberdeen International Airport as it is today

Dramatic Art before the First World War. He toured with his own company, with plays ranging from Shakespeare to light comedy and wrote at least one play himself. In his later years he visited Aberdeen on one occasion to receive from his many admirers a full-colour camera portrait, the work of Charles Skene, once a leading photographer at Studio Morgan and later a well-known property magnate.

There was one other romantic twist to his adventurous life. From his beginnings at Dyce in 1934 he had by his side the help of a loyal secretary, Miss Caroline Brunning of 159 Mid Stocket Road. They remained unmarried companions for all those years, but in 1978 Gandar Dower, by then aged eighty-three, came north again to lead his beloved Caroline down the aisle of Queen's Cross Church. The Rev. Dr Edmund Jones performed the simple ceremony before they were whisked away in a Daimler to a reception at the Station Hotel.

As for Aberdeen Airport, civil flights were back in business by the middle of the century, with routes to the Highland and Islands and a regular service to London. From glorified huts on the Dyce side of the airfield you boarded the old 32-seater Dakota plane, renamed the Pionair for civil purposes, and embarked on a four-hour journey south, stopping off at Renfrew and Manchester on the way to Northolt, which was the London terminal before they built Heathrow.

For those major forms of transport, trains and planes alike, that early enthusiasm for state control began to diminish and they were gradually released from the ties of nationalisation. Even the major haulage companies had gone through that phase of state control before returning to private hands. Considering the scale of Aberdeen Airport today, Gandar Dower could have had no conception of what he was starting that day in 1931. He added colour and excitement to North-east life and deserves to be remembered as one of the pioneers of air travel, and an example of what can happen when the entrepreneurial spirit is allowed to flourish.

CHAPTER 40

A City in Two World Wars

1914–1918

The generation which witnessed the dawn of the twentieth century, and which shortly after mourned the death of Queen Victoria, who had reigned for more than sixty years, would not have believed what the fates had in store for them. Until the recent invention of the motor car – and the even more bewildering business of the Wright Brothers taking off in a flying machine in 1903 – they had jogged along sedately in their horse-drawn carriages, fashionable in their crinolines and contented with a pace of life that had endured for centuries.

How could our ancestors have guessed that within a few years into the new century, they would be plunged into the biggest war the world had ever seen, and that given another twenty years or so after that, they would suffer an even more devastating global catastrophe?

One of the most seminal events in all history occurred that first Tuesday of August 1914, when a royal assassination in Sarajevo, which seemed to have little to do with the folk in Fittie, caused Britain to declare war on Germany. In a rush of patriotic euphoria, tens of thousands joined up to serve King and Country in the innocent belief that it would all be over by Christmas. By the middle of October, the first 10,000 men of the British Expeditionary Force were engaged in the battle that was raging around them in the Belgian town of Ypres (our soldiers called it 'Wipers'), and in a bizarre yet touching incident on Christmas Day, British and German troops came out of their trenches, shook hands, exchanged comforts and joined in a game of football.

If only it could have ended there. The succeeding years would devastate the human race, through horrific battles that ranged from the Somme (July to November 1916, with more than a million casualties for an advance of ten miles) to Passchendaele (July to November 1917, again with shocking losses). To walk across those battlefields today is the sharpest lesson you can ever learn about what that war does to mankind. It becomes all the more heartbreaking when you go from one cemetery to another and find the little crosses that tell of young lads from Torry to Turriff, Kittybrewster to Auchnagatt, for whom life went no further.

Can you lose the cream of a generation, sacrificing a great raft of the nation's skills and intelligence, from doctors, scientists and artists to engineers, poets and artisans, without seriously damaging the genetic strength of society? Historian Alexander Keith, a keen observer of the human condition, made the point that losing so many of our best young brains gave an opening to the politicians whose principal attribute, he dared suggest, was opportunism in the interests of their own order. As Keith saw it, 'They proceeded between the wars, using the depressive weight of the Civil Service, to reduce the country to a sombre uniformity of conduct.' He deplored the Tory–Lloyd George Education Act of 1918 for dulling public recognition of what was happening and for damaging the kind of robust structure of education for which the North-east was noted.

Within weeks of the outbreak of war the hospital ship *Rohilla* made its first dash for Aberdeen with forty-five invalid sailors on board, including His Royal Highness Prince Albert, later to become King George VI and father of the present queen. He was serving with the navy when he was brought ashore, suffering from appendicitis, and operated upon at the Northern Nursing Home. But the future king was back to full fitness in time to serve with the Grand Fleet at the Battle of Jutland in 1916. The German U-boats were soon attacking British ships, and by July 1915 no fewer than twenty-nine of Aberdeen's fishing fleet had been sunk. Within sight of the city, HMS *Hawke* was torpedoed with the loss of 500 men. Survivors were landed at the harbour.

The drama of war brings its own peculiar excitement to civilian life. As a diversion from the newspapers' regular lists of killed and wounded, crowds of Aberdonians turned out to see Britain's new weapon, the tank, when the one called Julian came on a campaign to encourage the sale of Defence Bonds. Unloaded at the Joint Station, it was escorted by a bodyguard of bobbies to the Castlegate, where it caused a great stir, particularly for the young who had not yet encountered the weapons of war. At the beginning of 1916 the control of street-lighting brought Aberdeen a black-out from 10 p.m. On 2nd May, the city had a narrow escape from an air-raid when a Zeppelin lost touch with the rest of a German attack on Edinburgh and, following a string of misleading lights, landed over Aberdeen, where it dropped a bomb, thankfully without damage. On the domestic front, the cost of living had risen by 40 per cent since the beginning of the war, with a glass of whisky reaching the giddy height of sixpence (two and a half pence in modern money).

A schoolboy's-eye-view of those days came later from Henry Shewan, who went on to become a distinguished Queen's Counsel, recalling the scenes at the end of the war when the streets of Aberdeen were filled with severely disabled men. Going home at lunch-time, Henry found his tramcar crowded with ex-servicemen on their way to Forbesfield Road, where the Government had set up a factory for training and rehabilitation. Young Henry was appalled by their wounds and could not believe the cheerfulness of their banter. But for all their limbless devastation, they were still the lucky ones, at least with the gift of life that had been denied their fallen comrades who would, in Binyon's words, 'grow not old as we that are left grow old'. Historian Fenton Wyness was another schoolboy with indelible memories of the wounded as they arrived back at the Joint Station. He and his fellow Boy Scouts were detailed to meet them off the train with their trek-cart, shocked to see soldiers with dressings unchanged since the battlefields of France.

Those four years were labelled the Great War – there was no reason to call it the First World War until there was a Second – and it came suddenly to an end on 11 November 1918, retained to this day for memorial purposes on the neat premise that the armistice was signed at the eleventh hour of the eleventh day of the eleventh month. German surrender took place in a railway carriage in the forest of Compiègne as the guns fell silent and the world took stock of one of the most shocking episodes in all history. There was relief that it was all over but, in the tragic circumstances, little sense of celebration. Aberdeen marked the occasion with a solemn service of thanksgiving, a parade of the ex-servicemen who had already been discharged and a students' torchlight procession. What else was there to do?

As the lights went up again on 12th November our ancestors saw a world they scarcely recognised. For those who had lived in Victorian times, life would never be the same again. It had taken only four years of war to gouge that great divide of history. The turmoil had been further complicated in its last year by the Bolshevik Revolution and the overthrow of the Czar of Russia. It sparked off political action in Aberdeen as elsewhere, with socialist extremists to the fore in some wild scenes, one of which involved the Lossiemouth-born Ramsay MacDonald, due to become Labour's first prime minister, who was howled down and pelted with vegetables. There were street riots and baton charges by the police.

On the lighter side, the young reporter called James Leslie Mitchell, who had joined Aberdeen Journals at the tail-end of the war, was sent by his news editor to cover a meeting in the Adelphi, the purpose of which was to form an Aberdeen Soviet, in keeping with the radical mood of the time. As the night grew late, without sign of young Mitchell, Mr Catto, the news editor, put on coat and hat and went to investigate. To his astonishment, he entered the crowded hall to find his reporter far from the press desk. Instead, he was up on the platform giving a rabble-rousing speech in support of the Aberdeen Soviet! Forcibly marched back to Broad Street, young Mr Mitchell did survive his misdemeanour but was soon on his way to being a great Scottish novelist under his pen-name of Lewis Grassic Gibbon. By the time of his premature death, before his thirty-fourth birthday, he had mellowed somewhat, though still a serious champion of social justice.

1939–1945

If the Great War of 1914–18 seemed short of purpose, its successor of 1939 at least had the justification that the war-like ambitions of the German chancellor, Adolf Hitler, had to be countered. The former corporal from the First World War who had driven his motorcycle at Passchendaele had been on the political rampage since the early 1920s. Having gone to Munich from his native Austria, he had sought, and failed, to gain power in Bavaria for his National Socialist Party (the Nazis). By 1933, however, he had indeed reached his objective as ruler of all Germany, moving the entire entourage to Berlin.

Set largely to the mellow dance music of Carroll Gibbons, Lew Stone and Henry Hall (broadcasting from Gleneagles Hotel), the mood of the 1930s emerged from the Depression with a veneer of sophistication – and a hope that the rumbling undercurrents of Hitler would somehow go away. The death of King George V in 1936 brought the crisis of his eldest son, Edward VIII, abdicating in favour of marrying the American Wallis Simpson, and the subsequent coronation of the next son, George VI, already married to Elizabeth Bowes-Lyon of Glamis.

But Hitler's march on Czechoslovakia in 1938 and on Poland the following year made it plain that a Second World War was inevitable. The last day of peace would be that Saturday, 2nd September 1939, when Territorials of the Gordon Highlanders were mobilised from towns, villages and farms across the North-east, heading to the local railway stations to join trains that would take them to Aberdeen and beyond. The vacuum left in local communities as loved ones waved off their loved ones to a fate unknown was filled that afternoon by train-loads of Glasgow children who came as evacuees, in the belief that Clydeside shipyards and factories would become early targets for German bombers. This would be a different war, fought as much in the air and at sea as on land.

Aberdeen was declared a neutral city, neither giving nor receiving evacuees, but subject to the immediate and general upheaval in schools which were due to resume after the summer

War didn't stop work – a gas mask drill at an Aberdeen telephone exchange

holidays. Part-time education was introduced while air-raid shelters were hastily provided to cover the school populations and every citizen was issued with a gas mask, in the fear that the Germans might possibly resort to that form of warfare.

The actual declaration of war came at 11 a.m. on Sunday 3rd September 1939, broadcast by Prime Minister Neville Chamberlain as the entire nation gathered round the wireless set in thoughtful silence. Unlike the previous war, there was no immediate engagement of land troops but the period of the so-called Phoney War did not apply to the sea. On 28th November, Aberdeen's own ss *Rubislaw* was sunk and thirteen men drowned. A few weeks later a ship was bombed and wrecked off Girdleness and another ship bearing an Aberdeen name, the *Ferryhill*, was sunk by the enemy. Into 1940 and a German aircraft flew over the city, pursued by planes which took off from Dyce and shot it down. By now, Gandar Dower's civil airfield had been commandeered by the Air Ministry.

Physically, Aberdeen now looked like a city at war. If it took time for military combat to engage, there was no delay in bringing in the dreaded black-out, the blotting out of lights from every window after dark, with drivers compelled to fix a mask on vehicle lights, giving only a slanted minimum filter to guide them on their way. Iron railings were removed from public buildings and private houses, to help the war effort. All entertainment was banned in those early days. In a slight over-reaction, no cinemas, theatres or dance halls were allowed to operate and even football matches came to a halt. In time, the restrictions were eased but even then the public found it eerie to be groping their way into the darkened foyers of entertainment. After the bright neon of carefree days, it was a grim reminder of what the world had come to.

Food rationing was soon in full swing and all road signs were removed, intended to baffle German spies who might be seeking direction in a strange land but more likely to baffle and frustrate those home-bred motorists who were lucky enough to have a petrol allowance. The Beach Ballroom was commandeered for troop accommodation and substantial concrete blocks were installed along the beach (indeed around the whole coastline) as a barrier to invasion by enemy tanks. The exteriors of public offices and buildings were fortified with sand-bags in case of bomb-blasting and, except on a moonlit night, a walk down Union Street would reveal little but the glow of a pedestrian's cigarette or the faint, ghost-like reflection of a tramcar. To give some assistance to vision, rings of white paint appeared on lamp-posts and trees, with kerbs, car wings and bumpers similarly adorned.

Not that everyone was complying with the rules. In the first month of the war, the police decided to fly over the city one night for an enemy's-eye-view of how effective the black-out was proving. As a result, a string of culprits appeared in Aberdeen Sheriff Court for contravening the Lighting Restriction Order. Mrs Brattesani of 46 Justice Street was fined ten shillings for showing a brightly lit window, having been previously warned. Mrs Margaret Thomson of 1 Links Street paid a fine of five shillings for a misdemeanour that was more understandable. She too had received a previous warning, but when the police arrived, Mrs Thomson was washing her stair by the light of a candle in an uncurtained window. 'I'm damned if I'll put it out until I've washed my stairs!' said the house-proud Aberdonian lady. The bobby extinguished the candle nevertheless. In another instance, one of the memorable 'Burnett's buses' from Mintlaw was spotted on the Aberdeen–Ellon road showing too much of a glare, with the result that Alexander Burnett, the proprietor, and Alexander Brown, his driver, were each fined £2. Pedestrians had shaken warning fists at Mr Brown who, when finally stopped by two special constables, explained that he had been given a fright when he nearly ran into a cyclist in the dim light.

In preparation for the air-raids that would surely materialise in time, Aberdonians were given a dry run of what the sirens would sound like. The warning call would be a fluctuating wail lasting two minutes while the 'all-clear' would be a sustained, unvarying note of similar duration. All too soon that first, screaming alarm would become a familiar sound to be dreaded, with sirens blaring from Walker Road, Broomhill, Mile End and Hilton Schools, the old Royal Infirmary building at Woolmanhill and the Tramway Depot in King Street. The Old Aberdeen and Seaton district would later get their warning from a siren at King's College.

For security reasons, newspaper reports were censored and Aberdeen became merely 'a North-east town', without further identity in reports of the German bombing raids which were now on their way. The city's first real experience of enemy bombers came around midnight on 26th June 1940, with a hit-and-run raid which damaged a bungalow at Tullos, followed a few days later by a much more serious attack in which a hundred incendiary bombs were dropped in the Torry district. Victoria Road School was destroyed. If any doubts remained, the people of Aberdeen knew for sure they were at war a week later, on a July day that produced a memory they would never forget. As the sirens sent them scurrying to the shelters, a German bomber came thundering in from the bay to drop a stick of bombs that sent fountains of black smoke pluming into the air. Three Spitfires came roaring in from Dyce, all guns blazing as the enemy plane dropped its bombs in a line from the university sports ground at King's College to Urquhart Road and finally to York Street, near the shipbuilding yards of Hall Russell and Alexander Hall and Co.

Shipyard workers enjoying a lunch-time pint in the popular Neptune Bar were among the casualties as the building was largely destroyed. The final tally would show that thirty-two people lay dead and eighty more were injured. Among the victims from Hall Russell's yard that day was a brother of Harry Gordon, the well-known comedian. As the Spitfires caught up, the German plane took a last burst of machine-gun fire over Pitstruan Place, momentarily recovering before swinging towards Broomhill School, missing it narrowly and heading for the site of a new ice-rink being built near the Bridge of Dee, where it crashed in flames. The crew all perished. In broad daylight, that unprecedented drama of a dogfight in the skies above Aberdeen was watched by thousands in the streets below, though the future pattern of air-raids would tend to belong to the night. Either way, the limited newspaper reports could tell only of the attacks on 'a North-east town.'

Individual tragedies soon mounted. A high explosive bomb scored a direct hit on the Shirriffs' house in Forbesfield Road, killing Mrs Shirriffs while her husband George, sitting across the same room, survived. There were further casualties in Oscar Road and Wellington Road. There was no let-up in the next two years, the German raiders destroying the large Ogston and Tennant soap factory in Loch Street (the casualty list mounted when they hit the Loch Street Bar on that same stormy night). They bombed Poynernook Road, sank the ss *Highlander* off Aberdeen and targeted Henderson's engineering works in King Street. On one particular night, people were out of their beds for three separate alerts.

Throughout these nerve-racking experiences it was hard to believe that some semblance of normal life was being maintained. Cambridge won the Boat Race and two British actors

The aftermath of the Wellington Road air raid

picked up Academy Awards, Vivien Leigh as best actress for *Gone With The Wind* and Robert Donat as best actor for *Goodbye, Mr Chips*. Bizarrely, with America still to be convinced that this was their war as well as ours, President Roosevelt's private envoy was meeting up with Adolf Hitler.

Aberdeen's biggest air-raid of all was reserved for Wednesday 21st April 1943, the day after Hitler's fifty-fourth birthday. In the whole history of the city there has never been a night quite like it. There is also an extraordinary tailpiece to this particular night – but first to the story itself. As a wave of Dornier planes came swooping in from the sea and people ran for the shelters, all hell broke loose from the skies above the Granite City. Flying low across the roof tops, the Germans unleashed a terror attack of frightening intensity, dropping bombs and raking the streets with machine-guns and cannonfire till parts of the city resembled a sea of flame. The attack was concentrated on George Street and the adjacent areas of newer housing districts, all in

Crowds line Seaforth Road for funeral of 1943 air-raid victims from Bedford Road and Cattofield

that northern half of the city taking in Kittybrewster, Hilton and Woodside. Whole families were buried as tenement homes received direct hits and burst into flames.

Yet it was a night of miraculous escapes. As the people ran from one particular tenement towards the air-raid shelter, they were just filing through the exit when a bomb exploded behind them, and the building they had just left collapsed into rubble. Only one little girl received a minor cut. Firemen strove to quell the flames and dampen the embers to give rescue squads a chance to dig their way through. The stoicism of the Aberdonian saved many a life, as people lay bravely under piles of wreckage and waited while the policemen, ARP (Air Raid Precautions) workers and neighbours tore away the debris that buried them.

A squad of soldiers at the Bridge of Don Barracks would figure among the dead, in addition to the mounting list of civilians. As upwards of thirty tons of high explosive bombs rained down on the city, the Germans had had a lucky break with their very first strike, which put out of action an anti-aircraft battery on the eighteenth green of Balgownie Golf Course. As the mayhem continued, two churches fell victim to the bombs, including St Mary's Episcopal, better known as the Tartan Kirkie, in Carden Place. When the bumble-bee hum of the German bombers finally faded in the distance of the night sky, heading back to their base at Stavanger, Aberdeen licked its wounds and counted the cost.

It must be hard for subsequent generations to grasp the reality of that infernal night, as their parents and grandparents crawled out of the shelters, many of them finding there was no home to go to. They were accommodated in church halls or schools, taken in by relatives or billeted in private homes – a domestic arrangement that didn't always work! The death-toll in that raid was 98 civilians and 27 soldiers, with another 235 injured, 93 of them seriously. Considering that no fewer than eight thousand houses were either completely destroyed or damaged, the small consolation is that, but for some of those miraculous escapes, it could have been worse. In reporting that horrifying night, the *Evening Express* defied the censorship law, showing up its futility with the introductory sentence: 'A North-east of Scotland town – the Germans say it was Aberdeen . . .'

A remarkable record of the bombing raids on Aberdeen and the North-east was compiled by Albert Annand, a wire-room operator at Aberdeen Journals who later became overseer of his department. As the details of war news poured into the office, Albert was among the first to know what was happening, before it was censored for publication. Meticulously, he made a note of every raid, location and casualty (including bombs dropped on Maud on 24th April 1941!), a document that has now been preserved for posterity.

In the wake of the massive death-tolls in London, Coventry and Clydebank, the walled garden at Hazlehead contained a grim secret which would not have been good for morale. Within its seclusion – and in the belief that Aberdeen was a ready target for the Germans based in Norway – the authorities had prepared a huge pit, intended as a mass grave. Fortunately the casualties did not reach the proportions necessary to fill it. On an equally macabre note, and remembering the shortage of timber, the authorities were also considering the use of cardboard coffins, initially encased in a proper wooden box for decency's sake but so hinged that they could be readily removed and the wooden coffin recycled another day.

That was overtaken by a scandal at Kaimhill Crematorium when relatives were charged for coffins that were indeed being retrieved and reused with profit in mind. Councillor James Dewar was sent to prison for his part in scam. Dewar, who was managing director of the crematorium and a councillor for the Woodside ward, was jailed for three years after being found guilty of stealing 1,044 coffin lids and two coffins. A Woodside undertaker, Alick George Forbes of Great Northern Road, was given six months for reset. Dismissing Dewar's appeal, the lord justice-general said: 'I don't suppose that a case has come into these courts which contained details so horrifying and so outrageous to public feeling and so repugnant to ordinary decencies as this case has been.'

But what of that tailpiece to the most frightening night of devastation in the history of Aberdeen, 21 April 1943? It is an intriguing human story, unearthed at a much later date by two of my former colleagues on *The Press and Journal*, Jim Kinnaird and Arthur Binnie. The source of their revelation was Mr Norman Beattie, former general manager and secretary of Aberdeen Harbour Board, who went on a post-war Board of Trade promotion to Hamburg, the largest port in Germany, which had a long trading connection with Aberdeen.

Mr Beattie, who retired in 1978, had addressed a meeting one afternoon when he was approached by a German journalist who was covering the event and wanted to walk back with him to his hotel because there was something he wanted to chat about. Having established that Mr Beattie was indeed in Aberdeen during the war, the man then asked if he remembered a massive air-raid on the city on 21st April 1943. Yes, he remembered it vividly as the heaviest raid of the war. He had been in his garden at 42 Woodend Place when it started but was soon dashing for shelter because of the tracer bullets.

Did Mr Beattie realise that the attack was concentrated on the northern half of the city, with no damage at all from the harbour southward? Yes, indeed. He had wondered why the harbour had been spared on a night hell-bent on destruction; the assumption had been that the German planes avoided it for fear of gunfire from naval ships and land defences in the area.

The journalist said this was not the explanation. He then went on to say that his own brother-in-law had come to Aberdeen in March of 1939 to marry a girl from Torry. They returned to Germany in time for Hitler's war, in which the bridegroom became a Luftwaffe pilot – the pilot who was detailed to lead that raid on Aberdeen! Grappling with his dilemma, and determined to spare his wife's relatives who still lived in the Torry district, he instructed his squadron to concentrate their attack exclusively on the area between Kittybrewster and the harbour. At all costs, they had to avoid anything south of that.

Mr Beattie, who has survived into his nineties and lives in Cults, was privy to information that would have fascinated the press even though, in the heat of a delicate moment, he had not sought more details about the pilot. However, he belonged to a generation that took its responsibilities seriously and, not seeking to cause repercussion in those post-war years, he kept the encounter mainly to himself. Jim Kinnaird, a Peterhead man who used to cover the harbour for *The Press and Journal*, gained first hint of Mr Beattie's information and, in retirement many years later, passed it on to Arthur Binnie, who was preparing a booklet on Aberdeen's wartime experience intended for perusal in local schools. Of course it is a story without corroboration. But it helps to make sense of German strategy that night, and Norman Beattie felt he had no reason to disbelieve the man. It has been my own experience as a veteran journalist never to discount anecdotal evidence.

There is a further twist to the story. Though no link has yet been made to the relatives in Torry, Arthur Binnie's pursuit of wartime records disclosed that the pilot who led the attack that night was also an artist, who proceeded to sketch an impression of the raid for publication in the *Berliner Illustrierte Zeitung*.

It appeared in the magazine on 10th June 1943 under the heading 'The Way We Saw Aberdeen', with a chillingly graphic account of the night as seen from the German cockpits. The name of the pilot/artist was given as Captain Walter Bornschein, who described in word and sketch how he led the whole squadron on a sweep over the town, taking 'the great straight street' (George Street) as his guide. Given as present-tense captions, he writes:

With the targets in sight in front of us, the group roars in a broad, moving front tightly over the houses below – weaving, dipping and soaring over the towers and chimney tops. We have

Air-raid of 1943 – a German pilot's dramatic sketch of the night

to take care not to collide with the neighbouring aircraft. On the horizon, the outlines of industrial installations and the massive gasometers loom into sight . . . None of the heavy bombs miss their aim. The machine-gunners fire at whatever targets offer themselves. The air is filled with the brilliant tracery of our weapons and the light anti-aircraft. Explosion after explosion flashes in the night. An enormous dark red cloud wells up in the heavens. The gasworks!

For the translations, I'm indebted to Jim Pittendrigh, an Aberdonian who has worked as an accountant in Switzerland since 1961 and who, by coincidence, had been doing his own investigation into that April night he remembers so well from his boyhood.

On that same night, Sunnybank School was badly damaged and houses around the Bedford Road and Elmbank Road area were destroyed. Five pupils were killed in their homes. On the very night Walter Bornschein was leading thirty German bombers over the city, the RAF was wreaking its own vengeance on the strategic river port of Stettin, with a force of 300 planes! The pilot/artist had already been honoured with the Knight's Cross in 1942 but met his own fate exactly a year after his raid on Aberdeen.

Mention of Jim Kinnaird brings a postscript to the story of the air-raids. Not all the victims of the Hall Russell raid were in the Neptune Bar that lunch-time. Jim's uncle and namesake, Jimmy Kinnaird, a marine engineer, was with several workmates who sought refuge in an old ship's boiler that served as an air-raid shelter. Their packed lunch that day would be their last, for the old boiler proved to be not a sanctuary but a death-trap. The blast from high explosives killed them all.

Lord Haw-Haw

In the final reckoning of wartime bombing it was found that Aberdeen had been the object of thirty-four air-raids, in which 178 people were killed and 588 injured. The number of houses completely destroyed was 333 with a further 13,198 badly damaged. Remarkably, the Home Office figures show that in comparison to the bombing raids on Aberdeen, the second largest number of attacks in Scotland affected the Fraserburgh–Peterhead area, while Edinburgh had twenty-three raids, Glasgow ten, and Dundee five.

But bombs were not the only hazard. As part of his psychological warfare, Hitler had the help of an Irishman, William Joyce, better known in Britain as 'Lord Haw-Haw', whose propaganda broadcasts were designed to undermine British morale. People tuned in nightly as the sinister, drawn-out voice began with 'Gairmany calling, Gairmany calling'. He would then go on to alarm us with authentic items of news about ourselves, showing that his network of spies was working in our midst, completely up-to-date with information. Typical of the local detail was: 'The town clock at Forres stopped at one minute to midnight last night.' On another occasion: 'Hitler will be in Scotland in time to perform the opening ceremony of the new bridge over the Ythan at Ellon.' Neighbours looked around suspiciously, wondering who the informants might

Cowdray Hall, Aberdeen's War Memorial

be. Many a North-east community had its rumours, spreading tales of transmitters that were allegedly heard in the night and casting doubt on many an unconventional character who was probably perfectly innocent.

Adding further colour to the civilian scene was that gallant army of fire-side soldiers, known originally as the Local Defence Volunteers, parading with only a khaki armband and a forage-cap before they were transformed into a fully-kitted force as the Home Guard. A modern audience would know them better as the blueprint for *Dad's Army* of television fame, a motley mixture of men who were either too old or unfit for active service or who were working at home in reserved occupations. They were the butt of many a later joke on the basis that if Hitler happened to reach as far as Fittie he was unlikely to be deterred by Captain Mainwaring and his mob!

But in reality, many of those men who formed the three Aberdeen battalions – the 4th or City, the 6th or Post Office, and the 7th or Works – were brave survivors who had fought and beaten the Germans as Gordon Highlanders in 1914–18. Their mettle was tested in 1942 when the active soldiers of the 52nd (Lowland) Division attacked the city's Home Guard defences in a mock encounter, labelled the 'Battle of Bon Accord'. The old boys of the 51st Division were determined to show their southern rivals that they had not forgotten what warfare was all about. Despite some dubious umpiring of the event, the invaders were declared to have been 'eliminated'. Two years later, when those same men of the 52nd scored a major success in capturing a German town, the Aberdonians were not slow to claim credit for having taught them a lesson or two at the 'Battle of Bon Accord'.

As the tide of the Second World War began to turn, with General Montgomery in North Africa and beyond, air-raids petered out and the general view that the war might last ten years now seemed over-pessimistic. After five years, the adrenaline of danger had lost its buoyancy and a weariness set in across the nation. The so-called Second Front of June 1944, when Allied troops landed in Normandy, was the beginning of the end, leading to Victory in Europe, known as VE-Day, on 8th May 1945. We lit bonfires of celebration and faced a bleak post-war world of austerity, lightened in Aberdeen on Saturday 27th April 1946 by the particularly warm welcome to Winston Churchill, the man who had led us to victory and had now come to receive the freedom of the city.

A Heroine

Of the many stories of heroism from the war, none was more impressive than that of Marion Patterson, a senior fire-guard based at the civil defence headquarters in Marischal Street. It was during an air-raid on 7th August 1942 that a German bomb destroyed a building in South Market Street where sailors were guarding an ammunition dump. Many were trapped inside, and when Marion and her colleagues arrived they could hear only the knocking and tapping of desperate men. With bare hands, they set about digging into the rubble, tearing it clear until they reached the survivors. One sailor had to be freed from beneath a beam.

Marion Patterson had cour-ageously crawled through a small opening to effect the res-cue. When she went to wash lime from her face, she looked back in time to see the collapse of the whole building. Three rescue workers, including a newly married nurse, were among seven dead that night. Dozens more were injured. For her bravery, Marion was presented with the George Medal by King George VI,

Air-raid heroine Marion Patterson re-visits the scene in South Market St

the first fire-guard in Britain to receive the honour. Along with her other awards, that prestigious medal is now in the Aberdeen Art Gallery and Museums' collection. As Marion Hay, she had emigrated to Canada with her parents before the war but returned as a married woman when her husband, Guthrie Patterson from Dundee, came to join the RAF. She lived at 1 Littlejohn Street and opened a hairdressing business in Broad Street, also taking up the duties as a fire-guard. The sailor she rescued made a good recovery and she later met his family when they came visiting from Glasgow. Sadly, there was no happy ending to the story. Marion, who later returned to Canada, received word that the sailor went back to the navy and, in his first week at sea, his ship was torpedoed and all hands were lost. Scottish artist Robert Sivell painted a picture of Marion Patterson which now hangs in the Imperial War Museum in London. The preliminary sketch is in the possession of Aberdeen Art Gallery.

CHAPTER 41

Industry at War

With the interruption of air-raid sirens and the sleepless nights of tension and uncertainty for the civilian population, there was still a job to consider in the grey dawn of a new day. With a 'piece' tucked under their arms, those men and women who kept the home fires burning were on their way by tramcar or bicycle to a place of work, so often engaged on a task quite alien to their pre-war role.

Take, for example, the Belmont Street premises of J.S. Sharpe, who had earned a high reputation as the fishing-tackle people. Of the Sharpe family, Jack was the technical and inventive chap, now faced with turning the machines which had produced the apparatus of contemplative pleasure towards the vastly different purposes of war. Whether it was producing parts for aero-engines or shells, the demands were met by a workforce, including women, that expanded to a night-shift and attained a high quality that brought its own handsome compliment when the war ended. So much so that, when Sharpes readjusted to their pre-war expertise in making fishing-rods, landing nets, gaffs, artificial flies and tackle, they were invited by one of the leading companies to take on the machining of aero-engines and other intricate parts. A separate factory was opened in John Street, with metal-working machines for the new contracts, leaving Belmont Street to its traditional role in the fishing-tackle business.

Employees of William McKinnon and Co. took pride in the fact that their engineering firm had once been headed by John Gray, the public-spirited gentleman who founded Gray's School of Art. At the premises in Spring Garden, however, they found themselves transformed into a munitions factory during the war, turning out shells, mortar bombs and rockets by the tens of thousands, as well as a range of parts for the Hercules aero-engine. Across at Great Western Road, the Lisco fabrication company, which had started life as a blacksmith, was caught up in contracts for the Admiralty, producing watertight doors, hatches and ships' scuttles and ventilators. In the return to peace-time work, the firm (full name Light Iron and Steel Constructions) led the field with aluminium fish containers, a more hygienic successor to the fish box.

Harrott and Co., glove and knitwear manufacturers in Rose Place, were soon turning their efforts towards all form of clothing for the Forces, including pullovers, gloves and underwear, while James L. Archibald of Great Western Road, having lost all their able-bodied cabinet-makers and upholsterers to the Services, still managed to accept contract furnishing work for Government departments. At their Union Works, Wiggins Teape (Stationery) Ltd replaced their manufacture of envelopes with the whole new experience of producing paper components for the Forces – shell containers, oil containers and, most adventurous of all, large tanks that could be jettisoned from the Mosquito aircraft of the RAF and the Mustangs of the American Air Force.

The concrete firm of George W. Bruce faced the war without its managing director, an enthusiastic Territorial, who was off to France as second-in-command of the 5th Gordons, only to find himself captured at St Valery in 1940 and despatched to various German prisoner-of-war camps for the next five years. The company's pre-war production of road kerbs, paving slabs and fencing posts turned swiftly to air-raid shelters and concrete blocks for the coastal defence of the country.

The large contractors were forced into major expansion. Brought from Yorkshire to Aberdeen at an early age, William Tawse had become one of the North-east's most dynamic figures, building harbours, bridges and hundreds of miles of the nation's roads, extending his creativity to a deft literary style aided by the phenomenal vocabulary of a well-read man. In the war, Tawse's men built those early coastal defences from Aberdeen to Peterhead and went on to surface airfield runways throughout Britain. But that was just the beginning. Other achievements of William Tawse Ltd included a commando camp in the Highlands, the Churchill Causeway in Orkney and the Ministry of Aircraft Production factory at Tullos, regarded as a model of industrial layout in its day.

Alexander Hall and Son was a builder's business founded at Durris in 1880, Mr Hall then moved into the city to be a carpenter in the Mile End district. Pre-war expansion came as builders took the wise decision to embrace all the major trades in the industry within the one company. Alexander Hall and Son was therefore well placed for the war effort, building army camps and aerodromes as well as fabricated huts. From that latter development, the company moved into prefabricated houses, so much in demand to meet the crisis in living accommodation after the war, when it built 15,000 'prefabs' throughout Scotland. But the repetitive nature of wartime and post-war work had diluted the builders' skills and Hall and Son quickly sought a return to contracts that would revive the craftsmanship and technical ingenuity of their workforce.

Down at the shipyard of John Lewis and Sons they were soon converting trawlers into minesweepers and boom defence vessels. As well as thirty-nine ships built for the war effort, including corvettes, the yard was coping with an annual average of 400 vessels arriving for conversion, repair and refit, among them tank landing-craft. Many were equipped for arctic or tropical conditions, new skills that proved useful after the war.

Lewis's also built for the Admiralty a portable floating dock at Torry, an American design operated from the quay by air compressors. Its post-war achievements included an order from Salvesen's to build the world's first stern-trawling factory ship, the *Fairtry*, which revolutionised deep-sea fishing, against the odds of skulduggery and industrial espionage as the Russians tried to get hold of the plans. (The *Fairtry*, incidentally, introduced us to fish fingers!)

The John Lewis shipyard Home Guard

The industrial machines of the home front played a major part in keeping up the war effort. At Crombies of Grandholm, famous for their overcoats and much else, they were producing cloth for the Forces in numbers that could only astound. The yarn produced was bound into bales of wool which, if placed on top of each other in a single year's production, would have topped Mount Everest by 5,000 feet. By that same calculation, the annual consumption of thread would have gone from Grandholm round the moon and back more than six times! In more practical terms, a year's output included overcoats for 125,856 soldiers, sailors and airmen and a further 142,542 for civilians, mainly for abroad since the Government was demanding dollar exports to buy munitions from Canada and the United States.

Each firm had its own problems. The large timber companies, like John Fleming and Co., were acting as store-keepers for the Government. But Fleming's premises at Baltic Place was counted too close to the docks for safety and they removed much of their stock to the car park at Pittodrie. A further order in 1941 said all timber had to be cleared from the port areas, and the Aberdeen stocks were directed to the policies of Dunecht.

CHAPTER 42

The Post-War World

The war did not end completely until mid-August when the dropping of atomic bombs on Hiroshima and Nagasaki brought the Japanese swiftly to their knees. Victory over Japan (VJ-Day) brought a modified repeat of VE-Day but an air of relief and celebration tapered through the rest of 1945. Servicemen in uniform were still a common sight in the streets of Aberdeen, not least the sailors on shore from ships in the bustling harbour, which had become an important naval base during the war.

Inevitably, in the general upheaval of a world conflict, the ties of morality had been loosened. And if the drug culture had not yet reached the commonality, the drinking one was long established, by now embracing women to an extent unknown before the war. Within that carefree atmosphere, the low-life of Aberdeen simmered in the shadows of quayside pubs. Weird noises in the night were not enough to disturb the slumbers of nearby residents, not even the piercing shriek of a woman's voice at two o'clock on a December morning causing more than a minor flutter.

In the bleary-eyed break of dawn the tramcars clanked along Union Street and carters' horses pulled their loads up Market Street. Another normal day in the life of Aberdeen was just beginning. That was, until an elderly man walking on the foreshore by the mouth of the River Dee in search of firewood froze at the sight of an object that sent him scurrying to the nearest telephone-box. The police removed the grisly exhibit to headquarters at Lodge Walk and began a murder investigation that has not been solved to this day. What the old man had found was a human arm, crudely sawn off and with the fingers arched as if scratching at a killer in self-defence. Whose arm could it be?

Superintendent John Westland ordered a check of fingerprints which paid off. The prints belonged to seventeen-year-old Betty Hadden, who had once been in minor trouble. But if Aberdeen knew nothing of Betty, it was well versed on the regular court appearances of her mother, Kate Hadden, a notorious name in the shadows of Aberdeen's low-life. A check at Kate's house confirmed that Betty had not been home for several days. Further checks showed she had been seen with sailors in the Castlegate on the eve of the gruesome discovery. Ships and sailors were pursued in all directions but not a clue was found. The theory was that the killer had disposed of the body in a trunk but was unable to tuck in the arm. So he sawed it off and rather carelessly disposed of it in the river.

An alternative theory was that the murderer was a local person who knew the area well, perhaps a quiet inhabitant of Torry who continued to live out his life without detection. An able detective, Superintendent Westland had his private suspicions, but in the absence of proof was never able to make an arrest. So, in case of future developments, the severed forearm of Betty Hadden was properly preserved and labelled by the distinguished Professor R.D. Lockhart at the anatomy department of Aberdeen University. Some years after his retirement, at home in Rubislaw Den North, I gave him the news that a disposal of materials at his old department had carelessly included the only clue to the murder of Kate Hadden's daughter. It was not his happiest moment. And thus the fate of good-time girl Betty Hadden remains a great unsolved murder in the criminal history of Aberdeen.

Rounding the corner into 1946, the bleakness of the post-war period was relieved for Aberdonians by colourful events like the Freedom Ceremony for Winston Churchill on 27th April and the first-ever celebration for the Dons of Pittodrie who, after forty-three years in existence, won the Scottish League Cup at Hampden Park, Glasgow. They beat Rangers 3-2 with a last-minute goal by left-half George Taylor. The date of that Hampden victory, incidentally, was 11th May 1946, perhaps an omen for greater things to come thirty-seven years later when, on that same date in 1983, the Dons reached their pinnacle of glory by beating Real Madrid in the final of the European Cup Winners' Cup.

Moments of relief were badly needed in a post-war world where food rationing would linger long and currency restrictions would render even a simple visit to France a rather hazardous undertaking. The Labour government of 1945 had to face the monumental task of rebuilding a war-torn society with all its debts, and the cramped air of austerity did little to boost the spirits of a wearied people. Identifying with such gloom helped to remove a government deemed unbearable after the first post-war years. The return of the deposed Winston Churchill as prime minister, even at the age of seventy-seven, was taken as a symbol of hope that better times might be at hand.

In the event, the 1950s did herald a swifter return to a better life than we had the right to expect. Social habits in a city like Aberdeen were largely a carry-over from the 1930s, when the people still walked 'The Mat' of Union Street on a Sunday evening; went to the pictures; or danced at the Beach Ballroom to the music of Leslie Thorpe, Charlie Wall at the Palais in Diamond Street, or Fred Cowie and his orchestra at the Douglas Hotel on a Saturday night. The popular music remained largely that of the great American composers like Irving Berlin, Cole Porter, George Gershwin and Richard Rodgers, with post-war shows like *Oklahoma!* and *Annie Get Your Gun* taking Britain by storm.

Mingled with that, the pre-war *Ruritania* of Ivor Novello was still alive at His Majesty's, with its clientele spilling on to Union Terrace to end the evening at the Caledonian Hotel, which had taken the place of the Palace, burned down in 1941. 'The Caley' seemed like the last word in sophistication, with its plush dining-room (where its café-bar is today) and a spacious lounge, complete with palm-court trio, where the after-show people came to mingle in a convivial social scene that has gone out of fashion. The suave figure of head waiter Charlie Bultitude, all bow-tied and tailed, floated discreetly about the hotel, which sported a very superior American

Bar on the first floor supervised by Big Andy, and a more pub-like Back Bar that was ruled by Jean, one of the city's more colourful characters.

The Caley played host to the stars appearing at His Majesty's, glamorous figures fleetingly glanced by their audience of that evening as they crossed the foyer en route to their suites. The hotel also housed the footballers of Rangers and Celtic, who would spend Friday night in the city before a match at Pittodrie. The Caley was the focal-point of social activity before the oil boom brought rivalry from the big hotel chains, as well as the upmarket enterprises of men like Donald Macdonald, who developed Ardoe House, and Stewart Spence, who did similar wonders with the Marcliffe at Pitfodels.

Aberdonians were doing their best to regain that pre-war spirit. Lovers walked on the Promenade from Dee to Don and found further joy in Harry Gordon's old Beach Pavilion, revived with shows that would bring everyone from great comedians like Dave Willis to the singing sensation of the day, the Beverley Sisters. Then the coronation year of 1953 brought a curious stirring, as if a new age might be about to break upon us. It was the time of the 'Teddy Boys' in drainpipe trousers, but that fashion was soon overtaken by musical events in America. Bill Haley burst on the scene with rock 'n' roll, followed closely by the king of that genre, Elvis Presley, whose gyrations were mirrored in Britain by Tommy Steele, sparking off a public hysteria when he appeared at the Capitol Cinema in its alternating role as a variety theatre.

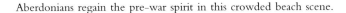

Aberdonians regain the pre-war spirit in this crowded beach scene.

The sixties brought The Beatles, who toured the North-east, and a swinging culture of sexual freedom, exposed and encouraged in 1963 by the public scandal of the century in which the Tory Secretary of State for War, John Profumo, husband of musical comedy star Valerie Hobson, finally admitted that he had shared the favours of London call-girl Christine Keeler with a Russian diplomat at the height of the Cold War. Sexual matters became the favoured topic of discussion.

The Beatles playing at the Beach Ballroom, 1963

Nearer home in that same decade, eyes were opened and public curiosity aroused by a murder trial in Aberdeen which laid bare such carnal ongoings as had never been imagined in the douceness of North-east respectability. That trial, in which Sheila Garvie, wife of prominent Laurencekirk farmer Max Garvie, was found guilty of his murder together with lover Brian Tevendale, lifted a lid that would not easily be replaced. There is little doubt that as Aberdonians spluttered over their porridge in an unprecedented burst of disbelief and excitement the moral tone of the area took a bend in a new direction. Within two years, however, there was another focus of attention, one that would engage public interest on a monumental scale, if only because it was destined to change forever the foundations of life in Aberdeen and the North-east.

CHAPTER 43

The Wonder of Oil

Casting an eye over history, it is tempting to think that the high points must surely have occurred long past. Yet, in considering a millenium of Aberdeen's economic history, there is little doubt that the most significant years have been within living memory, in the last quarter of the twentieth century and into the twenty-first.

For all the shrewdness of the Aberdonian, there was not even a glimmer of awareness that a fortune of liquid gold had been lying on the doorstep for 75 million years or more. The oil industry was for Americans and Middle Eastern potentates and had nothing to do with the more down-to-earth, substantial pursuits of farming and fishing. A world scarcity had certainly raised the question that there might well be oil in the North Sea – it had already been extracted from shallow waters in the Middle East – but who was going to tackle the unthinkable and drill it out of such stormy waters?

In the 1960s, therefore, it seemed like an academic exercise when the British and Norwegian governments, having been granted any ownership rights that might exist either side of a line in the middle of the North Sea, offered 'parcels' of that sea for exploration. The American companies moseyed in to have a look but found little to excite. British Petroleum opened a small office above the Wimpy Bar in Bridge Street, Aberdeen, but the forecasts spelt doom and gloom, revealing one dry well after another. There was even pressure within the company to sell its acreage and chairman Sir Eric Drake uttered words he would come to regret: 'There will not be a major field in the North Sea.'

Ted's 'Scoop'!

But suddenly there was oil. The sensational news was broken to the world by a delightfully modest and quietly shrewd North-east journalist called Ted Strachan, an Elgin man who was industrial editor of *The Press and Journal*. Underplaying his world scoop, Ted explained: 'I just picked up the story from the Phillips guy in London.' The story was that a consortium,

Journalist Ted Strachan

headed by Phillips Petroleum, had discovered an oilfield with 2.8 billion barrels of reserve. It lay hard upon the dividing line, but on the Norwegian side.

Anyway, what did it matter? If this was a sign of what lay elsewhere beneath the North Sea, then a bonanza of unimaginable riches had come to revolutionise the British economy. The future prime minister, James Callaghan, exclaimed: 'God is once more on our side!' Now that the hunters were on the scent, it would be only a matter of time before all was revealed. With British Petroleum's discovery of what they would call the Forties Field on Britain's side of the line came final proof that oil was here in large quantities. That was followed by Shell's discovery of an even bigger field, the Brent, which would give its name to the benchmark price for North Sea crude oil.

Aberdeen was now in line to become the focal point of this sensational development. But Ted Strachan's exclusive story was just one half of a remarkable day for Ted and his newspaper. As his report dropped on the editor's desk, he followed it with another story that would surely demand front-page treatment. The famous Rubislaw Quarry, symbol of Aberdeen and its granite industry for nearly two and a half centuries, was closing down. The editor's dilemma was solved by dividing the front page, left and right, bringing the uncanny news that just as one significant industry was coming to an end an apologetic nature had come along with a replacement. What a consolation! That historic day for *The Press and Journal*, incidentally, was Tuesday 28th April 1970.

As a North-east journalist who had gone off to be a feature writer with the *Daily Express*, I came back with a curiosity to trace the first signs of what was happening to my native land. This was history in the making and the recording of it would be a particular excitement. First stop was the Cromarty Firth and the shelter of Nigg Bay, where they were scooping out a dock for the building of the first gigantic oil platform to be towed out to the Forties Field off the North-east coast of Scotland. Once that field was operating, four years ahead, the oil would be brought ashore at Cruden Bay, just south of Peterhead. So I drove along the Moray Firth, by Elgin, Banff and Fraserburgh, to that Buchan land I knew so well. It was here at Cruden Bay that we would picnic in childhood days, remembering that Bram Stoker came this way when creating his tales of Dracula.

But it was oil, not blood, that would be sucked from the depths of the great North Sea. Jimmy Cantlay, the farmer at Nether Broadmuir, had sold fifty acres that would become the gathering point for the oil that would flow along the seabed and gush ashore, before starting its landward journey south, via Aberdeen, to the British Petroleum refinery at Grangemouth 140 miles away. From this return to see what was happening to my homeland in 1971, I sent this despatch:

The whole vibrating atmosphere of a prosperity just round the corner is there to be absorbed in Aberdeen, whether you are walking down the grey granite splendour of Union Street, breathing in the fishy smell of Market Street, joining in the football enthusiasm of Pittodrie Park or relaxing with a pint in a cocktail bar. Aberdeen has never been a dull city, given its abundance of cinemas, dance halls, pub entertainment and concerts. This week's diversions include the Stanley Baxter Show at His Majesty's and Dickie Henderson's All-Star Show – and now there is the attraction of the roulette tables at the Blue Chip, the Cheval or the Maverick.

The Press and Journal

223rd Year   No. 35,978   TUESDAY APRIL 28 1970   6d

A NEW SOURCE OF RAW MATERIALS OPENS UP—AS AN OLD AND FAMOUS ONE CLOSES

2000-barrel a day gusher

NORTH SEA OIL STRIKE BOOM DAY

By TED STRACHAN

A NEW oil strike in the Norwegian sector of the North Sea about 200 miles from Aberdeen, described as "significant" yesterday by an oil company chief, is comparable with the sort of discovery expected in North Africa.

This emerged last night from inquiries which suggest that the announcement of the strike by Mr John Houchin, head of

Phillips Petroleum, in Oklahoma, was "conservative" about the facts of the discovery.

According to the announcement by Phillips, the operator for a four-company consortium, oil has been flowing from a test well, Ekofisk 2-X, at up to 2000 barrels a day.

DRILLING RIG

This is a rate comparable to flows from single wells in North Africa. Average Middle East wells produce 10,000 barrels a day. The oil from the North Sea well, which is almost equidistant from Norway, Scotland and Denmark, is of a high quality.

The discovery has been kept secret for the past three weeks during tests. Partners with Phillips in the consortium are Agip, Petrofina and Petronord, of Italy, Belgium and France.

Mr Houchin said: "No discovery could be significant because of the thick perforation encountered and the size of the structure on which wells were drilled."

The find, made from the drilling rig Ocean Viking, is about two miles from another well site where oil was struck last winter. But full tests were not carried out on this previous well because of bad weather and drilling problems.

The accident happened at a test opposite Dalmore Farm cottage, only yards from the farmhouse.

the well. "This is only an initial announcement," he said. It would take about three or four weeks to complete the tests.

ABERDEEN BASE

If they indicate development of the find as a commercial proposition, months of engineering evaluations may follow to determine whether to bring the oil ashore in Norway, Denmark or Scotland.

Existence of a deep-water trench in the seabed off the Norwegian coast means the oil could be landed in Scotland. Where? "Well, we would have to have a fair-sized port and Aberdeen is as near as any," said the spokesman.

But he emphasised that a decision on where to land the oil was still "wide open."

Even if oil is found in commercial quantities at a point in the North Sea off Aberdeen, it does not follow that Aberdeen would be the chosen landing point.

Other East Coast ports are known to be interested in the possibility of becoming the North Sea oil terminal in Scotland and to have considered contingency plans to seize the opportunity. Most obvious rivals to Aberdeen are Dundee and Grangemouth, neither of which have been idle in planning for it.

Alness boy dies in crash

THE 10-YEAR-OLD son of a prominent Ross-shire farmer was killed last night when his car struck by a car on the main A9 road between Alness and Invergordon while sight of his home.

He was William David Oag, son of Mr David William Oag and Mrs Oag, Dalmore Farm, Alness.

The car, travelling towards Invergordon, was driven by Mr Bertram Macdonald, 34 Coulhill Road, Alness.

Commons question on UK shipbuilding sales

By BILL DOULT

BRITAIN'S shipbuilding balance of trade deficit has shot up by more than £30,000,000 in two years—and while the proportion of world trade has gone down.

This was the depressing picture revealed in the Commons last night during a series of probing Opposition questions about the state of the nation's shipyards.

Junior Technology Minister Dr Ernest Davies said that in 1967 Britain's £70,000,000 worth of foreign shipping more than she sold.

In the following year the deficit had risen to £76,000,000 and by last year Britain was buying £50,000,000 worth of ships from abroad than she was managing to sell to the rest of the world.

Questioned about the proportion of world trade Dr Davies revealed that although Britain's total output had gone up their share of the market had gone down.

For, while world orders between 1960 and 1964 averaged 9,300,000 tons a year Britain managed to build an average of 1,300,000 tons of that trade.

Trade Minister Mr Keith Joseph asked why, if the world boom, Britain had been unable to maintain her proportion of the market.

The Minister insisted, however, that "the plain fact is that the United Kingdom's industry has now doubled their orders from the time when the Opposition was in government."

Ready for battle of the Boks

BATTLE plans of the anti-South African cricket tour demonstrations were uncovered last night.

And violence is out.

Mr Peter Hain, chairman of the Stop the 70 Tour committee, said protests would be by running on the field and sitting down.

Their intention was not to stop the tour by violent means, he said on BBC-TV's "Panorama."

But Shadow Attorney-General Sir Peter Rawlinson warned that demonstrations would turn the streets around Lord's into battlefields.

Protesters were prepared to go to violence to impose their will on others and that struck at the very fabric of the rule of law, he said.

SAD DAY

Former England captain Mike Smith said: "If this tour is stopped it would be a sad day for cricket, a sad day for democracy in this country."

Mr Leslie Rhodes, chairman of Lancashire County Cricket Club, said he was opposed to demonstrations on the field of play.

"This is a kind of violence," he declared.

Mr Maurice Allom, the MCC's president, said he was against apartheid, but he did not think the tour would endanger community relations.

£500 CHEQUE

David G. Foster writes — A cheque for £100 was presented to the 1970 Cricket Fund last night by Mr Desmond Donnelly, M.P. for Pembrokeshire, on behalf of the Democratic Party.

The presentation, at Westminster, was made to Mrs Betty Nettleton, English widow of the South African VC, John Nettleton.

Mr Donnelly hinted that there would be more to follow and added: "I feel the strong belief that it is vital in the country's national interest to promote good relations with South Africa, Rhodesia and Portugal to end their isolation. You do not do this by pouring world killer on cricket pitches and this summer's tour must go through for the sake of Britain."

DJ index at seven-year low

The New York Stock Market suffered another major decline by the close, with prices continuing to slide to new lows.

The closely-watched Dow Jones industrial average closed at a new seven-year low of 733.13 — off more than 12 points on the day. The new low penetrated the previous low of 744.06 set on January 10 and left the average at its lowest since November 22, 1963, the day President Kennedy was assassinated.

Declines fell gains by 1153 to 231 at the close.

BIG POLICE TATTOO

About 400 police officers from all over the world will stage a spectacular tattoo in the Kelvin Hall, Glasgow, in August. Taking part will be dare-devil motor cycle riders from the Metropolitan Police Band and a massed Scottish pipe band.

Proceeds of the show, which is being run jointly by Glasgow police and the Stars' Organisation for Spastics, will go to the spastics and to the Police Dependants' Fund.

Beer haul ends

Eight naval apprentices pulling a beer barrel on a trolley have raised well over £250 for the Royal National Lifeboat Institution. They covered the 350 miles from Rosyth to Burton-on-Trent, Staffs., in 14 days.

What do we do with big hole now?

It's Rubislaw Quarry's last blast —after 200 years

RUBISLAW Quarry, Aberdeen—the deepest granite quarry in the world, from which half the Granite City has been built—is to close after almost 200 years in production, writes Ted Strachan.

A new quarry may be opened on the site, just to the north of the present quarry, depending on the findings of test borings being made there this week.

But the main quarry, an immense chasm 465 feet deep with its floor 180 feet below sea level, and 900 feet long by 750 feet wide at its rim, gouged out by generations of quarrymen in the past two centuries, will definitely close.

Announcing the closure decision yesterday, owners of the quarry, Aberdeen Construction Group Ltd., revealed that world-famous, Rubislaw had been approaching exhaustion for the past two years. No worthwhile rock had come out of it for two years with the result that the quarry had now become uneconomic.

LABOUR FORCE

Some of the quarry's labour force of 35, including quarrymen, crushers, masons and stone-cutters, will be placed elsewhere in the group, but some will be redundant, the extent of redundancy depending on whether a new quarry can be opened on the site.

Already rock borings have been made at a point just north, north-east of the present quarry—to a depth of 40 feet. These have revealed poor quality rock. Now fresh bores are being made further west.

The findings of these, in dictating whether or not further development is worth while, are expected to be available within a month. If a new quarry is opened, about 30 men will be employed to operate it, about a half dozen more each will be placed elsewhere in the group. Efforts will be made to keep redundancy to a minimum.

PRESTIGE

The process of closing the main quarry is expected to take about four to six months. Closure will start at the end of May.

What then for the awesome pit, which is part of Aberdeen's history and a major attraction for sightseers in the city? Managing director of Aberdeen Construction Group, Mr T. K. Hall said yesterday: "We have not yet decided what we are going to do with it."

Left to nature, the quarry would certainly flood. It is located in a high-amenity, high-value residential district of the city.

But to restore the ground, which has yielded blue-grey granite not only for Aberdeen but for prestige buildings and civil engineering works in every continent for 200 years, could take many years. And it is rich in historical associations.

Rubislaw Quarry was first opened by Aberdeen Town Council in 1741. But apparently the town council failed to get the satisfactory quality material near the surface and in 1788 sold it back to the Skene family, from whom they bought it for £130 Scots.

Working of the rich strata which, according to one estimate, had yielded more than 6,000,000 tons of granite by 1853, began in 1788.

TO LONDON

A great boom in demand for Rubislaw granite began in 1811. Stanes for the old Waterloo Bridge in London were quarried and dressed at Rubislaw and shipped direct to London.

And, when Rennie's Waterloo Bridge was replaced in the 1930s, one of the builders was encouraged to Aberdeen by the London County Council as a source of the 1200 which had been cut and dressed by the Rubislaw craftsmen.

At one time in the quarry's history 60 sett makers worked there squaring off pieces of waste rock for granite setts.

FEARS

An awesome pit — so deep that bystanders on the edge look down on birds flying in its depths, and direct sunshine never reaches its floor, which remains in perpetual shadow—Rubislaw Quarry has attracted daredevils during Aberdeen University Charities and Rectorial campaigns. More than once the Blondin which spans the quarry's tower and rims men and materials to its floor have been festooned with banners.

In 1964 stone from Rubislaw was used for the Bruce Monument at Bannockburn. A year later fears were expressed that closure faced the famous quarry—recalling similar fears of its impending exhaustion in the 1930s. That was nearly premature.

But now, having yielded stone for half Aberdeen and to grace cities such as London and San Francisco besides, Rubislaw passes into history with many another quarry which helped make Aberdeen the "Granite City."

200-YEAR-OLD RUBISLAW QUARRY, ABERDEEN

RIVER NESS RESCUE HERO — AT 74

A WAR veteran of 74 leapt into the icy, swollen waters of the River Ness to save a woman from drowning. Yesterday, the modest pensioner-hero, Mr William Anderson, a resident in the British Legion Home, Island Bank Road, Inverness was still in bed recovering from his ordeal.

"I was walking back to the home after doing some shopping in the town just before lunch," Mr Anderson said. "I spotted this woman on the bank. The next thing I knew she was in the water.

"I scrambled down the bank, waded in after her and pulled her to the side."

RECOVERED

The alarm was raised from a nearby house and police and an ambulance arrived on the scene. The woman who is 60, was taken to hospital and a police spokesman said yesterday that she had recovered.

A Native of Tain, Mr Anderson has been in the home since it opened two years ago. During World War I he served as a private with the Army Service Corps and saw action in France.

Last night Mr Jack Stuart, area secretary of the British Legion, paid tribute to Mr Anderson's bravery.

"It was an exceptional act," he said. "Willie is receiving treatment for his heart—the shock of the cold water could have killed him.

"There was nothing to it," Mr Anderson said. "What else could I do? I couldn't leave the woman in the water.

Pledge after Govt. switch on pensions

THE GOVERNMENT pledged yesterday to protect fully the occupational pension schemes of millions of workers if they change jobs. But not for "some years."

It will mean a major change in Labour's National Superannuation and Social Insurance Bill which has already had its second reading.

The Minister of State at the Department of Health and Social Security, Mr David Ennals, gave details of the plan last night.

He said without the changes in the Bill only about 40% of the 12,000,000 members of occupational pension schemes would have been assured of collecting all their pension rights on changing jobs.

PRESERVATION

The Bill, introduced last December, originally gave protection only to those pension rights which were earned after the Bill became law.

Mr Ennals told the Folkestone Chamber of Trade that the change would cost employers' pension schemes £23,000,000 a year.

He added: "We do not believe an increase of this order will really have a serious effect on soundly managed pension schemes.

"But we have told the Confederation of British

Industry that we recognise some schemes will be more seriously affected than others and it is only right that all schemes should have a breathing space at some years in which to make necessary preparations for full preservation."

The length of the breathing space would be discussed with the CBI, the Trades Union Congress and other interested parties, said Mr Ennals.

The new plan would not interfere with any other options which a member might be offered on leaving an employer's pension scheme.

Nor would it interfere with arrangements for the transfer of pension rights between one employer's scheme and another.

Mr Ennals disclosed that the Government had tabled a new amendment aimed at helping any scheme facing technical or procedural trouble in making a transfer arrangements.

He said that the Bill originally provided that an employer would be obliged to offer a remaining pension scheme member the benefits which he had earned after the Bill took effect.

But any pension rights which he had earned before that would have "remained, as now, at the mercy of his employer."

DEPLORABLE

The decision had been made largely because of complaints about employers and the TUC and others had been "keenly disappointed at the inadequate protection proposed."

Mr Ennals described as "absolutely deplorable" the abandonment of social justice that fewer than 50% of pension scheme members would be able to take his pension with him to his new job.

He hoped that when the right to a preserved pension became general many more workers would realise how much they stood to lose by withdrawing their contributions and would exercise their right to claim a deferred pension.

"But we recognise that there will always be some cases where an employee, for personal reasons, feels that the immediate sum represents a better bargain in his own interest.

"And we stand by our view that this is a decision which each man should make freely for himself," said Mr Ennals.

67 Tories are ready to fight in Scotland

THERE are now 67 Tory candidates ready to tilt for General Election in Scotland's 71 constituencies. Four remaining four constituencies are in the process of selecting candidates.

This was stated at a news conference in Glasgow yesterday by Sir Alexander Menzies Anderson, chairman of the Scottish Tory Party.

He was outlining the party's financial position. This showed that in 1969 the party increased their political activity and expenditure rose. Although income also increased in 1969 and expenditure was held within their estimates, a net deficit rose from £8000 to £6400. The deficit in 1967, however, was £16,000.

The financial statement comments: "If constituency contributions under the quota scheme had been met in cash and in full the deficit would have been virtually eliminated.

Total income for the year amounted to £54,600 while total expenditure was £103,200.

TV COOK HARBEN DIES

TELEVISION'S first cook, Philip Harben, died last night in St Mary's Hospital, Harrow Road, London. He was 63.

Mr Harben—complete with pointed beard and ready wit—became a household name soon after the war with his fancy recipes.

Thousands of housewives used to write to ham for advice and his culinary fame was worldwide.

In 1969, however, Mr Harben gave up television and started his own "pots and pans" business.

Mr Harben leaves a widow Katherine, and a son and daughter.

Body in Tay identified

Perth police announced late last night that the body of Mr Allan Alexander Mark (37), lorry driver, 2 Paradise Avenue, Craigie Farm, had been recovered from the Tay at Balmerino Fife.

Mr Cormack went missing on April 5.

Oban mine

Naval divers today found a 250lb. light explosive mine off the bed of busy Oban Bay, Argyllshire.

Mr WILLIAM ANDERSON
who rescued a woman from the River Ness

Aberdeen Harbour – transformed by oil industry

Even before the promise of oil, Aberdeen's unemployment was running at 3.6 per cent, against the Scottish average of 6.3. As the regional capital, it has long been more of a servicing than an industrial centre, a hub of financial operation which includes an incredible total of nearly two hundred insurance offices. But with a population of 180,000 it had slipped below Dundee to become the fourth city in Scotland, a situation which will soon be reversed.

As to how long the bonanza will last, Lord Provost John Smith says 'We are assured by the oil companies that, whatever the final outcome, there are twenty-five or thirty years of production lying out there in the Forties. The marine industry will play an increasing role for renewal work and light industry is bound to benefit from what they now call spin-off work. The hotels, restaurants and pubs, as well as the whole food and drinks industry will benefit.'

Outside, as the November sunlight catches the grey granite from the spires of Marischal College right uptown to the posh dwellings of Queen's Road and Rubislaw Den, the tangible signs of oil begin to mushroom. One telling sign was the decision of British European Airways to move the headquarters of its entire helicopter service from Gatwick to Aberdeen Airport because of the volume of work now involved in carrying personnel to and from oil rigs and bases. Around the local folklore place-names like Fittie and Point Law and up by Old Torry to Girdleness, broader names like Global and Transcontinental appear on modest shore bases, announcing that the big oil men are here to probe, while not wishing to make too much noise about it until they are sure the liquid is gonna gush.

Crowds gather to gaze at the floodlit spectacle of a new breed of ships in port, with names like Seismic Explorer, Cromarty Service or Lido Supplier, while divers and roughnecks of sundry nationality come and go in a buzz of activity. Across in Torry you will find a long, lean Texan, name of Calvin Seidensticker, draping himself over a desk and drawling words like 'gee' and 'mighty fine' into a telephone.

Actually, things are not so fine as they might have been for Mr Seidensticker. As drilling supervisor for Mobil in Aberdeen, he says 'Yeah, I suppose you could say we are a little disappointed that we have not so far found oil. It has been costing us £10,000 a day, but we are not giving up hope . . .' Other companies, like British Petroleum, have found oil all right and it is now mainly a question of how many of the giants strike it lucky enough for a final decision to go ahead.

Not everyone in Aberdeen wants oil. There are fishermen who fear it will alter the eating habits of the fish as well as provide difficulty for their nets. There are sectional business interests which don't particularly relish the rising demand on harbour accommodation, nor the rising level of wages that an oil bonanza will bring. But these are minor considerations. Aberdeen is on the march as the centre of a prosperity which will stretch right down the east coast from Orkney to Dundee and beyond.

So there is oil and business and finance and research; there is still a substantial fishing industry as well as papermaking and some granite and a vast agricultural hinterland creating its own industrial structure.

Inevitably there are the camp followers, the women whose nose for an opportunity is as sure as their profession is old. Taxi-drivers are already well versed on the habits and the hang-outs, whether they be in downtown dockland bars or the plush surroundings of a west-end cocktail lounge. One luscious lady from London was reporting that she was doing business in Aberdeen that surpassed her achievements in the metropolis. And her pad is not in a seamy backstreet but in a swanky Deeside suburb where ladies play golf and bridge and raise teacups with pinky held high. All part of the business of prospecting for prosperity, I suppose, the only difference being that, unlike the ladies of easy virtue, Aberdeen has been sitting primly on a fortune all those years – and didn't know it!

Thus I recorded the growing excitement about oil in the North-east of Scotland in 1971. But the oil itself had yet to come, soon to be disturbed from its slumbers, several miles beneath the bed of the sea, lying not in wells of liquid, as we might imagine, but within layers of rock in which, over the millennia, marine organisms had been transformed into gas and oil and would now have to be extracted like water from a sponge.

With the demands of modern civilisation, its moment had arrived. But to suck it from the sea and turn it into the fuel of everyday living would call for a technology still in its infancy. Gigantic platforms, with as much steel as the Forth Railway Bridge, would have to be built and towed far out to angry waters. Beyond all that, there was the drilling operation, reaching down, down, till it shattered the rafters of hell, to a depth which, if it went upwards instead of downwards, would reach the summit of Mont Blanc.

This, perhaps the greatest engineering feat in all history, had been achieved by the time I returned and now the pipes were rising out of the sea at Cruden Bay, hitting land first at Hay Farm before setting forth on the subterranean journey to Grangemouth. Geordie Carnie's land had been temporarily disturbed but now he had grown and harvested a crop of oats on the restored soil. When I visited him on the morning of Monday 3rd November 1975 he was ploughing his stubble field, little thinking of that liquid gold now flowing under his feet, en route to the lubrication of Britain's economy.

'I'll jist ploo awa,' said Geordie. 'I dinna expect the queen will bother comin' oot this wye.' In fact Her Majesty was less than thirty miles away, about to preside over a very special day.

The Great Day

So I left Geordie to his ploughing and headed towards Aberdeen. Once again, with a front-seat view of history in the making, I sent my despatch for the morning readership:

What a glorious occasion it was – a royal occasion, a Scottish occasion, blessed with sunshine and colour and the atmosphere of a gala celebration. It was the day when Britain became an oil-producing nation. The presence of Her Majesty the Queen and the prime minister [Harold Wilson], his Cabinet colleagues and a thousand invited guests suddenly crystallised the distant myth of North Sea oil into a living reality. Here at the village of Dyce, on the outskirts of Aberdeen, we were witnessing the creation of that chapter of history that will tell our grandchildren of the new industrial revolution.

From all the talk and argument and barrage of statistics it now became clear, even to the least technically minded, that the miracle had worked. The oil was flowing from the silent depths of the North Sea bed, a hundred miles east of Peterhead, ashore to the Scottish coast and south to the BP refinery at Grangemouth, all symbolised by the pressing of a button by the queen. Here we were, marking a memorable event with one of the biggest sprees ever seen in Scotland, costing British Petroleum around £700,000. But what was that compared to the £745 million it has already cost the company to bring the oil ashore?

Significantly perhaps, the pipeline comes ashore in the political constituency of East Aberdeenshire, a Tory stronghold until last year but now part of that North-east shoulder of Buchan, Banff and the Moray coast which has gone solidly over to Scottish Nationalism. Douglas Henderson, the Nationalist member for East Aberdeenshire, was at Dyce yesterday declaring to all who would listen that this was a great day for 'Scotland's oil'. Undoubtedly Mr Henderson and the people of his constituency, whose close contact with the activity of oil has sharpened their awareness of the new-found wealth, echo a broader cry across Scotland for a greater say in the running of their own affairs. Today, however, the oil and the running of Scotland belonged to Westminster, symbolised by the full array of first-team members, making it plain to those who had any doubts about the matter that this was a British occasion.

Mr Wilson was here to greet the queen and speak about this milestone in Britain's economic history. Mr Callaghan, the foreign secretary, and Mr Benn, the energy minister, were here and so was Mr Ross, the Scottish Secretary, and his Tory predecessor, Lord Campbell of Croy, the Liberal leader, Jeremy Thorpe, the Nationalist chairman, Willie Wolfe, shadow energy minister Patrick Jenkins, Reginald Maudling and so on. Aberdeen had never seen a gathering like it. Whoever owns the oil, the main function of this day was to rejoice in the fact that it was flowing in quantities that would soon reach 400,000 barrels per day, a statistic that can be meaningless until you calculate that each barrel carries about forty gallons. (This field alone will provide a quarter of Britain's oil needs.)

So we rejoiced in a £48,000 tent that was reminiscent of Bertram Mills Circus, with its dais of radiant red and muted blue, with concealed television sets to show the spectators what they might be missing in the flesh. Television's Donny B. MacLeod compered the show and jollied the audience into a warm-up session before the queen arrived. The Grampian Police Pipe Band skirled a real Scottish welcome and the regimental band of the Gordon Highlanders, flown home specially from Singapore, was given a heroes' reception in the land where they belong.

The Queen

Then came the Queen in emerald green, serene and thoughtful, turning to face the audience as they joined in the National Anthem. Prince Philip looked on tenderly and Prince Andrew stood straight as a guardsman. Among those presented to Her Majesty was Mr Matt Linning, the engineer who masterminded the North Sea operation. The Royal Family met other BP workers and walked out among the flag-waving children from local schools before the Queen moved into the main BP operations centre from which the whole flow of oil from the Forties Field is controlled.

There she pressed the button which inaugurated, with ridiculous simplicity, a whole new age for Britain. We awoke from the technological dream and finally accepted the fact that it was all for real. The battle to wrest the liquid gold from the vaults of nature had been won against heavy odds. 'Oil Strike North' was no longer just a series on television; as from this moment, Britain was now an oil-producing country, its citizens the blue-eyed Arabs of North-West Europe.

In the words of Her Majesty, it was a story of excitement and romance. And, as she drove out of the tented arena on her way to the nearby airport, the crowd rose and cheered, waved and rejoiced. The band struck up 'God Save the Queen'. In such a setting of historic splendour, it would have been a hard man who did not have a lump in his throat.

In less than three years the queen returned to the Buchan coast, four miles on the other side of Peterhead from Cruden Bay, to lead a similar ceremony for the arrival of gas. Nothing much had ever happened in the parish of St Fergus, though it gained its name from an early Christian preacher who was credited with performing miracles in the Buchan area. Whether he had anything to do with the creation of gas is a matter for idle conjecture. Finding oil was basically an American skill, and as Aberdeen began to assume the mantle of Western Europe's oil capital you

The Queen presses the button to start flow of oil

could have been forgiven for thinking the Wild West had come to Union Street. Rednecks in buckskin jackets and cowboy boots became a familiar sight as thousands of Americans and other nationalities came crowding in to make their homes in the Granite City.

Families arrived in such numbers as to justify the opening of an American School at Cults and a French School attached to the Grammar. The offshore workforce rose above the 30,000 mark, with skilled workers earning 18 per cent more than their counterparts in other industries and professional people taking that figure to 30 per cent. Inevitably, the new prosperity brought problems for the modest artisan not involved in oil and for companies seeking to attract recruits to a city with an inflated housing market. In a convenient location like Carden Place, for example, a house costing £5,000 in 1964 was changing hands for £250,000 twenty years later. If this was not exactly typical, it was explained by the demand from companies to convert a house into a modest-sized office and the front garden into a car park.

Apart from the Wild West swagger, the tangible evidence of oil's impact on Aberdeen was to be found originally at the airport but increasingly at the harbour, where the fleet of supply vessels built up to thousands by the 1990s. Traditional ships took a back seat as Aberdeen became a major European port with bases for the oil companies of the world, which were joined by three local companies of immense significance – the Wood Group, Seaforth Maritime and the Craig Group.

Local Leaders

The Wood Group was soon rising to a staff of 10,000 and a turnover of more than £600 million. Other local entrepreneurs included Jim Milne, a country lad with a good Doric tongue in his head, who started with five employees in 1980 making plastic products and built up his Balmoral Group to 600 employees and a turnover of £100 million. Venturing out by Albyn Place and Queen's Road you found that those miniature palaces of granite, once the residences of well-to-do Aberdonians, were emerging as offices while great blocks of headquarters announced the names of Conoco, Marathon or Britoil from their elevated perch on the very edge of the old Rubislaw Quarry. Was there no sense of decorum or respect for the lady's feelings?

The public mind could scarcely grasp the enormous scale of North Sea oil, with hundreds of miles of pipeline being laid along trenches on the seabed, from well-head to shore and beyond. At the high point of production in the 1980s, the oil and gas industry in the North Sea was giving work to 52,000 people, with upwards of 20,000 working offshore. The helicopter had broadened its potential in the Vietnam War and found a new role as the ideal means of transport from shore to rigs and platforms. Aberdeen Airport was on course to become the biggest helicopter base in the world, a development that brought the added bonus of a search-and-rescue service to the North-east, provided by British European Airways. Offshore, more than a thousand divers were at work by the mid 1970s – a harum-scarum breed apart but brave men nevertheless, facing big dangers in the uncertainty of the deep.

In 1986 there was crisis. With the kind of periodic panic which afflicts the industry, the price of oil crashed from $30 to $10 a barrel. Profits fell, companies cut back their costs and in Grampian Region alone no fewer than 10,000 jobs were lost, raising unemployment from three per cent to 11.2 per cent. Signs of recovery appeared the following year and the crisis came to be regarded as a blessing in disguise, forcing the industry to find cheaper ways of doing things. The days of big spending were over.

Piper Alpha

But there is always a price to pay. From 1971 till 1978 forty-two men had died in the North Sea operation. In that crisis year of 1986, disaster struck the helicopter service when a Chinook coming in to land at Shetland from the Shell Brent field plunged into the sea, leaving forty-five dead. But the biggest disaster had yet to happen, forever to be remembered as Piper Alpha. And there were offshore veterans ready to link that tragedy with the financial cuts that followed the crisis of 1986. Not that the dangers had been ignored. In fact, with the death-rate reaching 50 per year, Shell Expro and its main drilling contractors, SEDCO, approached Dr Peter Clarke, principal of Robert Gordon's Institute of Technology (now Robert Gordon University) on the subject of training and education. As a result, safety and survival courses were soon added to the higher national certificate courses in oil technology, and RGIT was on its way to becoming the industry's world centre of excellence.

But nothing quite prepared the oil world for Piper Alpha, the name of a platform owned by Armand Hammer and his Occidental company. Hammer, born in 1899, was an extraordinary American businessman, uniquely placed as one who had never allowed even the Cold War to interrupt his cordial connection with the Soviet Union. From a very early age he had dealt successfully and face-to-face with every leader from Lenin to those of modern times and acted as a trusted link between his own government and the Soviets in times of political crisis. In 1957 Armand Hammer bought the small Occidental Petroleum Corporation of California and turned it into something massive. Predictably, he was there with all the big company names and legendary individuals like Paul Getty when North Sea oil presented its potential of riches.

In what was said to have been a clandestine arrangement with the Foreign Office, Hammer gained the Piper and some other platforms in the Moray Firth sector of the North Sea. As far as single platforms were concerned, Piper was deemed the world's most prolific oil producer. But it had had its technical troubles and, with cutbacks in maintenance, was said by some to be a disaster waiting to happen. When it did, on 6th July 1988, it was the biggest tragedy in the history of the oil industry, with 167 dead and sixty-two others lucky to survive. Those men came from all over the United Kingdom but Aberdeen and the North-east naturally felt the brunt of it most of all.

As Bill Mackie wrote in his splendid book *The Oilmen*: 'It marked the end of a romanticised dream of an industry known to the uninitiated only through the celluloid glamour of Hollywood. Suddenly it had become shockingly and brutally real.' The tragedy had been sparked off during maintenance by the removal of a pressure safety valve, a fact not communicated to the oncoming night-shift. In a massive explosion, the men in the accommodation module stood no chance as their living quarters plunged to the bottom of the sea. The sixty-two who did survive the heat and flames had to find their escape routes across scorching hot decks before jumping from a great height into the water.

It was the ultimate nightmare, with the helicopters unable to penetrate the heat and smoke. Those in melting survival suits had to plan their own salvation, faces blackened with smoke. Men like electrician Bob Ballantyne were eventually taken to Aberdeen Royal Infirmary by helicopter. Bob never went back. Instead, he gained an honours degree in cultural history at Aberdeen University and gave his life to the teaching of people with special educational needs. Mike Jennings, a former RAF radio officer who was Piper Alpha's flight information man, was in the packed cinema at the time of the first explosion.

Mike dropped a hundred feet into the water and surfaced amid a sea of fire, grasping a piece of partition as it floated past. He was picked up and taken to hospital in Aberdeen, where he was

Smoke and flames pour from the stricken Piper Alpha platform

visited by Prince Charles and Princess Diana, as well as Mrs Thatcher but not, he pointed out, by anyone from Occidental or his own company. Unlike Bob Ballantyne, however, he went back to another platform after three weeks. 'If I hadn't done it then, I would never have done it,' he said. Thirty men were never found. After Piper Alpha, Occidental paid compensation to survivors and families then sold up its assets and left the North Sea.

Sadly for Aberdeen, the heaviest loss was suffered by the local Wood Group: 47 of the 167 victims. Chairman Ian Wood, who had shown so much enterprise in joining the big players of the oil world, was later to say: 'Piper Alpha has left me deeply scarred. You have to live through it to understand, finishing up with huge amounts of guilt and concerns that you have to come to terms with over a period of time. But it never leaves you.' A memorial to the oilmen, a stark sculpture, stands in the serenity of Hazlehead Park, Aberdeen. After Piper Alpha it took five years for new legislation to come into force. But men like Mike Jennings retained an uneasy feeling that it could all happen again.

Place for Women

Contrary to the image of macho oilmen, from the early days there was always a place for women, first in the domestic and medical departments with a 1996 figure of 429 female employees. But the range of jobs increased till you found ladies like Sarah Wingrove working as a roustabout and Alison Gallagher, a physics and petroleum engineering graduate, reaching the position of regional managing director for the Schlumberger organisation. That kind of policy was encouraged by the chief executive of Schlumberger who was, interestingly, the Aberdonian Euan Baird, son of the distinguished Dugald Baird, world-famous professor of midwifery at Aberdeen University, and Dr May Baird, a formidable lady in North-east administrative circles in the middle of the century.

Through all the revolution of oil and its impact on North-east life, there was inevitably a social downside from the effects of family separation. There was a temptation for wives left alone on shore and for the men coming home there was the added problem of alcohol. At one stage Aberdeen had the highest divorce rate in the United Kingdom (7.5 per cent, against the average 6.4 per cent), perhaps due as much to the affluent lifestyle as anything. Some oilmen were reported to be leading double lives, saying they were offshore for a month when it was only two weeks, so that they could disappear somewhere else. Calls for compassionate leave ashore were said to increase when Rangers were playing Celtic, raising to insupportable levels the number of grannies who could die at any one time. Even resurrections, for a second time round, were not beyond the bounds of holy miracle.

Through all its ebbs and flows the oil industry has built a tale of industrial romance that remains hard to grasp even after all these years. Aberdeen has been transformed from a provincial city with strongly rural overtones into an international centre, with a new swagger of confidence and an economic prosperity beyond belief. Hotels and restaurants have mushroomed in all directions while the general standard of living has broadened horizons immeasurably. Of course it is always difficult to separate how much change is due to oil and how much would have happened in the normal course of time.

Returning exiles in search of the city they knew still find reassurance in familiar landmarks, like the statue of Robert Burns, brooding as ever in Union Terrace, perhaps in disapproval of the passing pigeons, or the heroic figure of William Wallace, flashing his mighty sword in the direction of His Majesty's Theatre. But the average Aberdonian seems to talk with less of the native tones than their parents or grandparents, especially the young, who follow a kind of modern-speak which may owe less to oil than to the general effects of television and popular culture. The accent is still there, producing an amusing hybrid of conversation, such as this, overheard in a restaurant: 'Ach, I dinna like praans wi' ma avocado!' Straight from *Scotland the What?!*

So the clubs and pubs and disco dens have spread themselves in psychedelic flare and blare, spilling on to Union Street the detritus of a consumer society more concerned with self than with the well-being of community. That main street of wonderful creation has followed others, like Edinburgh's Princes Street, to the realms of cheap-john shops and architecture, with their look of fickle transience. Of course by no means all of that can be laid at the door of oil, which has bestowed a bounty of such unbelievable riches as to far outweigh its disadvantages.

So how long will oil last? When British Petroleum sold its Forties Field to a new entrant, it seemed like the beginning of the end for what had come to be known as the United Kingdom Continental Shelf. Shell, too, were on the move. The big boys were pulling out. The party was over, they said, and Aberdeen would have to think about a life after oil. It had been good while it lasted, generating more than £300 billion and reinvesting more than £200 billion. For the United Kingdom as a whole it had meant tax revenues of £100 billion and oil-related jobs of one kind or another amounting to 265,000, one-third of them in Scotland. But life is short on certainties. By the dawn of the twenty-first century there was clear evidence that oil was far from finished. Though the Shells and BPs were now searching in other parts of the world, it emerged that they had brought up no more than 'the easy stuff'. With new techniques, the pundits reckoned there could be as much again to be harvested from under the sea, taking us deep into the new century.

New Breed

Small and medium-sized companies, now labelled 'the new entrants', cropped up from all directions to see what they could do with the leftovers now that the main banquet was supposed to be finished. A company like Cairn Energy, led by former Scottish rugby captain Bill Gammell, had shown what could be done. Buying up wells from Shell off the coast of India, at rock-bottom prices, it raised its share-price within eighteen months from £2 to £20, joining the Stock Exchange's Footsie 100 in the process. In the face of pessimism, a company like EnCana discovered a lucrative new field called Buzzard, sixty miles north-east of Aberdeen, with an estimated 1.2 billion barrels and reserves beyond that. With oil prices soaring in 2005–06, the latest round of licences on offer drew the biggest ever rush of bidders.

So who knows what lies ahead? Future historians will bring us the answers. Meanwhile, Aberdeen's own Wood Group built a worldwide reputation, employing 13,000 people in thirty-four countries, with 3,000 engineers based in Houston alone and manufacturing plants as far afield as China and Russia. Ian Wood, who collected a well-merited knighthood for his example, diverted his company into areas like gas-turbine overhaul and became such an international figure that the North Sea came to account for only 20 per cent of its activities. Like Ian Wood, David Craig and family

Sir Ian Wood joined the oil industry in a big way

emerged from a fishing background to become another large international conglomerate, offering everything from supply boats to catering services.

The expertise created in Aberdeen would follow the oil industry no matter where it went, in similar fashion to the big oil producers. But the vision of the Woodses and the Craigses was shared by far too few leaders of British industry who, by and large, missed the boat of opportunity when it sailed their way in the twentieth century. It was said to be God's last chance for the British. But could there be a second chance? Would the oilmen of the new century have the vision, the drive and the nerve to create a new age of North Sea oil?

Bill Mackie recalled one of the early American bosses, Jack Marshall, who said he lived at a time when they had been given 'the centre cut of the melon'. There was a real possibility that a mouth-watering portion of the fruit would still be there for an adventurous taker.

CHAPTER 44

A Place in Our Time

A prestigious dinner at the Aberdeen Music Hall in May 2005 was more than a social night-out for the large gathering that represented the full spectrum of local life, from business and the professions to trade unions, churches, voluntary services and the armed forces. It marked a new beginning for the Burgesses of Guild, one of the city's oldest institutions, which was seeking to redefine its role in the twenty-first century. Long gone were the days when the burgesses were charged with guarding the burgh's laws and customs, even standing up to fight and die as its protectors.

How serious that duty had been can be seen from the Battle of Harlaw, near Inverurie in 1411, when Provost Robert Davidson led his men to help defeat the invading Highlanders. The provost himself fell in that battle and was brought back to be buried in St Nicholas churchyard. The burgesses were responsible citizens involved in business and trade (fishermen, clergymen and lawyers were excluded!) whose loyalty to king and community was rewarded with trading privileges. Their numbers were divided between the Craft Guild and the Merchant Guild, according to whether you were a craftsman creating the goods or the merchant selling them. The latter tended to be a smaller elite of the most influential merchants in town who, in time, came to be known simply as the Guild, or the Guildry, the word 'merchant' dropping out of use.

There was a history of friction between the two groups, the craftsmen feeling that they had the lesser of the deal. The situation was not helped by a charter issued to all Scottish burghs in 1364 which favoured the merchant class and undermined the position of the craftsmen burgesses. The merchants had exclusive rights to conduct all export and import trade. The craftsmen found strength in their Incorporated Trades, formed in the sixteenth century to protect their rights and promote their standing within the burgh. Their headquarters were to be found in the Green until 1847, when they moved to the magnificent Trinity Hall in Union Street. That endured until the more commercial days of the 1960s, when it was sold to become the shopping mall opposite Belmont Street.

The Incorporated Trades, which had become a highly influential body in town, then moved to a new purpose-built Trinity Hall on Holburn Street, housing as ever the seven members: Hammermen, Bakers, Wrights and Coopers, Tailors, Shoemakers, Weavers and Fleshers. In earlier times they were dealt another blow by the Government Act of 1846 which removed privileges and trade monopolies. They managed to survive as a provident and charitable institution, living up to their motto, 'Force is stronger by union', and prospering into the modern age.

Meanwhile, the merchants had continued in their more privileged position, buying and selling at home and overseas and importing manufactured good and agricultural produce. For all of this, however, they paid a considerably higher entry fee to the town council. But their role as virtual guardians of the burgh began to be eroded in the 1830s, with the Burgh Reform Act which set in motion the slow democratisation of local government. Their trading privileges diminished and their numbers declined to a point where they faced possible extinction. Whereas there were a thousand burgesses at the beginning of the nineteenth century, when the population was 40,000, that number was down to 337 by 1867. It remained at that level for the next hundred years until the discovery of oil in the North Sea, proving once again that nothing stands still forever.

With the city population standing above 200,000, membership had reached beyond 900 in the new century. In 1983 a major change in the rules admitted women as full burgesses, marked by an historic ceremony at the town council meeting when seven women received their certificates. For the record, they were Lilian Stephen, Freda Mutch, Diane Morgan, Dorothy Grassie, Anne Cocker, Marjorie Bosomworth and Elizabeth Blacklaw. Through all the changes, the senior official continued to bear the title of dean of guild, dating back to 1427. At one time his duties ranged from the upkeep of council property and exercising the authority of a judge to supervising the burning of witches. His right to vote on certain town council matters survived until 1965. In 1996 a Guildry Award Scheme was introduced, giving financial support to selected citizens in educational and vocational training.

So to that Music Hall dinner of 2005, presided over by the reigning dean of guild, Mr Andrew Lewis, member of the well-known shipbuilding family, and addressed by Malcolm Brinded, executive director of Shell. With the theme of the evening, 'A Place In Our Time', Mr Lewis was seeking a modern definition of the burgess role. He said, 'We no longer ask that you take up arms to defend the city but we do ask that you become ambassadors, at home and abroad, to protect and promote its good name. We want to help Aberdeen to become an even better place than it is.'

To that end, he foresaw a role in which the burgesses would offer their vast range of knowledge, skills and expertise, covering all aspects of local life, to those in need of them. It was a starting-point, led by a member of that Lewis dynasty that had included his grandfather, Sir Andrew, the lord provost who inspired the massive fundraising scheme to build a new Royal Infirmary in the 1930s.

CHAPTER 45

Labour Takes Control

In much the same way as the charismatic Winston Churchill was replaced as prime minister by the inscrutable and rather colourless Clement Attlee, so was his friend Sir Thomas Mitchell followed into the provost's chair by Duncan Fraser, a Rothes man who had worked as a commercial traveller in Glasgow before coming to Aberdeen in 1903 to manage a drapery store.

Duncan Fraser had the distinction of being the first-ever Labour lord provost of the city, at a time when men of socialist principles were reluctant to have much to do with capitalism. That did not, however, prevent some of them becoming businessmen and Mr Fraser opened his own shop in Schoolhill in 1912. He was an intelligent and decent man but sober-faced in a jowly kind of way and not blessed in the personality stakes. In his drapery business, he imagined himself in some kind of competition with the much bigger Isaac Benzie's shop round the corner in George Street.

That gave rise to a story about one of his young assistants who was giving advice to a customer one day. As Duncan Fraser passed across his shop floor he overheard the young girl say to the lady: 'No, but ye'll get it roun' the corner at Isaac Benzie's.' As the lady left, he stalked across to remonstrate with the assistant and to say, 'What on earth can the lady get at Isaac Benzie's that she can't get here?' The young girl looked up into his face and said quite innocently, 'A bus to Culter, Mr Fraser!'

So, the arrival of a Labour lord provost on Aberdeen Town Council coincided roughly with the situation at Westminster, where Mr Attlee's government was embarking on the first real bout of socialism that Britain had experienced. The National Health Service and a full programme of nationalisation were on their way and local government would now be largely influenced by dictates from afar, with less sign of local flair and imagination. Lord Provost Fraser's time, therefore, was not one of notable initiatives, nor was the recent expectation of knighthoods likely to affect him. But he did collect a CBE in 1950 and two years later he became a chevalier of the Legion of Honour. He retired in 1951 and died in 1965.

T. Scott Sutherland

The Conservatives, who had dominated local politics in Aberdeen for so long, generally labelling themselves as 'Progressives', were still a lively element into the 1950s, even if their day seemed to be drawing to a close. They had fiery debaters in men like Frank Magee, an Englishman with a fine turn of phrase, and T. Scott Sutherland, local architect and entrepreneur who tended to swat his socialist opponents verbally as if they were a troublesome infestation. Scott Sutherland, whose name arises elsewhere, was that same remarkable man who had suffered a horrifying accident as a child and later wrote his revealing book called *Life on One Leg*. He did, however, appreciate the pitfall of an *Evening Express* reporter who, in the haste of catching the late edition, wrote of a heated debate one day that 'Councillor Sutherland sprang to his feet!'

T. Scott Sutherland, architect and entrepreneur extraordinary

William D. Reid

But for all the power of their rhetoric, neither of these two men was destined for the civic chair. Indeed, there would be only one more incumbent from the right-wing of politics before that brand went into a lengthy decline. For a brief spell, after Labour's Duncan Fraser, they made a comeback in the person of William D. Reid, a Peterhead man who became a lawyer in Aberdeen and had served on the town council since 1934. Of dignified appearance, Lord Provost Reid suffered from a persona which suggested superciliousness but may have been no more than natural reserve. His skill as a bridge player and deep interest in cricket and the art world may give us a clue to his inner self.

During the Second World War he had occupied a key role as controller of civil defence and the city's emergency committee, terms which may sound alien to a modern audience but were vital at a time of bombing raids and the possibility of a German invasion of Britain. Big changes in the distribution of town council seats in 1952 meant that Lord Provost Reid's flirtation with the top position lasted for just one year. As far as the Conservative element was concerned, the party was over for the foreseeable future, with Labour returning to establish themselves. For a city well removed from the industrial grime and hardship of the Central Belt, with a vast influence from its rural hinterland, it was something of a puzzle that Aberdeen had developed such a left-wing bias.

Bob Cooney

In a way rather hard to imagine today, the Communist Party was not insignificant in its ability to stir political feelings, with outstanding orators like Bob Cooney spouting invective from their soap-boxes towards the capitalist system in general and the United States in particular. Another leading Communist of the day was Archie Lennox, grandfather of rock singer Annie Lennox and brother of Lord Provost Robert Lennox.

A veteran in the International Brigade in the Spanish Civil War, Bob Cooney had his hard knot of followers not only in the city but in the douce little burghs around the North-east like Turriff and Peterhead, where Communists even gained a toehold on the local councils. That extremity of politics, however, took an almost fatal blow when the Soviet tanks rolled in to suppress local opposition in Hungary in 1956 and later in Czechoslovakia. It was a brutality too far for many dedicated Communists, who threw away their party cards in disgust. Back in Aberdeen, however, a minor matter in the 1950s gives some hint of the left-wing mood, when the trades council discussed a motion from a prominent little postman, who suggested that he and his colleagues should refuse to deliver postal copies of *Readers Digest* because of its 'American propaganda'!

Professor John M. Graham

The Labour Party returned to power in 1952, proud to elect a lord provost who was also a professor of theology, a man of fair face and sound reason whose high professional standing would surely defuse any west-end criticism that the Labour councillors were a bunch of rabble-rousers. Nobody could object to Professor John M. Graham, a West of Scotland man who was indeed a good advertisement for his party and ambassador for the city, and who would serve three years in the fifties and return for a second term in the sixties.

After such lofty beginnings, the Labour group settled to provostships that would draw from the more likely ranks of artisan pursuit, not necessarily the worse for that, and producing people of integrity and diligence who would work hard for their community, albeit in a less colourful age. Professor Graham's first term ended in 1955, when he was succeeded by George Stephen, a postal worker with a penchant for writing poetry. Graham remained as leader of the socialist group on the town council but caused a stir two years later when he resigned from that position, strongly disagreeing with his Labour colleagues in their determination to scrap the primary departments of the Grammar School and the High School for Girls.

Postie and Poet

Like so many of his predecessors, George Stephen was not a native of the city but a Forgue man, who arrived in time for Skene Street School and later the Central. Out of school at thirteen, he was a postal messenger before becoming the country postman at Cruden Bay. It was during his time as a Buchan postie that George Stephen took to writing vernacular poetry, a hobby which had its first public exposure in the local paper in Peterhead but proceeded to engage him for the rest of his life. He shared that enthusiasm with his fellow pioneer of socialism, Prime Minister Clement Attlee, who later discovered they had both served in the fierce encounter of Gallipoli in the First World War and presented him with a poem he had written as they landed there. George Stephen served a double term, after which Professor Graham was persuaded to return to the provost's chair in 1961. It was rumoured that even Labour councillors wanted to avoid appointing city treasurer G.R. McIntosh, a rugged individualist to whom charm was something of a stranger. The professor was re-elected lord provost but ran into ill health before taking early retirement to live in Comrie.

Norman Hogg, once an apprentice baker with Mitchell and Muil, went from national organiser of the Scottish Bakers' Union to the role of lord provost in 1964, little knowing that he had produced a namesake who would take matters even further from his working-class roots. Son Norman, a product of Ruthrieston School, became Labour MP for Cumbernauld and Kilsyth, as the first step on a political journey that would transport him to the Upper Chamber of Westminster as Lord Hogg of Cumbernauld, with other accolades including that of lord high commissioner to the General Assembly of the Church of Scotland.

A painter to trade, Robert Lennox was next on the block for the first of two terms as lord provost, fiercely opposing the reorganisation of local government in the 1970s but nevertheless taking up his position as the first civic leader of the new Aberdeen District Council in 1975. As housing convener, he was once carpeted by his own Labour group for opposing a rent increase for municipal houses. He eventually broke ties with the Labour Party and stood as an independent in 1980. True to a family spirit of independence, Robert Lennox also refused to sit for the provost's portrait, dismissing a custom dating back to 1600 as 'a largely superficial affair' costing thousands. Even when he died in 2001, aged ninety-two, he had decreed that there would be no announcement until after his cremation. And so it was. Some people prefer to be different.

Between the two terms of Provost Lennox, Aberdeen ran into a problem with the appointment of Labour's James Lamond in 1970, when he was already the prospective parliamentary candidate for Oldham East. That general election came within months and Provost Lamond, who worked for the North-East Regional Hospital Board, was faced with a double life that seemed unsustainable. After a year, he resigned and devoted himself to the parliamentary role, which he maintained for the next twenty-two years, after which he returned to the civic scene of Aberdeen. Mr Lamond was followed by another of the younger breed who would also take the political road south. John Smith, a charismatic figure around town, was northern manager of the Dunfermline Building Society when politics beckoned. He entered the town council and became lord provost at the age of forty-one, among the youngest in the history of the city. By the mid 1970s, however, he went from lord provost to Lord of the Realm, whisked off to Whitehall as minister of state at the Scottish Office, bolstering Harold Wilson's Labour government, with the title of Lord Kirkhill, which reflected the Torry ward he had served for twelve years.

Alex Collie

After Robert Lennox's second term, the civic chair was occupied for three years by William J. Fraser, a postal superintendent and former Scottish chairman of the Labour Party, giving way in 1980 to a man who was destined to set records. Alexander Collie, who was born above the Prince of Wales Bar in St Nicholas Lane in 1913, continued that Labour tradition of tradesmen stepping into the role of lord provost. Alex was a baker with the Co-op for more than forty years but topped that length of service with close on fifty years on the town council, a feat of endurance that gained him the freedom of his native city. Alex Collie was one of those cheery little figures who earn themselves labels like the People's Provost, striding out with the long step of a short man but blessed with a big heart. As parks convener, he headed that phenomenal run of success when Aberdeen claimed the Britain in Bloom trophy on a record eight occasions. Since he was also a fanatical supporter of Aberdeen Football Club, it was a clever trick of nature to have him in place as lord provost in 1983, chest bursting over the balcony of the Town House as 100,000 Aberdonians lined the streets to welcome home the triumphant Dons team from Gothenburg, fresh from their European Cup Winners' Cup victory over the great Real Madrid.

Growing up in Willowbank Road during the Depression shaped the political future of men like Henry Rae, who became lord provost in 1984. But he would serve in the navy during the war before venturing towards the civic scene, returning first to life as a conductor and then a driver on the tramcars, later recalling the passengers he would convey to the greyhound stadium at the Bridge of Dee and the football at Pittodrie. An active trade unionist, he was a Labour councillor for twenty-two years and died in 1999 at the age of seventy-three.

Robert Robertson

From a tram driver to a railwayman was the move that brought Robert A. Robertson to the provostship in 1988, during a political career that was marked by controversy. Having joined the old Aberdeen Town Council in 1965, Mr Robertson then opted for the new-fangled Grampian Regional Council in the massive reorganisation of 1974. But there he was at loggerheads with the ruling Conservative group as he pressed for changes in policy. He returned to the Town House in 1980, became lord provost eight years later but ran into open conflict with his own Labour group, sticking resolutely to his opinions, refusing to toe the line and finally losing the party whip. Mr Robertson was in office as the city faced the tragedy of the Piper Alpha disaster in the oil-fields of the North Sea.

James Wyness

James Wyness, who took the chair in 1992, was a Labour activist from his teenage years, becoming a shop steward in Lewis's shipyard while serving his time as an electrician. He then followed a career in the merchant navy as an engineering officer, after which his life took a totally different course. Jim Wyness proceeded to Aberdeen University, where he gained a joint honours degree in history and politics, applying that education to his subsequent career as a teacher at Hazlehead Academy and then to Aberdeen District Council, where he gained the lord provost's chain.

A Woman at Last

Margaret Farquhar, the city's first woman Lord Provost

In 1996 the mould of male domination was finally broken with the election of Margaret Farquhar as the very first lady to hold the office of lord provost in its 724-year history. No better representative of down-to-earth Aberdonianism could have been found. Mrs Farquhar entered the town council in 1971, following in the footsteps of her husband, William. That arrival at the Town House, representing the Northfield ward, was occasioned by the resignation of the short-term lord provost, James Lamond MP, who was on his way to Westminster. Her involvement in a plethora of public duties, from St Machar Housing Co-operative to the Grampian Girls Brigade, was hardly lessened when she took on the ultimate responsibility at the Town House. Two hip operations for Mrs Farquhar brought her colleague, Margaret Smith, to the task of deputising in the absence of the lord provost. It proved a suitable apprenticeship for the lady who would indeed succeed her.

A native of Leicester, Margaret Smith trained as a PE teacher and moved on to community roles in local government before her career brought her to the North-east. She entered the council in 1988 and became its leader in 1996. Aberdeen was now acclimatised to the idea of a woman lord provost and Ms Smith took over in 1999. Her four years of endeavour, however, were overshadowed by controversy on a single issue – the fact that she embarked on a number of overseas trips on which she took as a travelling companion, a lady she had met on a community project in Glasgow thirty years earlier. At one point, the *Evening Express* alleged that taxpayers had forked out £33,770 on the travel costs of the lady in question, revealed as Mrs Lesley Baird, an Aberdeen graduate who lived with her husband and children in Lenzie, near Glasgow. It became a major topic around the city and, in an interview, Lord Provost Smith expressed her hurt and anger at the inference of 'scandal' and defended her right to have the help of a companion.

In the curious way that events are shaped, that controversy played a major part in breaking more than fifty years of Labour domination in the municipal affairs of Aberdeen. There were other matters in the equation but the Margaret Smith issue was the catalyst, proving that the power of the press is by no means a thing of the past. Labour's dogged defence of their colleague was taken as arrogance and brought a public outcry that was promptly reflected in votes. In 2003, when the whole council was up for re-election, the previous balance of twenty Labour and fourteen Liberal Democrat seats was reversed precisely enabling the Lib Dems to gain power in an alliance with the three Conservatives. Six Nationalists made up the complement.

John Reynolds

In 2003 John Reynolds became the first non-Labour Provost for fifty years

That change of fortune brought John Reynolds to the lord provost's office, introducing a new breed to the civic office, less entrenched in the political predictability to which Aberdonians had long become accustomed. After the bakers, electricians and posties, here was a Blackpool man from an occupation quite different to those of his predecessors. The affable John Reynolds, the second successive incumbent from England, came north in 1969 as a twenty-year-old trouble-shooter for the ABC entertainment organisation after their manager at the bowling alley in the former City Cinema in George Street was badly beaten up.

He met his future wife within days and decided to settle for life as an adopted Aberdonian! After various managerial posts, he eventually became self-employed as a newsagent through a franchise with the newsagents R.S. McColl. John Reynolds faced up to the innovations of a new century, not least on his own municipal doorstep, where, on the very first day of gay marriage legality, two of the Lib Dem councillors, Neil Fletcher and John Stewart, went down the aisle of King's College chapel to declare their civil partnership.

Revolution was in the air. As John Reynolds completed his term of office in 2007, to be followed as lord provost by his colleague Peter Stephen, the Council then made a dramatic appointment. For the post of deputy lord provost they chose a newly elected Nationalist, John West, an eighteen-year-old law student whose duties would include chairing meetings (though he had never attended one), hosting civic events and representing the Queen when dignitaries visited the city. Some older councillors fumed in disbelief. Had the world gone mad? Young John just beamed the smile of innocence – and welcomed his sister Kirsty, another new arrival at the 2007 election, who was promptly appointed the city's spokeswoman on education. At least she was twenty-one.

CHAPTER 46

The Fourth Estate

In a modern world of instant communication, with television cameras now taking you live to the heat of battle zones, it is hard to imagine a time when there wasn't even a newspaper. How did people know what was going on outby? In the age of horse and carriage, augmented only by the flight of the homing pigeon, how did people know about composers like Johann Sebastian Bach in far-off Germany, or what was happening to Henry VIII and his many wives, or Mary, Queen of Scots down south? How did a boy from the North-east, John Ogilvie by name, find his way to Rome to become such a figure of significance in the Catholic Church as to be hanged for treason back at Glasgow Cross in 1615 – and later canonised?

Since news was not exactly hot off the press, the citizens in an age of reason and patience would presumably await the messenger on horseback who would eventually relate happenings in the wider world, with whatever accuracy, before it was further spread by word of mouth. (The notorious fallibility of that process may have given rise to that earlier comment from Carlyle about rumour.) The mechanics of all this are hard to imagine.

The situation did change, however, at least as far as Aberdeen and the North-east were concerned, with an historic event of great importance to Scotland – the Battle of Culloden in 1746. And the man who brought about that change was a young Aberdonian, James Chalmers, whose father was professor of divinity at Marischal College and who himself seemed destined for the Church when he went to Oxford University.

Before we entertain the story of James Chalmers, however, it is worth recalling that the art of printing had actually been introduced to Aberdeen in 1621 by Edward Raban, who was born in England of German parents and had worked in Edinburgh and St Andrews before being invited north as the town's printer. In 1643 he took over a bookseller's shop in Broad Street. A man of refined taste, Raban produced books of the highest artistic standard, his finest venture being the *Aberdeen Almanac*, a periodical that reached a circulation of 50,000 by 1677 and proceeded to have a long and healthy life. The first attempt at an Aberdeen newspaper took place in 1657, when the town council commissioned Raban's successor, James Brown, to produce a weekly journal and a stationer, John Forbes, to sell it. Little is known of this venture, but when Brown died in 1661, Mr Forbes and his son took over its production at Raban's old shop in Broad

Street. Son John continued after his father's death and he in turn was succeeded by his son-in-law, James Nicol.

We can now catch up with James Chalmers, the professor's son who had gone off to Oxford. While in the City of Dreaming Spires he became so intrigued with the art of printing that he moved to London, where he joined the House of Watts, the leading printer of the day. He had also gained experience with James Nicol back home, and on the day in 1736 when the latter gave up the post of town printer, James Chalmers applied for the job, little knowing the significance that this would have in the history of newspapers in Aberdeen and the North-east. Setting up his own printing works in Castle Street, he took on the role of official printer to the city and the University of Aberdeen. Forever a Royalist, Chalmers was inevitably caught up in the events of the '45 Rebellion, when Bonnie Prince Charlie marched south as far as Derby, only to turn back and be hounded by the Duke of Cumberland all the way to Culloden via Aberdeen. There are differing reports as to how Chalmers arrived at that decisive battle. One said the city asked him to go north and bring back an account of events for the people of Aberdeen. His own grandson later said he had actually served with Cumberland's army.

In 1748 James Chalmers founded the *Aberdeen's Journal* (now *The Press and Journal*)

News-sheet

Either way, within two days, the defeat of the Jacobites at Culloden on 16th April 1746 was fully described in an eye-witness account, and contained in a news-sheet which rolled off the Chalmers press in Castle Street. Aberdonians absorbed this novelty with great interest, but were not to know what seeds were being sown in the history of journalism. That news-sheet gave James Chalmers the idea of starting a regular newspaper. His military and other duties delayed the process but, on 5th January 1748, the very first copy of *The Aberdeen's Journal* (as it was called before they dropped the clumsy apostrophe *s*) landed in the homes of the city, at first a weekly production but later the daily paper which flourishes to this day as *The Press and Journal*. It is not only unbroken in sequence since that very first issue but also one of the oldest surviving newspapers in the world.

That original paper amounted to a single sheet, folded over to give four pages of foolscap size, divided into three columns. In days before competition, the newspaper 'scoop' was of less significance, but James Chalmers was soon presented with a gem of a story, albeit one that came a little too close for personal comfort. Having occasion to visit London, he was travelling by ship, the fastest means of transport at the time, when the vessel fell into the hands of a French privateer. He and his fellow passengers were held prisoner for five days before being relieved of all their possessions and dumped in London.

His success encouraged others to follow the inky way, beginning in 1752 with the *Aberdeen Intelligencer* (where did they find those clumsy names?) and extending to the twentieth century, with publications that ranged from the *Aberdeen Almanack* to the *Citizen*, an attempt by the Labour Party to run its own newspaper. There was no more reputable rival than the *Aberdeen Herald*, a Liberal paper founded in 1832 and edited by James Adam, a south-west of Scotland man whose fearless attacks on legal and political figures were the stuff of first-class journalism. In the *Herald* he fostered a poet's corner which highlighted the talents of writers like William Thom, Alexander Taylor, William Cadenhead, William Anderson and William Forsyth (editor of the rival *Journal*), a literary feature that has never been surpassed in the history of North-east journalism.

In the main, however, the *Journal* was too well established and most of the opposition was either absorbed or died a death. Chalmers himself died in 1764, to be followed in the business by his son, James, who came to the task via Marischal College, Cambridge University and some printing experience in London. He was just twenty-three years of age, but no less a figure than his father in a career which would stretch for the next forty-six years. In that time he played host to such luminaries as Robert Burns and recorded events which ranged from the construction of Union Street and the Aberdeen–Port Elphinstone Canal to the visit of the inimitable Dr Johnson.

The influence of this remarkable family was far from over when Chalmers the Second died in 1810. Then it was the turn of his son David, only twenty-two, to extend the dynasty beyond the century mark with another forty-four years in charge. In matters of newspaper circulation, we need to keep in mind that the population of Aberdeen was only a tenth of what it is in the twenty-first century, and that each copy was passed from house to house and read by large numbers of people. The seemingly modest figures in David Chalmers' time show that the *Aberdeen Journal* was selling 2,231 copies, set against *The Scotsman's* 1,914, the *Glasgow Herald's* 1,615 and the *Dundee Courier's* 250. The *Glasgow Herald* came into existence thirty-five years after the Aberdeen paper but had the advantage of being a daily from the start. Even today, however, when they are all dailies, *The Press and Journal* still outsells the other three with a circulation of around 84,000, all of them having dropped back from peak sales in the previous century. The *Dundee Courier*, which used to out-sell the *P&J*, now takes second place with a circulation of 80,000, followed by *The Herald* on 74,000, with *The Scotsman*, often regarded as the 'national paper', lagging in fourth place at 62,000.

Free Press

In 1854 David Chalmers handed over the management to his two sons, James and John, no doubt sensing that a new-found opposition might need the energies of younger men. A year earlier, after previous contenders had failed, a serious challenger arose in the form of *The Aberdeen Free Press*, a paper that became a daily publication in 1872, four years before the *Journal*.

Its first two editors were impressive North-east figures: William McCombie, a talented essayist and journalist, followed by Dr William Alexander, who wrote the great Doric classic of Aberdeenshire rural life, *Johnny Gibb of Gushetneuk*, in 1871. While the *Free Press* espoused the Liberal cause, the *Journal* had maintained political neutrality, a matter of concern for local Conservatives, who felt their lack of success at that point was partly due to an absence of newspaper backing. After toying with the idea of starting their own newspaper, the Conservatives took a more decisive step, formed a company called the Aberdeen and North of Scotland Newspaper and Printing Company, and bought *The Aberdeen Journal*.

So after 128 years of Chalmers family ownership the paper was sold, though the reigning brothers were taken on board as directors, along with names like Colonel Innes of Learney, Alexander Davidson of Desswood, William Ferguson of Kinmundy, Henry Wolrige-Gordon of Esslemont and Thomas Balmer of Gordon Castle, Fochabers – a considerable gathering of landed gentry from outside the city. However, the arrival of new brooms may have been the fillip required. Immediately, *The Aberdeen Journal* became a daily paper, and engaged in a regular battle for circulation, in which editor William Forsyth pointed out to the directors that his four-page paper was competing against the eight pages of the *Free Press*.

Evening Express

But they had other things on their minds. Soon they were announcing the arrival of the *Evening Express*, launched with very little publicity but making its mark in spectacular fashion from the very beginning. It consisted of four pages, with six columns each, and the printing machines were hard pressed to meet the demand. Emphasising the immediacy of the news, they peppered the pages with a sub-heading: 'This Day'. With stories like court cases, it caught readers' imaginations.

Returning to William Forsyth, editor of *The Aberdeen Journal*, his high intellect was in contrast to the impossible nature of his handwriting in an age when the legibility of handwritten copy was important, especially to compositors, who set the type on piece-rates. In their 1978 chronicle of Aberdeen Journals, George Fraser and Ken Peters, both distinguished editors of the group, tell the amusing story of one compositor, completely defeated by Forsyth's handwriting, who went back to seek clarification from the source. The editor stroked his chin for a moment . . . and finally had to confess that he couldn't make head or tail of it himself. On the same theme, another compositor claimed that, if given his fiddle, he might be able to turn the editor's hieroglyphics into a tune!

Broad Street

Aberdeen Journals had its ups and downs, including a move to the Adelphi, but finally it settled in Broad Street in 1894, next door to the Town House, and that would remain its home for the next seventy-six years until it moved out to the present site at Mastrick in 1970.

The old Broad Street office of Aberdeen Journals as many remember it, before the move to Mastrick in 1970

But nothing stands still. With the First World War, all human activity was thrown into confusion as the able-bodied men headed off to fates unimaginable. Keeping a newspaper alive was a struggle against rising costs and falling revenues, even if that was offset by the public appetite for news of Passchendaele and the Somme. The circulation of the *Evening Express* went up from 45,500 in 1914 to 56,700 in 1916.

If there is any consolation in war it is, ironically, that people behave towards each other in a more civilised manner. Even the rivalry between the two Aberdeen daily papers gave way to co-operation in matters of working agreements and mutual reporting. When the war was over, the benefits of such co-operation were not lost on either side and the further help that was given when the *Free Press* suffered a disastrous fire in 1919 perhaps set the scene for what happened next. In 1922 the *Free Press* and the *Journal* agreed to amalgamate, with a combined name that rolls off the tongue more easily now than it did when the North-east public was first adjusting to the *Aberdeen Press and Journal*.

Derby Pictures

Before the marriage, however, the old *Journal* had one last fling of enterprise which took its place in local folklore (and was no doubt intended as a reminder of seniority to the new partner). Since the train provided the fastest link with London, it had never been possible to publish pictures of the Derby in next morning's paper. But in 1922 William Maxwell, the editor, struck a deal with the old Picture House in Union Street to fly from London a film of the Derby for showing in the cinema, along with photographic prints for the *Journal*.

What's more, they would engage that distinguished pilot of the day, Sir Alan Cobham, to fly the plane. It went so well that Sir Alan established a record for the longest, non-stop flight in the British Isles. His target for dropping the film and prints by parachute was Torry Hill. That they landed in the backyard of a tenement at 161 Victoria Road had nothing to do with the fact that Sir Alan had never seen Aberdeen before! The parachute came unstuck in the rudder wires but landed in time for a Torry youngster, Alexander Russell, to pick up the package and run all the way to the Picture House (later the Gaumont). On that Wednesday evening of 31st May 1922 Aberdonians watched the silent movie of Captain Cuttle winning the Epsom Derby, while next morning the *Journal* had pictures of the parade before the start, a head-on at the finishing line and a side view of Captain Cuttle winning by four lengths from Tamar, with Craiganour in third place.

Having thus edged progress on its way, editor Maxwell (later to be Sir William) used his influence to ensure that the amalgamated paper would be housed in his inferior Broad Street premises and not in the far superior *Free Press* building on Union Street, which was sold off to become part of Esslemont and Macintosh's department store. To his mind, this had been a take-over. A committed Conservative, he and his paper had certainly played a part in raising that party's fortunes at the expense of the Liberals. The *Free Press*'s favourite party was already coping with the rise of socialism.

Predictably, Maxwell became editor of *The Press and Journal* but, to show it was not all one-way traffic, his London office at New Bridge Street gave way to the *Free Press* office at 149 Fleet Street. Two of the *Free Press* directors who joined the new board, Henry Alexander and Edward Watt, would later emerge on the civic scene, one following the other as lord provost of the city in the 1930s. Maxwell was still around in 1928, when the company became a take-over target involving some of the biggest names in newspapers: the Harmsworth family who gave us Lord Northcliffe and Lord Rothermere and would later own the *Daily Mail* among others, and the Berry brothers, whose modest home in Wales would produce three major press barons, Lord Kemsley, Lord Camrose and Lord Buckland.

Kemsley

The Berry company of Allied Newspapers won control, and when Camrose went off to head up *The Daily Telegraph* the Broad Street papers became part of Kemsley Newspapers. By now they had gained their current name of Aberdeen Journals. Lord Kemsley's strapping sons came north to learn the business in Aberdeen, as did his only daughter Pamela, who not only played an active part as a director but stayed on to become the Marchioness of Huntly, marrying the premier Marquis of Scotland and becoming a major figure in North-east social life from her home at Aboyne Castle. They seemed an unlikely pair: the tall, elegant lady from London and the smaller, kilted Deeside laird whose position carried the colourful label of Cock of the North. It would not be too cynical to say that she had the money and he had the title, a mutual convenience not unknown in rarefied circles. The union lasted for twenty-four years until 1965, when Lady Huntly divorced her husband, who later married Elizabeth Leigh, with whom he moved to Cranleigh, Surrey. He died there in 1987. A pilot who used to fly her Piper Comanche all over Europe, Lady Huntly lived on at Aboyne, where she died in 1998 at the age of seventy-nine.

The youngest of Lord Kemsley's sons, Oswald Berry, was not such a popular figure as his sister. Something of a tearaway who was known to wrap his car around a city lamp-post, he would appear in the office late at night, much the worse for drink and trying to tell good, solid journalists how to produce the paper. On one such occasion, a sub-editor with a short fuse, who had stood young Mr Berry till he could stand him no longer, rose from the desk and delivered a knock-out blow in the manner of Joe Louis, the reigning hero of boxing. He put on his hat and coat and went home, returning next day to accept his inevitable dismissal. His boss sympathised with the action but agreed that he could no longer work for Lord Kemsley. He would, however, recommend him to Lord Beaverbrook, and the young man became assistant editor of the *Scottish Sunday Express* in Glasgow. As for young Oswald, he met a sticky end on 8th June 1952, at the age of thirty-four, when he slipped between quayside and yacht while returning from a night out.

By the reign of Lord Kemsley, Sir William Maxwell had given way to another formidable editorial figure, William Veitch, an Edinburgh man who joined the company in London in 1910

Lord Kemsley's daughter, Pamela Berry, with her husband, the Marquis of Huntly

and had become a major force in Fleet Street as chairman of the Parliamentary Press Gallery, among other things. As editor-in-chief of *The Press and Journal*, *Evening Express* and *Weekly Journal* William Veitch proved himself a shrewd and capable leader, but a wily old fox with the twinkle of mischief about him.

St Valery

The Press and Journal and *Evening Express* had long been in the forefront of fundraising in the wake of disasters and in support of good causes. After the debacle of St Valery-en-Caux in 1940, when Gordon Highlanders were among those of the 51st (Highland) Division who were sacrificed to stave off the Germans while the Dunkirk evacuation took place, the North-east felt a debt of gratitude to the French. At risk from discovery by the Germans, the good folks of St Valery had tried to protect our men and care for the wounded. *The Press and Journal* launched a St Valery Remembrance Appeal, raising £8,700 to help rebuild their town. In the end, the money was used to build a gateway to the military cemetery, with pillars made of Kemnay granite and the gate itself made of oak from Aboyne. Lady Huntly and William Veitch were there for the presentation ceremony on 10th June 1950.

Though Veitch was in overall command, there was an obvious need for the three papers to have their individual editors, a matter that was rectified during the war. *The Press and Journal* post went to James M. Chalmers, a former compositor on the *Banffshire Journal*, who became the Buchan correspondent of the *Free Press* before his promotion to Broad Street. The first editor of the *Evening Express* was George Fraser, a railway signalman's son from Newmachar, while the *Weekly Journal* editorship went to Cuthbert Graham: two distinguished North-east journalists about whom there is more to come.

Cuthbert Graham, distinguished journalist and friend of Lewis Grassic Gibbon

Two Hundred Years

The 200th anniversary of *The Press and Journal* was celebrated on 5th January 1948 in a grand reception in the Music Hall, which was also the venue of a magnificent pageant about life in the early days of the paper, written and produced by two legendary journalists on the staff at the time, George Rowntree Harvey and W.A. Mitchell. King George VI sent his congratulations, as did the prime minister of Canada, Mr Mackenzie King, a courtesy which would have amused the founder, James Chalmers. While the latter was engaged at Culloden, very much on the side of the Hanoverians and soon to launch his newspaper, two of Mr King's great-great-grandfathers were battling on the side of Prince Charlie.

By 1950 *The Press and Journal* had a new editor in George. E. Ley Smith, a corpulent character who had joined the paper in 1915 as a boy but was soon off to the First World War in time to be wounded. A swimmer and water-polo player of international repute, he once swam out to a stranded ship offshore at Belhelvie to carry a lifeline – and to get the story to himself. The succession of editors thereafter fell to Kenneth J. Peters, whose father had run the business side of the paper as a director; Jimmy Grant, an Elgin man, who joined in 1936, working in both Edinburgh and Glasgow before serving in the Royal Artillery during the war; and Peter Watson, a native of Buckie, who followed a tradition of stepping from the technical side to the editorial having spent his early years in the Broad Street wire-room. In 1986 Mr Watson was succeeded by Harry Roulston, an Edinburgh man who was moving over from the editorship of the *Evening Express*. When Mr Roulston went back to Edinburgh as editor of the *Evening News* in 1992 he was followed as editor of *The Press and Journal* by Derek Tucker, a Liverpool man who had spent more than twenty years with the *Express and Star* in Wolverhampton.

Meanwhile, at the *Evening Express*, George Fraser was succeeded by Kenneth Peters, then Robert Anderson from Elgin, whose departure to edit the *Sunday Graphic* in London brought Rex Bawden from Newcastle. In 1962 the chair was filled by Robert Smith, a local journalist who served in the RAF during the war and remained for the next twenty-two years, putting him into an elite of long-serving editors in British journalism. Bob Smith's successful role in administration perhaps delayed his talent as an author which blossomed when he took early retirement in 1983, producing books like *Grampian Ways* and *The Granite City*.

He was followed by Harry Roulston and, in 1986, by Dick Williamson, a Morayshire man who had started his career with the Highland News Group. Jeff Teather had a brief tenure before leaving to be assistant editor of the *Evening Standard* in London. Editorship of the *Evening Express* then fell to Donald Martin, a Glaswegian who arrived from editing the *North West Evening Mail* in Barrow-in-Furness. (Mr Martin's grandfather was the distinguished Scottish journalist Jack Campbell, a leading light in the Beaverbrook organisation.) When Martin left to edit the *Evening Times* in Glasgow, his position was taken by Damian Bates, who was promoted from within.

By the late fifties, circulation was in a healthy state, the morning paper approaching 90,000 copies a day and the evening paper standing at 80,000. As ever, of course, newspapers were changing hands. An ebullient media magnate from Canada, Roy Thomson, son of a Scottish barber but a name unknown this side of the Atlantic, arrived in Edinburgh to buy *The Scotsman*, before gaining the country's first commercial television franchise. With previous experience in North America, he could confidently declare that his successful bid for Scottish Television was 'a licence to print money'. By 1959 this jolly tycoon with the bottle-bottom spectacles had largely satisfied his appetite for expansion when he bought out the entire Kemsley empire, complete with *The Sunday Times* and later *The Times*. His acquisition came as a bolt from the blue, not least at Aberdeen Journals, where Roy Thomson and his right-hand man, James Coltart, were joined as directors by William Veitch and later by Kenneth Peters, William J. Pattillo, long-time secretary and chief accountant, and Harry Robertson, the circulation manager.

Lang Stracht

So began yet another new phase of ownership in the history of James Chalmers' famous *Journal*, one which would soon face a nightmare in the 1964 outbreak of typhoid in Aberdeen – and then the upheaval of relocation. The Broad Street office of 1894 was still a warren of corridors and little rooms, warm and friendly and overflowing with legend but no longer suitable in an age of city-centre congestion and the peril of double-yellow lines. There had been several plans to move but the one that mattered came into being in 1970, when the town council acquired the old site for its own Broad Street expansion and Aberdeen Journals moved out to the heights of Mastrick, where Cockers used to grow their roses. The logistics of that flitting defy understanding, but it happened just in time for the new age of technology, and the arrival of that oil industry which would bring such unthinkable prosperity to Aberdeen and the North-east. Roy Thomson, by now Lord Thomson of Fleet, presided at the official opening in December 1970 and, some time later, the Queen Mother came with a royal endorsement of the premises, spending an afternoon at Mastrick, shaking hands with dozens of people and confirming that she had for long been a reader of the company papers.

So Aberdeen Journals went from strength to strength until 1995, when the merry-go-round of newspaper ownership took yet another spin. On this occasion the buyer was none other than the *Daily Mail*, in a reminder of the 1920s, when Lord Rothermere had failed in his take-over bid. This time it succeeded, and the James Chalmers enterprise of 1748 was set fair to continue its illustrious contribution to the history of newspapers. But that ownership lasted only until 2006, when Aberdeen Journals was put on the market once more. If the D.C. Thomson organisation, best known for its *Dundee Courier*, *Sunday Post* and popular comics, seemed an unlikely buyer, at least it brought the Aberdeen papers into Scottish ownership for the first time in generations. It was a case of Oor Wullie meets Robbie Shepherd.

Of other papers now gone, the most popular was the *Bon Accord*, a glossy-covered weekly, strong on the pictorial side and published in Union Row by Henry Munro. It ran from the 1800s through to 1959, when a strike finally closed its doors. In journalistic terms, its later figures of note included people like Philip Purser, who became a major writer in Fleet Street, and Cuthbert Graham, subsequently editor of the *Weekly Journal* in Broad Street and a significant force in North-east letters. None of this takes account of the fact that the local press, then as now, had fierce competition from national papers, many of which had fully-staffed local offices. In the mid twentieth century those competitors were headed by some memorable newspaper-men, like Adam Borthwick of the *Daily Express*, Stanley Maxton of the *Daily Mail*, Charlie Easton of D.C. Thomson papers, Ted Kidd of the *Daily Record*, Harry Dunn of *The Scotsman* and two generations of George MacDonalds of the *Glasgow Herald*. The elder of those two had the good fortune to be a close friend of Leslie Mitchell (novelist Lewis Grassic Gibbon) when he was a reporter in Aberdeen and lodged with George's mother.

Leopard

One of the most imaginative publications to grace the North-east scene took its name from the graceful animals to be found on the Aberdeen civic arms. *Leopard*, which came into existence in 1974 as a glossy magazine devoted to local life and letters, was the brainchild of one enterprising lady, Diane Morgan, who rightly sensed a gap in the market and set out to fill it. As Diane Scott from Ferryhill, she went from the Girls' High to Aberdeen University and onward to Cambridge before settling back in her home town, equipped with a law degree. She lectured at what is now the Robert Gordon University and became known as a freelance writer under her married name of Diane Morgan, contributing to national publications. With the emergence of a North Sea oil industry, Aberdeen was alive with the buzz of prosperity and about to become the oil capital of Western Europe. Colourful characters striding down Union Street with Stetson hats and big cigars were symbols of a cosmopolitan community that had brought its expertise to the new industrial revolution. Oil companies in search of good reports were keen to sponsor local events and it all added up to a business and social whirl quite novel in the douce environs of Aberdeen.

There was so much to write about, and Diane Morgan felt that magazines like *Scottish Field* and *The Scots Magazine* tended to focus on the Highlands and the Borders, Edinburgh and Glasgow, and that the North-east could stand a monthly magazine of its own; thus *Leopard*. The

timing was immaculate. She shared the view that the oil was the catalyst for a new-found confidence in Aberdonians, affecting everything from business to sport, not least the monumental achievements of Aberdeen Football Club in Europe. Coinciden- tally, there was an abundance of local literary figures in existence, both worthy of examination in themselves and available as contributors to *Leopard*. They ranged from Cuthbert Graham and David Toulmin to Hunter Diack and his great friend and controversial educationalist R.F. Mack- enzie, as well as others whose names appear in the following chapter. For the next fourteen years Diane Morgan edited *Leopard*, putting the heritage and life of Aberdeen and the North-east into clear perspective and earning herself a place in the custodianship of her native city. For a time, the magazine also benefited from the support of the Scottish Arts Council through its literary director, Trevor Royle, who authorised a North-east sup- plement within the covers of *Leopard*.

Diane Morgan, eminent local historian and founder of Aberdeen's *Leopard* magazine

Having achieved her ambition and given so much of her life to the project, she was ready to bring it to a close when she received offers for its continuance. Subsequent owners have included Outram Newspapers (the *Glasgow Herald*); local farmer and writer Charlie Allan and his daughter Susie; and the current editor and publisher, Lindy Cheyne and Ian Hamilton, who produce it from Auld Logie at Pitcaple. *Leopard* flourishes into the twenty-first century, finding its way to exiled Aberdonians in the far corners of the earth and retaining popular items like the comedy feature on 'Councillor Swick' written by local favourites Buff Hardie and Steve Robertson, with drawings by Sandy Cheyne. As for Diane Morgan, she moved into authorship with a series of popular books on the villages of Aberdeen, dealing with areas of the city once known for their own distinctive identities. She also cast a critical eye on architectural developments in 'Lost Aberdeen'. In her farewell to *Leopard* in 1988 she painted a vivid word-picture of that local genius and former pupil of Aberdeen Grammar School, Lord Byron. Ironically, it was the bicentenary of Byron's birth, and Aberdeen had scarcely noticed the event.

CHAPTER 47

Writers and Artists

The history of newspapers in Aberdeen, quite naturally, cannot be separated from the array of distinguished writers produced by the North-east over the years. Since journalism is an obvious way to earn a living while developing any talent as a writer, many of them did indeed work for Aberdeen Journals; others managed to hone their skill in prose, poetry or plays while doing something else.

William Alexander

From the nineteenth century, the name which springs instantly to mind is that of William Alexander, editor of the *Aberdeen Free Press*, who owes his fame to that classic of North-east rural life, *Johnny Gibb of Gushetneuk*. First published in 1871 and written in the so-called Doric dialect of the area, his novel had the advantage of belonging to an age when that was the everyday speech of the North-east. William Alexander was the son of a crofter and blacksmith at Rescivet, Pitcaple, who intended to be a farmer but turned to writing after losing a leg in an accident. His entrée came through William McCombie, farmer at Cairnballoch, Alford, who also owned the *North of Scotland Gazette* and later the *Aberdeen Free Press*. Alexander, who turned the *Free Press* into a daily paper, settled into family life in Aberdeen when he built the house at 19 Watson Street and brought his wife from Chapel of Garioch.

William Alexander, who wrote
Johnny Gibb of Gushetneuk

One of ten children from a hardy country lineage, he was followed into the editor's chair by a younger brother, Henry, again a man who started life elsewhere and turned to journalism only when he lost an eye at work. Though *Johnny Gibb* ran to nineteen editions, with the 1912 version enhanced by the illustrations of that distinguished Aberdeen artist, Sir George Reid, its local language would inevitably restrict its appeal beyond the area.

Lewis Grassic Gibbon

The North-east's greatest writer, J. Leslie Mitchell
(Lewis Grassic Gibbon)

No such inhibition applied to Lewis Grassic Gibbon, who, in his tragically short life, still managed to become one of the great international writers of the twentieth century, without equal in the history of his native North-east. Best known for his 1932 classic, *Sunset Song*, Grassic Gibbon achieved a spectacular feat of linguistics by creating a form entirely his own – the English language moulded into rhythms and cadences that make it sound distinctly Scottish. Thus he reached that wider audience by whom *Johnny Gibb*, sadly, would never be fully understood.

Born James Leslie Mitchell at the croft of Hillhead of Seggat, Auchterless, in 1901, he grew up at Arbuthnott in the Mearns, a lonesome boy with a head full of genius. He rebelled against the 'shoddy erudition' of teaching at Mackie Academy, Stonehaven, and marched out to become a reporter on the *Aberdeen Journal* at the age of sixteen, in the last year of the Great War. There he lodged with the mother of fellow-reporter George MacDonald, who became a life-long friend, and who spent most of his career as the *Glasgow Herald*'s man in Aberdeen. A roving spirit of the 1920s, Leslie Mitchell (for that was what he was still called) joined the army and then the RAF, pursuing his interest in archaeology through a posting to the Middle East at much the same time as Lawrence of Arabia. But it was not until 1928, aged twenty-seven, that he wrote his first book and a further two years before his first novel. In those few remaining years of his life, he wrote seventeen books, fifteen of them between 1931 and 1934.

In February 1932, that painfully shy but brilliant young Aberdeen journalist, Cuthbert Graham, wrote a criticism of one of his novels but added constructively: 'How will Mr Mitchell develop? It is to be hoped that he will settle down to give us novels of the North-east. After all, he must know the countryside of his birth and upbringing best, and the Mearns, unlike the

Wessex of Hardy or the Argyll of Neil Munro, has not been made to live in a novel, and Mr Mitchell could do it.' Little did Cuthbert Graham know what he was doing. Mitchell didn't like the criticism of his last book but vowed that he would 'show Mr Graham' by writing that novel one day. Well, not only did he proceed to write his greatest book, *Sunset Song*, within a few weeks but had it in print before the end of that year. In the next two years he completed the now-famous trilogy *A Scots Quair*, which rocketed him to international fame.

Often at loggerheads with his dour, crofting father, he came back to the Mearns in the summer of 1934, proudly displaying his first new car, which drew only sarcastic comments from the old man. Leaving in some disgust, he drove south with the manuscript of *Grey Granite*, the last of the trilogy, now accompanied by Cuthbert Graham who had become a trusted friend. He was complaining of stomach pains and was rushed to hospital in Welwyn Garden City, where he lived. After an operation for a perforated gastric ulcer, peritonitis set in, and the North-east's greatest literary son died on the operating table. He was not yet thirty-four. In an introduction to one of Grassic Gibbon's books, I wrote of his style: 'Narrative was blended with italicised dialogue in such sweet harmony that, when linked to the depth of his passion and the height of his imagery, it could stir a rare excitement in the reader. I must be far from alone in saying that the encounter with *Sunset Song* in the teenage years was to open my eyes to the life around me and let me view it with a new enlightenment. For the aspiring writer it was also a lesson on what could be done with words.' That lesson was not lost on the following generation of North-east writers, many of whom, like David Toulmin and David Kerr Cameron, openly stated their debt to Grassic Gibbon for showing the way to new vistas of expression.

George Fraser

In his time at the *Aberdeen Journal*, Grassic Gibbon was surrounded by an abundance of writing talent, like George Rowntree Harvey, brilliant author, critic and eccentric, who refused the temptations of London; Alexander Keith, the classic lad-o'-pairts, a rich mixture of outstanding academic, major historian and rugged Aberdeenshire farmer (he farmed Eigie of Balmedie), who was also secretary of the Aberdeen-Angus Cattle Society; and George Fraser, later editor of the *Evening Express*, whose staying power as a brilliant columnist was tested when he began writing during the First World War and was still producing his perfectly crafted prose for *The Press and Journal* eighty years later, by then having passed his centenary! George Fraser had a very personal memory of Leslie Mitchell, who became his rival for the hand of a girl called Peggy in the cashier's office of the *Aberdeen Journal*. In the end Peggy married George but always kept the loving poems that were penned for her by the suitor who gained fame as Lewis Grassic Gibbon.

John R. Allan

Within that same Broad Street office of what became *The Press and Journal* there was writing talent on a level that would not have been surpassed in Fleet Street – erudite people like Grassic

Gibbon's critic and friend, Cuthbert Graham, who chronicled North-east life in weekly articles with such skill and craft. Falling into place in the wake of Grassic Gibbon were men like John R. Allan, farmer at Little Ardo of Methlick, who gained fame in 1935 with his brilliant reconstruction of a bygone age in *Farmer's Boy*. It prompted Howard Spring to write that 'The breath of the wind is in this book, and the growing of the corn and the dumb patience of beasts and the splendours and follies of men'. Back from the war, he wrote at least one other classic, *North-east Lowlands of Scotland*, described by Cuthbert Graham as 'a triumph of interpretation of the North-east.'

David Toulmin

John Reid (David Toulmin) – farm worker turned novelist

The remarkable range of writing talent produced in Aberdeen and the North-east has by no means been wholly dependent on journalism. A Buchan farm servant, John Reid, born at Rathen in 1913, spent most of his life in the hard grind of the ferm-toun, fee'd at Kinmundy and dairyman at Newseat of Peterhead. But he was nearly sixty before that burning desire to write introduced him to the bookshelves with titles like *Hard Shining Corn, Straw into Gold* and *Blown Seed*. He adopted the pen-name of David Toulmin. Some compared him to Grassic Gibbon, an unrealistic and unfair burden, but he certainly gathered up a following of loyal readers who brightened his latter days when he moved into Aberdeen, exchanging the sharn and pleiter of the country for a job in landscaping, happily settled at 7 Pittodrie Place, within earshot of the football.

David Kerr Cameron and Eric Linklater

If justice was done to David Toulmin, it fell far short in the case of another writer from rural Aberdeenshire, who came half a generation after Toulmin and stuck to his own name of David Kerr Cameron. His grandfather was grieve to Lord Aberdeen at Haddo House and his father was a typical horseman of his day, moving from place to place according to the fee'd-man's pattern of the time. Cameron was born in March 1928 and went to school at Tarves and Pitmedden, leaving at fourteen to be a milk-boy at Cairnbrogie. After RAF service, he went to work as an agricultural engineer but remembered his headmaster's suggestion of journalism on the basis of his imaginative essays. Little did the headmaster realise he was encouraging a talent that would make David Kerr Cameron one of the outstanding North-east writers of the twentieth century.

Gingerly entering journalism with the *Kirriemuir Herald*, he then became a sub-editor on *The Press and Journal* before leaving the calf country in the mid 1950s and moving south to work as a sub-editor on *The Daily Telegraph* in Fleet Street, in charge of the feature pages.

Correcting other people's work served only to delay the blossom of his own talent, with the result that he was fifty before he saw his first published word. That, and his disappearance down south, almost certainly hindered a proper persona being established back home with the result that many people have yet to catch up with his brilliant trilogy of rural life, *The Ballad and the Plough*; *Willie Gavin, Crofter Man*; and *The Cornkister Days*. He followed that in 1987 with a splendid novel, *A Kist of Sorrows*. Throughout his work there is a beautifully lyrical and thoroughly authentic portrayal of a vanished world, one that so many of us have known and cherished. You could hear the jingle of the harness in his words: 'It was a land above all where life moved against the tapestry of the year, the immutability of the seasons, absorbing their rhythms and immemorial rituals: ploughing, harrowing, sowing, reaping, threshing and the tending of livestock. It had a soul and a pulse-beat, a dreichness that was not unlovely. Sometimes it stole the heart.'

David Kerr Cameron died in February 2003, aged seventy-four, and one day perhaps he will receive due recognition. No such neglect has attended Eric Linklater, product of the Grammar School and Aberdeen University. A failed medical student, Linky cut his journalistic teeth at *The Press and Journal*, went to work on *The Times of India* and served in the First World War before returning to Aberdeen as assistant to the professor of English. He then developed as a prolific and popular novelist with titles like *Juan in America*, *Poet's Pub*, *Magnus Merriman*, *Private Angelo* and *The House of Gair*. His autobiographical works were *The Man on My Back* and *Fanfare for a Tin Hat*.

Jessie Kesson, famous North-east author whose novels include *The White Bird Passes*

Jessie Kesson

But North-east writers have by no means confined themselves to novels – and women have suffered not at all from discrimination. Who could have suppressed the talent and personality of women like Jessie Kesson, taken from her mother in Morayshire to the orphanage at Skene in the 1920s and fated to a hard life as a cottar wife in the rural North-east before emerging as a major writer, with books like *The White Bird Passes*, *Glitter of Mica* and *Another Time, Another Place*? Her work dramatised well for BBC Television and she and husband Johnnie moved to London, where they combined a care-taking job with her writing career. Jessie was a free spirit, at home with a cigarette in one hand and a dram in the other. When she didn't have a phone, they could always fetch her at the Green Man Pub in Muswell Hill. Skene Orphanage was used for much of the filming of *White Bird Passes*, the book of which she dedicated to her dominie, Donald Murray, who used to speak in glowing terms about the potential of this orphaned girl when he moved to my own school at Maud in 1937. And if Mr Murray was headmaster at Maud, the minister in that village for thirty-five years had fathered another outstanding North-east talent. After graduating from Aberdeen University in 1917, Mabel Cowie took on the name of Lesley Storm and became one of the most popular British playwrights of the twentieth century, with West End successes like *Black Chiffon*, *Tony Draws a Horse* and *Roar Like a Dove*, some of them turned into films.

Lorna Moon

A girl from the neighbouring Buchan village of Strichen, Nora Low, took issue with the great Cecil B. DeMille about his cinematic treatment of J.M. Barrie's *The Admirable Crichton* – and accepted his challenge to come to Hollywood and see if she could do any better. Under her pen name of Lorna Moon, she became one of the top three earners among Hollywood screenwriters in the 1920s, along with DeMille's brother Bill, with whom she had an affair and a child, Richard DeMille, who is still alive in Santa Barbara, California. Lorna's own life story, wildly adventurous and ending tragically in a sanatorium in 1930, when she was in the prime of life, would make a dramatic screenplay in itself. It has been told in book form by son Richard who, to save embarrassment for his married father, was brought up as part of the family of his uncle Cecil, producer of such screen classics as *Samson and Delilah*, *The Greatest Show in Earth* and *The Ten Commandments*. Lorna had no contact at all with Richard and little more with another son by marriage or her daughter from a third liaison. When she died in Albuquerque, New Mexico, in 1930, aged forty-three, her ashes were brought home to Strichen by a young lover, who accompanied her father, Charlie Low, to the top of Mormond Hill, where they scattered them to the wild winds of Buchan. A suitable end for such a free spirit.

Neil Paterson

Still in Hollywood, another of its most successful writers, Neil Paterson, a solicitor's son from Banff, gained initial recognition as a novelist with such books as *The China Run* and *Behold Thy Daughter*, for which he was hailed as Scotland's greatest story-writer since Robert Louis Stevenson. The literary world anticipated that he might do for the coastal communities what Grassic Gibbon had done for the rural ones. A tall, distinguished-looking, athletic man (he was captain of Dundee United FC at the age of twenty) Paterson was born in 1916 but, by his mid-thirties, had found a diversion that deprived his readers of another novel for the next twenty years.

That diversion was the writing of his 1953 film *The Kidnappers*, starring Duncan Macrae and two North-east schoolboys, Vincent Winter from Aberdeen and Jon Whiteley, the headmaster's son from Monymusk. As a professional writer he could not turn his back on the lucrative career that now beckoned, going on to write films like *High Tide at Noon*, *The Shiralee*, *Innocent Sinner* and

Room at the Top, collecting an Oscar for his screenplay of John Braine's novel. Through all the overtures from major studios to live and work in Hollywood, however, Neil Paterson refused to budge from his sleepy Perthshire haven of Crieff, from which he could still act as production chairman for Films of Scotland and serve as a director of Grampian Television in Aberdeen.

The Poets

The North-east poets are a brilliant cluster in their own right, with outstanding women like Nan Shepherd, Helen Cruickshank and Flora Garry (she was a cousin of Cuthbert Graham and was also related to Lesley Storm), whose *Bennygoak and Other Poems* catches the flavour of her native Buchan, even if she came late to the genre. But if Charles Murray, born in the Vale of Alford in 1864, is hailed as the greatest exponent of the native verse, you will immediately run into the counter-claim of J.C. Milne, a native of Memsie, near Fraserburgh, who came a generation later. Like Nan Shepherd, John Milne made his mark on North-east life and letters through the Aberdeen College of Education, that fruitful source of literary talent better known as the T.C. It was there that he attracted an incomparable devotion as principal master of method, from which he was on the point of retiring in 1962 when he died at the age of sixty-five.

Milne, who lived at 19 Albury Place, Aberdeen, was the archetypal Buchan loon, warm and understanding of humanity in all its shades, apparently plain and uncomplicated yet an academic genius who followed a first-class honours degree in mental philosophy with another 'first' in moral philosophy while lecturing in logic at King's College. Then, taking an interest in geography, he proceeded to yet another 'first', all the time keeping close to his Buchan tongue. Among his many achievements, he is credited as the man who gave poetic dignity to that favourite North-east greeting 'fit like?', as well as its standard response of 'nae bad'. But there was so much more. As with all writers, he needs to be read to be appreciated. You gain a whiff of the man in *Fut Like Folk?* which begins:

> Fut like folk in you braid Buchan lan'?
> Folk wha ken their grun like the back o' their han,'
> Divot and clort and clod, rock, graivel and san'.

And it ends:

> Folk wha say their say and speir their speir,
> Gedder gey birns o' bairns and gey muckle gear,
> And gang their ain gait wi' a lach or a spit or a sweir.

Charles Murray

The richness of that poetic tradition is seldom bettered than in the work of Charles Murray, who captured public imagination from the distance of South Africa, where he landed a major post as secretary for public works and wrote in dialect with the exile's yearning for home. The North-east public keenly awaited his every offering, as in the 1930s when his latest poem, *There's Aye a Something*, appeared in *The Press and Journal* one morning and caused such a rush on sales that a reprint had to be quickly arranged. That poem tells of Sandy, the farmer whose wife is town-bred and genteel and for whom he is regarded as a bit of a come-down. You get the flavour of Sandy in rich verses like:

> He's roch an' oonshaven till Sunday comes roon
> A drap at his nose and his pints hingin' doon
> His weskit is skirpit wi' dribbles o' kail
> He drinks fae his saucer and rifts ower his ale

('Pints' is the North-east word for boot-laces.)

With such contrasting parents, Sandy's children have clearly entered into a genetic gamble, which Murray sums up brilliantly:

> They're like her in looks as a podfu' o' piz
> But damn't, there's aye something – their mainners are his.

Charles Murray, leading Doric poet

With such universal popularity and affection for Charles Murray, there would inevitably be other opinions. John R. Allan took the view that his work was more observed than felt, while the irascible Hugh MacDiarmid wrote, 'Charles Murray has not only never written a line of poetry in his life but he is constitutionally incapable of doing so.' (For the comfort of Murray devotees, I was once told by MacDiarmid that 'Robert Burns was no poet at all!')

Murray came back to the North-east for his retirement and developed a strong friendship with his fellow poet, Nan Shepherd, who was living in Cults. They used to be seen holding hands in public, not at all fazed by the twenty-nine-year difference in their ages. In later life Nan Shepherd gave this vivid description of him:

Charles Murray was a man you could not miss in company. He had presence, not self-assertive but dynamic – one felt more alive from being with him. When he spoke he had compulsive listeners. Droll, witty, solemn, seemingly nonchalant but with a delightful relish in what he related, he was a raconteur of genius. He was company for a duke or ditcher and imperturbably himself with both. His lean, hawk face was warm with interest – sheer simple interest in people, what they were, what they did, how they did it.

In an introduction to his poems, she summed him up in a sentence: 'The seed of Charles Murray's power is that he said yes to life.'

To London

The further you delve into the pool of North-east writing talent the more you realise the task is fraught with the pitfalls of omission, doing less than justice to people like George Bruce from Fraserburgh and that other poet and novelist George MacDonald, born in Huntly in 1824 and a graduate of Aberdeen, who became a professor at Bedford College, London and a major figure in that city's literary life. Many of his fifty books were set in his native Aberdeenshire.

He was not alone in making his mark beyond the native land. Of the Victorian journalists, Archibald Forbes (1838–1900) left Aberdeen University and became a distinguished war correspondent, starting with the Franco-Prussian encounter and continuing with the Russo-Turkish, the second Afghan, and the Zulu wars. Aberdeen University gave him an LLD. The names already mentioned from Poets' Corner in the *Aberdeen Herald* are worth a study in themselves. They include a quintet of Williams, the best known of whom was perhaps William Thom, working in a cotton factory by the age of ten but soon invited to speak at big dinners as far as London. William Anderson (1802–67), born in the Green, became a city policeman, while his friend William Cadenhead (1819–1905) was an overseer at the Broadford works, best known for his light, convivial verse.

William Forsyth (1818–79), a native of Turriff, became editor of the *Journal* and was known in such national publications as *Punch*, *Blackwood's* and the *Cornhill*. William Carnie (1824–1909), another man from the Green, veered towards music and wrote popular songs of the day, rounding off that group of versifiers. In the twentieth century William Lints Smith, who started as a clerk in the Aberdeen Combworks before joining the *Aberdeen Journal*, was Lord North-cliffe's choice as manager of *The Times* in 1920 and guided that paper to its high point in fifty years, as recorded in the official history.

Something similar happened to William Will from Huntly, another product of the *Aberdeen Journal*, who became managing director of Allied Newspapers in London and was largely responsible for that group's takeover of his old Broad Street employer, leading to its ownership by the Kemsley family. Another Allied Newspapers man was John Malcolm Bulloch, who went from the *Aberdeen Free Press* to be editor of the *Daily Graphic* and Allied's noted literary and dramatic critic in London. A keen versifier while a student at Aberdeen, Bulloch was responsible for *The Scottish Students' Song-Book* and later for the three-volume *House of Gordon*, as well as a history of Aberdeen University.

London was overflowing with newspapermen trained in Aberdeen (the *Free Press* proved a particularly fertile breeding ground), a tradition that extended into the twenty-first century with names like James Naughtie, a former reporter on *The Press and Journal*, who fronts the *Today* programme on BBC Radio Four. Nearer home, Robert Bruce went from the *Aberdeen Journal* to be editor of the *Glasgow Herald* and was knighted.

Of those who ventured abroad, none was more distinguished than Francis Low, a Gordonian who turned his back on the family's farming tradition at Easter Clune of Finzean and became a journalist with the *Free Press*, thrown in at the deep end for a verbatim report of a Music Hall speech by David Lloyd George. Low was commissioned in the 4th Battalion Gordon Highlanders in the First World War, during which his commanding officer was Edward Watt, one of his bosses at the *Free Press* and later to be lord provost of Aberdeen. A posting to India whetted his appetite for the subcontinent so he returned there after the war and teamed up with fellow Scot, Eric Linklater, who was also best man at his wedding. By 1932 he was editor of *The Times of India*, on personal terms with leaders like Gandhi and Jinnah. He became Sir Francis Low for his advisory work on the lead-up to independence.

Spalding Club

Rounding off this tour of Aberdeen's writing scene would not be complete without mention of Joseph Robertson. Historical research having become a fashion in Scotland, he and a local advocate, John Stuart, came up with the idea of providing Aberdeen with a society for the publication of the literary, historical, genealogical and topographical remains of the North-east. At a meeting in the Royal Hotel on 23rd December 1839, with the provost in the chair, the Spalding Club was thus formed, taking its name from Aberdeen's first historian, John Spalding, and proving a major step forward in the city's cultural life. Robertson, who lived from 1810 till 1866 and was about to become editor of *The Constitutional*, wrote a delightful *Book of Bon Accord*, and that, along with his other researches, made him the fount to which historians down the years were bound to turn.

As for the Spalding Club, its noble concept did not prevent a rather chequered career. Among its splendid work, it spent £13,000 on producing thirty-eight volumes of local history. Nevertheless it was wound up in 1870, by which time the inspirational Joseph Robertson was dead. A New Spalding Club was formed in 1886, once again tackling major works, like J.M. Bulloch's *House of Gordon*, but it was killed off by the First World War with important projects not yet complete. For example, the club had commissioned Buchan scholar, playwright and musician Gavin Greig to collect the folk-songs of the North-east, a task he all but completed with the help of his friend, the Rev. James B. Duncan, minister at Lynturk and a native of the parish of New Deer where Greig lived.

Sadly, Greig had yet to reduce his conclusions to a final judgement when he died in the first days of the 1914 war, still in the prime of life. Historian Alexander Keith, who described Greig as 'that greatest of all folk-song collectors', edited a small portion of the work which was published as a book in 1925. But it was not until 2002 that the full eight volumes, hailed as the largest and richest collection of its kind in the world, was finally published for Aberdeen University in association with the School of Scottish Studies at Edinburgh University. An attempt at a Third Spalding Club in 1928 produced another thirty titles but that, too, went the way of its predecessors and was wound up in the 1960s.

The Artists

The name of George Jamesone (1588–1644) keeps recurring in the artistic life of Aberdeen, hailed as Scotland's answer to his Flemish contemporary, Van Dyck. Jamesone was the earliest of the nation's portraitists, and, without doubt, Aberdeen's finest. But he was given close company by others such as William Dyce, a local doctor's son who became professor of fine art at King's College, London, and was engaged on the frescoes of the House of Lords when he died in 1864; and John Phillip (1817–67), a shoemaker's son from Skene Square, who gained fame and fortune in Spain where one of his portfolios was said to have brought him £20,000.

Sir George Reid, celebrated artist

Not least of Aberdeen's famous artists was Sir George Reid (1841–1913). Son of the manager at Aberdeen Copper Company, George was a Grammar School boy who became an apprentice lithographer at twelve but harboured ambitions to be a portrait painter. After studying in Paris, Utrecht and the Hague he returned to Aberdeen and attained his ambition, becoming president of the Royal Scottish Academy in 1891, the year in which he was also knighted. A strong supporter of Aberdeen Art Gallery, he is well remembered for his illustrations of *Johnny Gibb of Gushetneuk*.

A native of newburgh, James McBey (1883–1959), started work in the North Bank but took up etching and decided to try his luck in London, travelling the world and gaining high praise for his talent as a war artist during the 1914–18 conflict. The spontaneity and strength of his etching was regarded as the best in the history of British print-making.

James Pittendrigh MacGillivray (1859–1938), a native of Port Elphinstone, divided his time between sculpture and poetry, his many well-known busts including that of Sir George Reid and William Alexander. He was also responsible for the statue of Lord Byron which stands in the grounds of the Grammar School.

CHAPTER 48

Lord Byron

When writing about the North-east's literary figures there has to be a special place for George Gordon of Gight, better known to the world as Lord Byron, one of the area's most famous poets and a man whose Aberdeenshire accent was said to have stayed with him till the very end of his short life. Gight (pronounced as in *richt*) was an estate with a castle near the Aberdeenshire village of Tarves and its heiress in the late 1700s was the orphaned Catherine Gordon, who had been brought up in Banff by her grandmother, the dowager Lady Gight.

Catherine was an aristocratic Gordon, tracing her line directly to James I, but she was left without guidance when her father drowned himself in the canal at Bath. It was in that same English spa that the young lady then fell under the spell of ex-Guardsman 'Mad Jack' Byron, a big-spending gambler and thorough waster whose charms she found irresistible. Mad Jack's ancestors had arrived in England with William the Conqueror, were given Newstead Abbey as a seat by Henry VIII and later a peerage for services to Charles I. He had already been married to the Marchioness of Carmarthen, who left her husband to elope with him. But when she died and her massive £4,000-a-year income came to an end, Jack was soon in a spot of financial bother and faced with a task of some urgency – to find another heiress.

Catherine Gordon from Aberdeenshire filled the bill to perfection. Romantic and naïve, and with a fortune of £23,000, she was the ready-made answer to a skunk's prayer. Within four months they were married in great style at St Michael's Church, Bath, much to the distress of her relatives. Two months later, however, she was back home in separation, soon to be pursued by Mad Jack who wasn't going to let a small matter like that upset his financial salvation. The charm, it seemed, had worked once more. They were settling down at Gight to a life of high festivity and much extravagance, according to the diary of William Russell, Catherine's cousin and Laird of Aden at Old Deer (the mother of Willie, Lord Whitelaw, the Conservative statesman of modern times, was also one of the Russells of Aden).

Jack Byron was playing the part of the Scottish laird; that was, until he could persuade his wife to pay off his creditors by selling the Gight estate. It went for £17,850, bought by the Earl of Aberdeen for his son, Lord Haddo. Within a year of marriage, therefore, Catherine's fortune had gone, except for £4,222, retained for the purpose of giving her an annual income of £135. When the timber of the estate was felled as part of the sale it was said that the noise put the ancient herons of Gight to flight, recalling the prophecy of Thomas the Rhymer, who had said:

> When the heron leaves the tree
> The laird o' Gight will landless be.

The Byrons left Gight for good that spring of 1786, returning to London, where Jack was soon imprisoned for further debt as Catherine counted the cost of her disastrous marriage. To complicate matters, she was now pregnant, giving birth on 22nd January 1788 to the boy who would take her own family name of George Gordon, destined to set the literary world alight one day under the title of Lord Byron.

She seemed to have gained some sense when she fled with her child back to the safety of Aberdeen, where she lodged first in the tenements of Virginia Street before moving to 10 Queen Street. But the susceptibility of women to the wiles of weeds and wasters remains one of life's eternal mysteries. No sooner had Jack Byron accumulated his latest raft of debt than he appeared once more on the doorstep, the creditors hard on his heels. Poor Catherine went out to borrow another £300, on which she would have to pay interest of £15 a year from her modest funds. Mad Jack disappeared, to stay with his sister Fanny in France and, mercifully, Catherine never saw him again. For there he died a year later, near starvation and in rags, one of life's disasters. For all that, however, she hadn't lost her infatuation. Down the length of Queen Street, it was reported, they could hear her cries of grief. She moved into a rented, first-floor flat at 64 (some say 68) Broad Street, a substantial tenement that lay between Queen Street and the present frontage of Marischal College. Her spacious sitting-room had three tall windows, identifiable from sketches of the time, which looked down on Broad Street. Taking care of her modest means, she now had the task of bringing up the boy George, who did not escape the local version of 'Geordie'. She managed to cope with the necessities of food, drink, heat and clothing, with a subscription to the library as her one luxury.

She did manage to employ a nurse to look after George, who proved a handful, a mischievous lad regularly chased from the courtyard of Marischal College by the old porter, George Pirie, who could easily spot him in his red jacket and nankeen trousers. There were also doctors' fees to contend with, for there was clearly something wrong with the boy's leg. He was sensitive about his disability which many thought to be a club-foot, but it was more a limp caused by a tightening of the Achilles tendon, preventing him from putting his heel to the ground. By the age of five George Gordon was off round the corner from Broad Street to a small school, a dilapidated room, run by John Bower where, it was said: 'The dialect was the broadest, the tone of the school the roughest and yet, at the bottom, there was genuine kindliness and humanity.' From there he moved to another small school run by a Marischal College graduate, John Ross, just off the Upperkirkgate by Drum's Lane. Ross instilled in the future poet a taste for reading and history that stayed with him for the rest of his life. Byron would later recall: 'Under him I made an astonishing progress and I recall to this day his mild manners and good-natured painstaking.'

To the Grammar

His contact with Mr Paterson the shoemaker, who made special footwear for his defect, led to the appointment of Paterson's son as the boy's tutor, in preparation for entry to the Grammar School. John Paterson himself was still a Grammar pupil but soon to be first bursar at Marischal College. The fact that George would be on his way to the Grammar School before the age of seven, when the normal age of entry was ten or eleven, had much to do with preparing for the title he would inherit one day from his grand-uncle. So he made his way down Upperkirkgate and up Schoolhill to the Grammar, not the sparkling granite building of today but that modest little place by the entrance to the more recent and much bigger Robert Gordon's Auld Hoose on the site to be occupied one day by Gray's School of Art.

Lord Byron, pupil at Aberdeen Grammar School at a remarkably early age

Joining a class of much older boys, he embarked on three years at an Aberdeen school of great antiquity, indeed dating back to the thirteenth century. While the Grammar may not have been in the same social category as the Harrow to which he would later aspire, he was mixing, nevertheless, with a substantial cross-section of North-east stock. His forty-eight classmates included boys like James Lumsden, the laird of Belhelvie's son; William Chalmers, grandson of the founder of the *Aberdeen Journal* and later a surgeon with the East India Company; John Greig, an army surgeon in the Napoleonic Wars; James Leith, soon to be first bursar at Marischal College, who then fought with great gallantry through the Peninsular War and died in action at the very end; and James Blaikie, lawyer and distinguished provost of Aberdeen, who persuaded the Government to provide funds for the rebuilding of Marischal College. As with Byron, Blaikie has a statue in the city, within the Town House.

The annual visitation of town and gown was a colourful occasion of pomp and ceremony, concluding with the presentation of handsome prizes. The age difference between George Gordon and his classmates accounts for the fact that you don't find him in the prize list, not that his intellect was ever in doubt. In the playground, incidentally, he was said to excel at marbles, better known to Aberdonians as bools! The rector of the Grammar School in his day was James Dun, a man of serious infirmity, whose house across the street from the school was still a well-known museum in modern times.

His Passions

On one occasion young George spent his summer holidays at what was then the rural village of Woodside with the family's former maid, Agnes Gray, who was now married. This served his fascination for all things mechanical since Woodside was at the heart of mills like Grandholm and the creation of the Aberdeenshire Canal. By then he had also reached a precocious stage in his further fascination with girls. In later life he would record: 'My passions were developed very early – so early that few would believe me if I were to state the period and the facts which accompanied it.' Agnes Gray's younger sister May, who followed her as maid to Catherine Byron Gordon, is generally held responsible for the boy's early initiation into sexual matters and, by inference, for setting him on the downward path. But during that summer holiday, according to Patrick Morgan's *Annals of Woodside*, he also fell in love with the attractive Lexy Campbell, who lived with a respectable spinster lady. According to Morgan, 'Poor Lexy lost caste by this affair and her subsequent history was unfortunate.' So May Gray may not have been alone in guiding the future Lord Byron towards the pleasures of the flesh.

A Title at Ten

The title, of course, was not yet his. And the poor boy was just approaching the age of ten when his life was about to face that major change. In the summer term of 1798 the pupils, assembled in the central block of the Grammar School, were answering the roll-call in Latinised form when the usual 'Georgius B. Gordon' was overtaken by 'Domine de Byron'. The Byron family in the south had been slow to inform Catherine that the grand-uncle had died of wounds incurred in the service of Horatio Nelson, and that ten-year-old George Gordon was now Lord Byron, heir to Newstead Abbey in Nottinghamshire.

All eyes turned on the embarrassed boy, who would now be heading for a very different life in the south and beyond. Before leaving Aberdeen, Catherine took her son and the maid, May Gray, to spend a few weeks in the countryside (actually no further than a cottage at Honeybrae, which stood where 91 King's Gate stands today). It may have been the end of his life in Aberdeen but Lord Byron did not forsake his roots. His fascination with Deeside brought him back to stay at Glentanar and to climb Lochnagar. The area had cast a spell over him, a spiritual connection that never left him.

It inspired him to write such verses as:

> I rose with the dawn, with my dog as my guide
> From mountain to mountain I bounded along
> I breasted the billow of Dee's rushing tide
> And heard at a distance the Highlander's song.

The Grammar School was followed by Harrow and Trinity College, Cambridge, before he embarked on an adventurous if dissipated life, much involved in London society, lover of Lady

Caroline Lamb and married to Anne Isabella Milbanke. A year later Anne left him after the birth of their daughter Ada, revealing shades of Catherine and Mad Jack as history repeated itself. He travelled the Continent, meeting the poet Shelley and gaining his own place in literary history. As a champion of political liberty he joined the Greek insurgents as they rose against the Turks but died of marsh fever in 1824. He was brought back to Britain and is buried at Hucknall Torkard in Nottinghamshire. A statue in his honour stands in the forecourt of the Grammar School today, the work of James Pittendrigh MacGillivray and unveiled on 14th September 1923.

CHAPTER 49

Will Doric Survive?

Of all the distinctive features that separate the folk of Aberdeen and the North-east from the rest of the world, by far the most immediate is the local dialect. Mistakenly, perhaps, we call it the Doric, a Grampian version of the Lowland Scots tongue spoken down that eastern side of Scotland from the far north to the Borders and westward by Ayrshire. From area to area that Lowland tongue has its variations but adheres to a broadly standard form of spelling – except in the North-east. We're a thrawn lot!

When English says *stone*, standard Scots says *stane* and we say *steen*. Similarly: *bone, bane, been*; and so on. We broaden the vowel sound on every possible occasion and emphasise our difference with an idiom to baffle the innocent. For example, the Doric (sometimes called 'the Buchan tongue' because that local area typifies its extremities) offers two forms of the English *have* – *hiv* and *hae* – each with a different usage applied instinctively by people who will most likely have no explanation for it. Translating an English sentence *You have to have something in your stomach*, the Doric version becomes *Ye hiv tae hae something in yer stamack*. To transpose those two forms of *have* would sound ridiculous. Yet, change that sentence into the future tense and it becomes *Ye'll hae tae hae something . . .* No logic. Just instinct. For those who speak the local dialect with ease, the traditional North-east greeting of *Fit like?* (*How are you?*) would most likely be answered in one of three ways: *Oh juist tyauvin' awa*, or *Warslin' throwe*, or *Knypin' on* – each with a subtle shade of difference.

So this is the Doric dialect of North-east Scotland, always rooted more powerfully in the rural districts than in the city. But to know it, you need to be brought up with it. Any form of language lives or dies by the willingness of sufficient numbers to speak it in a natural and everyday fashion. Even with the massive subsidies being poured into Gaelic, that other form of Scots speech, its survival remains in grave doubt. So, lacking that powerful lobby of Celtic support, the Lowland Scots tongue is fighting an equally desperate rearguard action. There are those who will dismiss this view as too pessimistic, but they need to face the facts. How many people are actually speaking our Doric language in their everyday lives? In the massive onslaught of outside influences, from television to the language of a worldwide pop culture, how long will it survive? Are the young people interested? Do they care?

In a society that credits itself with sophistication, people are geared to a modern jargon of imperfect English which leaves little room for the native tongue. That tongue was once a powerfully expressive form of speech, rich in its vocabulary, colourful in its purpose of translating our thoughts into words. It still is, for those who use it. For most, however, it has become a caricature of its real self, to be patronised as a relic that is quaint and amusing, to be illustrated with words like *dreich* and *scunner*.

But don't depend on my word for this declaration of decline. Listen instead to the man who was as great an authority on Lowland Scots as anyone who ever lived. The late David Murison spent the bulk of his life on the creation of the definitive *Scottish National Dictionary*, a mammoth task that proved him one of the great Scots of the twentieth century. A Buchan loon, whose carpenter father moved from Brucklay to find work in Fraserburgh and then Aberdeen, David Murison followed the Grammar School and Aberdeen University with a distinguished career at Cambridge, emerging as one of the great classical scholars.

The idea of a national dictionary for Scotland had been mooted as far back as 1907 and was later taken up by Dr William Grant of Aberdeen. By the end of the Second World War, however, it needed a full-time editor as well as fresh inspiration. Murison was the man for the moment, small of stature but a giant of intellect, a plain-spoken genius who could trace the

David Murison, Aberdonian editor of the *Scottish National Dictionary*

history and assess the health of our language with remarkable clarity. He assumed his editorship in 1946, when he was thirty-three, and had reached the letter *N* when I went to visit him eighteen years later. It was no great surprise that his own North-east corner was proving a major source of material.

By then, however, he had made some disturbing discoveries. For example, in that generation between the end of the nineteenth century and 1926, he calculated that about one-third of our vocabulary had disappeared from everyday speech. He reckoned that another third had gone by the 1960s, a deterioration that was accelerating with the rise of television. He completed his dictionary in time for retirement in the late 1970s, when he returned from his base in George Square, Edinburgh, to his native Fraserburgh. It was there, looking out on the infant school that had set him on his way to Cambridge, that I sought a revision of his views. The accent, the intonation and the vowel sounds would last for a long time, he said, but in a hundred years it was possible that Scots words would not be used at all, except perhaps as a fashion. That was the assessment of David Murison, a more realistic view than that of Robert Louis Stevenson, who had forecast a much earlier demise.

In a dialect born mainly to be spoken, giving full vent to its powerful rhythms, the written word has suffered from its phonetic freedom. It is a problem that has beset all but the very best of Doric writers, producing a residue of amateurish versifying that struggles towards mediocrity, mostly without success. Contemporary Doric writers face the added hazard that their audience is a million miles away from the understanding of Johnny Gibb's day, or even that of Charles Murray in more recent times. So the writing becomes skewed and self-conscious. Because of those phonetic variations, even a good Doric speaker will sometimes struggle to make sense of the written word. Of course, language will always evolve but when that comes from nothing better than basic ignorance, the result is a descent into the slovenly English and sloppy diction which so often passes for Scots speech today. The glottal stop, generally attributed to Glasgow, is by no means absent from the streets of Aberdeen.

So what of that word Doric (adopted as a label for our North-east speech in mysterious circumstances) upon which I cast some doubt at the beginning of this chapter? It certainly has an authentic Scottish ring but it comes, in fact, from Greece, where it was the dialect of the Spartans and found its way into the English language, bringing connotations of roughness, coarseness, lack of culture. Milton used it. David Murison disapproved of its application to his native dialect, protesting that there was nothing coarse about his Buchan tongue! Yet so many people speak about 'lapsing into the Doric'. Is it really a lapse? Or are we just once more being careless with words?

A man without vanity, rejecting all thought of being publicly honoured for his work, David Murison merely wondered if his life's devotion to the native tongue would have any lasting value. I suspect that he had his doubts. Before this century has gone, however, the matter will be settled, one way or the other.

CHAPTER 50

Lillie Langtry Woos the Laird

Though Aberdonians had an appetite for theatre as far back as the fifteenth century, it was well through the 1700s before there was a recognisable structure of playhouses. Pageants, plays and a variety of spectacles sprang up at places like the New Inn hostelry in the Castlegate, followed by Jackson's Theatres in Queen Street and Shoe Lane and Coachy's Playhouse in Chronicle Lane, named after the owner who was a well-known coachman in town. But theatre as we understand it today really arrived with the opening of the Theatre Royal at the foot of Marischal Street in 1795. That ran through till the 1870s, when it was superseded by Her Majesty's Theatre and Opera House in Guild Street.

George Washington Wilson, renowned photographer

Touring companies were now bringing the stars to the provinces and a group of enterprising North-east men decided it was time for Aberdeen to broaden the cultural horizons with a venue that could house grand opera. The company was formed by Newell Burnett, an advocate from Kyllachie; John G. Chalmers, publisher of the *Aberdeen Journal*; Alexander (Soapy) Ogston of Ardoe; John M. Clark of Garthdee House; John Willet, a civil engineer; William Duthie, a ship-owner from Cairnbulg; William Stevenson, a merchant from Viewfield; John Gordon of Craig-myle; and, not least, George Washington Wilson, Aberdeen's most famous photographer.

Built on a Guild Street site partly owned by Stevenson and Washington Wilson, Her Majesty's cost £8,400, with seating for 1,650, and was designed by the prestigious theatre architect of the day, C.J. Phipps. The name was in honour of Queen Victoria, whose North-east connection was now established at Balmoral, and the theatre opened on 19 December 1872 with a performance of Lord Lytton's play, *The Lady of Lyons*, starring James Rhind Gibson, an Aberdonian who was already a star of the London stage. It was proving a highly successful venture, with London musicals and other major productions like *The Mikado* by the D'Oyly Carte Opera Company on the bill. But in 1891 Her Majesty's was taken over by the powerful Robert Arthur, who owned the Royal Court Theatre in London and a chain of others around the country and who proceeded with a reconstruction, this time bringing in that other architect now famous for his theatre designs, Frank Matcham. Robert Arthur would play an even greater part in the theatrical life of the city.

Among those who appeared at Her Majesty's, none caused a greater stir than that infamous actress and great beauty of her day, Lillie Langtry, friend of Oscar Wilde and mistress of King Edward VII. Lillie played there in 1891, her only Aberdeen appearance, though she had already made a connection out Buchan way. Historian Alexander Keith, himself a son of the parish involved, gives a tantalising hint of how the promiscuous Miss Langtry managed to relieve an Aberdeenshire laird, George 'Abington' Baird of Strichen, of £100,000. The fuller version of the scandal does not disappoint.

Derby Winner

The Strichen estate in rural Aberdeenshire came into the hands of the Baird family in 1855, when they bought it from Lord Lovat. Son George turned out to be the ultimate reprobate, walking out of Eton at fourteen and landing at Magdalene College, Cambridge, soon to be caught up in the glamour of horse-racing – and to be the target of those who saw him as a source of easy money. Due to inherit millions at twenty-one, he was still under trusteeship, so to avoid detection he registered his racing name as 'Mr Abington', which he used for the rest of his short but extraordinary life as an owner and rider, achieving high success even though he fell foul of the stewards at the Jockey Club. One of his thoroughbreds, Merry Hampton, won the Epsom Derby in 1887.

Soon at the centre of a rough set in London's West End, and rather colourfully described as 'a hell-raiser and whore-master', George Baird (or Mr Abington) became infatuated with the great Lillie Langtry, who had taken a fancy to horse-racing. Lillie entered into an affair with the laird of Strichen, who would regularly batter her then pay £5,000 remorse money. Though she once landed in hospital with two black eyes and a swollen nose, she refused to press charges and instead accepted his £50,000 cheque and the yacht he had recently bought. George Baird was drawing £100,000 a year from his investments at the time. He followed Lillie north when she appeared in Aberdeen but was soon off for another round of debauchery in New Orleans. There he caught a chill and died within two days, still only thirty-one years of age but having condensed a few lifetimes into that short period. So much for Lillie Langtry, who lived on till 1929, when she died in Monte Carlo. Other major names of the day who trod the Guild Street boards in Aberdeen included Ellen Terry, Herbert Beerbohm Tree and Henry Irving, as well as a budding talent called Charlie Chaplin, not then distinguishable within the Fred Karno troupe.

CHAPTER 51

Charlie Chaplin in Town

Historians have agonised over the veracity of the claim but I can only present the evidence of my rendezvous with Charlie Chaplin at the Tor-na-Coille Hotel, Banchory, in 1970. There he confirmed to me what I had already heard in my childhood: that he appeared in Aberdeen in his lesser-known days. He added the further surprise that his fellow-troupers in the Fred Karno show had included Stan Laurel, before the two of them sailed for fame and fortune in America.

Chaplin expressed a wish to see the old theatre again and we drove in from Banchory on that fine summer day. Her Majesty's had become better known to later audiences as the Tivoli, but by then it was a bingo hall, mercifully retaining the general shape and ambience of its theatrical days. The little clown was touched that his unexpected visit had spontaneously produced a crowd, seeking confirmation that this could really be the great Charlie Chaplin. Photographic proof of his 1970 visit, incidentally, provided a scoop for Aberdeen cameraman Ron Taylor, whose picture graces the cover of one of my books.

The Palace, just off Bridge Street and best remembered as a cinema, was originally a variety theatre but was destroyed by fire in 1896 with the loss of seven lives and many more seriously injured in the stampede. When rebuilt it attracted top artistes like Harry Lauder, Charles Coburn, Dr Walford Bodie, Florrie Forde and Harry Tate, all huge names in their day. In her later years Florrie Forde returned to the Tivoli, where she had previously chalked up an impressive twelve seasons playing to capacity audiences at every performance. When there again in 1940, Florrie broke off to entertain wounded servicemen at Kingseat Hospital, a generous gesture with a dramatic sequel. She died in the taxi bringing her back to Aberdeen.

Frank Matcham's decor and splendid acoustics had turned Her Majesty's into a real treasure of British theatrical design, still retaining some of the C.J. Phipps features to add to its distinction. By then, however, Robert Arthur had other things on his mind and set about closing his Guild Street enterprise and disposing of it altogether. It was acquired by James Leith and a group of Aberdeen businessmen, with Horace Collins, the well-known Glasgow theatrical agent, looking after the bookings. By the terms of the sale, however, Mr Arthur had confined them to a limited range of entertainment, turning an opera house into a variety theatre, which would become known as the Tivoli when it reopened on the July holiday of 1910.

Charlie Chaplin visits the Tivoli with the author

Walter Gilbert moved round the corner from the Palace to be the first manager of a variety hall that soon wound its way into the Aberdonian heart. Down the years came the comedians who were household names – Dave Willis, Alec Finlay, Jack Radcliffe, Tommy Morgan, Lex McLean, Jimmy Logan and Jack Milroy, with singers and musical acts like George Formby, Donald Peers, Andy Stewart, Albert Sandler and Flotsam and Jetsam. The Tivoli orchestra benefited from some distinguished musical directors, men like Haydn Halstead who teamed up with the legendary Will Fyffe to give the city of Glasgow its own anthem. Ironically, the words of 'I Belong to Glasgow' were written by Fyffe, a Dundonian, and set to music in Aberdeen.

The last musical director when the Tivoli closed in 1966 was Clifford Jordan, who had decided, for his retirement, to open a hotel in Queen's Terrace. But what would he call it? Taking his wife's name of Margaret and his own one of Cliff, he came up with the sophistication of the Marcliffe Hotel, a splendid hostelry that may have moved site but, under the ownership of Stewart Spence, retained its high standard at Pitfodels.

The Tivoli came into the hands of such diverse figures as T. Scott Sutherland, the architect, and singer Calum Kennedy, but fell victim to bingo till that finally ran out of steam in 1999 when it was bought by another Aberdeen businessman, Mr Tony Donald, for £150,000. The Scottish Arts Council has since stated a need for a medium-sized theatre in Aberdeen and a Tivoli Trust was established to consider a combination of professional and amateur productions, a North-east cultural centre and the feasibility of a repertory company. The stumbling block proved to be the size of the insurance premium before funding could begin.

CHAPTER 52

Jewel in the Crown

So why did Robert Arthur lose interest in Her Majesty's Theatre and Opera House after he had undertaken the lease in 1891 and completely reconstructed it? Always a step ahead, the man from the south was sensing the need for a theatre of greater capacity, comfort and facilities to put Aberdeen even more in line for the size and calibre of companies now venturing out of London. His interest was firmly focused on a site in Rosemount Viaduct, where he would create the theatre of his dreams, the magnificent building we still know today as His Majesty's.

Having brought down the Guild Street curtain on Saturday, 1 December 1906, with Arthur Law's comedy *A Country Mouse,* he left his successors with those restrictive practices on the use of Her Majesty's that would clear him of all competition. Business is business, no doubt, whatever we

His Majesty's Theatre, with modern extension

may think of the morality. Two days later, on Monday 3rd December, His Majesty's Theatre opened its doors as one of the gems of British theatre, another work of art by Frank Matcham, top designer of his day, and costing £35,000 to build. (It remained 'His' Majesty's since it was built in the reign of Edward VII.) The site seemed a hazardous one, perched high above the Denburn while, at the low level of its back door, trains heading for Buchan and the north had no sooner left the Joint Station than they were stopping at the Schoolhill halt. That, however, turned out to be a godsend as an unloading point for scenery, props and costumes arriving from the south.

With customary foresight, Robert Arthur proved to have chosen a picturesque site in that triangular setting of the Viaduct and Union Terrace, opening out towards the gardens below and forming a vision to behold from the vantage point of Union Bridge. Arthur's judgement of people was confirmed again with his choice of manager for the exciting new venture. Harry Adair Nelson, a native of Bath, had owned and run the Prince of Wales Theatre in Liverpool, and when that came unstuck he became leading tour manager for the companies of George Edwardes, presenter of the famous Gaiety Girls. By 1906 he was on his way to Aberdeen, preparing for the grand opening night at His Majesty's, a glittering occasion such as the city had never seen, and for which the police were out in force to control the large crowds gathering by five o'clock.

In an Edwardian age of elegance, the horse-drawn carriages rolled up at the theatre entrance, gentlemen in white tie and tails stepping down to assist their ladies in full evening dress and jewels and conveying them to the foyer where Adair Nelson was waiting to greet his guests. He would later recall the names of his staff that night: Brown, the doorman, who opened the carriage doors; Benzie, who collected the tickets inside the vestibule; Miss Peters, who presided over the dress circle bar; Miss Moir, who sold programmes; Webberley, the head electrician; Johnnie Small, the scenery painter; and Waldie, the carpenter.

An Aberdeen audience, 2,550 of them in seats and others huddled on the dress circle steps, was taking its first-ever look at the magnificence of His Majesty's, all the craftsmanship coming from the city's own tradesmen. With its cantilever support for the balconies, there were no pillars to disturb the view of rich crimson in the velvet seats, carpets and curtains at the four boxes. Beneath the white ceiling, encrusted with crystal chandeliers, James Scott and Son crafted the decorative plaster work that formed a frieze above the proscenium, while W. Hamilton Buchan of Union Row designed the figures above the upper boxes, representing the goddesses of tragedy and comedy. The glamour of the occasion mattered more than the quality of the opening show, which happened to be an operatic pantomime version of *Little Red Riding Hood*, overflowing with scenery, costumes, choral singing and dancing. The lead part was played by a young lady called Nellie Wigley, who sang, 'I wouldn't leave my little wooden hut for you'. Aberdonians were certainly willing to leave their own little wooden huts for a show that ran to capacity audiences for four weeks.

The manager's daughter, Elizabeth Adair, became a star in her own right as actress and trailblazer for women in broadcasting, giving us a glimpse of her father's life in those early days at His Majesty's. Adair Nelson lived at 65 Osborne Place, at the corner of Prince Arthur Street, with his wife, two sons and two daughters. By the early 1920s he had the substantial salary of £400 per annum and coped quite adequately with school fees of £3 a term at the High

The magnificent interior of His Majesty's Theatre

School and the Grammar. His routine of a summer evening was to walk round his beautiful garden to pick a small carnation for the buttonhole of his immaculate suit, tailored at W.J. Milne's. Complete with starched wing collar and bow tie, a gold chain across his waistcoat, bowler hat and silver-topped cane, he set out to catch the tramcar at the junction of Albyn Place and Prince Arthur Street, alighting at Union Terrace for the final walk to the theatre. (You wonder why he didn't just walk down Skene Street!) Incidentally, one of his canes was actually a sword-stick for protection against muggers, who were not unknown in the 1920s.

Nevertheless, to him Aberdeen was always 'this enchanting place' and His Majesty's was 'his theatre'. Daughter Elizabeth wrote of childhood visits to the pantomime, when they would sit in the 'manager's box', absorbing the magic of theatre. She would then catch sight of her father, standing on the little balustraded balcony to the right of the dress circle, from where he surveyed his audience like a captain from the bridge. For seventeen years Adair Nelson was the boss, kind and tolerant, except on the night when the student show was wrecked by a rowdy section of the audience that embarked on an orgy of destruction, ending with police action and a ban on student shows for several years.

On another occasion, he noticed that a leading actor, due to appear in Hall Caine's religious play, *The Christian*, was too drunk and banned him from taking the stage. The actor and some friends vowed vengeance and were waiting for the manager in Lower Skene Street after the show. He was indeed attacked but resorted to the police whistle he always carried on his key ring! But these were minor blips in a life of friendship with the famous names that graced the stage of His Majesty's: Henry Irving, Frank Benson, John Martin Harvey, Fred Terry, Matheson Lang, Seymour Hicks, Fay Compton (sister of Compton Mackenzie). Everything from Dickens' *A Tale of Two Cities* to Franz Lehar's *The Merry Widow* came to Aberdeen. But if we are to pinpoint the most poignant moments in the history of His Majesty's, one night stands out as a strong contender.

On that morning of 11th November 1918, the Armistice had brought to an end the tragedy of the Great War, as we then called it. That evening, the O'Mara Opera Company was presenting Gounod's *Faust* at His Majesty's. The crowds who had packed the streets with mixed emotions that day now filled the theatres. When it came to the 'Soldiers' Chorus', Joseph O'Mara himself led his troops to the stage, carrying a Union Jack in each hand, followed by the cast as they marched and waved banners and flags and sang the rousing chorus. It was a night for memories, if not for dry eyes.

But in the transience of life there is always something lurking round the corner. In 1923 Robert Arthur, impresario extraordinaire and by now tied up with Howard and Wyndham in London, decided to sell his beloved theatre. It was acquired by Walter Gilbert of the Tivoli, with a view to putting his son Lothian in charge. So the first flourish of history for His Majesty's Theatre came to an end, as Adair Nelson bowed out with the dignity you would expect, moving over to the Palace Theatre in Bridge Street for the next few years, before taking over the Lyceum Theatre in Edinburgh. But there he took ill and came back to Aberdeen, which had remained his home, where he died in April 1929, a true gentleman who set a style for theatre-going in his adopted city.

CHAPTER 53

The Donald Family

In 1933 His Majesty's came into the ownership of the Donald family, by now a name that stood for everything connected with entertainment in the Granite City. Earlier that century the Donald dynasty had started humbly in the east end of Aberdeen, when James F. Donald saw the opportunity of catering for the coming craze of the day and opened up his Donald's Dancing Academy in North Silver Street. He lived above the premises and there he raised his four sons, James, Herbert, Dick and Peter, each in his own time becoming a dancing teacher downstairs. Meanwhile, father James was displaying the sure instinct of the entrepreneur and preparing for what would revolutionize public entertainment – cinema.

The family involvement in cinema follows as a story in itself. But now they had acquired the jewel in the crown, the plush splendour of His Majesty's in Rosemount Viaduct, with its velvet warmth and air of opulence, where they launched another chapter in the theatrical history of Aberdeen. The glamorous nights were there to savour for succeeding generations of Aberdonians, from the opera of Sadler's Wells and the Ruritanian romance of Ivor Novello to the finest Shakespearean actors of the day: Donald Wolfit, Alec Guinness, Sybil Thorndike, Vivien Leigh. The stars who trod those Aberdeen boards read like a Who's Who of world-class talent, from Robert Donat, Emlyn Williams, Anna Neagle and Cicely Courtneidge to comedy legends like Gracie Fields, George Robey and Scotland's own Harry Lauder, as well as that great voice of operetta, Richard Tauber.

During the Second World War a musical act of the day featured a popular tenor, accompanied by his wife, who was a brilliant pianist. In 1943 their touring act was billed as 'Ted Andrews and Barbara – and introducing Julie'. It was the first time we had heard the voice of the little girl called Julie Andrews, destined for fame in Broadway musicals (*My Fair Lady* and *Camelot*) and Hollywood stardom in *Mary Poppins* and *The Sound of Music*.

Aberdeen's native output of acting talent doesn't match the level of its writers but there are those worth noting. The High School girl called Lois Obree, born in 1909, gained fame in London under her stage name of Sonia Dresdel, appearing in a string of films from the 1940s onwards such as *The Fallen Idol, The World Owes Me a Living, The Trials of Oscar Wilde* and *Lady Caroline Lamb*. A former pupil of the Grammar School, Andrew Cruickshank (1907–88), became a well-loved figure of stage and films but will be best remembered as Dr Cameron in the 1960s television series *Dr Finlay's Casebook*. Balancing the school rivalries, David Wilson left Gordon's College in 1966, and after graduating from Edinburgh University and RADA embarked on a theatrical career in the 1970s under the name of David Rintoul. But television gave him his greatest exposure, ironically in a later series as the eponymous Dr Finlay of *Casebook* fame.

In BBC TV's commendable versions of the Grassic Gibbon classics, beginning in 1970, producers were badly hampered by the scarcity of authentic North-east voices and were forced into casting from the Central Belt of Scotland, where anything north of Stirling is perceived to carry a Highland lilt. As any Aberdonian knows, the local tongue is flatter than that. The only consolation was that actors with a reasonable North-east connection stood a good chance of a part, thus the high quality performances from Eileen McCallum, Derek Anders, Victor Carin and Billy Riddoch, son of Willie Riddoch, well-known Aberdeen cattle dealer.

It also gave a professional opportunity to a talented actor and broadcaster like William Gavin, who had largely confined himself and his players to the local stage. Bill Gavin worked as a clerk for a coal and agricultural merchant and had to delay his dream of a full-time stage career. He launched his William Gavin Players in 1949 (with Ben Travers' *Rookery Nook*), virtually giving Aberdeen the privilege of its own repertory company, such was the high standard of performance. It was in 1967 that he moved to Perth Repertory as an actor/writer before taking a chance in London. There he landed in time to play the part of Alexander Fleming, the Scot who discovered penicillin, in a high-profile television dramatisation of his life. Bill Gavin died on Christmas Eve of 1995 at the age of eighty.

That leaves us with a double phenomenon that makes up for whatever lack of volume there has been in Aberdeen's theatrical output. If the comic sense of Aberdonianism has been spread around the world, it is due mainly to two names from succeeding generations: comedian Harry Gordon and the triumvirate who chose to call themselves *Scotland the What?* Harry Gordon, born in Constitution Street in July 1893, was Aberdeen's contribution to that pre-war generation of Scots comic entertainers that included Harry Lauder, Will Fyffe, Tommy Lorne, Dave Willis, Tommy Morgan and Jack Radcliffe. They reflected the Scottish mood of the age, giants of their time, and little deserve the derision that a later breed of would-be sophisticates have heaped upon them. (When I interviewed Irving Berlin in New York, he simply couldn't stop speaking about the talent and universal appeal of Harry Lauder. Just as much, Dave Willis was one of the all-time geniuses of clowning and miming in the mould of Charlie Chaplin.)

Harry Gordon personified the characteristics that Aberdonians love to play up at their own expense, taking his act as easily to the stages of Canada, the United States or South Africa as to his own home venue of the Beach Pavilion, where he produced his variety show on an annual basis from 1924 to 1940. (Fenton Wyness was his programme illustrator.) Harry had started out as a teenager with the local Monty's Pierrots at Stonehaven and developed into the best pantomime dame in the business, writing his own material and creating character studies by the dozen. Short and smart in his Gordon kilt, he possessed that magnetism which made him popular not only with his vast audience but with fellow comedians like Will Fyffe, his close friend.

Lord Provost Mitchell with Harry Gordon and Will Fyffe on VE-Day

Harry's varied routine included a record run of eleven consecutive pantomimes at the Glasgow Alhambra, and he eventually moved home to that city's first block of luxury flats, Kelvin Court on Great Western Road, which became a popular choice for show-business people like Jack Milroy and Kenneth McKellar. In Harry's day, his Glasgow neighbour was that city's favourite son, Tommy Morgan ('Clairty, Clairty' himself!), and in later life they could be seen sitting on a bench outside Kelvin Court sharing memories of their glory years. Harry's popularity in the west of Scotland owed much to the fact that Aberdeen had always been a popular destination for Glaswegians during their Fair Holiday; the Beach Pavilion was the focal point of summer entertainment in the city.

Harry was otherwise known as the laird of Inversnecky, which explains the café of that name still to be found on the promenade. It is a sign of the times that his famous Beach Pavilion went from being Harry Gordon's to Harry Ramsden's, part of the seaside enterprise run for several years by another Aberdeen legend, Willie Miller of football fame.

Harry's wife Jose made a name for herself as one of the best Aladdins in pantomime and their daughter Bunty became a dancer, later marrying the Canadian Norman MacLeod, who led the harmony group, the Maple Leaf Four.

The Donalds set the tone for the city's theatrical life for years. James F. Donald's four sons grew up to support and succeed their father. Jimmy took his place in the foyer of His Majesty's to welcome the audience (and was followed in time by his own sons, James and Peter); the founder's second son, Herbert, ran the Capitol while third son Dick combined his interest in the family business with a separate career in football, not only playing for the Dons between 1928 and 1938 but emerging as the most successful chairman in the history of Aberdeen Football Club. His crowning glory came in 1983, when the Dons of Pittodrie became the European Cup Winners' Cup champions, beating the greatest club side in the world, Real Madrid. That left the youngest member of the Donald family, Peter, who went off to London and became chairman of the powerful Howard and Wyndham chain of theatres, completing a breadth of show-business connections that helped to explain why the Donalds of Aberdeen gained a significance well beyond their own parish. They were known to Hollywood legends like producer Sam Goldwyn, who was said to drop everything to entertain a visiting Donald.

His Majesty's remained the last privately owned theatre in Scotland until 1974, when it was bought over by Aberdeen Corporation for £350,000, the local authority wisely engaging the Donalds to retain their management role. Health and safety regulations brought about a major refurbishment in 1980–82, but an even bigger upheaval was contemplated twenty years later. Into the new century, the Aberdeen Performing Arts Trust, now charged with running the theatre as well as the Music Hall, faced the fact that this wonderful building was grossly underused, available to the public only when they turned up for a performance. It had a wider role to play within the cultural life of Aberdeen. For a start, it needed a restaurant and coffee shop to attract the daily custom and acquaintance of the general public. There was also a call for a separate corporate hospitality room, a rehearsal area with the same stage layout as the theatre and a green room for cast and crew to meet and relax, now a standard requirement in all major

The Donald brothers discuss the Kingsway plan with architect Leslie Rollo.
Left to right: Richard, Herbert, James and Peter

theatres. This would also be the opportunity to upgrade the sound and lighting systems, overhaul the stage hoist, and remove the famous old revolving stage which had been a novelty in its day but was no longer required.

All this would mean an extension to the Frank Matcham building which had graced that attractive corner of the city for nearly a hundred years, an adjacent structure reaching down for its foundations to the former car park by the Denburn. The logistical problems belonged to Trevor Smith, of the city council architects department, whose design for the Aberdeen Maritime Museum had brought him award-winning acclaim. There would be no competing with Matcham's original design, out of the question financially in any case. Instead, modern design and materials would hopefully give an open welcome, particularly to a younger audience, without jarring too much on traditional sensitivities. Needless to say, however, the juxtaposition of dignified granite and modern glass drew criticism of incongruity. The work was carried out by the Robertson Construction Group, with David Steel as project manager, at a cost of £7.8 million, provided by Aberdeen City Council, the Scottish Arts Council Lottery Fund and Scottish Enterprise.

During the eighteen months of rebuilding, His Majesty's found a temporary home at the assembly hall of the Aberdeen College of Education at Hilton, naturally limited in its facilities but well adapted for the duration. At least theatrical entertainment was kept alive until that evening of 8th September 2005, when the guests, resplendent in evening dress, walked up the red carpet to view their new-style theatre in all its refurbished glory. Prince Edward, Earl of Wessex, himself something of a thespian, unveiled a bust of Frank Matcham and declared the theatre open. If the occasion lacked the overall lustre of previous re-openings, there was at least a gala performance by Scottish Ballet to send His Majesty's on its way once more. The man at the helm was chief executive Duncan Hendry, a native of Glasgow whose father's job as a prison governor brought him at one stage to Aberdeen. A graduate of St Andrews, he returned north, became director of the Aberdeen Alternative Festival in 1988 before moving to His Majesty's in 1999. Duncan Hendry had a staff of a hundred and a turnover in excess of £5 million.

Another key figure in the story had been Edi Swan, by then the archivist at His Majesty's after a life-long connection in which he became the first technical director in 1979, in time to be plunged into the planning of the 1980–82 restoration. A Fittie loon, Edi was a student at Gray's School of Art and had been painting scenery for the student shows when he became even more deeply involved in the scenic design of the theatre, in everything from the Whatmore Players and Fol-de-Rols of the 1950s to memorable seasons of Scottish Opera, *The Five Past Eight Show* and twelve years of designing and painting for *The Andy Stewart Show*. Into that theatrical career, Edi managed to weave a life of teaching art at the academies of Peterhead, Turriff and Ellon, where he became assistant rector in 1972. He was also a member of the Munn Committee, which established the curriculum for Scottish schools, and has written a history of His Majesty's Theatre.

CHAPTER 54

Scotland the What?

If Harry Gordon, who died in 1957, belonged to a recognisable tradition of Scottish comedians, his successors as prime purveyors of Aberdonian humour need more explaining. Show business was in that post-war turmoil that brought the double challenge of television and rock 'n' roll. Entertainment as we had known it was swept aside by a fresh mood of musical energy, led by Elvis Presley (an American whose roots were later confirmed as being in the Buchan parish of Lonmay!), calling upon youth to take over the world.

Student shows survived as a popular form of satirical entertainment, and in Aberdeen that meant an annual week at His Majesty's Theatre, during which budding talent had its chance to flourish. Into that scenario in the early 1950s came William D. Hardie, a Hilton boy who had left Gordon's College in 1949, having made his stage debut in the 1946 production of the school play, *The Auld Hoose*, the story of the founding Robert Gordon. But his main talent, as a writer of satire, developed in the student shows at Aberdeen University, from which he moved on with a scholarship to Cambridge. Retaining the connection with Aberdeen, however, he teamed up with a leading light of student comedy, Steve Robertson, and then with another student, George Donald from Huntly, whose piano playing brought an extra dimension to their post-university adventure, the Aberdeen Revue Group.

The group was an amateur pastime that ran through to the 1960s while the three young men carved out professional careers – Steve Robertson as a lawyer, George Donald as a teacher of modern languages at Gordon's College (later assistant rector of Perth Academy) and W.D. Hardie, now better known as Buff, becoming secretary of Grampian Health Board. With these responsibilities, however, they decided to bring down the curtain on their stage careers, choosing the Edinburgh Festival Fringe of 1969 as the venue of their grand farewell. For this, they gave themselves a new name, *Scotland the What?*, a parody of that more-serious national boast, 'Scotland the Brave'. The *Daily Express* reviewer wrote that, of all the comedy shows on the Fringe, this was the funniest. So, with crowds flocking to their church hall, the Aberdonians had to rethink their future. The rest is theatrical history.

Instead of ending their time on stage, it was just the beginning for *Scotland the What?*, which proceeded to run for another twenty-six years of phenomenal success, during which each gave up his career to become a professional entertainer. The formula was simple: three personable

Legendary trio from *Scotland the What?*: George Donald
at the piano, with Steve Robertson (left) and
Buff Hardie (right)

Aberdonians in dinner jackets presenting hilarious sketches and musical novelties with a strongly North-east flavour but adjustable for an audience in Glasgow or London. The world got to know place-names like Auchterturra and characters like Sandy Thomson, the convener, phoning Her Majesty at Buckingham Palace, hilariously inviting her in broadest Doric to 'open the Oldmeldrum Sports a wik on Setterday'. This was Aberdonian humour to succeed Harry Gordon, a more sophisticated form of entertainment, with shades of what England could produce with Flanders and Swan, or Richard Stilgoe, or Kit and the Widow. They managed to perpetuate the dialect against the tide of its decline from what had been the everyday speech of Harry Gordon's day.

Reaching into their sixties, Steve, Buff and George decided for the second time to bring it all to an end, back at His Majesty's Theatre where they had performed as students nearly forty years earlier. The farewell of *Scotland the What?* ran for a month, with the final show on Saturday, 25th November 1995. His Majesty's had seen many a memorable occasion in its ninety years, but nothing that quite compared with this. It was one of the most emotional nights ever to grace a British theatre. Out they came to another packed house, the welcome resounding from stalls through dress circle and upper circle to the utmost rafters of the gods. There were tears of laughter before they took us, with a parody of Rod Stewart's 'We Are Sailing', to the touching conclusion that 'We Are Failing'. The audience wanted to call its denial of lines like 'We're a hat-trick . . . of geriatrics'. When the final curtain prepared to drop, the natural reserve of Aberdonians fell into disarray, with a show of affection that even Harry Gordon would have envied.

The audience rose and stood for ten minutes of unashamed adulation. The three performers seemed bewildered by the demonstration and then, with an old-fashioned courtesy, they turned towards each other and exchanged handshakes. Throughout their career this had been a ritual in the wings before going on stage, but it was the first time the audience had seen it. There wasn't a dry eye in the house. There was time to spare a thought, too, for the talented and ever-popular James Logan, their artistic director, who had not lived to witness this precious moment. His place had been taken by Alan Franchi, well-known director at Grampian Television. When they finally let them go, the audience hung around the bars and foyer of His Majesty's, unwilling to release the last remnants of a memorable night. Occasions like these become milestones in your own life, to be fixed in the memory forever.

CHAPTER 55

How Cinema Changed Our Lives

As much as anywhere in the world, Hollywood changed the face of entertainment in Aberdeen in the most dramatic fashion. Within living memory, that story of the silver screen is inextricably tied up with that one particular family: the Donalds. The founding father, James F. Donald, was an enterprising boy from Newhills who not only ran his own cycle shop in Rosemount but was a prominent cycle-racing champion of his day. As already mentioned, he was a keen dancer, becoming the Fred Astaire of Aberdeen and opening his own academy of dancing and deportment in North Silver Street.

But the entrepreneur within him was stirring once more as he observed the rise of Hollywood. By 1915 he had moved into the glamorous world of cinema, starting with the West End at the top of Union Street (later called the Playhouse) and proceeding to build or acquire a total of seventeen cinemas, as well as His Majesty's Theatre, in an empire which not only took its place in local folklore but spread its name far beyond his native city. Who could forget the scented allure of those foyers as you drifted off to the glamour of Beverly Hills at the Capitol, the Majestic, the Kingsway or the Astoria, the Queens, the Belmont, the Cinema House, the Playhouse, the Grand Central or the largest of them all, the City Cinema in George Street, which had seats for 2,500?

For all the dominance of that one family, however, the Donalds were by no means first on the scene. As already mentioned, when James F. made his first tentative approach to this mysterious new world in 1915 he was assured that he had already missed the boat. That opinion came from one of the early pioneers, Dove Paterson, an elocutionist from Newburgh who had been making a name for himself at the old Alhambra Theatre. Now the cinema was his preoccupation, along with others like William Walker, who ran a prosperous bookseller's business in Bridge Street, and Robert Calder, an amusing character from Moss-side Farm at Glassel who joined in the pioneering work of the old cinematograph. The first exhibition of cinema in Aberdeen was given at the Philharmonic Hall in Huntly Street in 1896 by R.W. Paul, inventor of an early type of projector. But Walker the bookseller was hard on his heels, having moved from lantern slides to film projector in October 1896. He travelled all over the country with the added attraction that he himself filmed local events like the Braemar Gathering. This led to a command

The old Capitol Cinema, Union Street

performance at Balmoral, when Queen Victoria was so intrigued by the new-fangled invention that she invited him to London, where he was gaining a national reputation. In fact Aberdeen was playing a more prominent part in pioneering the art of film than any other town in Scotland.

It was Dove Paterson from Newburgh who achieved the first permanent cinema in Aberdeen, taking over the St Katherine's Hall in the Shiprow in 1908 and calling it the Gaiety. He was followed into cinema operation by a Londoner, Henry Phillips, who came all the way to Aberdeen to open the Picturedrome at Union Terrace and Skene Terrace, later to be the Cinema House and a base for the Donalds; and also by Bert and Nellie Gates, a couple of stage entertainers who used to perform a 'Skating Carnival' entirely on roller-skates. The lure of the cinema was too strong for Bert, a Campbeltown man, who would give Aberdeen one of the best loved of its early cinemas, the Star Picture Palace, affectionately known as the Starrie, situated at the corner of Park Street and South Constitution Street in what had once been the East End Mission. He would then expand to a public limited company called Aberdeen Picture Palaces and open the Globe in Nelson Street with new backers like Alexander Hay of the soft-drinks family who found such a new lease of life that he left the family business and devoted himself entirely to the cinema.

For a touch of class, however, it was left to Mr H. Bannister Howard (of the Howard and Wyndham family) to turn the former Arcade Skating Rink into the Electric Cinema, standing precisely where the Capitol would arise in later years. The Electric was said to be for the 'leisured and fashionable' and lived up to that claim with daily matinees providing free tea in a club-like lounge, along with cigars, sweets, cakes, papers and magazines and even headed writing paper for those with a note to dash off. Such was the sophistication of a bygone day, complete, of course, with its cinema orchestra.

The Hollywood bug was contagious, affecting even men like J. Russell MacKenzie, the Belmont Street auctioneer who converted the former Queen's Restaurant at the corner of Union Street and Back Wynd and, on Hogmanay night 1912, opened it up as the Queen's Cinema. Just before the First World War, a Glasgow company claimed the first purpose-built cinema in Aberdeen, the La Scala on Union Street, later to be remodelled as the Majestic, diagonally opposite the Capitol. All of this before James F. Donald had appeared on the scene. But his day would come, starting modestly at the top of Union Street. Meanwhile, as cinema grew ever popular, expansion continued, creating the social flavour of the time.

Newsreels of fierce action from the Battle of the Somme in 1916 spared no detail of the horror, for mesmerised Aberdonians as they sat in cinemas the length of Union Street and absorbed, for the first time, what was actually happening to Willie and Sandy and Bob in the bloody battlefields of a foreign land. Those who survived the nightmare came home to former favourites like Mary Pickford, Mabel Normand and Lilian and Dorothy Gish and found there were newcomers to savour in Gloria Swanson, Tallulah Bankhead, Lon Chaney and Rudolph Valentino. There was special delight when they set eyes on their very own international star from Aberdeen, Mary Garden, appearing in her first film, a screen version of her stage success in Massenet's opera, *Thaïs*. There were, of course, limitations for an opera singer who was trying to display her vocal talents in a silent film! Thankfully, Mary Garden would go on to make her name where it mattered most – in the opera house.

The Poole family from Gloucester, already well known in the city, had turned the old Palace Theatre in Bridge Place into a cinema in 1929 and added the brand-new Regent at Justice Mill Lane, later to become the Odeon. The latter project was the first chance to design a cinema for that extraordinary architect, T. Scott Sutherland, who went on to give us the Astoria at Kittybrewster and what he regarded as his finest creation, the rebuilding of La Scala to become the Majestic.

It is hard for a modern audience to grasp the size and scale, not to mention the sheer glamour, of those picture palaces, a whole world away from the popcorn complex of today. Consider the fact that, in his 1933 design for the City Cinema in George Street, Scott Sutherland gave Aberdeen a picture house with a capacity as big as that of Glasgow Royal Concert Hall and well in excess of the much-vaunted Sydney Opera House. Sutherland, the ebullient architect-cum-entrepreneur, would later give rise to the Scott Sutherland School of Architecture and play a major part in the creation of the Robert Gordon University.

When Bert Gates and his Aberdeen Picture Palaces turned the Electric into the Capitol in 1933 at a cost of between £60,000 and £70,000, one of the great novelties was the appearance of the very first theatre pipe-organ in the North-east, a £2,500 John Compton console which rose from the depths in a glare of spotlight amid a massive orchestration of sound to play during interludes and raise hairs on the back of the neck. The first resident organist was Harold Coombs, who had been a boy wonder in his native Sheffield and proved a big hit when he came north for his first encounter with a modern cinema organ.

By the late 1920s the public was tiring of the silent film, and the so-called talkies arrived in the nick of time. Al Jolson in *The Jazz Singer* set the scene for a mixed response, with early reception of disappointing quality, movement severely restricted and performers with squeaky voices running for cover. Aberdonians came out of the cinema scratching their heads in puzzlement over the American accent. For many, it was the first time they had heard it, and the confusion could be equated with that of an American trying to decipher the Doric of the North-east. By 1930 matters had improved with *The King of Jazz*, in which Paul Whiteman and his Orchestra featured the young Bing Crosby and songs like 'It Happened in Monterey'. It also hit the high spots with the first performance on film of George Gershwin's 'Rhapsody in Blue'.

Films were also on show at His Majesty's Theatre, which was taken over by James F. Donald in 1933. In his renovations, he installed the first revolving stage in Scotland, employed a fourteen-piece orchestra under the baton of Lambert Wilson and held a gala reopening on 14th August of that year, supervised by his son Peter. But it was one of the last acts of the enterprising James F. Donald. In March 1934 he died at his North Silver Street home, aged sixty-four. Thousands turned out to line the streets for his funeral procession to St Peter's Cemetery, a fitting tribute to an outstanding Aberdonian. His four sons took over the business. Though they had not been the builders of the Astoria, the Donalds promptly bought it over in 1936, when it was failing to reach the expected business. Dick Donald, who had managed the Grand Central when only fifteen years of age, became manager of the Astoria, still in tandem with playing for the Dons. In that mellow decade of the thirties, before the amplified beat came to threaten not only the concept of melody but the tenderness of the middle ear, the Hollywood talents that flitted across the silver screen included the incomparable Fred Astaire and Ginger Rogers, that wonderful skater Sonja Henje, Myrna Loy, Charles Laughton and the Marx Brothers.

By contrast, Aberdonians were reminded that murder was not an American preserve when the cinema screens flashed up a request for information about eight-year-old Helen Priestly, whose body was found in a sack in the lobby of her tenement at 61 Urquhart Road in April 1934. A neighbour, Mrs Jeannie Donald, was found guilty of Helen's murder and sentenced to death by hanging. The sentence was later reduced to life imprisonment.

The glamorous film-star Anna Neagle caused a stir in the city in 1937 on her way back from filming *Victoria the Great* at Balmoral. And the crowds were out in force again two years later for the Aberdeen premiere of her follow-up film, *Sixty Glorious Years*, at the Regent. On that occasion she posed for pictures in the same room of the sumptuous Palace Hotel that Queen Victoria herself had used as a sitting-room on royal visits to the city.

Whereas Aberdeen had reached a peak of twenty cinemas, the Second World War now marked the closure of some old favourites – the Starrie, the Globe and the King's. As the shadow of that war approached, Aberdonians were watching the future president of the United States, Ronald Reagan, and co-star Dick Powell in *Going Places*. By 1940, the Regent had become the Odeon and Bobby Pagan had come to play the organ at the Astoria (it slid in from the wings, as opposed to rising from the pit) as one of a succession of cinema organists that would include memorable performers like F. Rowland Tims and George Blackmore.

Bobby Pagan at the organ of the Astoria

Just as the battlegrounds of France had riveted cinema audiences in the First World War, so did the carnage of war engage a later generation. Official newsreels from the war of 1939 kept them on the edge of their seats, not least to see if they could catch sight of a relative among the troops passing in front of the camera. There was one particularly poignant story from 1940. A lady sitting in the Odeon thought she spotted her brother who had been reported missing at Dunkirk. Next morning Eric Robyns, the manager, re-ran the film in slow motion to help her identify him. She was hopeful but still not positive. On arriving home, however, she was met with a telegram to say that her brother was indeed safe! Along at the News Cinema in Diamond Street they were making their own local newsreels, and in October 1941 Aberdonians were able to watch that disastrous fire on their own doorstep, in which the famous old Palace Hotel was destroyed with the loss of six lives.

The Donalds were now firming their grip on the Aberdeen entertainment scene, taking over

Aberdeen Picture Palaces in 1941 and using the Capitol, Astoria and Kingsway to spread across the city epics like *Casablanca*, that memorable Oscar-winner with Humphrey Bogart and Ingrid Bergman, and Dooley Wilson singing 'As Time Goes By'. In the post-war period, the Picture House in Union Street became the Gaumont, and the Capitol broke all box-office records when Irving Berlin's *Annie Get Your Gun* hit the screen in 1950. But a warning came rumbling across the Atlantic to the effect that American cinemas were feeling the effect of television. For the moment, at least, we could proceed as if nothing was happening, taking in the novelty of three-dimensional films which required the wearing of coloured spectacles so cumbersome that it was soon overtaken by the wide screen of Cinemascope. James Stewart starred in *The Glenn Miller Story* and the 28-year-old Marilyn Monroe showed up with Jane Russell in *Gentlemen Prefer Blondes*. Local interest was stirred by that delightful film of the time in which schoolboys Vincent Winter from Aberdeen and Jon Whitely from Monymusk starred with Duncan Macrae in the world-wide distribution of *The Kidnappers*, written by that other North-east talent, Neil Paterson.

Crowds had flocked to see the film of the queen's coronation on 2 June 1953, an ominous date for cinema, in that it was the day the BBC made its very first outside television broadcast (not that the new medium had yet reached the North-east of Scotland). But its arrival would not be long delayed and the consequences were totally predictable. Whatever form the cinema would take in the future, it would not be housed in the kind of buildings we had known. New preoccupations would arise, whether bingo, bowling or disco.

By 1961, when commercial television augmented the BBC in the shape of Grampian (housed in the old tramway depot at Queen's Cross), the Palace Cinema had become the city's biggest ballroom, en route to disco; the Kingsway Cinema made way for the city's biggest bingo hall; and the huge City Cinema closed down in 1963 to become a large bowling alley. The Astoria gave way to bingo too, and when that failed, it became yet another shopping centre. So the pack of cards collapsed: the Torry in 1966, Cinema House in 1971, the Majestic and Gaumont in 1973, while the Playhouse was demolished to make way for shops and offices in 1974. In 1981 the closure of the Queen's and Grand Central put the final nail in the coffin of Aberdeen cinema as we had known it, virtually bringing to a close the Donald empire in their role as cinema proprietors.

The Capitol had survived longer than most, having once flirted with a diversion that added its own lustre to the show-business scene of Aberdeen. That was back in the 1950s, when the Donalds took over the running of Harry Gordon's old home at the Beach Pavilion. Those variety shows were then transferred to the Capitol, bringing to Aberdeen an array of top performers that read like a Who's Who of show business. They ranged from comedians Vic Oliver, Arthur Askey, Chic Murray, Charlie Chester and Jimmy Edwards to Guy Mitchell, Petula Clark, Shirley Eaton and those wonderful pianists, Rawicz and Landauer.

Of course cinema re-invented itself in the multi-complex halls of today, and in Aberdeen that finds outlet in two centres, one in Cineworld at the beach and the other at Vue, in the Shiprow, where Associated British Cinemas had opened the Regal in 1954, fifteen years after the original plan was thwarted by the outbreak of war. On top of that, the old Belmont cinema has gained a new lease of life as the Belmont Picturehouse, an imaginative venture in which it not only shows top-class films but enters into educational projects like local film-making and scriptwriting, complete with a café-bar.

Harking back to cinema as we knew it, there are footnotes which stick in my mind. One is the story of what happened to Bobby Pagan's famous Compton organ at the Astoria. It was saved by Robert Leys, head of music at the nearly Powis Academy, and re-installed in that school as a commendable piece of enterprise, with an opening concert at which the great George Blackmore performed. In November 1982 a pupil broke into the building one night, set fire to the school hall and reduced the famous organ to ashes. Such was the bleaker side of a society that had taken vandalism to new depths. The Capitol organ still exists, though its fate has not been much better. When its cinema days were over, it was kept in order by devotees like Michael Thomson, a city librarian who used to play it on Saturday mornings, when the public could drop in to enjoy the recital. But the Capitol became a nightclub and the organ was not afforded the protection it required. As a result it suffered damage and needs more than £300,000 of renovation and a new venue. For all the weird and wonderful causes that can attract lottery money, there is apparently no chance that the last vestige of Aberdeen's cinema-organ history will even be considered. Michael Thomson is now assistant organist at St Machar's Cathedral and would dearly like once again to run his fingers over that memorable treasure of Aberdeen's musical heritage. His passion for the subject has at least left us with a memorable history of cinema in Aberdeen from 1896 till 1987, entitled *Silver Screen in the Silver City*.

As another point to arrest my attention, it was in the midst of the onslaught on traditional cinema in the mid 1960s that one particular film broke all box-office records. For nine solid months, and with return showings thereafter, it was not some modern format that caught the public's imagination but a thoroughly traditional, old-fashioned film: *The Sound of Music*. Working for a spell in New York at the time, I conveyed the phenomenal ratings to the man who wrote the music for that memorable show, the legendary Richard Rodgers. As we sat in his fourth-floor suite in Madison Avenue, the grand piano resting in the corner, he told me how he and his lyricist, Oscar Hammerstein, had written those famous musicals, from *Oklahoma!*, *Carousel* and *South Pacific* to *The King and I* and now *The Sound of Music*. Rodgers was deeply touched to hear how his music was faring in faraway Scotland.

CHAPTER 56

This is the BBC

In an age of radio and television signals bouncing off satellites in the heavens above, the origins of broadcasting are a reminder of how primitive it all was in the beginning. Not that that detracted from the sheer sense of magic. The 'wireless', as it was called, came to Aberdeen on the blustery evening of Wednesday 10th October 1923, the opening night of the British Broadcasting Company's modest studio at 17 Belmont Street, upstairs from the premises of Aberdeen Electrical Engineering. Folk gathered round their crystal sets at nine o'clock to hear the Marquis of Aberdeen give his opening address, which was followed by music from the band of the 2nd Gordon Highlanders.

The fact that Aberdeen had been chosen as one of the pioneering stations in this new wonder of science was due to a man who was present on that historic occasion. John Reith, who was born in Stonehaven, was known as the father of British broadcasting and managing director of the founding company before it became a public corporation, the BBC, of which he was the first director-general. A stern and lonesome figure of moral rectitude, Lord Reith set the standards of principle and formality with which the BBC was long identified. Aberdeen's first wireless station, given the code signal of 2BD, amounted to a large room overlooking the railway line, hung with heavy black curtains on the walls to help absorb the noise from passing trains.

Early days of the BBC in Belmont Street – Willie Meston, A.E. Cruickshank and Betty Craig are among those performing 'Torry to the Fore'

Initially there was just one large microphone, enclosed in a wire mesh, a real source of trouble on warm days when an entrapped bluebottle would find itself with a captive audience, as frantic attempts were made to swat the pesky thing.

By 1924, however, 2BD had its own twelve-piece orchestra, decked out in full evening-dress, just as Reith had insisted even for his newsreaders, with no jackets to be removed except on a particularly hot day! The new medium was, of course, a natural platform for people like Aberdeen's own comedian, Harry Gordon of the Beach Pavilion, whose broadcasts would reacquaint the listening public with his fictitious town of Inversnecky, a name that still survives in a promenade café. In a broadcasting day stretching to six hours of live transmission you would hear regular news bulletins and a sports programme from Peter Craigmyle, Aberdeen's own international referee, a charismatic figure whose authority on the field was so complete that few footballers risked the humiliation of a public dressing-down. Peter also had his own sports shop in King Street.

There was even a local repertory company, adapting the classics or breaking into short performances in Doric, a whole new platform for local talent like William Mair, Grace Wilson, George Dewar and Daisy Moncur. In those experimental days, when all you heard was the output of your own local station, the low-powered transmitters were aimed at the greater density of city populations. So there was little or no joy for country folk. In the growing confusion of too many wavelengths, however, there had to be a streamlining of the system. The BBC established a long-wave transmitter at Chelmsford, and the Post Office's development of land-lines meant that everyone could join the network. With the pioneering days over and the small stations all but disappearing, the call sign of 2BD in Aberdeen went out for the last time in 1929. But in view of its geographic position, not to mention a public outcry about cutbacks, Belmont Street survived better than most, becoming a relay station taking programmes from Glasgow, enjoying a limited opt-out facility, and transmitting the national programme that began in March 1930.

Its status was enhanced in 1932, when it became a feeder station for a new Scottish regional service. A splendid programme-maker, Moultrie Kelsall, was sent to Aberdeen, where he not only built a talented team and breathed new life into broadcasting but also met his wife, Ruby Duncan, a well-known pianist. Several programmes were originating from the city each week, involving local writers and actors like Arthur Black, Willie Meston and, not least, the colourful George Rowntree Harvey, brilliant author, critic and feature-writer with *The Press and Journal*. Belmont Street contributed to *Children's Hour*, the whole country tuning in for the latest adventures of the Aberdeen Animals, who were members of the local BBC staff, including Moultrie Kelsall himself and two highly talented broadcasters of the day, Alan Melville and Howard M. Lockhart. Alan Melville, who would succeed Moultrie Kelsall, went on to greater fame as a leading British playwright. He also collaborated with Ivor Novello in writing the composer's last production, *Gay's The Word*, for actress Cecily Courtneidge. Harry Gordon was in full flight and North-east listeners, caught up in the novelty of the new medium, also revelled in hearing other local singers and entertainers like John Mearns and Willie Kemp – and a regular programme of bothy ballads which came live from the farm of Crichie, near Fyvie, home of John Strachan, one of Aberdeenshire's most glorious rural characters.

But expansion through the 1930s meant that Belmont Street was being stretched beyond limit and a search for more spacious premises landed upon the former dwelling of Beechgrove House in the Mile End district of the city. For all the advances in technology, however, Alan Melville missed the more informal human contact when he could have a 'fly cup' with his staff. Within nine months of the move to Beechgrove, war broke out, with drastic effects on broadcasting. Regional programmes merged with national ones to become the Home Service. Change came swiftly and dramatically. Howard Lockhart and the Aberdeen Animals were rehearsing for *Children's Hour* one day when a phone-call from Edinburgh told them to go home. The programme was axed forever. Howard accepted the inevitable and took his cast down to the Caledonian Hotel for a farewell meal.

The pre-war ethos of the BBC wireless days in Aberdeen was never quite recaptured, and by the time Britain lived through the bleakness of post-war austerity television was ready to launch itself as a dominant influence on society. Spreading in stages from London, BBC Television reached the Central Belt of Scotland just in time for the coronation of Queen Elizabeth II in June 1953. North-east farmers attending the Royal Highland Show at Alloa were among the first witnesses as stand-holders invited them in to gape in wonder at the black-and-white pictures now flickering from a wooden box in the corner and showing the post-coronation royal visit to Edinburgh. Whatever would they think of next?

The first signals reached Aberdeen in December 1954 but the television service came fully to the North-east the following year, when a large trade exhibition in the Music Hall put the public in touch with the dealers who would provide their sets. The Beechgrove studios had gained a new lease of life, now producing television programmes, sometimes opting-out locally, as in the days when they were dealing only with radio, but also capturing the national audience on an impressive scale. With a good North-east pedigree, Pat Chalmers became the boss at Beechgrove before being whisked off to Glasgow and London and coming back again to be controller of BBC Scotland. It was a time of innovation, with producers like Mike Marshall and Arthur Anderson helping to establish Aberdeen's credentials.

Just as Beechgrove brought Robbie Shepherd to the fore on the radio as the voice of Scottish country dance music, so did it succeed with a national audience for two particular programmes on television. Pat Chalmers had been the driving force behind rural broadcasting in the early days. A monthly programme called *Farm Forum* had just been launched in January 1965 when the second edition had to be cancelled because the camera crews were required in London for the funeral of Sir Winston Churchill. *Farm Forum* was followed by *Landward*, again with Chalmers in charge, until he was succeeded as producer in 1978 by Arthur Anderson, a native of Dumfries, who proceeded to a twenty-three year connection with the programme, broadening it out to a countryside appeal and creating some gems of television production.

Along with producer Mike Marshall, Pat Chalmers was also responsible for launching *The Beechgrove Garden*, which became a national institution, featuring two of the most likeable characters the viewers had ever seen. Jim McColl was a Kilmarnock man who had come to work at the North of Scotland College of Agriculture and then for Morrison Bowmore, the distillers at Oldmeldrum. Through an inspirational piece of casting, he was teamed up with an archetypal man of the North-east soil, George Barron, whose practical apprenticeship in horticulture led him to the heights of his calling, at the Great Garden of Pitmedden. In 1952 Major James Keith, the last laird of the estate, had presented his mansion to the National Trust for Scotland, which decreed that the garden should be restored to its former glory.

That task was entrusted to George Barron, who ventured as far as the Palace of Versailles to study some of the techniques. At a later stage back home, he found himself plunged into the bewildering world of television, teaming up with Jim McColl to inform and entertain the viewing public from *The Beechgrove Garden*, which was indeed the back garden of BBC Aberdeen, just over the dyke from Mid Stocket Road. The two contrasting characters complemented each other to perfection, Jim McColl the more polished and articulate, while George Barron imparted his knowledge in a warm, down-to-earth and, above all, naturally spoken

A legendary partnership: Jim McColl and George Barron at the BBC TV's Beechgrove Garden

Doric that made few concessions to the English language. The chemistry turned them into national characters, producing one particularly hilarious moment when the pair were proceeding to their different tasks. It was a perfect example of how varied the dialects of Scotland are. In all innocence, George made a perfectly valid Doric statement when he said to Jim: 'Well I'll juist awa' an' dee a wee jobbie in the pottin' shed.' How was he to know that 'a wee jobbie' in the distant vernacular of Billy Connolly's Glasgow meant something much closer to functional necessity?!

Grampian Television

When the BBC faced commercial rivalry, a consortium gained the franchise to launch Grampian Television in 1961, replacing the old tramcar depot at Queen's Cross with brand new premises on Fountainhall Road, just round the corner from the BBC at Beechgrove. Though Scotland's John Logie Baird first demonstrated his television pictures in 1926, and the BBC made a tentative start with the new medium in the 1930s, it was after the Second World War before a service was properly established.

In the ravaged state of post-war Britain it was not a high priority. But the public appetite was certainly whetted by the arrival of television in the mid 1950s, even if it was a BBC monopoly with just one channel. The idea of commercial competition would follow only when an Independent Television Authority set out to evolve a structure of coverage for the whole of

Britain. In competing groups, shrewd business people geared themselves to apply for the new opportunity, making the origins of Grampian Television an interesting tale. One such group comprised the directors of Caledonian Associated Cinemas, who operated a chain of cinemas throughout Scotland from their headquarters in Inverness. Their formidable team consisted of CAC chairman Robert Clark, a Paisley man who ran Elstree Film Studios; Sir Alexander King, who was deeply involved in Scottish cinema; Provost Robert Wotherspoon of Inverness; and Captain Iain Tennant of Morayshire.

Though the intention had been to apply for the Central Scotland contract (Scottish Television), they decided instead to wait for the North and East of Scotland franchise, mainly because they were not quite prepared but also, no doubt, because the original companies down south, Rediffusion, ATV and Granada, were all losing money. By the time Grampian's franchise was advertised in 1960, however, the fortunes were turning and the experienced Lord Thomson from Canada, who landed STV, had made his famous remark about television becoming a licence to print money.

By now, the bees were buzzing round the Grampian honeypot, about ten swarms of them, with Sir Alexander King and his team facing strong competition, particularly from groups headed by Sir Tom Johnston, former secretary of state for Scotland, and an amalgamation of the theatrical Howard and Wyndham company and the Donald family of the Aberdeen cinemas. King's men won the contract but took on board former rivals like Lord Forbes, Tom Johnston and that fine North-east talent, Neil Paterson, distinguished novelist and Hollywood screenwriter. With the launching date aimed at the autumn of 1961, they set out to find a site for the studios, the possibilities including the old reform school in Whitehall Road, the Royal Northern Club building at the junction of Union Street and Huntly Street, and the Astoria Cinema at Kittybrewster.

They finally settled for the old Corporation tramway depot on Fountainhall Road at Queen's Cross. Ward Thomas came from Granada Television to be sales controller and the company secretary/accountant was Alex Mair, a North-east farmer's son who had worked for Gandar Dower, the founder of Aberdeen Airport. The studios were ready for an official opening on 16th September, and in the early afternoon of Saturday 30th September 1961, the station went on air with the face and words of actor James Copeland announcing: 'This is Grampian – the station serving the North and East of Scotland.'

Thus commercial television came to Aberdeen, under the name of the mountain range that roughly symbolised the area to be served. There was now a competitor for the BBC, with a local identity and flavour that brought its own special pride, even if North-east caution at first had reservations about the interruption of programmes by advertisements. For the next forty-two years Grampian would operate from Queen's Cross, building up its own tradition of newsreaders and presenters, including Jimmy Spankie, June Imray (the Torry Quine), Selina Scott and Kennedy Thomson. Keeping local culture in mind, programmes would range from *Bothy Nichts* and *Calum's Ceilidh* to *Living and Growing*, *Top Club* and *The Art Sutter Show*. A major milestone along the way was reached in 1997 when Grampian Television joined the Scottish Media Group, linking into Scottish Television in the Central Belt at a purchase cost of £106.7 million.

The new Grampian TV headquarters, opened in 2003

Then came the major upheaval of 2003, when Grampian Television said goodbye to Queen's Cross and moved across town to a brand new headquarters at Craigshaw Business Park in West Tullos. Most recently, in 2006, the Grampian name gave way to that of STV, a rebranding apparently made necessary by the modern mystery of multi-channel digital television. Along that route towards its first half-century there were, of course, many other milestones. In 1962 Ward Thomas became managing director and local programming increased from two to six hours per week, returning a first-year profit of £47,421. Whereas programmes had initially gone out through transmitters at Durris and Mounteagle, near Inverness, the Angus transmitter went into operation in 1965 to coincide with the opening of Grampian's news centre in the Marketgait, Dundee. By 1968, with Captain Iain Tennant now chairman, Grampian was claiming more than a million viewers and recording a profit of £340,926. It was also providing for ITN the coverage of the British Open Golf Championship from Carnoustie.

Into the 1970s, James Buchan became programme controller and Alex Mair chief executive, while Aberdeen lawyer Calum MacLeod joined the board. New transmitters were expanding the Grampian area at Rosemarkie in the Black Isle, Rumster Forest in Caithness, Gartly Moor near Huntly, Knockmore on Speyside and Tay Bridge in Fife. The documentary *What Price Oil?* collected the Shell Award for promoting an understanding of the new industry that had come upon Grampian's doorstep. And the station welcomed big names of the future in Isla St Clair and Billy Connolly. During the 1980s, Grampian marked the fortieth anniversary of the retreat to St Valery, involving the Gordon Highlanders of the 51st Highland Division, and kept up with the more cheerful happenings in Gothenburg, as Aberdeen Football Club beat Real Madrid to win the European Cup Winners' Cup of 1983. Employing a staff of 343 by 1987, Grampian appointed Donald Waters as chief executive to replace Alex Mair, who was retiring, and added Alistair Mair, head of Caithness Glass, to the board.

The 1990s brought highlights like evangelist Billy Graham at Pittodrie and Selina Scott's film on Prince Charles, followed by the opening of a new studio in Stornoway and the purchase, in partnership with Border TV, of the new Scot FM radio station. Crowning it all was Grampian's role in presenting the National Television Awards for the full ITV network, with a peak audience of 12 million. In 1998 Grampian mourned the sudden death of its popular controller, Alistair Gracie. He was succeeded by Derrick Thomson, who later became managing director.

Northsound Radio

The silver anniversary of commercial radio in Aberdeen was celebrated in 2006, by which time Northsound had moved from its original home to a brand new station across town at West Tullos, complete with five state-of-the-art studios and a large open-plan office. It was a far cry from that first day of broadcasting on 27th July 1981, when Northsound Radio burst into life at 6 a.m. from its modest base in the former Rubislaw Special School at the lower end of King's Gate, diagonally opposite the Atholl Hotel. The site completed a neat triangle of media buildings, with the BBC's Beechgrove House less than half-a-mile towards Rosemount and Grampian Television's headquarters lying a similar distance along Fountainhall Road.

Here was the less formal style of presentation, upbeat and chatty in the established manner of commercial radio, with local voices bringing local news and views and disc-jockeys engendering admiration by their aptitude for non-stop chatter. Northsound settled comfortably with its audience and provided a platform of advertising for local business. If it was all a novelty at first, Aberdeen soon embraced its own radio station. The founding company was led by Andrew Lewis, member of the well-known shipbuilding family who stayed the course and was still chairman at the twenty-fifth anniversary. Continuity was to be found elsewhere in a popular figure like Damien McLeod, who arrived in the first year and, apart from a brief departure in 1992, has covered the entire history of Northsound. In 2007 he was presenting the mid-morning show.

Others who learned their craft in Aberdeen and went on to greater exposure at national level included Nicky Campbell, who presented the Northsound breakfast show from 1983 till 1986 and gained a name on a variety of London-based radio and television programmes, such as BBC One's *Watchdog*. Bryan Burnett cut his broadcasting teeth in six years at Northsound before making a name for himself at the BBC and ITV. Alison Craig was among the women of the late eighties who went on to prominence in national broadcasting and journalism, while Bobby

Hain, a confident youngster from the early days, switched from disc-jockeying to management and became the big chief at Scottish Television in Glasgow.

Sports coverage benefited from the upswing in the fortunes of Aberdeen Football Club, which accompanied the rising fortunes of the oil industry, with the golden age of Alex Ferguson bringing the ultimate glory of Gothenburg, 1983. By 1995 the station had split itself into Northsound 1 and 2, but expansion beckoned and the company moved to Tullos in 2002, selling the old premises to CALA property developers, who turned them into luxury flats. Into the new century, Northsound was staging Aberdeen City Council's Hogmanay party in Union Street, with acts as big as The Proclaimers, Deacon Blue and Liberty X, while its 'Free at the Dee' open-air concerts became the launch pad of the biennial 'Offshore Europe', attracting crowds of 50,000. On a more formal note, Northsound became host to a prestigious annual business dinner, attracting as speakers political figures like Alistair Campbell, Peter Mandelson, Ken Livingstone and Michael Portillo.

CHAPTER 57

This Sporting Life

The Olympians

On the basis that Olympians represent the pinnacle of sporting achievement, Aberdonians have taken special pride in four swimmers who carried their name to the world stage. They also felt entitled to claim a fifth swimmer – gold-medallist David Wilkie, whose triumph at the 1976 Montreal Olympics was celebrated in his parents' home at 18 Viewfield Road and elsewhere in the city. The fact that his Aberdeen parents, Harry and Jean, were living in Ceylon when David was born, and that he was schooled at Daniel Stewart's College in Edinburgh, raised doubts about the claim. But Aberdonians don't give up so easily. They will point out that David Wilkie did attend Broomhill School and that he was sent to Edinburgh only because Gordon's College Boarding House didn't have a vacancy at the time.

Confining ourselves to the indisputable, Athole Still blazed the Olympic trail for Aberdeen when he went, after a royal send-off at Buckingham Palace, to compete at Helsinki in 1952. He was followed by fellow-Gordonian Ian Black, whose lead-up to the Rome Olympics of 1960 brought him newspaper acclaim as the greatest all-round swimmer in the world at the time. If that experience ended in a shocking tale of discouragement and disappointment, it does not prevent Athole Still insisting to this day that Ian Black remains the finest swimmer Britain has ever produced.

In that same Rome Olympics, Aberdeen's Sheila Watt went from her secretarial desk in the city to strike a splendid blow for her sex by gaining a fourth place in the 100-metre butterfly. And completing the Aberdeen quartet, David Carry was part of the British team at the Athens Olympics in 2004. But his greatest triumph to date came two years later, at the 2006 Commonwealth Games in Melbourne, Australia, when he won gold medals for both the 400-metre freestyle swim and the 400-metre medley to set Scotland on its way to a stunning achievement of twenty-nine medals, including an unprecedented eleven golds.

David, whose family name was already well-known through Jamieson and Carry, the Union Street jewellers, had swum for Scotland in the Commonwealth Games four years earlier. But in 2006 he helped to set the whole nation alight with a new pride in its young athletes, a fresh interest in sport and a determination to harness it all for the country's claim as a future venue for the Games. Sheena Sharp from Huntly gained her own share of glory and upheld Aberdeen-shire's name with another double gold for shooting. As part of the triumphant return on a fine spring day, David Carry went back to his old school, Robert Gordon's College, where he was welcomed home as a local hero by headmaster Hugh Ouston. As he proceeded to address pupils at their assembly, the emotion evoked by his presence was a clear illustration of how the young can be inspired by example. If one of their own pupils, so recently himself at school, could reach the heights in sport, then perhaps so could others.

The encouragement of his old school was sadly in contrast to what happened to his famous predecessor, Ian Black, who had since become his idol and inspiration and who had been there to welcome him home the previous evening. Black had been Carry's head teacher, having returned in 1990 to lead the Junior School at Gordon's. As an all-time sporting hero, he had achieved phenomenal success, beating the Scottish senior butterfly champion and swimming for the full national side when only fourteen years of age. By seventeen he was collecting one gold and two silver medals at the 1958 British Empire and Commonwealth Games in Cardiff and gaining five British titles before electrifying the European Championships in Budapest, winning three golds and smashing five European records.

Ian Black, Aberdeen's greatest swimmer

By eighteen, Ian Black had broken two world records and seemed set, as the golden boy of swimming, to collect gold medals at the Rome Olympics of 1960. Then it all began to go wrong. Scorning the chance of training in warmer climes, he stayed loyal to Andy Robb, swimming master at Gordon's College, who had done so much for his development. Unfortunately, in the build-up to the Olympics, the college pool was under renovation so he turned to the public baths at Justice Mill Lane. But Aberdeen Corporation would give him no 'clear time' to train on his own – and in any case the baths' management were under attack for over-chlorinating the water. So, while his leading opponents of the day were training with all the facilities and warmth of Australia and the United States, the Aberdeen boy was heading down the road to the open-air pool at Stonehaven. Athole Still was among those who railed against the neglect of his colleague, feeling he was only half-prepared for what should have been the greatest moment of his life.

Compounding the misery, the headmaster of Gordon's College, David E. Collier, a sternly unpopular figure, chose to launch an attack on the media for making such a fuss of Ian Black while giving little recognition to the school's academic achievements. Mr Collier failed to grasp that however many academics he might produce, there would be only one Ian Black. In a petty confrontation, he stripped the boy of his prefect's badge, at which point Black walked out through that vaulted gateway, never again to be seen as a pupil of Robert Gordon's College.

Through all this embarrassment, he set out for the Rome Olympics, denied the guidance of his mentor, Andy Robb, who had to stay behind for his duties at the college. Andy's wife went instead! The Scottish press made last-minute pleas for Robb to get himself to Rome, telling of a pessimistic protégé badly in need of guidance and support. Black was making his own decision to pull out of the butterfly event, but that was his best hope, they said. Instead, he went for the 400-metre freestyle, which was won by Murray Rose of Australia. In the absence of photo-finish equipment in those days, several judges pronounced a dead-heat for bronze between Ian Black and Jon Konrads of Australia. But the controversial verdict went to Konrads.

A committed Christian even then, Ian Black accepted his fate and retired from swimming two years later, when he was still only twenty-one. To this day, now retired in the west end of Aberdeen, he harbours no bitterness. But he will retain forever his place on the pedestal of international swimming. So, in that notable spectrum of Aberdeen swimmers, where do we now place David Carry, who has certainly benefited from the best of facilities in other lands – but has yet to meet that broader band of talent beyond the Commonwealth? Even now, with more Olympic days ahead, he must surely take his place immediately after his idol and former head teacher, dislodging Athole Still from second place.

If consolation were required, the glorious Athole has found it in a colourful life following a swimming career in which he was first capped for Scotland in 1950, when he was sixteen, and went on to swim for both Scotland and Great Britain for the next twelve years until he retired in 1962. His anticipation of two more Olympics after Helsinki was thwarted by the format and timing of events, which went against him. But if Athole Still was a wonderful swimmer, he could hardly have imagined what else lay round the corner. Back home in Aberdeen, he had a big win at the horse-racing and opened a betting shop with his father in Park Street, near their home in Summerfield Place. In all weathers you would find Athole shouting the odds on the greyhounds at the Bridge of Dee. He graduated in French and German at Aberdeen University and found another lucrative career, as a sports commentator with the BBC, not only covering every Olympic Games from 1964 until 1984 but sharing with Peter West the presentation of that long-running and highly popular television series, *Come Dancing*.

And even that was not the end. In his mid-twenties Athole discovered he could sing and was taken in hand by Willan Swainson, head of music at Aberdeen University. At Covent Garden they assessed a fine tenor voice and he was directed towards the Guildhall School of Music, where he financed his studies by working for ITV and also as swimming correspondent for *The Times* and *The Sunday Times*. The bold Athole, now married to Aberdonian Isobel Cordiner, a production assistant he met at Grampian Television, then emerged as an operatic star to take leading roles at Scottish Opera and Glyndebourne. After further studies in Italy, however, he made another change of career and embarked on personal management, starting with two famous clients from his own world of swimming, Duncan Goodhew and Sharron Davies. From there, his stable extended to people like the great Olympic rower, Steve Redgrave, with whom he co-owned a racehorse, and former Pittodrie favourite Gordon Strachan, as well as another football figure he once met in Italy. His name was Sven-Goran Eriksson, who would become the much-publicised manager of the England football team. Athole Still International became well established, a family company of high profile inspired by the irrepressible Aberdonian who had become a major figure on the London scene. Living in Dulwich, he would swim in an unheated pool every summer morning, drifting back in memory across a colourful career, beginning at Gordon's College all those years ago under the tutelage of the great Andy Robb.

The Glory of Gothenburg

For all the athletic achievements across the years, the main focus of sporting attention in Aberdeen, as elsewhere in Britain, falls inevitably upon the game officially known as association football, or soccer, to distinguish it from other forms of the ball game. That means Aberdeen Football Club, housed at Pittodrie Park for more than a hundred years, and which has built up a romance of high points and heartbreak that will be forever an essential part of the history of the city.

The fact that the club lived through its first forty-three years without a single sign of silverware, and a further thirty-four years of minimal success, speaks volumes about the loyalty of that cloth-capped brigade of Aberdonians you would find trekking down Merkland Road East,

Willie Miller and his Dons in Gothenburg – Europe's top team in 1983

week after week, in the belief that the so-called beautiful game might one day bring reward for their patience. And one day it did. It is one of the truly romantic stories in the history of football that a modest-sized club outwith the shadow of Rangers and Celtic had the gall and the gumption to strike out for Continental glory – and to bring home the European Cup Winners' Cup in 1983, having beaten the greatest football club in the world, Real Madrid, in the final.

Old men had lived and died and seen nothing of this, but their grandchildren cheered on their behalf and were grateful. There is a theory that such an unimaginable achievement owed something to the new-found confidence imbued in Aberdonians by the burgeoning oil industry. Whatever the reason, on a rain-soaked night in the Swedish city of Gothenburg, Aberdeen was placed firmly on the European map, going on to confirm its superiority by beating Hamburg in the subsequent Super Cup and being hailed as the number one football team in Europe. It was a bad time for atheists, who had to concede that miracles do happen after all!

The glory of Gothenburg was a far cry from the origins of Aberdeen Football Club, which grew out of three local teams deciding in 1903 to amalgamate: Orion, who played at Cattofield, Victoria United at Central Park, and an earlier Aberdeen FC which had gained tenancy of Pittodrie Park. Pittodrie was a Celtic name meaning 'the place of manure', lending the critics some ready-made ammunition when the quality of football was poor. At least the club had now joined the mainstream of Scottish football, even if it had to wait two years for election to the top league. That took them into the company of the twin giants of the Scottish game, Rangers and Celtic, which then, as now, have the advantage of that massive support of sectarian division in Glasgow and the west of Scotland. The farcical scale of the dominance of the two teams in Scottish football can be gauged from the fact that between 1904 and 1947, the Scottish League Championship was won either by Rangers or Celtic, with the exception of 1931, when Motherwell won. In other sports, such as horse racing, a handicap system would have been imposed, while in boxing a mismatch would have been declared.

It can be reasonably said that the real high points in Scottish football occur on those rare occasions when a team other than one of the Old Firm clubs scores a triumph. Having posed the only consistent threat to Rangers and Celtic in a hundred years, the success of Aberdeen Football Club in the 1980s was an outstanding achievement.

Fortunately there were consolations in those less-ambitious times, memories of loyal footballers with exquisite skills who were not so readily lured away by financial bait. In olden times, Aberdonians would rave about loyal footballers like Donald Colman and Willie Cooper, whose only thoughts were to play for Aberdeen. More surprisingly, such loyalty endured into modern times when the club's greatest-ever player, Willie Miller and his defensive partner Alex McLeish, spent their entire careers at Pittodrie. One of Aberdeen's best-ever and most creative ball-players, Gordon Strachan, gave seven wonderful years to Pittodrie before accepting an offer from Manchester United.

So the catalogue of famous names can be paraded by those with long memories: Alex Jackson (of the Wembley Wizards) and Benny Yorston in the twenties; Willie Mills and Matt Armstrong in the thirties; George Hamilton, Stan Williams and Archie Baird in the forties; Archie Glen, Graham Leggat, Harry Yorston, Paddy Buckley and Jackie Hather in the fifties; Charlie Cooke, Jimmy Smith and Zoltan Varga in the sixties; leading into the Golden Era of the late seventies and eighties. Success finally came to the club after forty-three years when the Dons, as they came to be called, won the Scottish League Cup in 1946, followed by the Scottish Cup a year later and, the prize above all, the Scottish League Championship in 1955. In the week of that 1955 triumph, a baby born in the east end of Glasgow was given the name of William Miller. The Dons did not win that top prize again until the day after his twenty-fifth birthday, when the same William Miller captained them to victory. It was the start of what became known as the Golden Era of Pittodrie.

Coincidence plays some strange tricks. On a wet summer evening in 1978 the first-ever history book of Aberdeen Football Club was launched at the Capitol Cinema in Union Street, marking the first seventy-five years of the club. Two thousand Dons' fans crowded in to take part in what was a gala night of nostalgia. Jack Sinclair and his band entertained, notable players dating back to the First World War were paraded on stage and the audience cheered as film clips from old newsreels recalled the limited occasions when the Dons had found success. At a more private cocktail party, the latest member of the Pittodrie staff, just arrived, came quietly on the scene in time to be interviewed by Arthur Argo of the BBC. What did he think of this milestone in the history of the club, he was asked.

'I'll just have to try to emulate the feats of the past,' he said modestly. Feats of the past? The interviewee was Alex Ferguson, former Rangers player and recently sacked manager of St Mirren. Who could have guessed that the new manager was about to render that history book out of date and create the golden age that would lead to European glory? In the process, he would write himself into the broader history as perhaps the most successful football manager Britain has ever seen, going on to dominate the English Premiership and to lead Manchester United to ultimate glory as European Champions.

All that was in the future as he settled to the task of shaping up a phenomenal run of success for Aberdeen. Within a few years he had finally broken the mould of Rangers–Celtic domination in Scotland, winning the League Championship three times, the Scottish Cup four times, the Scottish League Cup and Drybrough Cup – and crowning it all with those European triumphs in 1983. Winning the Scottish Cup in 1982 was the entrée to that European adventure which led to a quarter-final meeting with the famous Bayern Munich at the Olympic Stadium in the Bavarian capital. A goalless draw was still no guarantee of victory in the second leg back at Pittodrie on 16th March 1983, and that prospect seemed to have gone when Bayern were leading 2–1 with fifteen minutes left to play.

Not even an equalising goal would save Aberdeen now, since the away-goal rule would favour Bayern. But miracles can happen. Gordon Strachan and John McMaster executed a clever ruse that deceived the Germans and left Alex McLeish to head the equaliser. One more goal required. Could it possibly be done? Within a minute, the same John McMaster delivered the perfect ball into the Bayern penalty-box, Eric Black headed against the German goalkeeper, and the enigmatic John Hewitt was there to put it through between his legs. Aberdeen had

Willie Miller outwits Celtic's Frank McGarvey

never seen anything like it. The final thirteen minutes seemed like an age but, when the referee drew breath for the final whistle, the scenes of jubilation turned that March evening into the greatest occasion Pittodrie had ever witnessed.

A semi-final tie with Waterschei of Belgium was merely a rehearsal for the European final in Gothenburg on 11th May 1983. Upwards of 12,000 diehard Aberdeen supporters invaded Sweden in fifty plane-loads and by car, bus and, not least, by the P&O ferry *St Clair* for what would be, win or lose, the greatest adventure of their football experience. If someone had told them a few months earlier that the glamorous Cup winners of Europe, from Scotland to the Soviet Union and from the Baltic to the Mediterranean, would knock each other out in a contest that would leave the incomparable Real Madrid to face the Dons of Pittodrie in the final, there would have been calls for a psychiatric assessment. This was the stuff of David and Goliath.

But there was no lack of confidence as the Red Army of Aberdeen gathered at its focal point of the Europa Hotel and won over the hearts of the Swedish neutrals, charmed by the good humour of their Scottish visitors. In all truth, the Spanish supporters regarded the result as such a foregone conclusion that the bulk of them stayed at home. So those who came were well outnumbered. They all headed for the Ullevi Stadium amid gathering clouds and flashing lightning, a suitable background to a night of approaching drama. Eric Black's opening goal for Aberdeen was cancelled out by a penalty for Real and normal time ended in a draw. A penalty shoot-out would suit the Spaniards so Aberdeen had to settle it in extra-time. In many ways this had been Peter Weir's night and once again he embarked on a run and a pass to Mark McGhee, who rounded his marker and crossed the ball to the penalty area. That young man for vital moments, 22-year-old John Hewitt, was racing in to beat the goalkeeper with a magnificent header.

Eight more minutes of drama and the final whistle brought the finest moment in the eighty-year history of Aberdeen Football Club. Whereas they had once struggled to succeed in Scottish football, the players had now beaten the best that Continental Europe could provide. As Willie Miller received the European Cup Winners' Cup, bedlam broke out in scenes of ecstasy that spread across the city of Gothenburg. Back in Aberdeen, *The Press and Journal* would show the picture of a totally deserted Union Street during the match – and a contrasting one of two hours later as crowds spilled out in celebration. The 'welcome home' next day brought unprecedented scenes to the route from the airport, through Bucksburn and Woodside, up Anderson Drive and down Queen's Road and Albyn Place to Union Street. Estimates of 100,000 people were not an exaggeration. Aberdeen was having its hour of glory, unlikely to be repeated in another hundred years, so the moment had to be savoured with relish. There had been four key men in the creation of this fairy-tale: chairman Dick Donald of the cinema family, his vice-chairman, Chris Anderson (both former Dons players), captain Willie Miller and manager Alex Ferguson, the architect of victory.

Fergie, as he was commonly called, enjoyed three more years of success, but by 1986 no one could begrudge him accepting the top job in English football. At Old Trafford he went on to revive Manchester United with an unprecedented run of success, collecting his knighthood in the process as well as some racehorses, one of the accustomed trappings of his new-found wealth.

Triumphal homecoming for the Dons after their victory at Gothenburg

The boy from Govan had truly made good. Expectations were now so high that lesser days were an almost inevitable consequence. And so it turned out. Whereas the first three managers at Pittodrie – Jimmy Philip, Paddy Travers and David Halliday – had spanned a total of fifty-three years between them, the age of intolerance in which we live would bring something different.

The next eighteen years would see a string of nine different managers, none of whom could reasonably be expected to recreate the dream. They included the all-time hero of the playing field, Willie Miller, who did at least return at a later stage as an executive director. As the glory of Gothenburg took its place in history, it is hard to believe that, into the twenty-first century, there is now a whole generation of Aberdonians who remembered nothing of it. Nevertheless, it must surely remain not as an albatross of nostalgia to discourage future generations, but as a reminder that, in this troubled and unpredictable world, all things are possible.

As a footnote to the history of Pittodrie, there is a lingering regret in the fact that the boy who would one day be voted the greatest Scottish footballer of all time would never perform on his own home territory. Born in 1940 at Printfield Terrace, Woodside, a skinny little lad with a squint, Denis Law, was whisked away from his native city at the age of fifteen, before anyone at Pittodrie even knew of his existence. It was a stroke of luck for Andy Beattie, Aberdeen-born manager of Huddersfield Town, whose brother Archie happened to live near the Law home and spotted the talent of the local youngster. Denis Law would develop into the dashing figure of

British football, mainly with Manchester United, as part of a deadly triumvirate with the equally legendary George Best of Northern Ireland and Bobby Charlton of England. Who knows what he might have done for football in Aberdeen had he stayed in his native city?

When Paul Putted for Gold

The proudest moment in Aberdeen's golfing history came unexpectedly at Carnoustie on a summer's day of 1999, when Paul Lawrie was gifted the chance of a play-off in the most dramatic of circumstances. The Frenchman Jean Van de Velde was coasting to victory in the Open Championship when he embarked on a cavalier, even suicidal, course of rescuing himself from a spot of bother in the burn. The Aberdonian Paul Lawrie, former assistant professional at Banchory but by then attached to the modesty of Newmachar Golf Club, was suddenly thrust into the limelight of a three-way play-off, from which he emerged as the Open Champion of 1999. It was one of those incredible moments, the stuff of fairy-tales, leading to a place in the Ryder Cup and regular involvement in the United States and European tours. Paul settled into a new-found affluence at Milltimber, home as often as possible to see his beloved Dons and highly supportive of junior golf in the North-east, to which he had become a hero.

Golfer Paul Lawrie, Open Champion at Carnoustie in 1999

The little-known fact that Paul Lawrie was not the first Aberdonian to win the Open Champion-ship is just part of the fascinating story of how the game of golf evolved in the North-east. In the beginning, it was played on the Queen's Links, now part of the municipal course. The Society of Golfers at Aberdeen started life there in 1780, though golf had been around long before then. With King's College founded in 1492, scholars were continually passing to and from the Continental seats of learning, just as Aberdeen traders were doing business in the Baltic.

The Continental fashions they brought home included a variety of ball games, while golf had taken its place as a social pastime, played on Sunday after kirk. But with the coming of the Reformation and Calvinism, stricter attitudes drove golfers out of town, to the Links, still with the risk of prosecution for playing on a Sunday. A critic of Calvinist attitudes, Charles Smith, the first of Aberdeen's golfing historians, also pointed out that sport of all kinds fell into abeyance in the stormy days of the Jacobite Risings. During this time, he said, 'golf ceased to be a game of the masses', and well into the nineteenth century 'there was hardly a working-man golfer in Aberdeen'.

The Society of Golfers at Aberdeen was responsible for several of the rules of golf still fundamental today, including those which forbid improving the lie of the ball by beating down grass or earth and limiting the time available to search for a lost ball to five minutes. The Society became the Aberdeen Golf Club in 1815, a week before the Battle of Waterloo, and it is thought the country was so preoccupied with the possibility of French invasion that golf fell out of favour. When it revived, the members included names from the leading families of the time, like the Haddens, Piries, Burnetts, Crombies, Bannermans, Davidsons and Abercrombies, easily recognisable on the Queen's Links in their scarlet tailcoats and black lum-hats, which were eventually superseded by the large floppy velvet cap.

The first clubhouse was a room at the back of Alexander Munro's shop in King Street. But there were problems at the golf course. There had always been football on the Links but now there was also cricket and horse-racing. Herring fishermen dried their nets, agricultural shows were held, and there was a proposal to route the Buchan railway line that way too. Enough was enough and the golfers negotiated a lease on the Balgownie Links, on the north side of the Don, described as a waste ground covered in heather and whins. The land was cleared and the Aberdeen Golf Club found its permanent home, from where it encouraged others to take up the game. The Bon Accord Club was formed in 1872 and interest was further stimulated by challenge matches in which men like Old and Young Tom Morris from St Andrews took part.

The working-man golfer had reappeared, and the Victoria was the next club to come on the scene. When the Northern and the Caledonian Golf Clubs were formed in 1895 and 1899 there were then four clubs playing at the Links. Golf was now on the march and it was not long before Hazlehead became a municipal course. The course architect of the day, incidentally, was the famous Dr Alister MacKenzie, who designed the Augusta course on which the US Masters Championship is held every April.

Murcar took its place adjacent to Balgownie in 1909, and clubs had also been springing up along the River Dee: Deeside (1903), Banchory (1905), Aboyne (1883), Ballater (1892) and Braemar (1902). Balnagask completed the chain of links courses that stretched southward from Murcar, with interest spreading northward to the beautiful Buchan course at Cruden Bay. Aberdeen Golf Club had grown quickly, and in 1903 the royal title was conferred by King Edward VII. A year later it further encouraged golf in the city by presenting the Royal Aberdeen Medal for an annual competition at the Town Links, a championship that excited huge interest and drew crowds of more than 10,000.

Royal Aberdeen had the benefit of a crack golfer and able organiser in Macbeth Moir Duncan, an Aberdeen advocate with an illustrious sporting and academic background who was also club secretary from 1893 until 1921. A Cambridge graduate and rugby captain, he was also capped for Scotland at wing three-quarter. Moir Duncan recruited Archie Simpson, one of six golfing brothers from Carnoustie, to be the club professional and a formidable team was immediately in place. He organised exhibition and challenge matches between leading professionals of the day, especially when they were in the North-east for the highly popular

Cruden Bay tournament. At one time or another he had all the big names on show, including the famous triumvirate of Vardon, Taylor and Braid.

Serious inter-club competition in Aberdeen began with the Maitland Shield in 1913, in which an invincible university team was led by William Tweddell, a medical student from Yorkshire who came to Aberdeen after service in the First World War, during which he won the Military Cross and Bar. Later a member of Royal Aberdeen, Tweddell then became a doctor in Worcestershire, won the British Amateur in 1927, became captain of the Great Britain and Ireland Walker Cup team and captain of the Royal and Ancient Golf Club. He was back in the city as guest of honour at the Royal Aberdeen bicentenary in 1980.

Back at the old Town Links, the town council had engaged the famous English professional J.H. Taylor to redesign the course in 1911. Nearby tenements were teeming with young lads seeking an outlet for their energies. George Duncan, born in 1883, was the son of a local bobby at Oldmeldrum who was transferred to Aberdeen and lived in a house on the edge of the Links. Eight-year-old George had a passion for football but saw the chance to make a sixpence as a caddy for the golfers. A natural ball-player, he was offered terms as an outside-right by Aberdeen Football Club but also discovered there was a living to be made at golf. Turning down the Dons at eighteen, he applied for a professional's job in North Wales. That was the beginning of a remarkable career in which he won the Open Championship in 1920 and captained the Ryder Cup team of 1929, the first British team to win, with Duncan himself managing to hammer the great Walter Hagen in his 36-hole singles matches.

In the early days of the century the exodus of Scotland's professionals to make a living in America was at its height. Another Aberdeen loon who learned his golf at the Links, Willie Macfarlane, born in 1889, may have been an outsider when he approached the US Open at Worcester, Massachusetts, in 1925. But he tied with that other legend, Bobby Jones, and won the play-off for the title the following day.

The first tournament held under the auspices of the North-East District of the Scottish Golf Union was the Journal Cup, played at Balgownie in 1922, the year in which the *Aberdeen Journal* amalgamated with the *Free Press* to become *The Press and Journal*. Down the years *The Press and Journal* and *Evening Express* have been strong supporters of golf, with knowledgeable writers like Peter Craigmyle, Jimmy Forbes, Norman Macdonald, Alastair Macdonald, Gordon Simpson and Colin Farquharson.

An Aberdeen public starved of golf during the Second World War turned out in their thousands to watch new heroes like Jack Booth of Murcar, an insurance man pre-eminent in the local game. But he was challenged by a man whose ball skills were even greater elsewhere – Tommy Pearson, Aberdeen and Scotland outside-left, greatest exponent of the 'double-shuffle' and one of football's most artistic performers. By the late fifties another local name was hitting the headlines in the flamboyant personality of Harry Bannerman from Murcar, of whom it was said that he could putt like God. Harry, complete with big cigar, turned professional in the sixties, embarked on the European tour and had his moments of glory when he was chosen for the Ryder Cup of 1971, in which he had historic encounters with Arnold Palmer and Jack Nicklaus, two of the greatest golfers of all time.

The 1970s were also the heyday of men like Sandy Pirie of Hazlehead, who won a Walker Cup place, and the Chillas brothers from Huntly: David, who won a Scottish cap, and John, who became Scottish professional champion, with many other titles on the Tartan Tour. Other prominent names of the time included Frank Coutts, a Walker Cup player in the eighties who was then professional at Deeside for more than twenty years, and Ronnie MacAskill, appointed professional at Royal Aberdeen in 1975 and still there more than thirty years later.

The North-east's young golfers have benefited from the Grampian–Houston Initiative, given impetus by Stewart Spence (of the Marcliffe at Pitfodels), a former Royal Aberdeen club

Stewart Spence

champion, and providing a platform for promising talent to be seen in the United States.

Into the new century, the focus fell on Richard Ramsay of Royal Aberdeen, a full-time amateur with a Walker Cup cap and the prospect of a bright future. That future came closer in spectacular form in 2006, when Richie, as he is commonly known, captured world headlines by winning the United States Amateur Championship, following in the footsteps of golfing legends Bobby Jones, Arnold Palmer, Jack Nicklaus and Tiger Woods. That virtually made 23-year-old Richie the number one amateur in the world and earned him an honorary life membership at Royal Aberdeen, celebrated at a dinner in his honour, a unique distinction for one so young.

Richie Ramsay, winner of the US Amateur Golf Championships, 2006

A highlight of the Aberdeen golfing experience came in 2005, when the Senior British Open was played at Balgownie and was won in an exciting finish by another of the golfing legends, the ever-popular Tom Watson. From Watson's homeland of America came another stirring prospect in 2006 when the billionaire entrepreneur Donald Trump announced a £300 million plan to build a world-class golf complex on the Menie Estate, near Balmedie, to the north of the city. Many European sites had been considered but Scotland remained the favoured option, not only as the home of golf but because

Trump's mother, Mary McLeod, was a Stornoway lass who emigrated in 1932, when she was twenty. The economic benefits were said to be colossal but the main threat to Trump's ambition came from environmentalists, who feared for the sand dunes, and from those with thoughts of building a wind-farm. As Charles Murray said, there's aye a something!

The fact that an Aberdeen Ladies Club was formed in 1892 was due to the initiative of Blanche Harrower, daughter of the famous professor of Ancient Greek at Aberdeen University, William 'Homer' Geddes and wife of John Harrower, who succeeded her father in his university chair. The ladies rented the playing fields at King's College, a venture which failed miserably when their little course was hacked up by hammer-throwing students. So they moved to Balgownie Links. Having had nineteen secretaries in the first twenty-eight years, the ladies then struck luck with Charlotte Lyon, eighth child of the city's lord provost, Sir Alexander Lyon. Charlotte held the post for the next fifty-one years and proved herself a very fine golfer, on the verge of international honours.

Internationalists down the years have ranged from Kathleen Cochrane and Beatrice Mellis, in the early days, to Annette V. Laing in the sixties (she was also Scottish Ladies Champion) and Joan Hastings (Mrs Joan Rennie) in the seventies, another Scottish Champion who also played for Britain against the United States in the Curtis Cup. Then came Elaine Farquharson of Deeside Ladies with a wonderful career that saw her win international honours against Europe and the United States, her victory as Scottish Ladies Champion in 1990, and defeated finalist in the British Ladies. Into the new century, Elaine became non-playing captain of Scotland. The most recent internationalist has been Sheena Wood of Aberdeen Ladies. Outwith the amateur scene, there were also the professionals like Janet Wright, daughter of the professional at Aboyne, and Muriel Thomson, who had the unusual distinction of being appointed lady professional at Portlethen.

From Grace to Bradman

In those far-off days before film or television, special circumstances were required for the game of cricket to flourish in an area like North-east Scotland. For a start, it needed people who knew the game – and those who were willing to learn how to play it. The fact that it was well established by the 1840s is a good enough starting-point for an intriguing history. By the mid nineteenth century Aberdeen was a rapidly developing industrial town with new arrivals keen to continue the game they had played down south.

One such group were Customs and Excise men, sent north to ensure that tax was paid on paper, by then a major local product. Cricket was also played seriously in the public schools of the south, where the sons of many a well-to-do Aberdeen family were sent for their education. They, too, were keen to continue with cricket on returning home. One of those families was the Piries, who owned the Stoneywood Paper Mill. So, in 1850, with cricket-loving Excise-men keeping an eye on paper tax and the sons enthusiastic about their sport, the Pirie family laid out the first cricket ground in the area. From such beginnings came the Stoneywood Cricket

Club which, in the twenty-first century, has amalgamated with Dyce to become one of Aberdeen's two representatives in the Scottish National Leagues.

Indeed, several clubs have had an association with the paper industry, including printers, lithographers and the local press. Another interesting element is that, for nearly forty years from 1848, Aberdeen had its own boys' public school, called Chanonry House, which was not only successful academically but produced a remarkable number of graduates who played a part in the development of cricket in the city. The first, and probably most outstanding, was James Forbes Lumsden, whose name runs through the story of Aberdeen cricket for more than sixty years. In 1857, aged just nineteen and an apprentice solicitor with Smith and Cochran, he convened a meeting in the Aberdeen Hotel (situated off Broad Street) with the idea of starting a 'senior' cricket club in the city. That meant the club had to have its own ground – and players had to wear cricket flannels.

The main purpose of the club was to enable Aberdeen to challenge the top Scottish sides of the day – Lasswade, Grange and West of Scotland – an aim that gave rise to Aberdeen Cricket Club. Forbes Lumsden leased four acres at Queen's Cross, and for five seasons the town had a senior club. The end of that lease meant a return to 'junior' status, the players having to share fifteen pitches which the city council had provided at Aulton Links. In those days the clubs used to organise practice twice a week, starting at 6 a.m. – with a fine of two pence for any player who was late! By 1866, however, Forbes Lumsden had negotiated a new lease at the Holburn Ground (between Broomhill Road and Allan Street), and senior status was reclaimed under the broader name of Aberdeenshire Cricket Club, which has survived into the twenty-first century as the other of the two North-east members of the National Leagues. At a time when rugby, golf, tennis and even football had yet to gain real popularity, cricket was drawing large crowds to Holburn, with major attractions that included the great W.G. Grace and his South of England XI.

When housing became a more lucrative option for the Holburn ground, Aberdeenshire decided to seek new pastures, at which point two former Chanonry House pupils, the brothers James and Robert (later Sir Robert) Williams, took matters in hand. By 1890, Mannofield was purchased and made ready to become the permanent home of the county club, as it has remained ever since.

Meanwhile, the 'Links' clubs would come and go, with Hawthorn and Crescent ever-present as the star sides. In 1878, however, Joseph Ross not only founded a successful Caledonian club but recognised that the thirty or so clubs playing at the Links needed better organisation. His initiative brought about the Aberdeen Cricket Association, of which he was the first president. From that first season of competitive cricket in 1885, two clubs, Crescent and St Ronald, have a continuous history to the present day. When five sides from the county were added in 1887, they included Kemnay and Kintore, two more clubs with a continuous history. The name was then changed to the Aberdeenshire Cricket Association.

So the personalities began to emerge. Forbes Lumsden himself captained Aberdeenshire for twenty seasons and appeared in at least one Scottish team. James Williams, who procured Mannofield, was an outstanding bat for Aberdeenshire over thirty-four seasons until 1907. But the biggest headlines in those days belonged to F.A. Smith, who went from Chanonry House School to study medicine at Aberdeen. The Northern Cricket Annual of 1890 says of him: 'Ten years ago, in the Holburn Ground, that wild medical and brilliant cricketer popularised the game to enthusiasm, and electrified all onlookers by his brilliant defence and hard hitting. Was there a broken slate or window-pane for half-a-mile around the local "Oval" that Smith was not chaffingly blamed for . . .?' F.A. Smith went on to play for Somerset, the first player from Aberdeen to appear in English County cricket.

Two local families stood out in that period: the Lumsdens, who had seven members playing at different times for Aberdeenshire, and the Browns, who were the backbone of a very good Caledonian team, with five of the family involved. Morley Brown also found time to be the outstanding all-rounder for Aberdeenshire from 1890 until 1902. That was the first year of the Scottish Counties Championship, when Aberdeenshire came second to Forfarshire, going one better in the following year and winning the title on two more occasions before the outbreak of war in 1914.

The twentieth century brought the formation of the Scottish Cricket Union, the first national ruling body, and with it a more satisfactory method of selection for international caps. Mannofield's quality was quickly recognised. R.G. Tait first came to notice while still a pupil at Ashley Road Primary by scoring a century against the Grammar School. Having played his early senior cricket for Braemar CC in the Bon Accord League, Bobby joined the county side at seventeen and was soon top batsman. In his eleven years in county cricket (five seasons for Aberdeenshire before moving on to work in Dundee) he created all sorts of records. In each of five of those seasons, he scored more than a thousand runs. But his greatest moment came in 1909, when Scotland played the Australians. R.G. Tait top-scored in each Scotland innings in a game where the Australians just managed to escape with a draw. With the outbreak of the First World War cricket ceased completely and more than 550 of Aberdeen's regular players volunteered for service. Bobby Tait served under Brigadier-General A.F. Lumsden of the Royal Scots, a former team-mate at Aberdeenshire and son of Forbes Lumsden. Tragically, Bobby was so badly wounded that he never played cricket again.

During that war another of Aberdeenshire's internationalists, R.S. Clark, was distinguishing himself in a different field. As a biologist, he joined the 1914–17 Antarctic expedition led by Ernest Shackleton. When the *Endurance* was crushed in the ice, Clark emerged as the man of initiative. As Shackleton led his group of six to seek help, Clark stayed on Elephant Island with the remaining crew and was said to be the force behind many of the projects that kept them alive through months of isolation. On his return to Britain, Robert Clark was uniquely awarded the Polar Medal with Clasp. He returned to play for Aberdeenshire and Scotland in the 1920s and to have a distinguished career in marine biology.

With wartime hibernation, Aberdeenshire faced extinction in 1916, having only two paid-up members but still due the burden of local taxation for its large ground. Once more, Forbes Lumsden stepped in to save the club he had founded sixty years earlier. The new dawn of 1919 brought a fresh enthusiasm, led by the big clubs of pre-war days: St Ronald, Kintore, Balmoral, Stoneywood and, especially, Huntly. In fact the 1920s was really the era of Huntly CC, four times Grade I champions and six times Aberdeenshire Cup winners, while regularly supplying players for the county. These included J.G. Scott, G. Scott and G.J. Clemens, in a tradition that continued in future years, bringing Captain G.W.A. Alexander, J.C. Richardson, W.A. Donald and C.J. Mearns to play for Aberdeenshire and Scotland.

School cricket, notably at the Grammar School, had been played for many years, but in 1921 Aberdeenshire CC started a junior section, mainly with boys from Ashley Road School, Broomhill School, the Grammar and Gordon's College. Gordon's and the Grammar both opened new playing fields around this time and their former pupils' clubs established themselves in local cricket. The importance of a junior section at Mannofield became clear when two recent juniors, John Mortimer in 1932 and George T. Forbes in 1937, received their first caps for Scotland. They were the outstanding players of the 1930s, Mortimer taking more than half the wickets for Aberdeenshire over a number of seasons.

In 1932 the county club was able to enter its second XI in the recently founded Strathmore Union, a league of significantly higher standard than the local grades. Subsequently, the Mannofield XI finished top of the union in the three years leading up to the war. Unlike the First War, cricket survived throughout 1939–45, albeit on a reduced scale, after which it was another team from outside the city that dominated, just as had happened after 1918. This time it was Inverurie's turn for the limelight. In fact, for thirty-five years it shared supremacy in Grade I with Kemnay, Stoneywood, Kintore and Cults, all clubs with their own grounds. Until the 1980s only St Ronald, North and Artisans managed to break the monopoly.

Another similarity with the 1920s was the initiative taken by Aberdeen Grammar, Gordonians and Aberdeenshire. The former two clubs entered the Strathmore Union and employed professionals for the first time, with Grammar FPs winning the title in 1948, and on three more occasions without professional help, before they left the union in 2000. Gordonians won the league only once, in 1994, and bowed out of the union in 2003.

Aberdeenshire remained at the top of cricket, with four consecutive county championships, featuring a string of international players in R.H.E. Chisholm, F. Findlay, T.A. Findlay, G.T. Forbes, J. Mortimer, G.W. Youngson and, later, J.C. Richardson.

First capped in 1948, Ronnie Chisholm played regularly for Scotland until 1971, by which time he had accumulated eighty caps. George Youngson was one of the all-time great bowlers of Aberdeen cricket, topping the English first-class averages in 1949, thanks to his performances for Scotland.

The high point of cricket in Aberdeen throughout the century came in September 1948, with the Scotland v Australia game at Mannofield. It was all the more memorable in that it was the great Donald Bradman's last game in Britain, a farewell in which he scored his last first-class century in front of what is still the biggest crowd ever to watch cricket in Aberdeen. Another major milestone was Aberdeenshire's centenary celebrations in 1957, when the great Surrey side of P.B.H. May played at Mannofield. The game was sponsored by Sir John Hay, an Aberdonian cricket lover. At the end of the game it was revealed that Sir John had set up a trust fund on behalf of the club, a generosity with tangible results still evident in the twenty-first century.

Sir John Hay's XI v. Surrey, centenary match 1957. Fred Trueman is fifth from the left, back row

National cricket leagues in Scotland were introduced in 1996, when Aberdeenshire became the first Scottish League champions. Meanwhile, Stoneywood/Dyce was making remarkable progress. In just six seasons it came from being a 'small' club in the local grades to one of the elite ten clubs in the Premier Division. In the mid-sixties, Aberdeenshire had asked Vic Coutts and George Murray to organise coaching, a significant development that brought junior cricket to an almost unprecedented level of popularity, making up for the serious decline in schools cricket. Under this guidance, the players who rose to the top included G. Angus, A. Bee, D.B.S. Brown, N.W. Burnett, W.A. Donald, D.H. Johnston, H.G.F. Johnston, J.D. Knight, D.G. Moir, J.D. Moir (Grammar FPs), D. de Neef, F. Robertson, M.J. Smith, R.C. Smith (Grange) and D.E.R. Stewart.

As Stoneywood/Dyce rose to prominence it appointed Steve Knox as professional coach and benefited greatly from the organising skills of Allan Barron. That produced full Scottish caps in Kyle Coetzer, Stuart Coetzer and Gordon Goudie. Professionals, however, had an earlier history. From Harry Lillywhite in 1859, Aberdeenshire had engaged English pros until after the Great War, most notably Schofield Haigh, who had three distinguished years at Mannofield before playing for Yorkshire and England.

In 1934 the club brought Alma Hunt from Bermuda, one of the great personalities of cricket, an all-rounder whose presence brought tram-loads of spectators to Mannofield just to see the great man. Hunt was a fast bowler, a prolific, hard-hitting batsman and a brilliant fielder. A highly popular figure all over the city, he maintained his link with Aberdeenshire until 1947, when, on retirement, he introduced his cousin, Nigel Hazel, who carried on the family connection for a further seven seasons. He, too, was a prodigious hitter, later moving to Forfar and becoming professional for Strathmore.

After a lean spell in the 1950s, some of the Sir John Hay Fund was used to attract a top-class professional, Rohan Kanhai, already a star batsman with the West Indies. But the title remained elusive. In 1986 India's Sanju Mudkavi began a twelve-year engagement with Aberdeenshire, joined in the city by his brother Andhu, who became the first Gordonian professional in forty years. It was no coincidence that, in 1994, Gordonians won the Strathmore Union for the one and only time. When Inverurie (1993), Stoneywood/Dyce (1994) and Huntly (1999) joined the Strathmore Union they, too, realised the value of a professional and in recent times there have been more such appointments than at any time in the local history of the sport.

Just as the influence of the Lumsden family was beginning to wane at the end of the nineteenth century, another family came to Mannofield whose service would stretch, almost unbroken, for well over a hundred years. In 1892, John Mortimer became an honorary member, soon to be followed by three of his sons as players: John, Alex and Andrew. Thus began a highly impressive family record of playing for Aberdeenshire, holding office and keeping the club alive in the Great War. By the 1920s a third generation had arrived, through Alex's son John, who became the main strike bowler for five seasons.

After winning his second Scottish cap in 1933 he had the misfortune to be injured while playing football! – an incident that curtailed his bowling style. By now brother Arthur was joining him at Mannofield. However, John survived to play again for Scotland and to be part of that highly successful Aberdeenshire team of the post-war years. In fact he was still willing to turn out in the 1960s, forty years after his arrival, when he was also the club secretary. On his death in 1967 the Mortimer connection was broken, but just for five years, when his son-in-law, H.O. Smith, joined Aberdeenshire. Howard Smith, well-known in that other capacity as a master at Gordon's College, went on to serve the county as a committee member for more than thirty years. Having married John Mortimer's daughter, he and Sheila extended the connection with son Colin J.O. Smith, who went on to top all the family achievements, not only captaining Aberdeenshire but becoming the most-capped Aberdonian cricketer of all time. By 2005, Colin had gained 105 caps in seven seasons as a high-order batsman and specialist wicket-keeper, with the prospect of being the most successful Scottish wicket-keeper in history.

Over the years, more than 250 clubs can be identified as part of the Aberdeen cricket scene, more than half of them associated with employment, as seen in names like Aberdeen Comb-works, City Police, Culter (Paper Mills), Esslemont and Macintosh, Hall Russell, Hall and Co., Hendersons (engineering), Torry Research and University Press. With school cricket virtually dead, the requirement of the new century is for clubs to embrace the coaching process. There are hopeful signs at Banchory, Cults, Stonehaven, and the latest North-east club at Methlick, which farmer and writer Charlie Allan has proudly publicised as the MCC of Scotland!

Jason's Proud Moment

To the sporting public of Aberdeen, rugby has always been regarded as a minority interest. Nevertheless the roots of the game go back to the 1870s, when Aberdeenshire Rugby Club was first established. Until the First World War, however, it was played rather informally. You would find, for example, that the boys of the Grammar School had to play against adult teams, spurred on by H.F. Menzies, a Scottish internationalist who was on the school staff.

By 1911 a team drawn from the Grammar School and Gordon's College ventured south for the first time to play George Heriot's in Edinburgh – and won. Geographically, of course, Aberdeen was remote from the main centres of Scottish rugby and it was not until 1913 that the first Aberdonian was capped for Scotland. G.A. Ledingham was a Grammar FP who later played for Glasgow University. But a surprising number of teams began to appear, with names like Engineers, Queen's Cross, Nomads, University and the former pupil clubs of Gordon's and Grammar. By the 1920s the game had settled into a more structured set-up, with local leagues established and occasional forays south made either as district teams or as individual clubs.

Standards at both school and senior rugby levels were raised by the appointment of Duncan McGregor as games master at the Grammar School in 1920 and the subsequent arrival of J. Kerr Hunter at Gordon's College. Their coaching led to a rich crop of local talent in the later 1930s. Rugby was on the move. Dr J.R.S. Innes of Grammar FPs was capped before and after the Second World War and captained Scotland in 1948. That war had interrupted many a career but soon there would emerge a string of notable figures, from Dally Allardyce and Doug Smith of Grammar FPs to Bert Bruce and the Findlay brothers, Frank and Tom, of Gordonians. By the 1950s there were five main clubs established in the city: Aberdeenshire Wanderers (heirs to the Engineers), Grammar FPs, Gordonians, Aberdeen University and Aberdeen Academicals, which appeared for a time under the inspiration of Peter Glen but later merged with Wanderers. Since the Second World War some outstanding individuals have graced the rugby scene. The Grammarian E.J.S. Michie played for Aberdeen University, won fifteen caps and became a British Lion. Donald Macdonald, a Gordonian, played for Edinburgh University and was capped four times, while his school contemporary, Kenny Stephen, settled to a life in Brazil, where he represented Teacher's Whisky and went on to captain the Brazilian international rugby team.

The mercurial Gordonian scrum-half Ian McCrae was the North-east's most exciting player from the sixties into the seventies, not only capped for Scotland but excelling as a cricketer and as a footballer, to the extent of attracting the attention of senior soccer clubs. He also carved his own bit of history as the first-ever substitute allowed in international rugby. Other notables, like Ken Scotland of Aberdeenshire and Ron Glasgow of Gordonians (he was a PE teacher at Gordon's), enriched the local scene. And Aberdeenshire also had the benefit of a young Borderer called Bill McLaren, who came north to train as a PE teacher before gaining legendary status as the greatest of all rugby commentators on radio and television.

In the 1990s Stuart Grimes produced a remarkable tale. As a pupil at Gordon's College he was one of six brothers who created a record inasmuch as they were all at Gordon's at the same time. But Stuart showed little or no interest in rugby, applying his skills instead to basketball, squash, tennis, ski-ing and American football. He was already a student at Edinburgh University before he emerged as a 6ft 5in giant of rugby who went on to be one of Scotland's most-capped forwards of all time, approaching seventy appearances in the new century and having a spell as Scottish captain. With the coming of the professional game he went to play for Newcastle Falcons. A few years behind him, fellow Gordonian and school captain Chris Cusiter became Scotland's scrum-half, at the beginning of a promising international career. Upholding the reputation of his native city, he was joined in that task by another local rugby player who will have something to tell his grandchildren.

Scotland rugby captain Jason White

Jason White was a schoolboy at Cults Academy in 1994 when he took part in the Scottish Schools under-18 trials at Murrayfield. Still only sixteen, he was already a strapping 6ft 5in when his coach at Aberdeen Wanderers, Calum Johnstone, predicted that one day he would go on to captain Scotland at full international level. He said, 'Jason is a level-headed lad with tremendous presence and abundance of talent. Full Scotland honours are certainly within his capabilities if he maintains his current rate of progress.' At the same time, Jason himself added, 'My dream would be to lead Scotland out in a full international at Murrayfield one day.'

Predictions and dreams could not have been more accurately fulfilled when more than a decade later the same Jason White, already a British Lion, celebrated an exquisite moment in the Six Nations Championship of 2006. Having disposed of the much-vaunted French team at Murrayfield, he then led his country to a magnificent victory over the English, recently crowned as world champions. That moment of euphoria was shared with Chris Cusiter, another British Lion, who had the privilege of bringing the match to an end with the final kick into touch. Jason White went proudly up those steps as Scottish captain to receive the Calcutta Cup. Of such moments are dreams truly made. His season of glory was complete when he was voted Players' Player of the Year in both Scotland and England, where he played for the Sale Sharks.

As a sign of rugby's growing popularity in Aberdeen and the North-east, a capacity crowd of 23,000 turned out on a fine summer evening in 2005 to watch a historic event at Pittodrie Stadium. Achieving a support no longer found in soccer terms, the Scottish rugby team went out and beat the Barbarians for the very first time. With the fortunes of club rugby rising and falling over the seasons, it was suggested many years ago that until Aberdeen concentrated its resources on one team it would be difficult to make any sustained impact on the national scene. Gordonians shone briefly at that level but faded to a point of returning to local district competition, sadly as they approached centenary celebrations. Tribal loyalty to former-pupil clubs in the past had been an obstacle to amalgamation. But due to the scarcity of school players coming through, all clubs have now adopted an 'open' policy. In that context, Aberdeen Grammar FPs, drawing widely on local talent, have found success in the Scottish Premier League, virtually establishing the amalgamation that was mooted so long ago.

CHAPTER 58

And Twal' Mile Roun'

The city boundaries of Aberdeen have moved outwards over the years till they now encompass most of what lies within the proverbial 'twal' mile roun'', that phrase made famous by well-known Aberdeen artist James Cassie who, addressing the Royal Academy dinner in Edinburgh in 1870, said 'Tak' awa' Aiberdeen and twal' mile roun' an' faur are ye? (This hilarious warning to the wider world was later used by doctor-cum-poet David Rorie as the theme of his short poem 'A Per Se'.) Only the blossoming garden suburb of Westhill, that dormitory beyond Hazlehead, has managed to remain beyond the official boundary that now embraces surrounding territories from Torry and Cove in the south, via Cults and Peterculter, to Dyce in the north. Yet there was a time, now hard to imagine, when townships like Ruthrieston lay outside the burgh, with castle and keep and regular cattle markets, held on a stance still shown on the maps of 1869.

Torry

The community of Torry didn't come within the jurisdiction of Aberdeen until 1891, having been one of many fishing communities to the south of the River Dee, all within the county of Kincardine. Taking its name from a Gaelic word meaning rounded hill or mound, Torry nestled at the foot of the hill, close to the harbour in an area known as Old Torry. In December 1495 King James IV granted a royal charter creating the town of Torry, being an admirer of its patron saint, St Fittick. As a free burgh of barony it had many benefits, giving its inhabitants the rights to appoint burgesses, buy and sell goods and hold markets, a considerable advantage in those days of restricted trade.

King William the Lion granted the land to the Abbey of Arbroath in the late 1100s, reflected in local street names like Abbey Road in Torry and Arbroath Way in Kincorth. There was a house used by the abbot on visits to inspect his property (thus the name Abbotswell), and that included the ferry across the Dee, which provided him with income.

After the Reformation of 1560, all the lands of Nigg, including Torry, were acquired by the Menzies family of Pitfodels, an immensely powerful dynasty who dominated the provostship for more than 150 years. They remained the sole owners of Torry until Aberdeen bought part of the land in 1704.

From its early history Torry had depended mainly on fishing which, before the arrival of trawl fishing in the nineteenth century, was conducted from a fleet of yawls sailing the inshore grounds. Fish were caught by means of lines shot over the stern of the boat. Aberdeen was fast becoming a busy fishing port, with large numbers of people attracted by the boom in steam trawling. This prompted council plans to open the area south of Aberdeen for development, and Torry was to play a vital part in the expansion. The council tried to buy the 115 acres of Torry Farm Estate in 1869 but refused to meet the asking price of £28,000. This municipal folly becomes clear when you find that, after protracted discussion, the council later bought just thirty-one acres for £20,000, then a further seven acres for £56,500!

From a population of 370 in 1838, Torry had expanded to more than a 1,000 by the time the Victoria Bridge was built in 1881. Prospering from the fish-processing industry and ancillary businesses, its population had reached beyond 9,000 by the turn of the century. With the large influx of families came the need for tenements, the first of them built in 1883 at what became 104 and 110 Victoria Road. After the Great War, Aberdeen City Council took full advantage of the 1919 Housing Act, which offered generous funding for new projects. The Garden City was developed as a series of concentric streets centred on Tullos, with a mixture of tenements and semi-detached houses.

After the Second World War, housing needs prompted a further expansion of Torry's boundaries. Permission was given for building on the southern slopes of Torry Hill, with more houses on Balnagask Road and Wellington Road. The oil boom of the 1970s brought yet another dimension to the prosperity of Torry, even if it hastened the demise of the traditional industries. Oil support vessels replaced trawlers in Torry Dock and, worst of all, the picturesque area of Old Torry was swept away to make room for the various oil bases. The land near the river was essential for the economic prosperity of the city but local feelings about the impending demolition were mixed. The houses, built on reclaimed land, were also subsiding and in urgent need of improvement. So Old Torry was finally demolished in 1974.

From a little fishing village 150 years earlier, Torry had become part of a vibrant city, its fate intrinsically linked to the fortunes of Aberdeen. It had, in fact, become just another city suburb, yet somehow managing to retain its identity and spirit of independence. Even in this hurried world, there is a deep pride in the local heritage, ensuring that the name and ethos of good old Torry will not disappear.

Dyce

On the northern side of Aberdeen, the village of Dyce, now within the orbit of the city, dates back no further than the 1860s, though the parish itself is believed to have been inhabited as far back as 1000 BC. Its recorded history dates from about 1316, when Robert the Bruce gave the Forest of Cordyce to Sir James de Garviach in return for his loyalty during the Wars of Independence.

But the Dyce we know today did not exist until the arrival of the railways. The line to the north was already operating when the Aberdeen–Buchan line was built in the mid 1860s, turning Dyce into a busy junction. Railway workers had to be housed, and with the coming of a suburban service in the 1880s there were homes to be built for commuters who could now live in Dyce and work in Aberdeen. It had already lain on the route of the Aberdeenshire Canal that stretched from Waterloo Quay, through Aberdeen by Kittybrewster and on to Port Elphinstone, and was operational from the late eighteenth century until its path was drained and it became part of the foundation for the railway lines. The turnpike road to the north also passed through the parish, leaving a relic of the old toll house at Parkhill.

That the village dates largely from the second half of the nineteenth century can be gauged from names like Victoria Street and Gladstone Place. Yet however small Dyce may have been in earlier times, its name was better known around the country than most communities of its size. That was due to two factors: the novelty of having an aerodrome that would grow into the Aberdeen Airport we know today, one of the biggest in Britain, and the bacon factory with a national identity as 'Lawsons of Dyce'.

The aerodrome story, with all its romantic appeal, has already had a chapter of its own. But the Lawson business that brought 800 jobs to a small Aberdeenshire village needs more explanation. From a Glasgow background, Robert Lawson moved to Dunfermline, where he established a family business of general provision merchants. Returning from the Great War, son Frank developed the business towards the sale of bacon and ham, importing frozen pig carcasses from the Baltic countries. Then he met and married Annie Greenlaw, a teacher in Dunfermline who came from the Banffshire parish of Boyndie. It was on a visit to her homeland that Frank Lawson was introduced to a prominent farmer who tried to interest him in a bacon factory at Dyce. It had started as a farmers' co-operative in the early 1920s but went bankrupt during the Depression. Showing little interest at first, he was finally persuaded by John Boyd Orr, director of the nearby Rowett Research Institute and future Nobel Prize-winner, to take this defunct operation in hand.

Frank borrowed £8,000 while brother Bob and five employees came north to set the business in motion. There would be much competition from the Danish bacon industry, which had a virtual stranglehold on the Scottish market, but the Lawsons set out to persuade Aberdeenshire farmers to produce pigs for the resurrected business. Among those who responded were names like Mackie of North Ythsie, Innes of Dunscroft, Stephen of Conglass and Wishart from Hill of Fiddes. But to compete with the Danes they still needed a similar type of pig, as well as the butchery and curing techniques of that country. The master stroke was achieved in 1938 when they acquired the services of a young Dane, Harold Sorensen, who taught the Lawson brothers how to produce quality bacon. Harold had come on a two-year secondment but remained in Aberdeen for the rest of his life.

The Lawsons became major suppliers to the British market, with customers like J. Sainsbury plc. While Bob managed the day-to-day running of the business, Frank was the more extrovert one, travelling to London on a weekly basis, handling the marketing side and establishing contacts. They had able lieutenants in R.P. Wilkie, who came from Fife, and J.T. Alexander from Dyce, who became directors in the 1960s. The company went to the Stock Exchange and made major investment on expansion, returning an annual profit of around £350,000. Customers now included Marks and Spencer, who were buying £80,000 worth of goods a week and the workforce had reached 800 by 1964, when the typhoid outbreak in Aberdeen threatened serious implications.

However, it survived and, with several companies showing an interest, the Lawsons finally sold out in 1965 for £2.96 million, the entire shareholding being taken by Unilever, through its Wall's Meat Group. Frank died suddenly of a heart attack a few months later. With his son Francis appointed managing director and then chairman, the business continued to expand. But problems arose within the group, with serious competition among sister companies. That was compounded by union trouble and damaging strikes, the removal of subsidies for pig production and the arrival of the oil industry, with wage structures that made life difficult for indigenous companies. The last of the Lawson family resigned in 1977, the pig slaughter and processing was closed the following year and, in the early 1980s, Unilever disinvested from the area.

As for the village of Dyce, its main economic prop was replaced by that same oil industry, with its menfolk now liable to be climbing into helicopters and heading for the platforms of the North Sea, taking off from the biggest heliport in the world at what was once the modest little field we knew as Dyce Aerodrome. Alongside the airport there were now industrial estates, major hotels and housing areas, engulfing a bustling village of Dyce that once knew little more excitement than the steam trains puffing their way to Huntly or Peterhead.

Peterculter

Within that arc of the Aberdeen perimeter stretching from Torry to Dyce there lies a chain of communities, once noticeably separate but now more or less continuous from the time you leave Mannofield – Pitfodels, Cults, Bieldside, Milltimber and Culter. Indeed, there is little sign of countryside until you pass the statue of Rob Roy on that final bend of Culter and head out the Deeside road towards Banchory. The parish is that of Peterculter, into which even the village of Cults was transferred from Banchory–Devenick in 1891. And in 1975 the whole parish of Peterculter came within the boundaries of Aberdeen. Culter had long been the working end of the parish, noted for its paper mill established by England's Bartholomew Smith in 1751 and providing the economic backbone of the area for more than 200 years, its workforce standing at a substantial 600 as recently as the 1950s.

The mill passed into the hands of Alexander Pirie of Stoneywood in 1865 and maintained its reputation for high-class products well into the twentieth century, by which time it was owned by William Geddes and his family. Sadly, that all came to an end in 1981, when closure was announced by the last owners of the mill, Culter Guard Bridge Holdings of Fife.

The history of the parish dates back more than 700 years but Rob Roy, the freebooter portrayed as a kind of Scottish 'Robin Hood' after the 1715 Jacobite Rising, was not part of it. Local legend has it that the colourful Highland outlaw made a mighty leap over the Leuchar Burn at the point where his statue stands today. It is a good story for tourists, even if it doesn't stand up to scrutiny. If Culter had its paper mill, the general idea of industry was rather alien to that well-appointed royal route as it embarked from Aberdeen on its way to Balmoral and beyond. Donside was more in tune with that kind of thing. The ambience of Lower Deeside was one of terraced affluence: south-facing villas in sylvan settings, enclosing the well-heeled in their suburban privacy at a safe distance from the bustle of the city, to which they would no doubt make the short journey to earn a living, if that were necessary.

Cults

Within the parish of Peterculter, Cults lay nearest to Aberdeen. When Robert the Bruce, always partial to the burgh, rewarded it with the Freedom Lands and the Forest of Stocket, its boundaries stretched out to become the neighbour of Pitfodels Estate. For 400 years Pitfodels would be the home of the all-powerful Menzies family, whose Pitfodels Castle stood in the high ground of Norwood, one of the four small estates carved out of the former Menzies lands south of the Old Deeside Road.

Though Pitfodels remained with the family until 1843, the lands of Cults immediately to the west of it passed from the Menzies to the Thomsons in the seventeenth century. The Thomson name survives to this day. The man who observed the beginnings of modern Cults was Dr George Morison of Elsick, son of the provost of Aberdeen at the time of the '45 Rising. In 1785 he became minister at Banchory–Devenick and, in the Old Statistical Account of 1792, he wrote alarmingly about the River Dee being subject to very sudden and high floods. His personal contact with this phenomenon came from the fact that his parishioners from Cults, on the north side of the Dee, came to church in the kirk boat, which more than once was swept away by the floods. As if that were not enough, 'an evil disposed person' pierced holes in the bottom of the boat, prompting the kirk session to offer a reward for 'information so as to convict the delinquent'. Dr Morison found his own solution. Having inherited the estate of Elsick he was able to do many good deeds for the parish. Most spectacularly, in 1837 he forked out £1,400 to build St Devenick Bridge, better known as the famous Shakkin' Briggie, enabling his flock to walk safely to worship.

Into the modern era, the old Cults School was replaced in 1966 by Cults Academy, a fortuitous piece of planning considering that oil had not yet been struck. Cults now became an even more desirable settlement, a convenient home-base for incoming oil families who even brought their own International School, with its strong flavour of Americana, to Milltimber. One of the most desirable local mansions, Woodbank House at Pitfodels, became the training centre and social hub of the Shell oil company. It was once the grand residence of a prominent Aberdeen accountant, Dr Walter A. Reid, senior partner in James Meston and Co. of Golden Square.

Among the prestigious facilities that grew with oil's prosperity were some of the finest hotels in the area, notably the Marcliffe at Pitfodels, owned by Stewart Spence, and Ardoe House on the other side the Dee, flagship of the burgeoning Macdonald Hotels group, the success story of

Donald Macdonald, former hotel boss of the Stakis organisation. Between the two lay Norwood Hall, another Macdonald hotel, in that estate once graced by Pitfodels Castle.

Westhill

On that periphery of 'twal' mile roun', there is no more intriguing story than the origins of Westhill, now a garden suburb on a hillside leading down to the Aberdeen–Alford road and maintaining its own independence beyond the city boundary. It all began in 1963 as the brainchild of an Aberdeen solicitor, Ronald F. Dean, whose firm acted as factors for the trustees of Mrs Jane Farquhar. Westhill had been an estate of small farms and crofts of poor quality, peat bog and scrubland, for many years in the ownership of the Farquhar family but producing very little income for the beneficiaries.

Ronald Dean told them they could increase their income many times over if he could realise his dream of turning their 540-acre estate into a self-contained township. Seeking approval in principle from the joint planning authority of city and county, he made it plain that he would not be seeking public money. This would be a purely private venture. With such an attractive proposition, the authorities gave him the go-ahead for his Westhill dream, and left him to find the financial backing. He embarked on his ambitious scheme by creating a private company called Westhill Developments (Aberdeen) Ltd and received initial support from Commercial Union Assurance (he was chairman of its local board of directors).

But an unexpectedly adverse report caused the company to withdraw. Now faced with a dilemma, Ronald Dean turned for advice to a man with whom he had formerly done business, Sidney Denman, managing director of the London-based Ashdale Land and Property Company, a subsidiary of Eagle Star Insurance. Convinced that this was a worthwhile enterprise, Denman recommended it to his chairman, Sir Brian Mountain, and Ashdale became involved when house-building had already begun. Persley Development Company was the builder and the very first house in Westhill, 4 Arnhall Crescent, was officially opened on 1st October 1968 by the convener of Aberdeenshire, the Rev. P.C. McQuoid.

It was an historic day, from which the overall plan began to take shape. Sidney Denman decided to call the township the Westhill Garden Suburb, reflecting a concept of open spaces, landscaping, pedestrian walkways and play areas to cater for the young families that would no doubt grace the scene for a long time to come. From scenes like these, a town was born, growing to a population of around 10,000 at the beginning of the twenty-first century, complete with a variety of housing, a shopping centre, schools that include Westhill Academy, a golf course, offices, flats, car parks, a community hall and police station, and a forty-four-bedroom hotel that was later rebuilt as a much bigger Holiday Inn.

Provision was made for some light industry, but nothing that would affect the landscaping. After all, the majority of the working population would still be finding their employment in Aberdeen. But that did not prevent Westhill becoming attractive to a range of companies, leading to a sizeable industrial estate. One of the first to settle his headquarters in the new town was Stewart Milne, destined to be Scotland's biggest house-builder as well as chairman of Aberdeen Football Club. Others who followed the example included CHAP Construction, Technip Offshore, Elmar Services, Subsea 7, Divex, Helix RDS and Schlumberger Oilfield Services. Figures showing where local residents have their place of work are as follows: Aberdeen city – 66.5 per cent; Westhill – 18.7 per cent; rest of North-east – 12 per cent; others – 2.8 per cent.

Such a modern development as Westhill, arising from so little, gave a new focal point to the ancient parish of Skene, the history of which predates the life of Christ by centuries. A coffin discovered in a cairn at what is now the farm of West Hatton had been lying there for about five centuries before they started building the first pyramid in Egypt. The first church in the parish, part of the Church of Rome like all others at the time, was in existence by 1296. In more recent times there were just small settlements at Kirkton of Skene, Elrick, Garlogie and Lyne of Skene. The local orphanage took pride in its most famous resident, the writer Jessie Kesson, who attended Skene School from 1925 to 1935, and who dedicated one of her books, *The White Bird Passes*, to Donald Murray, her dominie at Skene.

Then suddenly, Westhill was developed. Later, an ornamental garden with a series of linked ponds using storm water drainage from the slopes of the town was dedicated to the man whose faith helped build Westhill, and named Denham Park. The original Westhill House would become the central point of the town and Ronald Dean, whose dream it was, would be the factor and manager. When parts of the estate were sold off in 1972, the auction caused something of a sensation when prices reached £20,000 per acre.

Predictably, Westhill has not escaped the ills of modern society, the vandalism and problems with youth. Campaigning for more amenities, the local people did secure such attractions as a swimming pool. Early complaints about shortage of shops would take them on excursions to Inverurie, nine miles away, but that situation improved, with additional arrivals like Tesco. An appealing aspect of the Westhill story is that its origins had nothing to do with the coming of the oil industry, which would later cause a flurry of opportunism in the North-east. Ronald Dean had merely visualised the potential of a fine new town a few miles to the west of Aberdeen. Oil was just a lucky break of the following decade that would hasten his dream to fruition.

Born in 1907 and originally from Elgin, Dean trained as a solicitor in Edinburgh before serving as an officer in the Second World War, in which he escaped capture at the debacle of St Valery in 1940. Ronald Dean became town clerk of Kintore, joined the legal firm of Davidson and Garden in Dee Street in 1949 and lived in the splendid Drumgarth House at Pitfodels. Among his varied achievements, he gained a reputation as an entertainer with a fine bass voice. However, there were those who regarded his Westhill ambition as a foolhardy pursuit, a judgement that had to be revised as its success unfolded. Just as Sidney Denman is remembered through the ornamental garden, the founder himself gains recognition by street names. He died in 2001 and Dean Gardens is a reminder of the man without whom a town called Westhill might never have existed.

CHAPTER 59

Names to Remember

The most notable names in the history of Aberdeen should have found their natural place in the context of this story. Some may have slipped through the net, and there are others to whom an oblique reference will not have done full justice. A few pen-portraits remind us of at least some of those figures who have made their contribution to the broad canvas of Aberdonianism.

Patrick Manson, a boy from Oldmeldrum, was regarded by many as the greatest Aberdonian of the twentieth century, taking his place in medical science alongside men like Joseph Lister and Louis Pasteur. Manson became known as 'the father of tropical medicine', the man who detected biting insects like the mosquito as the spreaders of malaria and other diseases, and who was credited in his obituary in *The Times* with having saved millions of lives with work that had been an inspiration to civilisation.

Manson was born at Cromlet Hill, Oldmeldrum in 1844, second eldest of the nine children of John Manson, a substantial farmer and local agent for the British Linen Bank. For the children's education, the family moved into Aberdeen, where Patrick started as an apprentice at Blaikie's, before developing a spinal curvature.

An accompanying defect of the right arm gave rise to a tremor which never left him through all his years as a skilled surgeon. In convalescence, he turned to the study of natural history, entered Aberdeen University in 1860, graduated in medicine and went to work in Formosa (Taiwan) and then Hong Kong. There he started what became the University and School of Medicine, before returning to set up as a consultant in London in 1890. One of the regular visitors to his laboratory was Joseph Lister, father of antiseptic surgery and former professor at Glasgow University, who took a deep interest in the malaria saga. The London School of Tropical Medicine was founded on Manson's suggestion and he was knighted in 1903. A broadly based man of robust and handsome appearance and great good humour, Patrick Manson produced many aphorisms. He said, 'Never refuse to see what you do not want to see or what might go against your own cherished hypotheses . . . The thing you cannot get a pigeon-hole for is the finger-point showing the way to discovery.' He died of gout in 1922 and was buried at Allenvale Cemetery, Aberdeen, along with the rest of the family. A telegram of condolence arrived from the secretary of state for the colonies, Winston Churchill.

George Washington Wilson went to school at Forglen, near Turriff, and was apprenticed to a local joiner by the time he was twelve. But greater things beckoned for young George, who showed an aptitude for drawing and painting and used to visit local mansions, such as Duff House, where the great masters inspired him. Determined to study art, he moved to Edinburgh and then the Royal Academy Life School in London, from which he returned to Aberdeen in 1848, when he was twenty-five, to work as a portrait painter. Fascinated by the new 'science' of photography, he used his technical skills to build his own equipment, for there was no camera shop round the corner.

By the 1850s he was establishing his own business in Crown Street, on his way to becoming a pioneering photographer of international repute when he received a command to take the first photographs of Queen Victoria and the Royal Family at Balmoral. It was a tricky assignment as Her Majesty kept moving at the wrong moment. There were retakes. Later, Washington Wilson went by pony with her head keeper, to take the first photograph of Lochnagar. When Victoria and Albert happened to pass by, she didn't miss the opportunity to say: 'You won't be able to blame the sitter this time, Mr Wilson. Lochnagar has never been known to fidget!'

He built a house at Queen's Cross, with a workshop in St Swithin Street, employing 150 people and producing half a million photographic prints per year. Having discovered by chance a new-style chemical developer, he stunned the profession in 1856 by producing the first two instantaneous 'snap-shots': a view of Princes Street, Edinburgh, and a broadside being fired from HMS *Cambridge*. His landscapes of famous beauty spots, taken with the eye of a true artist, became all the rage in Victorian drawing-rooms. It remains Aberdeen's good fortune to have had someone of Wilson's calibre producing such a unique legacy of local images. A man of wide reading and intelligence, he was a Gladstonian Liberal who held a seat on the town council between 1880 and 1882. He died in 1893, leaving four daughters and five sons, three of whom followed him in the business. Sadly, when a prosecution was raised by the Inland Revenue about the transfer of that business, the Wilsons lost the court case at great cost and closed down in 1902.

Thomas Glover, whose father was head coastguard at the Bridge of Don, went from modest beginnings in Aberdeen to become a massive figure in the business and industrial life of Japan in the second half of the nineteenth century where he is still revered today, even if his name means little in his home-town. Following the trail of traders from the west and encouraged when Japan emerged from 200 years of isolation, Glover arrived in Nagasaki in 1859. He not only supplied arms and money for the rebellion that brought down the last shogun ruler in 1868 but became a major influence in easing Japan into the modern world, helping to pioneer the Mitsubishi shipyard with a slip-dock that he arranged to be built in Aberdeen.

His coal-mine fired the industry of Japan and his ships became the basis of the country's naval and merchant fleets. With Aberdeen's reputation for building great clippers, he started a large trawling business and brought shipping orders to the city's Alexander Hall and Company. And if this industrial romance of an enterprising man from the North-east wasn't enough, his colourful private life is said to have been reflected in the realms of opera. Thomas Glover was reputed to

Thomas Blake Glover, the inspiration for Puccini's Lt B.F. Pinkerton?

have been the inspiration for Pinkerton in Puccini's *Madama Butterfly*, while his Japanese wife, Tsuru, who tried to commit suicide, was said to have been the model for the tragic heroine herself. What is certain is that his romantic affairs in Japan produced children to at least four different mothers.

This man with the complicated life story was born at 15 Commerce Street, Fraserburgh, in 1838, when his father was chief officer at Fraserburgh coastguard station. The family moved to Collieston and finally Aberdeen, where the Glover children attended the highly rated Gymnasium in Old Aberdeen. Joining the great trek to Japan when that opportunity presented itself, Glover formed his own company, acquired the agency of the prestigious Jardine Matheson company and embarked on a meteoric rise to fame, helped not only by his fluent grasp of the Japanese language but also by those shipping contacts in Aberdeen.

Glover, who was awarded the Order of the Rising Sun in 1908, died in his palatial residence in Tokyo in 1911. Ironically, when the Americans dropped the atomic bomb on Nagasaki in August 1945, the main target was believed to be the Mitsubishi shipyard which Thomas Glover had done so much to foster. After the Japanese surrender, the occupying forces took over the spacious Glover House in Nagasaki, though later Mitsubishi regained ownership and presented it to the city. It became a tourist attraction as 'the house of Madam Butterfly', and visitors are treated to a Japanese-style rendering of 'One Fine Day' as they make their way round the statue of Butterfly in the Glover Garden. Back home, Fraserburgh Library has a Glover Room, while Mitsubishi became involved with Aberdeen City Council in a plan to turn Braehead House, the family home at the Bridge of Don, into Scotland's own Glover House. This project took a step nearer to fruition in 2006, when the city council allocated £50,000 towards making the building accessible to the public during the summer months.

Mary Slessor, who devoted her life to missionary work in Nigeria and became known to the natives as 'Great Mother', was born in Aberdeen on 2 December 1848 at her grandmother's house in Mutton Brae, a poor little place near Belmont Street. Her parents, Robert and Mary Slessor, had their own home at Gilcomston, at that time regarded as being on the outskirts of the town. Robert was a shoemaker, but when three of the seven children died he found consolation in alcohol and drank himself out of business.

Mary attended Belmont United Presbyterian Church, where a missionary, home from Calabar, Nigeria, preached a sermon one Sunday, describing the fearful conditions created there by the slave trade. Her mother, a deeply religious woman, began to read her children reports from Calabar, telling of the courage of missionaries who were also coping with high casualties

Mary Slessor, who dedicated much of her life to the people of Africa

from fever in addition to their missionary work. The seeds were sown. Meanwhile, through economic necessity, the Slessors moved to Dundee, where there was more chance of work in the mills, especially for women. It was the age of the squalid single-end house, but at least Mary found work. She was also reading about the African adventures of David Livingstone, who became her hero, and when she heard of his death in 1874 her destiny became clear to her.

Having improved her education at night school, she applied to join the mission and arrived in Calabar in September 1876. There she saw herself as God's messenger and gave the rest of her life to tackling the poverty, deprivation, disease and downright cruelty in those tribal lands. Women had no rights, and in a market-place one day she came upon a girl pegged down and spread-eagled in readiness for the boiling oil that the chiefs had ordered to be poured over her. The fiery Mary Slessor, often called 'Carrots' because of her red hair, pushed her way to the front and challenged the head chief fluently in his own language. In doing so she risked being thrown to the scavenging leopards. But her determination prevailed. Mary saved the prisoner's life and took charge of her. And what was the woman's crime? She had offered food to a slave in her husband's absence. That was the power of Mary Slessor. She countered tribal laws, endured her own bouts of fever and finally, when the British accepted the chiefs' invitation to govern, she became the first woman vice-consul in the British Empire. Believing that, given a chance, the Africans could look after their own affairs, she trained teachers and left them to run their own schools.

Pulling back from death's door time and again, Mary finally succumbed and died in her mud hut in January 1915. At her old church in Belmont Street, by then part of Aberdeen Academy, the Rotary Club arranged a memorial tablet of Rubislaw granite, which was unveiled in 1958. It was the least that could be done for an Aberdonian lassie who had had the faith and the smeddum to give her life to the poor of Africa.

Isaac Benzie became a household name in Aberdeen and the North-east as the man who founded a department store in George Street that shared fame and popularity with its near neighbour, Raggie Morrison's, if on a rather different level. The Benzies were originally crofting folk whose land had a fine view of Bennachie, while Isaac himself started work in the wee country shop in his native village of Oyne. While still in his twenties, however, he moved into the city (in 1894) and opened a small drapery business at 185 George Street.

Working his own knitting machine for fingering wool, Isaac was soon producing hosiery which gained him the gold medal at the Industrial Exhibition of 1896. He and his wife lived above the shop in which they worked together, before moving out to 153 Clifton Road. Expansion came swiftly to Isaac Benzie, who typified that breed of businessman who makes up in practical wisdom what he lacks in the gift of speech. Branches opened all over town, with the top floor of the Gallowgate premises serving as a work-room where a dozen girls were engaged in the manufacture of stockings.

But his aim was always to bring the business under one roof, and that was achieved in 1924, after he had gradually bought up the properties from 143 to 167 George Street. Benzie's became the sophisticated store still remembered by generations of Aberdonians as a fashion house embracing everything from clothes, a hairdressing salon, a chiropody service and shower-and-spray baths to the spacious restaurant where the green-pea soup and mince-and-tatties went down to the accompaniment of a palm-court trio. A day out for country folk in Aberdeen was not complete without your 'denner' at Isaac Benzie's.

An advertisement for Aberdeen's premier department store, Isaac Benzie Ltd

The man himself, an elder of Causewayend Church and superintendent of its Sunday School, did not enjoy the best of health and died in 1926 at the age of sixty-one. He was succeeded by his elder son, another Isaac Benzie, who had inherited his father's business acumen and became a significant figure in the life of the city. But in 1935 he caught a chill and died of bronchial pneumonia when only forty-two. A picture of the large funeral procession, from his home at 48 Rubislaw Den South to Allenvale Cemetery, was not only a reflection of his popularity but an impressive reminder of the black-coat-and-tile-hat formality with which mourners used to treat the dead.

Control of the business then passed to his younger brother, Athol Benzie, of 68 Queen's Road, who won the Military Cross with the London Scottish in the First World War and proceeded to uphold the family tradition of public service. A burgess of the city and deacon convener of the Seven Incorporated Trades, Athol Benzie was also senior elder of St Machar's Cathedral, a prominent Rotarian and a keen golfer and tennis player. But he, too, suffered ill health and took the opportunity to sell out in 1955, when the House of Fraser Group bought the entire shareholding as part of its take-over spree. The name of Isaac Benzie survived until 1973, when it was changed to the House of Fraser Group name of Arnott's. But the door of a great local institution wasn't finally closed until 1986. The Benzies were distant cousins of the Fraserburgh family who spread themselves around the North-east as partners in the Benzie and Miller chain of stores.

Raggie Morrison's was the popular name for what was perhaps the best-known shop in Aberdeen, situated on St Nicholas Street, precisely where Marks and Spencer stands today, at the very heart of Aberdeen's shopping district. It ranked high among the institutions of the city, a great conglomeration of a place, boasting bargains yet claiming, with justification, that it could furnish anything from a cottage to a mansion. Above the door, its official name was Morrison's Economic Stores, but few people could tell the origins of Raggie Morrison, who became rather overshadowed by one of his employees, a human dynamo called James Mearns (born in 1863), the eventual owner of the business and the man mainly responsible for its rise to legendary status. Mearns grew up in the Aberdeenshire village of Logie Coldstone with little education and no money but with enough ambition to declare that one day he would own Aboyne Castle, a stately pile he greatly admired. Incredibly, one day he did.

James Mearns worked first with his father in a stabling business at Inverurie before deciding to seek his fortune in Aberdeen. He was first apprenticed to Baillie Henry Gray, who ran a drapery store in Broad Street, before moving to the unlikely little shop belonging to the Morrison family, then situated in Black's Buildings, opposite the old infirmary at Woolmanhill. William Morrison was building up the business that had been started by his sister but now, in 1882, he was joined by James Mearns, and it was not long before he realised he had discovered a young man of energy and ideas. When the shop was destroyed by fire, Morrison acquired modest premises at the corner of St Nicholas Street and Netherkirkgate and began to build afresh, this time with Mearns becoming the manager.

The two men worked well together. William Morrison retired and James Mearns eventually gained ownership of the business as well as becoming the very personification of all that Raggie Morrison's stood for. He travelled all over Britain and the Continent, buying up huge quantities of merchandise, sometimes bankrupt stock of wonderful silks, satins and brocades. All this would take its place alongside the rolls of linoleum, scrubbing brushes, pails, umbrellas, mousetraps, the shop becoming a real Aladdin's Cave that raised its own scent and excitement. He knew the power of advertising, as witnessed in his imaginative displays in *The Press and Journal* and *Evening Express* offering 'ladies' interlocking knickers for sixpence, tenpence and a shilling'! By October 1922 James Mearns had achieved his ambition of buying Aboyne Castle, for a sum said to be in six figures. He spread his talents to Aberdeen County Council, where he represented Aboyne and Birse. Mearns died in 1943, aged eighty-one, and in the post-war years yet another business that was founded purely on local ingenuity went into the hands of the multinationals and became the Marks and Spencer of today.

Jimmy Hay's remained the popular name for Aberdeen's most prestigious restaurant, the Royal Athenaeum, long after the man himself died in 1908. It was a tribute to the son of a local shoemaker who rose to the very top of his profession as a royal caterer and man of the highest integrity. As part of the Union Buildings standing opposite the Town House and designed by Archibald Simpson, the Athenaeum was the height of sophistication for Aberdeen diners, in an age of tail-coated waiters and cigar-smoking clients. In its day it was without equal, eventually to be replaced by the rash of trendy restaurants with which the oil boom came to enliven the city.

Jimmy Hay was born in 1853 and learned the business under David Robertson of the Royal Hotel (situated at that time in Union Street), the last of that band of Aberdeen innkeepers that flourished in the days of the stagecoach and a man he revered as a host par excellence. Jimmy Hay gained further experience in Edinburgh, where he met his wife, but was back in his native city by 1888, acquiring the restaurant business of McKilliam and Co., adjacent to the one he really wanted. He did indeed buy the Royal Athenaeum and began his rise to fame in the city and far beyond.

He became known as the Royal Caterer when King Edward VII and Queen Alexandra employed his services on Deeside, and his reputation made him first choice for banquets in Aberdeen and further afield. That included the great royal occasion when the king and queen came to open the new Marischal College in 1906 and were entertained in the Town and County Hall. Even when the royal couple visited Glasgow, the corporation luncheon was personally supervised by Jimmy Hay. Out of his humble beginnings came a man of distinction, a devout Catholic who spread kindness among the poor of the city. In 1903 he bought the estate of Binghill, in the parish of Peterculter, where he treasured his marvellous collections of gold and silver plate, glass and crystal of unique design, a fine collection of pictures and a splendid set of prints of Aberdeen in bygone days.

The Athenaeum was sold to John Mitchell of the County Hotel and survived until 1973, when it was destroyed in a fire believed to have started in a lounge above the Scotch Corner public house and which spread throughout the building. Crowds gathered to see the spectacular end of Aberdeen's most famous restaurant, which took its well-deserved place in the history of the city as a local institution of real distinction. The Royal Athenaeum's only rivals had been the Palace Hotel, another victim of fire, in 1941, and the Caledonian Hotel, which thereafter became the social centre of the city.

Ma Cameron's in Little Belmont Street provides a fascinating link with the coaching-house days of another age. It was a hostelry of old-world charm, known by the less appealing name of the Sow Croft, established towards the end of the 1700s, long before Ma Cameron appeared on the scene. The family origins remain obscure but Peter Cameron is believed to have taken it over in the nineteenth century, with three more generations taking over the reins through to the 1930s. The first Mrs Cameron seems to have been the memorable hostess who gave it a popular name and character, quaint and intimate, and frequented by a broad clientele that included academics and journalists. But the Ma Cameron name was passed down the generations when Alex Mitchell became the licensee in 1933. His wife was frequently referred to as Ma Cameron, such is the public fondness for a legend.

One of the pub's popular features has always been a fine pictorial record of Aberdeen as it used to be, brought together by William Geddes, who was manager during the time of the Mitchell family. The last Cameron connection was severed with the death of John A. Cameron's widow Amelia in 1933. She left two sons and three daughters, both sons being medical students at Aberdeen University. (Older residents of New Pitsligo will tell you their life-long village doctor was John Cameron, whom they believed to be Ma Cameron's son.) The old cobbled courtyard has now been covered, with more alterations that inevitably dilute the earlier atmosphere. But Ma Cameron's still retains a comfortable sense of Aberdeen in a bygone era, popular as ever in its convenient city-centre location.

Soapy Ogston was the popular name of Alexander Ogston, whose family ran a soap and candle manufacturing business with a worldwide reputation, their premises occupying a solid block of land bordered by the Gallowgate, Loch Street, Innes Street and McKay's Court, locally known as the Candle Close. Soapy is perhaps best remembered today as the man who built the large mansion of Ardoe House in a splendid baronial style, later known as the flagship of Macdonald Hotels, in the picturesque setting of the South Deeside Road. While that was his own residence, the anecdotal evidence suggests that he acquired the neighbouring Norwood Hall, just across the Dee at Pitfodels, as a home for his mistress.

In 1898 Soapy Ogston amalgamated with an even bigger company, Charles Tennant of St Rollox in Glasgow, at that time running the largest chemical works in the world and making a fortune from the creation of dry bleaching powder. (The company later became the foundation of ICI.) Sir Charles Tennant's daughter Margot was the second wife of Prime Minister Herbert Asquith and a lively mistress of 10 Downing Street. Sir Charles himself fathered fifteen children, the last two of whom were conceived when he was in his eighties. One of those belated daughters became Baroness Elliot, wife of Walter Elliot, the distinguished Scottish statesman. Ogston and Tennant became a major name on the international scene, despite suffering a disastrous fire at its Aberdeen premises in 1905, and survived until after the Second World War, when it was taken over by Unilever. It also had a spell as the Waldorf School, a private establishment. While Soapy Ogston had Ardoe House, his brother owned Kildrummy, now the Castle Hotel. Both houses show the individual coats of arms of the brothers in mosaic and as newels on the banisters.

Cocky Hunter was a name in North-east folklore that applied to father and son in the same way as did Isaac Benzie. In the case of the Hunters, it was synonymous for a prosperous business in junkyard dealing where they were said to buy and sell anything from a needle to an anchor. The range of merchandise between those two extremes was a bewilderment to behold. In a variety of locations, but latterly behind the Castlegate, Sheraton tables, Regency chairs and potentially valuable original paintings took their precarious place alongside (or beneath!) brass bedsteads, sewing machines, cat's whisker wireless sets, old bicycles, bolts and screws, clocks without hands, perhaps an Edison phonograph or a set of carving knives. It was the place to visit for a rummage – and the chance that you might pick up a bargain or some obscure object you had given up hope of ever finding.

The first Cocky Hunter, who gained his name from a dapper appearance in which he took some pride, was born in 1867 at Water Lane, by Virginia Street, overlooking Aberdeen Harbour. Out of school by thirteen, he ran a pony and cart for Mary Fletcher, the fish dealer, before he became a boiler-maker in the shipyards. By 1903, however, he had opened a second-hand furniture store in East North Street, from which he could be seen in the early morning on market days pushing his cart-load of goods to the Castlegate. In all this he had the help of his substantial wife, who broke off from her twelve-hour day to produce sixteen children from her eighteen-stone frame, none of which prevented her from living to the creditable age of eighty-six.

Cocky himself, whose real name was Thomas, became a kenspeckle figure in the city, hard-working, kindly and good-humoured, his dapper appearance in stark contrast to the apparent disorder of the business premises. He opened a second shop in Commerce Street, where you would find him until his death in 1925 at the age of fifty-eight. At the end of the

Cocky Hunter (right), at Aberdeen beach
in the early 1900s

day, Aberdonians are quick to honour their local characters and Cocky Hunter's funeral was another spectacle, large crowds lining the route from Commerce Street as boiler-makers carried the coffin to Trinity Cemetery. They kept open the gates until dusk as hundreds more came to visit the grave.

Several of his family were already running their own kindred businesses around town, including four of his daughters, who could be found selling prams, bicycles and a variety of second-hand goods at shops in Castle Street, George Street, Queen Street and the Gallowgate. A young son, Bill, maintained his father's base at Commerce Street, but the name of Cocky Hunter was inherited by the eldest son, Alec, who had sizeable premises enclosed by South Mount Street, Leadside Road, Richmond Street and Kintore Place. He stocked it from displenish sales and bankrupt stock and built up a highly successful enterprise that was known throughout Scotland. In the early hours of a morning in 1937, however, Cocky was called from his home at Nigg to find the whole business up in flames. The site was later occupied by the Rosemount Flats, an early example of the massive council-house blocks to be built by the city. By the following year Cocky had taken over the old Sick Children's Hospital in Castle Terrace beside the Castlehill Barracks, where he used his expert knowledge of antiques to add to the great conglomeration of goods overflowing on to surrounding pavements.

Elizabeth Adair, the actress and broadcaster, who knew Cocky's place from seeking out stage props, recalled the humorous side of the man. A large coffin in the shop bore a sign that read, 'Please do not lift this lid.' Those who took it as a challenge were themselves stiffened when confronted by a skeleton! After years of ill health, Cocky Hunter the Second died in 1961, aged sixty-nine. The family was still involved in its various enterprises but the store in Castle Terrace was taken over by a development company and Commerce Street gave way to the inner ring-road that ran from Virginia Street to East North Street. Cocky's brother Bill lived at 56 Castle Street, a handsome eighteenth-century home looking on to the old heart of Aberdeen, where he died in 1982 at the age of seventy-five.

William Watt Hepburn. Few men have grasped the business opportunities of Aberdeen with such flair and vision as Watt Hepburn, a Victorian figure who came modestly from the pious parish of Gamrie, intending to study theology, but ended up with an empire that extended to 150 companies. From Gardenstown, where his parents had a bakery and general store, he had walked along the cliff path to school at Macduff before the family moved into business in Aberdeen, building a block of four flats in Blenheim Place and occupying the ground floor at number 59.

Having developed tuberculosis, the young Watt Hepburn turned from thoughts of the ministry to a fresh-air job as a commercial traveller, visiting village shops around the North-east in a horse-drawn buggy. Men of such acumen soon find their opportunities, and he went from the partnership of Horne and Hepburn in Frederick Street to his own enterprise in Bridge Place. His notepaper heading announced him as 'W. Watt Hepburn, Produce Importer and Provision Merchant, Aberdeen, London and Dundee. Factories: Silver City Preserving Works, Aberdeen;

Fishing Works: Palmerston Road, Aberdeen and Ribby Street, Grimsby; Herring Curing: Lerwick; London Office: 115 Lower Thames Street, E.C.'

He was forty-four before he married Elsie McKerrow, on New Year's Day 1918, and moved into Kingshill House, a splendid home in what became King's Gate before the full grandeur of that street materialised. By then he was established as a wholesale grocer, buying up shops in town and country which he supplied from his own source, with a chain that ran from Dornoch to Montrose under the name of Slater in honour of his father's original occupation. His distribution company and some of his shops went under the name of Wilburn (made up of elements from his own name).

The slump of the 1920s and 1930s took its toll on industry but provided business opportunities for men like Hepburn, who aroused criticism for buying up ailing factories at a bargain price. Moving into textiles, he spread his ownership to firms like the Aberdeen Glove and Hosiery Co. in Chapel Street; Kilgour and Walker, woollen manufacturers in Berryden Road; Gordon and Co. in Union Glen and Spring Garden; and extending his empire as far as John Martin and Co. in Anstruther. In his defence, it has to be said that this was no asset-stripping exercise with the intention of closing the acquisitions down. Watt Hepburn's philosophy was to reorganise a business and find new ways of operating that would keep the employees in work. 'I want to make two blades of grass grow where one grew before,' he once said, summing up the outlook of a man who was certainly fascinated by the art of making money, especially on the Stock Exchange, but who also had a more worthy purpose in mind.

So the Hepburn empire expanded to a jute factory in Dundee, exclusive woollens in Dumfries and a wholesale clothing warehouse called Kerr Leid in Aberdeen. He bought the department store of Smiths in Dundee, the restaurant chain of Craigs in Glasgow and the Equitable in George Street, Aberdeen. His genius for management was so much in demand from firms in trouble that he became chairman of Richards Ltd at the Broadford Works, and managing director of Alexander Hall and Co., the shipbuilders, keeping them alive between the wars. He was also a major shareholder in the Northern Agricultural and Lime Company.

In those earlier days, when the herring trade faltered with the Russian Revolution, he was not afraid to modify his living with a move from Kingshill House to Beechgrove Terrace. But his recovery towards prosperity was later reflected in the subsequent flitting to 32 Rubislaw Den South. His only concern in employing people was how well they could do a job. Class or gender meant nothing. At a time when women had fewer opportunities to succeed, Watt Hepburn encouraged them to take responsibility and had a number of well-paid ladies in his management team. Mrs MacLeod, for example, was a war widow with children to bring up. Though she worked as a humble clerkess, he quickly spotted her understanding of finance and put her in charge of accounts for all his business. She became a lady with money to spare and he took pleasure in helping her to invest it. That's the kind of man he was.

Businessmen tend either to spread themselves to public service or shun it altogether, seeking no publicity for themselves. Watt Hepburn was of the latter, a supporter of the Bakers Incorporation at Trinity Hall but little else outwith his own life. His private interests, however, were broadly based. A keen student of history as well as theology, he travelled with his wife across the American continent between the wars and visited the Nile and the Biblical sites of the Middle East. He and his friend Tommy Mitchell, lord provost from 1938 till 1947, were in their late seventies when they went on a fishing boat to the Arctic Circle to see the Northern Lights. One of Watt Hepburn's other interest was cars, starting with a two-seater sports model before the First World War and graduating to his chauffeur-driven vintage Rolls-Royce. As often as not, however, he would simply travel on the tramcar. His daughters, who retain vivid memories of their father, have lived into a new century: Ann Sants, who became a clinical psychologist, still living in Oxford, and Mary Lauder, who studied social science, is now in Devon. Watt Hepburn died on 14th August 1953, in his eightieth year. At a time when being a millionaire was something special, his personal estate was valued at £1,143,869.

Charles Pirie Skene There is no proof that Charles Skene, the serial entrepreneur of Aberdeen, has any connection with the famous Skene family of Rubis-law, but there are common traits to suggest the possibility. In bygone days the Skenes, who were friends of Sir Walter Scott, owned those lands to the west of the city on which they developed some of the finest granite residences in Aberdeen. They began with one side of Albyn Place, engaging the famous Archibald Simpson to design a series of villas, and followed it up with an imaginative parallel of terraced mansions, set back from the other side of Albyn Place with the name of Rubislaw Terrace, with communal gardens to lend an air of space and grace.

In turn, this handsome route pointed to the west end of the city, setting a standard of gracious architecture that would fan out to Queen's Road, King's Gate and the Rubislaw Dens, North and South,

Charles Skene, entrepreneur

where lawyers, bankers, surgeons and businessmen could settle into their secluded opulence. Apart from Albyn Place and Queen's Road, which have largely surrendered to the commercial overture, the social cocktail is not vastly different today, given that the residences of the Rubislaw Dens, with the gentle valley separating them in picturesque splendour, could still produce an impressive Who's Who of the Aberdeen elite.

And that would include Charles P. Skene, whose Rubislaw residence is a reflection of how far he has come in a career of extraordinary drive and diversion. His grandfather, James R. Skene, left Aberdeen around 1860 to settle in Rhodesia, where Skene and Simpson became a partnership of entrepreneurial butchers trading cattle to South Africa. From his acquaintance with Cecil Rhodes, he named his son Cecil Skene, father of the present-day Charles. When his business partner died, James Skene married the widow and inherited the business. By the age of forty, he had retired to his native Aberdeen, living at 129 Desswood Place, with a shop in

Fountainhall Road and a portfolio of tenement property in Union Grove. But James Skene gambled on the Stock Exchange and lost. When he died, his wife and son moved in to live with relatives, the Morgan family, who had owned a photographic studio in Market Street. Around 1890, Studio Morgan moved to a magnificent building at 393 Union Street, where a grand piano in the reception area set the tone of the business. From there, it spread out to a vast complex, still with enough space to house a large family, complete with five bedrooms, wine, a billiard-room, and a garden which accommodated a tennis court, croquet lawn and stables.

Photography had followed and recorded the British Empire to the height of its glory, with noble families taking their cue from Queen Victoria to buy estates on Deeside and rich merchants spending lavishly on such luxuries as portraiture. Queen Victoria herself commissioned the Morgans to photograph the Royal Family and that extended to her guests at house parties, including the Czar of Russia and the Shah of Persia. Bob Morgan, a brilliantly creative man, was leading the family business with bohemian flair but began to give it less of his attention, finally selling out to his near-relative and assistant, Cecil Skene, in 1938. By then Studio Morgan had moved again, and operated on a much-reduced scale in Alford Place. There were no further changes until well after the Second World War.

Cecil's son Charles was a boarder at Drumtochty Castle before going on to Loretto School, Edinburgh, where he claimed to have 'excelled in mediocrity'. He had already acquired a taste for photography, but it was while serving in the navy during national service at the age of eighteen that he set his ambition. He was going to be a millionaire. That was inspired by reading the biography of Andrew Carnegie, the Scots boy from Dunfermline who became the steel king of America and the richest man in the world. Charles Skene made his own start with the family business, helping to turn it into one of the most profitable photographic studios in Britain.

But that alone would not be enough. With thoughts of expanding into property, he found himself at a dinner one night sitting beside a top man from a national property company which happened to own tenement buildings in Aberdeen. Would he ever consider selling them? By coincidence, yes, the company had decided to dispose of its residential properties. 'I'll buy them!' said the bold Charles, without knowing how many were involved. A deal was agreed in principle before he discovered he had just become the owner of 425 properties throughout Aberdeen! It was the beginning of a remarkable career that would turn him, overnight, into the largest owner of residential property in Aberdeen, and later one of the largest in Glasgow, when he went back to the same company which had sold him the Aberdeen properties and bought an additional 250 flats.

It all coincided with the arrival of oil and a pressing demand for accommodation. International staff and their families were moving to Aberdeen for a period of years; VIPs came visiting from all corners of the world; roustabouts required a base before flying out to the oil-platforms. Charles Skene had struck at the right time. Yet, long after he had fulfilled his ambition to be a millionaire, he was still dashing around with his beloved camera to photograph weddings and graduations! As a property magnate, he was also spending large sums with removal companies. So he bought his way into Rapid Removals, acquired a new fleet of pantechnicons, gaining a contract to deliver household goods from Harrods. Even that was just a stepping-stone to an even more imaginative idea. By 1984 he had spotted the opportunity for geriatric healthcare and went to America to study the new concept of the Continuing Care Retirement Community, groups of houses or flats built around a nursing home, with the owners or tenants able to call on nursing support if required. One of his senior employees, Barbara Whiteman, had been a nursing sister before moving to general management and supported the idea.

Royal Deeside had served Studio Morgan well in the past. It could do so again, this time for Charles Skene and his new enterprise. He fixed on the Georgian mansion of Inchmarlo House, near Banchory, where the River Dee flows past from Balmoral on its way to the sea at Aberdeen. What more appealing location? The estimated cost of converting Inchmarlo was £1.5 million and the cost of building the first phase of forty-one houses and apartments was £1.7 million. Barbara Whiteman was appointed matron designate and Inchmarlo was soon collecting enterprise and design awards. The venture was not without its problems, caused by the fluctuation in oil prices and its effect on house-buying confidence, but Skene weathered the storm and brought Inchmarlo to fruition as a self-contained community of 135 houses and a nursing home, with more development to come – a haven within the attractive setting of Deeside. Seeking to spread the gospel of entrepreneurship, Charles Skene raised awareness of its merits in educational circles, endowed it as a chair at the Robert Gordon University and became a visiting professor of the subject, believing in the ultimate benefits for society. In 2005, Charles P. Skene OBE went to Buckingham Palace to receive the Award for Enterprise Promotion from Her Majesty the Queen.

CHAPTER 60

So What of the Future?

Whatever rewards may lie in wait for the courageous, there will of course come a day when the oil will finally and irrevocably run out. That leaves a question mark on what Aberdeen and the North-east authorities are planning for the dawn of that day. For as much as the good Lord may favour Aberdonians, He is unlikely to bring forth a second dose of His benevolence. So, instead, a large part of the task will fall to those entrusted with our civic wellbeing who, as a breed in the modern world, are not always disposed to plan that far ahead. It carries no votes and would bear such belated glory as to deny them the pride of a polished ego. Yet our leaders will have to show that kind of vision and enterprise if an unthinkable depression is not to descend on Aberdeen and the North-east of Scotland around the middle of the twenty-first century. Failure to do so could bring about such a cataclysmic scenario that they would stand condemned forever by future generations. The fact that, by then, they may be grazing on distant pastures will do nothing to save the blushes of their descendants.

That worst-case scenario is not too hard to envisage: companies, feeling that the glory days are gone, deciding to relocate nearer the markets of the south; jobs disappearing with no prospect of being replaced; failure to attract new people to new industries – and encourage what already exists – resulting in an ageing population; a housing market inflated by the prosperity of oil now entering an age of decline and decay. Too pessimistic? Not if you believe some of the people who have helped to create a parallel prosperity for Aberdeen and the North-east, if not directly connected to oil then happily in conjunction with its confidence and achievements.

At least three major names spring to mind: Fred Duncan, creator of Grampian Country Foods, Britain's biggest supplier of fresh food, employing 22,000 people; Moir Lockhead, the general manager who led a buy-out of Grampian Transport and, in the name of FirstGroup, went on to run so much of the transport of this country, as well as school buses across Canada and the United States, employing 70,000 people in the United Kingdom and North America; and Stewart Milne, one of Britain's biggest private house-builders, with headquarters at Westhill and bases at Tannochside (Glasgow) and Oxford, a man to be measured by the fact that, in 2005, he became Scotland's highest-paid citizen. In the jargon of the day, these are some of Aberdeen's leading movers and shakers, men with a vested business interest of course, but one that is tied to the prosperity of the North-east. Fred Duncan, who lives in Banchory, is the son of a Buchan

Fred Duncan, creator of Grampian Foods

banker, while Stewart Milne, just down the road at Bieldside, is the son of a drainer and ditcher from Alford, men with a rooted loyalty to their native corner. Moir Lockhead, a welcome Englishman, has the Glassel estate near Banchory.

But they deal in the hard facts and realities of business wisdom and are unlikely to allow their emotional attachments to influence a common-sense decision. These and many others thrive in a prosperous community but might need persuading to stay around when the golden era fades and the geographic disadvantage of Aberdeen as a centre of United Kingdom convenience becomes a valid issue. Two of those industrial giants have already fallen foul of public opinion in their bid for change. In 2005 Moir Lockhead sought to move his First Bus base from the old Corporation depot at King Street to a more suitable world headquarters at a spacious site at Woodside. An inference that planning rejection could take this major international company elsewhere in the United Kingdom showed the difficulty facing the planning authority, especially when the application came up against thousands of local objectors. In the event, the authority approved the move, knowing the final decision would rest with the government powers in Edinburgh.

Stewart Milne also faced public wrath, not so much in his own business as in his other role as chairman of Aberdeen Football Club. For a variety of reasons, the directors of the club were keen to sell off their spiritual home of Pittodrie Park, within chilling distance of the grey North Sea, and move to the western outskirts of the city. Many years before, Stewart Milne had taken a buying option on Robbie Mann's 150-acre farm of Bellfield, near the village of Kingswells, and that was where the new stadium would arise, complete with soccer academy and training grounds, ample parking space and a major leisure and sports centre, including an Olympic-size swimming pool. The local authorities would participate and the complex would be completed with a hotel, restaurant and bowling alley. It all boiled up in the early years of the new century, accompanied by a predictable hullabaloo from the folk of Kingswells, who had no wish to see their comfortable little community

Moir Lockhead: his First Group spans the world

Stewart Milne, house-builder and chairman of Aberdeen FC

expanded and disturbed by football hordes on a Saturday afternoon. The planning factor also came into play, and the outcome was that the Kingswells project died a death, with Aberdeen FC left to consider whether they would move next door to a site on the Links or perhaps move outside the city boundary.

Stewart Milne had discovered the force of people power. But that did not divert him from the broader question of what would happen to Aberdeen when the days of oil are over. So he formed an alliance with the two men already mentioned, Fred Duncan and Moir Lockhead, and drew up a document for discussion on the future of Grampian. There is no doubt that all three men were already looking to the future of their own organisations and assessing whether they might have to move the emphasis of their business England. What was in their own minds would just as surely apply to others. At the first stage, their document would be discussed with the local authorities of the city and county. Among the general observations, it was pointed out that the city population was declining (dropping towards 200,000 in 2005, overtaken by the county to the extent of 20,000). That decline became even more worrying when the registrar general's demographic report of December 2005 predicted a further loss of 48,000 by the year 2024, almost one quarter of an ageing population in an area that was struggling to attract young families. Disagreeing with that forecast, the city nevertheless conceded a likely loss of 7,000.

The Three Wise Men from the North-east were pointing out the obvious: that many of the companies that had grown up in the past twenty or thirty years had become vitally important to the economy but were, increasingly, finding their workload belonged outwith the Grampian Region. Many were considering not only where their headquarters should be located but where their manufacturing base should be. Putting it bluntly, those company bosses were expressing alarm at the lack of thought within the civic leadership. They could see no sign of vision, of ambitious targets for the future needs of business and housing. Current means of assessing such needs were outdated. Posing a serious risk to inward investment, this would fuel the belief that the region was in serious decline, the consequences of which would be catastrophic. The document also highlighted the competition from other Scottish cities, like Edinburgh, where planning was being made for a major increase in population, airport expansion and better rail and inner-city transport; and Glasgow, where substantial family housing was planned within the city boundaries as well as extensions and improvements to the surrounding motorways.

Messrs Milne, Duncan and Lockhead were pulling no punches. What the North-east needed was council leadership that would set out a blueprint of how the area could develop over the next twenty or thirty years. It needed councils with the desire and ability to see the bigger picture and to focus more strongly on the benefits rather than the possible obstacles. They needed to seek an understanding of what would encourage business to stay. They should examine what was happening in Ireland and Wales. And, not least, they should be more open and accessible and demonstrate a real desire to work with the private sector. So in 2005, seeking urgency in planning the future of the North-east, they discussed their document with Aberdeen's lord provost, John Reynolds, council leader Kate Dean and chief executive Douglas Paterson, and their counterparts in Aberdeenshire, Provost Raymond Bisset, council leader Audrey Findlay and chief executive Allan Campbell. They, in turn, discussed it internally and raised some of its contents with NESEF, a body taking in the city and county councils, Scottish Enterprise Grampian and the Chamber of Commerce. By December 2005 a new threat to North-east jobs and prosperity arose when the chancellor of the exchequer, Gordon Brown, announced a major tax increase on North Sea oil, raising alarm in particular among the smaller companies by then emerging as the best hope of an extended lifetime for the industry.

So Aberdeen was on fresh alert. Coincidentally, the Scottish Executive produced the long-awaited plan for a western peripheral bypass road that would arc its way from Stonehaven, cross by Milltimber and Kingswells, round the airport and link up with the Aberdeen–Ellon road at the Blackdog. Aimed for an opening in 2011, the new road was designed to ease the pressure of traffic converging on the city and was seen as an essential starting-point in arresting the decline of the North-east. Aberdeen City Council showed further initiative by appointing a director of strategy, and the planning authority paved the way for 24-hour operation at Aberdeen Airport, where an extension to the runway was being built. These were some of the indications that Aberdeen and the North-east were engaging more deeply in shaping the twenty-first century.

If a catalyst was required for the next phase in Aberdeen's economic history, could it come in the form of American tycoon Donald Trump and his massive plan for a golf and leisure complex at Balmedie? Would that alert others to the attractions of Aberdeen and the North-east after the days of oil? In my brief encounter with Mr Trump at the Beverly Hills Hotel in 2006, he was keen to gauge from an Aberdonian how local opinion was shaping up. What did I think of his chances for planning permission? Americans will tell you that wherever Donald Trump goes, others tend to follow. So if it all works out according to plan, wouldn't it be an extraordinary stroke of fate for Aberdeen and the North-east if the decline of oil was matched by the rise of a leisure industry? Even before the appearance of Trump, leisure had already been raised as a possible replacement. Could the good Lord possibly be considering an extension to his Aberdonian bias? Only time will tell.

Donald Trump plans 'the world's best golf-course' near Balmedie

CHAPTER 61

The Northern Lights

In the grey dawn of Thursday 12th May 1983, a lonely old lady turned on the radio in her backstreet hovel in London and heard the celebrations of a football crowd in the Swedish city of Gothenburg. Mary Webb knew nothing about football, unaware of the sensation of the previous evening, when Aberdeen FC met the greatest football team in the world, Real Madrid, in the final of the European Cup Winners' Cup and won! But her eyes lit up with joy as 'The Northern Lights of Old Aberdeen' came swelling into her room-and-kitchen and she called out to herself 'They're singing my song!' And so they were. For Mary Webb was indeed the lady who wrote that anthem of Aberdonianism, sung around the world as part of the Scottish repertoire but most of all when folk are gathered with nostalgic thoughts of their native North-east.

There is still a general misconception that 'The Northern Lights' belongs to ancient times and that the composer must be long since dead. But Mary Webb, a charming English lady, produced her masterpiece as recently as 1951 and was still with us until 1989. One day, perhaps, she and her song will be given due recognition in the place where they belong, although precious little was shown in her lifetime. For all the wonders of modern communication, our ancestors were sometimes better at preserving their heritage.

So how did the song come about? Mary Webb was born in 1901 and grew up in Leamington Spa, Warwickshire, where she played the piano in a concert party, sometimes for the local Member of Parliament, Anthony Eden, who succeeded Winston Churchill as prime minister in 1955. It was while working in the kitchens of West London Hospital that she met an Aberdeen girl and invited her home to tea. Guessing that the lass was homesick, Mary vowed she would write her a song, and crossed to the piano. It so happened that her husband, Mel Webb, a news sub-editor at Broadcasting House, London, had met a colleague from BBC Scotland during the war. Archie P. Lee, well-known radio producer, had an Orkney background and could satisfy Mel's curiosity about the Northern Lights, those merry dancers in the sky seen most clearly the nearer you come to the polar regions. 'When I was a lad, a tiny wee lad,' said Archie, 'my mother said to me: "Come see the Northern Lights, my boy . . ."' As Archie expanded on the phenomenon, Mel Webb had the seeds of a verse, if it was ever required.

It all came together that night when Mary Webb sat down at the piano and thought of a song for the girl who came to tea. The tune unfolded from the keys of her old Broadwood piano as if it had been plucked from the ether. Mary was astounded, even unnerved, by the ease of the exercise. As she refined a few chords and Mel supplied the verse, the natural anthem of a city 600 hundred miles away was taking shape in the dim anonymity of a London flat. It was good enough to send to Robert Wilson, the great Scots tenor, who introduced it at London's Royal Albert Hall in 1952 and announced that the composer was in the audience. On her first ever visit to Scotland, she was coaxed on stage at the Tivoli Theatre to play her tune and take the applause of her one and only Aberdonian audience.

Mary Webb, who composed 'The Northern Lights', at her piano

Then Mary disappeared into widowhood and had no further contact with the city – until that morning when she heard the strains of the Gothenburg celebration. Five years after Gothenburg she suffered her first stroke and passed away penniless in 1989 at Charing Cross Hospital, London, lying on her deathbed for three weeks before a relative could be found. Half a dozen people gathered at Oakley Wood Crematorium, near Leamington, for a brief and pathetic finale; few even in her own native area having the slightest idea of her significance. A last-minute intervention secured her battered old piano, which was presented to the city of Aberdeen. After the cremation, her ashes were made available too. So they were brought to Aberdeen and scattered in the grounds of Kaimhill Crematorium on the morning of Wednesday 23rd August 1989. It seemed as suitable a resting place as any for the woman who had given us the tune and the chorus:

> God speed the day when I'm on my way
> To my home in Aberdeen.

There was a weeping in the wind as the melody soared into the northern sky and somehow brought the whole story of Aberdeen into focus. What a city! What a history! As we offer belated homage to Mary Webb, a forgotten figure from the past, it is perhaps a symbol of how readily we neglect our heritage. It demands our knowledge and appreciation if we are to carry it forward as a guide to whatever lies ahead. That Northern Light of Aberdeen is the torch we need to pass on, before we slip into our own modest place in the spectrum of time.

The Story of Aberdeen's Coat of Arms

If the ancient practice of heraldry fails to attract the public attention it merits, it is nevertheless an interesting study in how we are marked, decorated and identified as a community. In fact, Aberdeen's heraldry vies with that of Glasgow in being among the most widely used of any council in the United Kingdom. The city coat of arms appears on books, badges, banners, bollards, buildings, furniture, flags, clothing, vehicles, road-signs, uniforms and even litter bins. It appeared on the side of tramcars and buses until the trams disappeared in 1958 and Aberdeen Corporation buses went over to Grampian Region in 1975.

Yet the origin of Aberdeen's symbolism remains shrouded in mystery and conjecture. We know for sure that today's ensigns stem from a grant to the city in 1674 by Sir Charles Erskine, Lord Lyon King of Arms, who indicated that the town heraldry had been in existence long before then. What we now call heraldry first appeared on seals, those wax impressions which formed simple signature and identity a thousand years ago. In royal burghs such as Aberdeen, Banff and Montrose, the earliest seals generally showed the local saint. The first known use of a burgh seal in Aberdeen was in 1271 on a charter by Adam Gley in favour of the Black Friars, and this seal depicted St Nicholas, the town's patron saint.

By 1350 another seal had appeared, this time showing a building with a central doorway and three pyramidic spires, each bearing a cross at the apex. What these spires or towers symbolise is open to question. Aberdeen Castle, the Mither Kirk of St Nicholas, or the Holy Trinity? This design continued until 1424 when it changed to a wall of dressed masonry, a closed gate and three spires rising above the coping of the wall, taken to be the kirk of St Nicholas. It is more than coincidence, however, that the three-towered gateway occurs in cities across Europe, from Cracow to Oporto.

Even more coincidental, our nearest medieval trading partners of Bergen, Hamburg and Antwerp not only bear arms similar to the Aberdeen seal but copy our red-and-silver as their city colours. Within a few years a very different burgh seal showed a shield with a single tower enclosed by the familiar border and supported by two lion-like animals, holding between them a scroll with the motto 'Bon Accord'. The building is a triumphal arch rather than a tower.

When and why Aberdeen broke away from the European style of three-towered gateway to the three separate towers of today is a matter of speculation. The shield we now recognise appears alongside the name 'New Aberdeen' on the heraldic ceiling of St Machar's Cathedral. Aberdeen Castle had vanished by the reign of King Robert III (1390–1406), so why the three towers? Does the trio recall the fortifications of the Castle Hill, the Port Hill and St Catherine's Hill? There are so many stories but few facts.

Similar confusion surrounds the border containing the towers. This tressure is granted only by royal command and Perth is the only other Scottish burgh to bear one. Tradition says it was given by King Robert Bruce (1306–29) in gratitude for the help he received from the citizens in the War of Independence. Equally, he is held to have granted the additional heraldic honour of the leopards and even to have been the source of the motto 'Bon Accord', reputedly the password used by townspeople in 1308 when they destroyed the Castle of Aberdeen, then held by the English.

Leopards have a rare existence in Scottish heraldry, with Aberdeen the only town to use them. But as ever with Granite City heraldry, nothing is straightforward. The familiar leopards actually originated as lions, as can clearly be seen from their manes in the seal of 1430. The transformation from lions to leopards arose from confusion over the early French terminology! And there is still confusion. The leopards should be facing each other but their poses and attitudes vary, as shown on the burgh arms at the Mercat Cross, Aberdeen Grammar School, the Town House and the Town and County Hall. The splendid granite carving above the balcony of the Town House shows the leopards correctly facing each other, though the muscular beasts are clearly lions rather than leopards!

That re-granting of burgh arms by Sir Charles Erskine in 1674 followed a disastrous fire in Edinburgh when Scottish heraldic records were lost. That gave Aberdeen the coat of arms we know today, complete with silver towers on a red shield, which explains why the city livery colours are red and white – and why Aberdeen Football club plays in the same colours. Apart from the Mercat Cross in the Castlegate and the granite carvings at the Grammar School, good examples of city heraldry can be found at the War Memorial and at the Monkey House, that pillared doorway at the corner of Union Street and Union Terrace – well known as a rendezvous point for Aberdonians. There are painted stone panels on Marischal College and the Elphinstone Building, plus many fine examples inside the Town House.

As ever, Aberdeen has a final sting in the heraldic tail. It is one of only four burghs with two coats of arms, the others being Kirkcaldy, Linlithgow and Montrose. In Aberdeen's case, the alternative shows St Nicholas, patron saint of the burgh, dressed as a bishop above three children in a cooking pot. The original Nicholas rescued three children who, during a famine, were salted in a tub prior to being cooked. St Nicholas is the patron saint of children, sailors and pawnbrokers, as well as being the original Santa Claus.

Index

Note: Page references in **bold** indicate a picture (often with associated text). 'Mac', 'Mc' and names beginning 'St' are entered as spelt but Christian saints are listed under their names.

Reid, William D.   198
Reid and Leys (agricultural supplies)   95
Reith, John   258
religious education   126
Rennie, Joan   279
Rennie, John   59
Rennie's Wynd   63
Restoration of Monarchy   33
Reynolds, John   **203**, 311
Rhodes, Cecil   305
Rice, C. Duncan   73, 78–**79**, 130
Rice, Susan   79
Richards and Company   40, 304
Richardson, George   147
Richardson, J.C.   282
Richardson, Ralph   143
Richmond, Duke of   69
Richmondhill House   113, 115
Riddoch, Billy   245
Riddoch, Willie   245
ring-road   100
Ritchie, Anne   139
road transport   86, 310, 311
roads   84
Roar Like a Dove   221
Rob Roy   290
Robb, Andy   267, 268
Robert Gordon University   42, 103, 128, 134,
   190, 254, 307
Robert Gordon's College (earlier Hospital)   1,
   15, 36, 53, 95, 99, 125, 127, 128, 129, 131,
   131–136, 133, 267, 282, 285
   see also Auld Hoose; Robert Gordon
   University
Robert Gordon's Hospital *see* Robert Gordon's
   College
Robert Gordon's Technical College   134
Robert I (the Bruce)   10, 19–20, 288, 291, 316
Robert II   21
Robertson, Alexander   102
Robertson, David   300
Robertson, F.   283
Robertson, Harry   213
Robertson, James   95
Robertson, John W.   147
Robertson, Joseph   225
Robertson, Robert   201
Robertson, Steve   130, 215, 249
Robertson Construction Group   248
Robey, George   157, 244
Robinson, Crum and Co.   40
Robyns, Eric   255
Rodgers, Richard   178, 257
Rogers, Ginger   255
Rohilla (hospital ship)   160
Rollo, Leslie   **247**
Romans   16
Rommel, Erwin   152
Room at the Top   222
Roosevelt, Theodore   138
Rose Street   65
Rose, Beatrice   145
Rose, Murray   268
Rosehill   118
Rosemarkie   263
Rosemount   90, 91, 96, 97
Rosemount Flats   303
Rosemount School   125, 131
Rosemount Viaduct   82, 97, 99, 101
Roslin Institute   135
Roslin Terrace   96
Ross and Hutchinson   95
Ross Clinic   68
Ross, Alexander   40

Ross, John   228
Ross, John A.   40
Ross, Joseph   280
Rothamsted Agricultural Institute   150
Roulston, Harry   212, 213
Rowett Institute for Animal Research   150
Rowett, John Quiller   150
Royal Aberdeen Golf Club   276, 277, 278
Royal Academy Life School   295
Royal Athenaeum   60, 61, 300
Royal Bank of Scotland   50
Royal British Legion   115
Royal Cornhill Hospital   68
Royal Hotel   300
Royal Mental Hospital   65
Royal Regiment of Scotland   151
royal visitors   23, 108–109; *see also under*
   individual names
Royle, Trevor   215
Rubislaw   90, 96, 97, 124
Rubislaw Academy   127, 131
Rubislaw Den North   100
Rubislaw Field   131
Rubislaw Place   61
Rubislaw Quarry   6, 44–**45**, 182, 189
Rubislaw Terrace   96, **97**, 305
Rubislaw, SS   163
rugby   284–286
Rumster Forest   263
Russell, Alexander   209
Russell, Christine   144
Russell, Sheriff Muir   141
Rust, James R.   117–118
Rutherford family   22
Rutherford, Sir John   22
Ruthrieston   82, 116, 287
Ruthrieston School   125
Ryder Cup   275, 277

Sainsbury's *see* J. Sainsbury plc
Saint (drapers shop)   99
salmon   39
Salts (company)   95
Sandilands   95
Sandilands, Patrick   40
Sandler, Albert   239
Sants, Ann   305
Scatterty, Peter   135, 136
Schlumberger Oilfield Services   192, 293
School of Scottish Studies   225
School Road   124
Schoolhill   16, 17, 24, 37, 40, **53**, 56, 97, 99,
   128, 129, 133, 134, 197
schooling   125–127, 128–149
   see also under names of individual institutions
Scot FM radio   264
Scotch Corner public house   300
Scotland the What?   192, 249–250
Scotland, Ken   285
The Scots Magazine   215
A Scots Quair   218
The Scotsman   206, 213
Scott Sutherland School of Architecture   254
Scott, Alexander   147
Scott, G.   282
Scott, Hugh   104
Scott, J.G.   282
Scott, Selina   262, 264
Scottish Arts Council   215, 239
Scottish Arts Council Lottery Fund   248
Scottish Bakers' Union   200
Scottish Ballet   248
Scottish Cricket Union   281
Scottish Cup   271

Scottish Cyclists' Union   117
Scottish Enlightenment   56–57
Scottish Enterprise   248
Scottish Enterprise Grampian   79
Scottish Field   215
Scottish League Championship   271
Scottish League Cup   178, 271
Scottish Maid (clipper)   48, 82
Scottish Media Group   262
Scottish Medical Journal   78
Scottish Midland Railway   85
Scottish National Dictionary   233
Scottish Nationalism   186
Scottish North-Eastern Railway   85
Scottish Opera   79, 268
Scottish Television   213, 265
Scottish Wholesale Co-operative Society *see*
   Co-op
Scottish Youth Hostels Association   130
Scottish-American Investment Trust   113
Sculpture Gallery   111, 112, 116
Seaforth Maritime   189
Seaforth Road   124, **166**
search-and-rescue services   189
Seaton   124
Seaton House   72
Sedburgh School   141
Seidensticker, Calvin   185
Seton, Sir Alexander   28
sewerage   81
sex mores   180, 192
Shackleton, Ernest   281
Shakespeare, William   23
Sharp, Sheena   267
Shell   182, 193, 291
Shepherd, Nan   143, 222
Shepherd, Robbie   135
Shewan, Harry   160
Shewan, James   147
shipbuilding   48–49, 121, 175
shipping   39, 120
Shiprow   256
The Shiralee   221
Shoemakers (craft guild)   195
Shorelands   96
Shuttle Lane   124
Sick Children's Hospital   66, 303
Sievwright, John   51, 134
Sillerton House   136
Simmons, Jean   143
Simpson, Archibald   59, **61**, 69, 82, 142, 305
Simpson, Archie   276
Simpson, George   277
Simpson, H.F.S. Morland   131
Simpson, J.R.   66
Simpson, Dr W. Douglas   74
Simpson, Wallis   108, 162
Sinclair, Sir Archibald   157
Sinclair, Jack   271
Sir John Hay Fund   282, 283–284
Sir John Hay's XI   **283**
Sivell, Robert   173
Skene   293
Skene Orphanage   220–221, 293
Skene Street   99
Skene Street School   125, 199
Skene, Alexander   36, 37
Skene, Cecil   305, 306
Skene, Charles Pirie   158, **305**–307
Skene, James R.   305–306
Slains Castle   85
slave trade   63–64
Slessor, Mary   146, 296, **297**, 298
slum clearance   124

Tree, Herbert Beerbohm 236
Trinity Friars 24, 53
Trinity Hall 195, 304
Trueman, Fred **283**
Trump, Donald 278–279, **311**
Tucker, Derek 213
Tullos 164, 175
Tung, C.Y. 135
Turiff Pipe Band 152
turnpikes 84
Turriff 199
Turriff Advertiser 1, 77
Tweddell, William 277
tweed 39
Tweeddale, Marquis of 55
typhoid 34–35
typhus 35, 68, 96
Tyrebagger 46
Tyrie 14

Unilever 99, 290, 302
Union Bridge 7, 44, 59, **60**
Union Grove 96
Union Place Ladies School 140
Union Row Academy 137
Union Street **6**, **7**, 36, 38, 44, 59–61, **89**, 90, 92, 97, 99
Union Terrace 42, 60, 90, 178
Union Terrace Gardens 61, 82, 116
Union Works 41, 175
Union Wynd 136
United Free College 71
universities in Scotland and England 11, 13, 14–15
see also under individual names
University Press Cricket Club 284
university principals 75–79
University Rugby Club 285
Upper Docks 120, 123
Upper Stocket Road 96
Upperkirkgate 37, 72
Urquhart Road 124

Valentino, Rudolph 253
Varga, Zoltan 271
Veitch, William 210–211, 212, 213
Victoria, Queen 33, 81, 85, 108, 253, 255, 295, 306
Victoria Bridge 46, 288
Victoria Cross 130, 136, 152
Victoria Docks 120, 123
Victoria Golf Club 276
Victoria Park 82
Victoria Road School 164
Victoria Street 61
Victoria the Great 255
Voltaire 2–3
Vue 256

W.J. Anderson (contractors) 43
Waldie, Mr. (carpenter) 241
Waldorf School 302
Wales Street 60
Walker Park 116
Walker Road School 125, 164
Walker, George 101
Walker, James 115
Walker, Miss 141
Walker, William 251
Wall, Charlie 178
Wall's Meat Group 290

Wallace, A.G. ('Toby') 146
Wallace, Jim 135
Wallace, William 19, 20, 82
Walter Hood and Co. 48
War Memorial 99, 108, **171**
War of Independence 19
Warbeck, Perkin 35
Ward, Lucy 145
Warrack, Harriet 140, 141
Warrack, James 140
Watchdog 264
water supply 81, 116
Waterloo Quay 95, 289
Waterloo, Battle of 152
Waters, Donald 264
Watson Fraser Nursing Home 68, 108, 119
Watson Street 96
Watson, Peter 212
Watson, Tom 278
Watson, William 111
Watt, Edward G. 118, 137, 210, 225
Watt, Eric 130
Watt, Dr. George 65
Watt, James 56
Watt, Sheila 266
Waverley Place 61
The Wealth of Nations 56
Weavers (craft guild) 195
Webb, Mary 312, **313**, 314
Webb, Mel 312, 313
Webberley, Mr (head electrician) 241
Webster, Jack
    this book 1–3
    and Betty Hadden murder case 178
    and Charlie Chaplin 237–**238**
    on discovery of oil 182, 186–187
    and Richard Rodgers 257
    rides last tram 91
    and Donald Trump 311
Webster, John 1
Weekly Journal 214
Weir, Peter 273
Wellington Road 164, **165**, 288
Welsh, Nathaniel 24
Wernham, Bertha 147
West End Cinema *see* Playhouse Cinema (earlier West End)
West Hatton 293
West, John 203
West, Kirsty 203
West, Peter 268
Westburn Park 96, 116
Westburn Road 124
Westfield Model Gardens 129
Westfield School 131
Westhill 287, 292–293
Westhill Academy 292
Westhill Developments (Aberdeen) Ltd 292
Westhill Garden Suburb 292
Westland, John 177–178
The White Bird Passes 220, 293
White Friars *see* Carmelite Friars
The White Heather Club 147
White, Jason **286**
White, John Forbes 41
Whiteley, Jon 221, 256
Whiteman, Barbara 307
Whiteman, Paul 254
Whymper, Edward 115
Wiggins Teape 41, 95, 175
Wigley, Nellie 241

Wilkie, David 266
Wilkie, R.P. 289
Will, William 224
Willet, John 235
William Gavin Players 245
William I (the Lion) 17, 287
William McKinnon and Co 174
William Paterson and Sons 42
William Smith and Son (nurserymen) 95
William Tawse Ltd. 43
Williams, Charles 143
Williams, Emlyn 244
Williams, James 280
Williams, Robert 280
Williams of Park, Sir Robert 66
Williams, Stan 271
Williamson, Dick 213
Williamson, Peter 63–64
Willie Gavin 220
Willis, Dave 179, 239, 245
Wilson, Alexander 116
Wilson, David 245
Wilson, Dooley 256
Wilson, George Washington 100, 235, 295
Wilson, Grace 259
Wilson, Harold 186
Wilson, Robert 313
Windmill Brae 43, 58
Wingrove, Sarah 192
Winter, Vincent 221, 256
Wischert, Janet 25
witchcraft 25, 196
Wolf of Badenoch *see* Stewart, Alexander
Wolfe, Willie 187
Wolfit, Donald 244
Wolrige-Gordon, Henry 207
Wood, Brian 147
Wood, Ian 51, 134, 191, **193**
Wood, Sheena 279
Wood Group 189, 191
Woodbank House, Pitfodels 291
Woodend 66, 124
Woodend Hospital 68
Woodend Old People's Hospital 147
Woodlands Hospital 68
Woods, Tiger 278
Woodside 40, 82, 90, 91, 96, 103, 104, 166, 230
woollen industry 39–40
Woolmanhill 16, 17, 37, 58, 61, 65, 66, 68, 117, 164
Woolworth 99
World War I 47, 109, 136, 152, 159–161, 209
World War II 42, 103, 109, 119, 120, 122–123, 152–153, 161–173, 198, 255
Wright, Edward Maitland 76–77
Wright, Janet 279
Wright, John 77
Wrights (craft guild) 195
writers 216–225
Wyffe, Will 239
Wyness, Fenton 145, 160, 245
Wyness, James 139, 201–202

Yorston, Benny 270
Yorston, Harry 271
Young Street 124
Youngson, George W. 282
Ypres 159

Zeppelins 160